Praise for
Armin A. Brott

"Brott writes honestly and earnestly.
His wry sense of humor will be
a relief to hassled parents."
—*Time* magazine

The Expectant Father

"Quite simply the best guidebook to date for both the prospective father and his partner in their journey through the nine months of pregnancy.... A must for fathers-to-be." —John Munder Ross, Ph.D., author of *What Men Want* and editor of *Father and Child.*

"Don't get pregnant without it! A first-rate guide for all dads-to-be." —Vicki Lansky, author of *Feed Me, I'm Yours* and contributing editor to *Family Circle* and *Sesame Street Parents*

"This book is the *What to Expect When You're Expecting* for men.... If you know an expectant father, first baby or not, make sure he has this book." —*Full-Time Dads*

"For fathers soon expecting the ultimate gift—a new member of the family—*The Expectant Father* is his best friend."—CNN Interactive

"One would be hard put to find a question about having a baby that's not dealt with here, all from the father's perspective."—*Library Journal*

Winner, 2005 Adding Wisdom award from *Parent-to-Parent*

"...a terrific gift, offering insight into pregnancy and the first few weeks of parenthood."—BabyCenter.com

Also by Armin Brott in the New Father series

The New Father:
A Dad's Guide to the First Year

"This book would make a great gift for any new dad."
—Lawrence Kutner, Ph.D., columnist, *Parents* magazine

"...stood out immediately...because of its perceptive insights."
—*San Francisco Chronicle*

"Read a book? Who has time? But you'd be wise to find some so you can take advantage of a fabulous resource...*The New Father*."
—*Sesame Street Parents*

Fathering Your Toddler:
A Dad's Guide to the Second and Third Years

"...Brott demystifies child development...and make[s] fathers...enjoy the vital role they play in their kids' lives even more. A great addition to any parenthood library." —*Child* magazine

Fathering Your School-Age Child:
A Dad's Guide to the Wonder Years: 3 to 9

"Brott...drolly delivers readable, practical guidance on fathering."
—*Library Journal*

"This, thankfully, is not another one of those goofy, dumbed-down books... In fact, this is as informative as any traditional parenting book out there (including those aimed at the moms), and in some ways even better. Busy dads will be grateful for Brott's accessible tone and quick-and-painless format..."
—*Newsday*

The Military Father:
A Hands-on Guide for Deployed Dads

"As an Army brat I know firsthand that it's not only our military men and women who serve the country—their spouses and children serve proudly as well. Armin Brott has contributed his own brand of service with this wonderful book...."—Linda Powell, daughter of General Colin Powell, US Army Ret., former Chairman of the Joint Chiefs of Staff

"A much-needed salute to the importance of these unique dads...a 'field manual' for their most important front of all—the home front."—Roland C. Warren, President, the National Fatherhood Initiative

"Tackles everything."—*The Washington Times*

"We highly recommend that you obtain this book...."—The Men's Health Network

The Single Father:
A Dad's Guide to Parenting Without a Partner

"Brott...offers the tools to help men become and remain actively involved parents."—*Fresno Bee*

"Armin Brott steers divorced, separated, gay, widowed and never-married fathers through every aspect of fathering without a partner."—*New Orleans Times-Picayune*

"Brott offers a solution for all problems big or small..."
—*Ft. Lauderdale Sun Sentinel*

Father for Life:
A Journey of Joy, Challenge, and Change

"An essential guide for every dad."—MSN.com

The New Father series
by Armin A. Brott

The New Father
A Dad's Guide to the First Year
SECOND EDITION

Fathering Your Toddler
A Dad's Guide to the Second and Third Years
SECOND EDITION

Fathering Your School-Age Child
A Dad's Guide to the Wonder Years, 3 to 9

The Military Father
A Hands-on Guide for Deployed Dads

The Single Father
A Dad's Guide to Parenting Without a Partner

Father for Life
A Journey of Joy, Challenge, and Change

Also available in e-book format

The
Expectant
Father

—

Facts, Tips,
and Advice
for Dads-to-Be

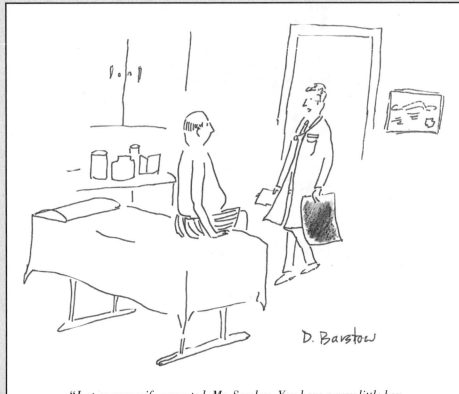

"Just as your wife suspected, Mr. Sanders. You have a very little boy growing inside you."

The
Expectant
Father

Facts, Tips, and Advice for Dads-to-Be

THIRD EDITION

Armin A. Brott and Jennifer Ash

Abbeville Press Publishers
New York • London

To Tirzah and Talya, who showed me how to do it the first and second times, and Zoe, who reminded me of just how much fun being a dad can be.—A.A.B.

For Joe, Clarke, and Emmy, and my parents Clarke and Agnes Ash, with love and affection.—J.A.

Editors: Jacqueline Decter and Susan Costello
Copyeditors: Austin Allen and Ashley Benning
Production Manager: Louise Kurtz
Designers: Celia Fuller and Misha Beletsky

Third paperback edition
10 9 8 7 6 5

Cover photograph by Geoff Sprear
For cartoon credits, see page 375

Library of Congress Cataloging-in-Publication Data
Brott, Armin A.
  The expectant father : facts, tips, and advice for dads-to-be / Armin A.
Brott and Jennifer Ash. —3rd ed.
      p. cm.
  Includes bibliographical references and index.
   ISBN 978-0-7892-1077-7 (pbk. : alk. paper)—ISBN 978-0-7892-1079-1
(hardcover : alk. paper)
  1. Fathers. 2. Pregnancy—Popular works. I. Ash, Jennifer. II. Title.
  HQ756.B76 2010
  649'.10242—dc22

                         2010015973

For bulk and premium sales and for text adoption procedures, write to Customer Service Manager, Abbeville Press, 137 Varick Street, New York, N.Y. 10013, or call 1-800-ARTBOOK.

Visit Abbeville Press online at www.abbeville.com.

Contents

Acknowledgments

So many people have had a hand in creating this book—from the first all the way through this third edition—that it's nearly impossible to thank them individually. Andrea Adam read all the early drafts, encouraged me, and helped hone my ideas while adding a few of her own. David Cohen and Jackie Needleman and Matt and Janice Tannin also contributed stories, recipes, advice, and friendship to the first edition. Keri Schwab and Megan Lee, research assistants extraordinaire, helped come up with some of the most amazing studies. Certified financial planners Joe Pitzl (mindfulplanning.com) and Jackie Weitzberg (GuideMyFinances.com) reviewed the sections on finances and made some great suggestions.

In previous editions, the team at DrSpock.com and, in particular, Marjorie Greenfield, M.D., reviewed everything and anything medical. This time, I had a whole medical review board, well stocked with OBs and fertility specialists: Elan Simckes, Saul Stromer, Saul Weinreb, Susan Warhus, and especially Lissa Rankin. All took the time—a lot of it—not only to fact-check chapters, but also to add their own insights, wisdom, and stories. There's more information on all of these great docs in the Resources section at the end of the book.

Behind the scenes, Bob Abrams and Cynthia Vance Abrams have championed *The Expectant Father* and helped turn a book from a first-time author into a bestselling series. Jackie Decter edited the first edition, correcting my mistakes and massaging my prose while leaving my ego intact. She passed the baton to Susan Costello, who has done an equally masterful job of keeping me on track. Celia Fuller and Misha Beletsky are the brains behind the wonderful design. Austin Allen and Ashley Benning did a fine job copyediting and proofreading. Michaelann Millrood deserves praise for her publicity efforts, Briana Green keeps our Web presence up to date, and Nadine Winns somehow manages to keep our customers happy. Jim Levine and Arielle Eckstut were there from the beginning and facilitated the early connection with Jennifer, which ultimately made the whole thing possible. After that, Melissa Rowland kept all the paperwork (you can't imagine how much) straight.

But even with all that help, this book would not be here today if it weren't for the thousands of expectant and new dads (and plenty of new moms too) who contacted me with their suggestions, comments, complaints (usually constructive), and anecdotes.

Armin Brott

While awaiting the arrival of our first baby, I vowed to read every piece of printed advice on pregnancy and motherhood. It quickly became apparent that nine months wasn't sufficient time to digest all that was available for expectant mothers. However, my husband's bedside table remained bare, not for lack of interest but for want of resources. A heartfelt thanks to Joe, who convinced me men do want to know more about pregnancy and thus encouraged me to embark on this project. I'm also grateful to my brothers, Eric and Jim, and to the many friends who candidly discussed impending fatherhood and made insightful suggestions. Virginia Webb's and Esther Williams's advice about newborns was invaluable.

Sincere thanks to everyone at Abbeville, especially Alan Mirken, who supported this project from the onset. The enthusiasm of Bob Abrams and Mark Magowan kept it on track. Jackie Decter deftly guided the book to completion and her friendship made the journey a joy. Thanks to Armin Brott for agreeing to provide the narrative, which breathed male life into the book. Laura Straus made the inclusion of cartoons possible, and Celia Fuller's inspired design brought all of this to life.

Jennifer Ash

Introduction

When my wife got pregnant with our first child, I was the happiest I'd ever been. That pregnancy, labor, and the baby's birth was a time of incredible closeness, tenderness, and passion. Long before we'd married, my wife and I had made a commitment to participate equally in raising our children. And it seemed only natural that the process of shared parenting should begin during pregnancy.

Since neither of us had had children before, we were both rather ill-prepared for pregnancy. Fortunately for my wife, there were literally hundreds of books and other resources designed to educate, encourage, support, and comfort women during their pregnancies. But when it finally hit me that I, too, was expecting (although in a very different kind of way), and that the pregnancy was bringing out feelings and emotions I didn't understand, there simply weren't any resources for me to turn to. I looked for answers in my wife's pregnancy books, but information about what expectant fathers go through (if it was discussed at all) was at best superficial, and consisted mostly of advice on how men could be supportive of their pregnant wives. To make things worse, my wife and I were the first couple in our circle of close friends to get pregnant, which meant that there was no one else I could talk to about what I was going through, no one who could reassure me that what I was feeling was normal and all right.

Until fairly recently, there has been precious little research on expectant fathers' emotional and psychological experiences during pregnancy. The very title of one of the first articles to appear on the subject should give you some idea of the medical and psychiatric communities' attitude toward the impact of pregnancy on men. Written by William H. Wainwright, M.D., and published in the July 1966 issue of the *American Journal of Psychiatry*, it was called "Fatherhood as a Precipitant of Mental Illness." (Another wonderful title that came out at about the same time was: "Psychoses in Males in Relation to Their Wives' Pregnancy and Childbirth.")

As you'll soon find out, though, an expectant father's experience during the transition to fatherhood is not confined simply to excitement—or mental illness; if it were, this book would never have been written. The reality is that men's emotional response to pregnancy is no less varied than women's; expectant fathers feel everything from relief to denial, fear to frustration, anger to joy. And for up to 80 percent of men, there are physical symptoms of pregnancy as well (more on this on pages 88–93).

So why haven't men's experiences been discussed more? In my opinion it's because we, as a society, value motherhood more than fatherhood, and we automatically assume that issues of childbirth and childrearing are women's issues. But as you'll learn—both from reading this book and from your own experience—this is simply not the case.

Who, Exactly, Has Written This Book?

When Jennifer Ash (who is not my wife) approached me about collaborating with her on *The Expectant Father*, we agreed that the goal was to help you— the father—understand and make sense of what you're going through during your pregnancy. The rationale was simple: the more you understand about what you're going through, the better prepared you'll be and the more likely you'll be to take an interest in—and stay involved throughout—the pregnancy. Research has shown that the earlier fathers get involved (and what could be earlier than pregnancy?), the more likely they are to be involved after their children are born.

All that's very nice, of course, but it's clearly dependent on your partner's *being* pregnant. So a good understanding of *her* perspective on the pregnancy—emotional as well as physical—is essential to understanding how *you* will react. It was precisely this perspective that Jennifer, along with my wife and hundreds of other expectant and new mothers I interviewed, provided. Throughout the process of writing the book, all of these women contributed valuable information and comments, not only about what pregnant women are going through but also about the ways women most want men to be involved, and the impact that involvement has on the entire pregnancy experience.

A Note on Structure

Throughout the book I try to present straightforward, practical information in an easy-to-absorb format. Each of the main chapters is divided into four sections, as follows:

What's Going On with Your Partner

Even though this is a book about what you as an expectant father are going through during pregnancy, and how you can best stay involved, it's critical that you understand what your partner is going through and when. For that reason, we felt that it was important to start each chapter with a summary of your partner's physical and emotional pregnancy experience.

What's Going On with the Baby

You can't very well have a pregnancy without a baby, right? This section lets you in on your future child's progress—from sperm and egg to living, breathing infant.

What's Going On with You

This section covers the wide range of feelings—good, bad, and indifferent—that you'll probably experience at some time during the pregnancy. It also describes such things as the physical changes you may go through and the ways the pregnancy may affect your sex life.

Staying Involved

While the "What's Going On with You" section covers the emotional and physical side of pregnancy, this section gives you specific facts, tips, and advice on what you can *do* to make the pregnancy "yours" as well as your partner's. For instance, you'll find easy, nutritious recipes to prepare, information on how to start a college fund for the baby, valuable advice on getting the most out of your birth classes, great ways to start communicating with your baby before he or she is born, and tips about how to be supportive of your partner and how to stay included in the pregnancy.

The Expectant Father covers more than the nine months of pregnancy. We've included a detailed chapter on labor and delivery and another on Cesarean section, both of which will prepare you for the big event and let you know how best to help your partner through the birth itself. Perhaps even more important, these chapters prepare you for the often overwhelming emotions you may experience when your partner is in labor and your child is born.

We've also included a special chapter that addresses the major questions and concerns you may have about caring for and getting to know your child in the first few weeks after you bring him or her home. If someone hasn't bought you them already, I'd recommend that you rush right out and get copies of *The New Father: A Dad's Guide to the First Year* and *Fathering Your Toddler: A Dad's Guide to the Second and Third Years*. These books pick up where this one leaves off and continue the process of giving you the skills, knowledge, confidence, and support you'll need to be the best possible dad.

Toward the end of this book there is a chapter called "Fathering Today," in which you'll learn to recognize—and overcome—the many obstacles you may encounter along the road to becoming an actively involved dad.

As you go through *The Expectant Father*, remember that the process of becoming a dad is different for every man, and that none of us will react to the same situation in exactly the same way. You may find that some of what's described in the "What's Going On with You" section in the third-month chapter won't really ring true for you until the fifth month, or that you already experienced it in the first month. You may also want to try out some of the ideas and activities in the "Staying Involved" sections in a different order. Feel free.

A Note on Terminology

Wife, Girlfriend, Lover, He, She...

In an attempt to avoid offending anyone (an approach I've discovered usually ends up offending everyone), we've decided to refer to the woman who's carrying the baby as "your partner." And because your partner is just as likely to be carrying a boy as a girl, we've alternated between "he" and "she" when referring to the baby (except where something applies specifically to boys or girls).

Hospitals, Doctors...

Not everyone who has a baby delivers in a hospital or is under the care of a medical doctor. Still, because that's the most frequent scenario, we've chosen to refer to the place where the baby will be born as "the hospital" and to the people attending the birth (besides you, of course) as "doctors," "nurses," "medical professionals," or "practitioners"—except, of course, in the sections that specifically deal with home birth and/or midwives.

As a rule, today's dads (and expectant dads) want to be much more involved with their children than their own fathers were able to be. It's my firm belief that the first step on the road toward full involvement is to take an active role in the pregnancy. And it's our hope that when you're through reading *The Expectant Father*—which is the book Jennifer wishes she could have bought for her husband when she was pregnant and the one I wish I'd had when I was an expectant dad—you'll be much better prepared to participate in this important new phase of your life.

So why should you get involved now, before you actually become a dad? Simply put, because it's good for your child, your partner, and yourself. As mentioned above, involvement during pregnancy is a good predictor of involvement after the pregnancy. And children who grow up in homes where dad is involved do better in math and science, are more sociable, are more tenacious when solving problems, and, thinking *waaaay* out into the future, they're less likely to use drugs or alcohol or become teen parents.

When the dad-to-be is involved during the pregnancy, he and his partner are more likely to be together for their child's third birthday than couples where dad isn't as involved. Pregnant women whose partners are involved prenatally are more likely to get prenatal care and, if they smoke, to quit. And according to researcher Jacinta Bronte-Tinkew, women whose partners aren't supportive during the pregnancy are "more likely to view their pregnancy as unwanted." Finally, your being involved now makes it more likely that your partner will breastfeed your baby (we'll talk about why that's so important later on).

For you, being an involved dad will reduce the chance that you'll engage in risky behavior. You'll probably start taking better care of yourself, you'll be happier in your relationship with your partner, and you'll even perform better at work.

Some Special Additions to This Edition

In the years since the first edition of *The Expectant Father* was published, I've received literally thousands of letters and e-mails from readers offering comments and suggestions on how to make this book better. I've incorporated many of those suggestions into this edition and believe that the book is greatly improved as a result. Let me give you a quick rundown:

♦ **Adoptive fathers.** Although your partner may not actually be carrying a baby, the two of you are still very much "psychologically pregnant." There's a lot of research, in fact, that suggests that in the months leading up to the adoption of their child, expectant adoptive fathers deal with many of the same emotional and psychological issues that biologically expectant fathers do.

♦ **Multiples.** We've expanded the sections geared toward expectant fathers of twins, triplets, and so forth.

♦ **Overcoming infertility.** As the average age of new parents increase, more and more couples are experiencing infertility. So we've included a new section on infertility in the Appendix as well as information on what you can do to increase the chances that you and your partner will conceive.

♦ **The ART of fatherhood.** An increasing number of couples are conceiving through the use of ART (assisted reproductive technology), which includes IVF (in vitro fertilization), artificial insemination, donor sperm, donor eggs, and gestational carriers (who used to be referred to as surrogates). We've included a number of sections that deal with the fascinating issues facing ART dads and their partners.

♦ **GI Dad.** Every year, a huge number of men from all branches of the service spend at least part of their partner's pregnancy thousands of miles away. And many of them come home to a child who was born while they were stationed elsewhere. As a Marine myself (not anymore, but there's no such thing as an "ex-Marine"), I knew I needed to do as much as I could to help our troops. For that reason we've included several sections in this book designed to help deployed expectant dads stay involved throughout the pregnancy so that they can hit the ground running when they get back home. I go into these issues in much more detail in my new book, *The Military Father: A Hands-on-Guide for Deployed Dads.*

We Need Your Help

I'd love to hear your experiences, feelings, comments, and suggestions, and I'll try to incorporate them into future editions of this book. You can contact me in writing c/o Abbeville Press (the address is on the copyright page of this book), or by e-mail at armin@MrDad.com. And please check out my Web site (www.mrdad.com).

Good luck as you start this new and wonderful stage of your life!

The First
Decisions

A mong the first major questions you and your partner will face after learning she's pregnant are: *Where are we going to have the baby?*, *Who's
going to help us deliver it?*, and *How much is it all going to cost?* To a certain
extent, the answers will be dictated by the terms of your insurance coverage,
but there are still a range of options to consider. As you weigh all your choices,
give your partner at least 51 percent of the vote. After all, the ultimate decision really affects her more than it does you.

Where and How

Hospitals

For most couples—especially first-time parents—the hospital is the most
common place to give birth. It's also, in many people's view, the safest. In
the unlikely event that complications arise, most hospitals have specialists
on staff twenty-four hours a day and are equipped with all the necessary life-
saving equipment and medications. And in those first hectic hours or days
after the birth, the on-staff nurses monitor the baby and mother and help both
new parents with the dozens of questions that are likely to come up. They also
run interference for you and help fend off unwanted intrusions. If you have a
choice among several hospitals in your area, be sure to take a tour of each one
before making your decision.

Most of the time, you'll end up going with the hospital where your partner's
doctor or midwife has privileges (or where your insurance plan says you can

go). Some people do it the other way around: they select the hospital first and then find a practitioner who's associated with that hospital.

Many hospitals now have birthing rooms (or entire birthing centers) that are carefully decorated to look less sterile and medical and more like a bedroom at home, although the effect is really more like a nice motel suite or a quaint bed-and-breakfast. The cozy decor is supposed to make you and your partner feel more comfortable. But with the wood furniture cleverly concealing sophisticated monitoring equipment, the cabinets full of sterile supplies, and nurses dropping by every hour or so to give your partner a pelvic exam, it's going to be hard to forget where you are. Keep in mind that at some hospitals, birthing rooms are assigned on a first-come-first-served basis, so don't count on getting one—unless you can convince your partner to go into labor before anyone else does that day. In other hospitals, *all* the labor rooms are also birthing rooms, so this won't be an issue.

Hospitals, by their nature, are pretty busy places, and they have all sorts of rules and policies that may or may not make sense to you. Giving birth in a hospital generally involves less privacy for you and your partner, and more routine procedures for her and the baby.

That said, if your partner is considered "high risk" (meaning she's carrying twins or more, is over 35, has had any complications during a previous delivery, had complications during this pregnancy, has any medical risk factors, or was told as much by her practitioner), a hospital birth will—and should—be your only choice.

Freestanding Birthing Centers

Of the 1–2 percent of births that take place outside a hospital, about 30 percent happen in private birthing centers. Staffed by certified nurse-midwives (CNMs), these facilities tend to offer a more personal approach to the birthing process. They look and feel a lot like home—nice wallpaper, hot tubs, and sometimes even a kitchen. They're generally less rigid than hospitals and more willing to accommodate any special requests your partner or you might have. For example, there are fewer routine medical interventions, your partner may be allowed to eat during labor (a big no-no at most hospitals), and she'll be able to wear her own clothes—none of those unflattering hospital gowns unless she really wants one. The staff will also try to make sure your partner and baby are never separated. One downside is that you and your newly expanded family may need to check out as soon as six to ten hours after the birth.

Private birthing centers are designed to deal with uncomplicated, low-risk pregnancies and births, so expect to be prescreened. And don't worry: if something doesn't go exactly as planned, birthing centers are always affiliated with a doctor and are usually either attached to a hospital or only a short ambulance ride away.

If you're interested in exploring this option, start by getting a recommendation from your partner's practitioner or friends and family. Or, contact the American Association of Birth Centers at www.birthcenters.org.

Home Birth

With all their high-tech efficiency and stark, impersonal, antiseptic conditions, hospitals are not for everyone. As a result, some couples (less than 1 percent) decide to have their baby at home. Home birth has been around forever (before 1920, that's where most births happened) but has been out of favor in this country for a long time. It is, however, making something of a comeback as more and more people (most of whom aren't even hippies) decide to give it a try.

My wife and I thought about a home birth for our second baby but ultimately decided against it. While I don't consider myself particularly squeamish, I just couldn't imagine how we'd avoid making a mess all over the bedroom carpet. What really clinched it for us, though, was that our first child had been an emergency Cesarean section. Fearing that we might run into problems again, we opted to be near the doctors.

If you're thinking about a home birth, be prepared. Having a baby at home is quite a bit different from the way it's made out to be in those old westerns. You'll need to assume much more responsibility for the whole process than if you were using a hospital. It takes a lot of research and preparation. At the very least, you're going to need a lot more than clean towels and boiling water.

Making the decision to give birth at home does *not* mean that your partner can skip getting prenatal care or that the two of you should plan on delivering your baby alone. You'll still need to be in close contact with a medical professional to ensure that the pregnancy is progressing normally, and you should make sure to have someone present at the birth who has plenty of experience with childbirth (no, not your sister or your mother-in-law, unless they happen to be qualified). So if you're planning on going this route, start working on selecting a midwife right now.

Statistically, it's pretty unlikely that you'll go this route. But in case you're considering it, I want to take you through some of the reasons people commonly give for wanting to have their baby at home, and some situations that would make a home birth unnecessarily risky.

WHY HAVE THE BABY AT HOME

- The surroundings are more familiar, comfortable, and private.
- You don't like—or are afraid of—hospitals and doctors. Or you had a negative experience with a previous birth.
- You've already had one or more uncomplicated hospital births.
- You can surround yourselves with anyone you pick.
- The birth is more likely to go exactly as you want than it might anywhere else. And your partner will be treated less like a patient than she would be in a hospital.
- You can pay attention to the spiritual aspects of the delivery, an intimate matter that you might be discouraged from, or feel embarrassed about, in the hospital.
- Hospitals are full of sick people and it's best to stay far away from them.
- It's cheaper.

WHY NOT TO HAVE THE BABY AT HOME

- Your partner is over 35 or has been told by her doctor that she's "high risk."
- She's carrying twins (or more) or you find out that the baby is breech (feet down instead of head down).
- She goes into labor prematurely.
- She developed preeclampsia, a condition that affects about 10 percent of pregnant women and that can have very serious complications if it's not detected and treated early (see pages 73–74 for more on this).
- She has diabetes or a heart or kidney condition, has had hemorrhaging in a previous labor, has had a previous Cesarean section, or smokes cigarettes.
- No insurance coverage.

Natural vs. Medicated Birth

In recent years giving birth "naturally"—without drugs, pain medication, or any medical intervention—has become all the rage. But just because it's popular doesn't mean it's for everybody. Labor and delivery are going to be a painful experience—for both of you, although in different ways—and many couples elect to take advantage of the advances medical science has made in relieving the pain and discomfort of childbirth. Whichever way you go, make sure the decision is your partner's. Proponents of some childbirth methods (see pages 178–84) are almost religiously committed to the idea of a drug-free delivery, to the extent that they often make women who opt for any pain medication feel as though they're failures. Besides making a lot of new parents feel bad about themselves when they should be celebrating the birth of their baby, that militant attitude is simply out of touch with reality. Nationwide, about half of women give birth using an epidural (which is the most common method of pain relief), and in some big-city hospitals that rate is north of 85 percent.

There are advantages and disadvantages to both medicated and unmedicated births, and we'll talk about them when we get closer to your baby's due date. But for now, the most important thing is to be flexible and not let your friends, relatives, or anyone else pressure you into doing something you don't want to do.

You and your partner may be planning a natural childbirth, but conditions could develop that necessitate intervention or the use of medication (see pages 73–74). On the other hand, you may be planning a medicated delivery but could find yourself snowed in someplace far from your hospital and any pain medication, or the anesthesiologist may be at an emergency on the other side of town.

Who's Going to Help?

At first glance, it may seem that your partner should be picking a medical practitioner alone—after all, she's the one who's going to be poked and prodded as the pregnancy develops. But considering that more than 90 percent of today's expectant fathers are present during the delivery of their children, and that the vast majority of them have been involved in some significant way during the rest of the pregnancy, you're probably going to be spending a lot of time with the practitioner as well. So if at all possible, you should feel comfortable with the final choice, too. Here are the main players.

Private Obstetrician
If your partner is over 20, she's probably been seeing a gynecologist for a few years. And since many gynecologists also do obstetrics, it should come as no surprise that most couples elect to have the woman's regular obstetrician/gynecologist (OB/GYN) deliver the baby.

Private OB/GYNs are generally the most expensive way to go, but your insurance company will probably pick up a good part of the bill. Most private OBs, however, aren't strictly private; they usually have a number of partners,

What to Ask Your Prospective Practitioner

Besides a medical school degree, OB/GYNs may have little else in common. Each will have a slightly different philosophy and approach to pregnancy and birth. The same (except for the medical school part) can be said for midwives. So before making a final decision about who's going to deliver your baby, you should get satisfactory answers to the following questions and any others you can think of. (If at all possible, make a separate appointment to do this. You'll never be able to get everything in a fifteen-minute appointment. And no, there are no stupid questions—we're talking about your partner and baby here.)

ESPECIALLY FOR OB/GYNS

♦ How do you feel about the father being there for prenatal exams and attending the delivery? Are you enthusiastic about it or just tolerant?

♦ Do you recommend any particular childbirth preparation method (Lamaze, Bradley, and so on)?

♦ At which hospital(s) do you deliver your babies?

♦ Are you board certified? Do you have any specialties or special training?

♦ How many partners do you have and how often are they on rotation?

♦ What percent of your patients' babies do you deliver? What are your backup arrangements if you can't be there?

♦ Do you perform amniocentesis yourself?

♦ Where do you stand on the natural-vs.-medicated debate?

♦ What's your philosophy about Cesareans, labor inductions, and episiotomies?

♦ What's your C-section rate, and how do you make the decision to proceed with the surgery?

♦ Do you permit fathers to attend Cesarean sections? If so, where do they stand (up by the woman's shoulders or down at the "business end")?

♦ What is your definition of a "high-risk" pregnancy?

♦ What kind of monitoring do you recommend? Require?

♦ How do you feel about the mother lifting the baby out herself if she wishes?

♦ How do you feel about the father assisting at the birth?

♦ Do you routinely suction the baby or use forceps during delivery?

♦ Do you usually hand the naked baby straight to the mother?

♦ Do you allow the mother or father to cut the umbilical cord?

ESPECIALLY FOR MIDWIVES

- Are you licensed or certified? By which organization?
- How many babies have you delivered?
- Which physicians and hospitals are you associated with?
- How often does a physician get involved in the care of your patients?
- What is the role of the physician in your practice?
- What position do most of the women you work with adopt for the second stage of labor?
- How do you make the decision to transfer the patient to a hospital or the care of a physician? How often does that happen?

FOR BOTH OB/GYNS AND MIDWIVES

- Do you have an advice line we can call when we panic about something?
- What are your rates and payment plans?
- What insurance, if any, do you honor?
- What percentage of your patients had natural, unmedicated births in the past year?
- What's your definition of "high risk"?
- If labor starts when you're not on call, will you come in anyway?
- What and who (besides you, Dad) is allowed in the delivery room (friends, relatives, doulas, cameras, webcams, etc.)?
- Are you willing to wait until the umbilical cord has stopped pulsating before you clamp it?
- What prenatal tests do you suggest getting? Which ones do you require?
- Which tests do you usually order for women like your partner (her age, race, medical history, and risk factors)?
- How many sonograms (ultrasounds) do you routinely recommend?
- Are women free to walk, move, and take a shower throughout the early stages of labor? Can the baby be put to the breast immediately after delivery?
- Are you willing to dim the lights when the baby is born?
- How much experience have you had with twins or more? (This is a very important question if you and/or your partner have a family history of multiple births or if you suspect that your partner is carrying more than one baby.)

which means that the doctor you see for your prenatal appointments might not be the one in attendance at the birth. So make sure that you're aware of and comfortable with the backup arrangements—just in case your baby decides to show up on a day when your regular doctor isn't on call. Labor and delivery are going to be stressful enough without having to deal with a doctor you've never met before.

Researcher Sandra Howell-White found that women who view childbirth as risky, or who want to have a say in managing their pain or the length of their labor, tend to opt for obstetricians.

Family Physician (FP)

Although many FPs provide obstetrical care, not all do, so check with yours to see whether he or she does. If not, he or she will refer your partner to someone else for the pregnancy and birth. One of the big advantages of going with your family doctor is that after the birth, he or she often can see your partner and baby on the same visit. The time saved running around from doctor to doctor will be welcome.

Like most doctors, FPs are frequently in group practices, and there's no guarantee that the doctor you know will be on call the day the baby comes. So, if you can, try to meet with the other doctors in the practice, as well as any OB/GYN your family doctor might work with. (Most FPs can't do C-sections or assisted delivery, and will need OB/GYN backup. Make sure you're comfortable with this person, since he or she may be doing the delivery if things get complicated.)

Midwife

Although midwives are not as common in the United States as they are in Europe and other parts of the world, they're becoming increasingly popular. And you might want to consider bringing one into the process, even if your partner has a regular OB.

In Howell-White's study, women who expect their partners to be actively involved in labor and delivery and who place a high value on getting information on the birth process are more likely to opt for a midwife. Interestingly, so are women who have no religious affiliation.

Certified nurse-midwives (CNMs) are licensed nurses who have taken a minimum of two or three years of additional training in obstetrics and passed special certification exams. They can deliver babies in hospitals, birthing centers, or at home. But because their training is usually in uncomplicated, low-risk births, CNMs have to work under a physician, just in case something comes up.

Some states have created a new designation, certified midwife (CM), which allows practitioners who aren't nurses, but who go through the same training and take the same exams as CNMs, to work as midwives.

Many standard OB/GYN practices, recognizing that some of their patients might want to have a midwife in attendance at the birth, now have a CNM (or in some cases a CM) on staff. Officially, then, your partner is still under the care of a physician—whose services can be paid for by insurance—but she'll still get the more personalized care she wants. Keep in mind, though, that because midwives aren't MDs, they can't perform surgery and they're able to handle only low-risk cases. Hopefully, neither of these minor limitations will be an issue for you.

If you're considering using a CNM or a CM and need some help with your search, the American College of Nurse-Midwives can put you in touch with one in your area and fill you in on any applicable regulations. Their Web site is www.midwife.org. If you've already found a midwife but want to be sure she's properly certified, visit the American Midwifery Certification Board's Web site, www.amcbmidwife.org.

There are also plenty of midwives out there who are neither certified nor licensed. Lay midwives have a lot of experience working with pregnant women and may even have a lot of specialized training. But they're not regulated and may not have passed any specific midwife exams, which means that in most cases they aren't certified to work in hospitals or birthing centers, but only in home settings.

Like CNMs or CMs, lay midwives must work with a physician, in case of an emergency. The Midwives Alliance of North America, at www.MANA.org, can help you find out more about lay midwives and make contact with one near you.

Doula

Although it sounds like it should mean "a little duel," *doula* is actually a Greek word that means "a woman caregiver of another woman." Many doulas have had children of their own, and all of them go through an intensive training period in which they are taught how to give the laboring woman *and* her partner emotional and physical support throughout labor, and information about the delivery. Doulas have become increasingly popular over the years, and we'll talk a lot more about them on pages 185–87. For now, though, as

"Listen, are you absolutely sure *you want to have kids?"*

you're just beginning the process, there's one very important thing to think about.

Doulas are *not* medical professionals, and they may not be particularly welcome in hospitals. Here's how childbirth educator Sarah McMoyler and I described, in our book *The Best Birth*, the sometimes-combative relationships that can develop. "The problem is that some doulas have an agenda and see their role as protecting mom and baby from what they believe are unnecessary interventions. Sometimes they take that agenda a couple steps too far and start playing doctor, inserting their non-medical opinion into a science-based hospital arena. As you can imagine, this can create tension and confusion, and is, frankly, completely inappropriate. In San Francisco, at least one major OB/GYN practice banned doulas from its delivery rooms after several of them persuaded patients to delay necessary procedures and interfered with the medical team's ability to do its job."

Bills

Having a baby isn't cheap. Exactly how much you have to come up with will depend on how and where your baby is born, and which of the infinite combinations of deductible, coinsurance, copays, and out-of-pocket maximums you have. According to the Agency for Healthcare Research and Quality, a part of the U.S. Department of Health and Human Services, the average charge for a vaginal delivery is just under $9,000—nearly triple what it was in 1993. And the average charge for a Cesarean is almost $16,000—2.5 times higher than in 1993. Private insurance covered an average of 80 percent of prenatal care charges and 88 percent of delivery charges. But even if you have good insurance, that 12–20 percent can still add up in a hurry. Do keep in mind, though, that what the practitioner receives will almost always be quite a bit less than the sticker price.

In the sections that follow, you'll get an idea of how the costs for a typical—and a not-so-typical—pregnancy and childbirth experience might break down. It's a good idea to look over your insurance policy, find out how much it will be picking up, and start figuring out now how you're going to pay for the rest of it. Oh, and all of this is in addition to anything you might have paid for fertility diagnosis and treatment. What we're talking about here are just the costs that come up after your partner gets pregnant. Putting together a budget can be important even if you're adopting. In many cases, adoptive parents are in close contact with the birth mother throughout her pregnancy and delivery. You and your partner might go with her to the doctor's appointments, see the ultrasound, hear the baby's heartbeat, and pick up the bills—most of which won't be reimbursed by your insurance company—for everything. If you're doing an international adoption, you won't have to worry about covering the birth mother's medical expenses, but you'll probably need to budget in the cost of several overseas trips. In addition, you'll need to take into account the many other adoption-related expenses you're likely to incur, including agency fees, attorney's fees, and the home study you'll have to go through.

Pregnancy and Childbirth

Most doctors charge a flat fee for your partner's care during the entire pregnancy. This generally covers monthly visits during the first two trimesters, biweekly visits for the next month or so, and then weekly visits until delivery. But don't make the mistake of thinking that that's all you'll pay. Bills for blood and urine tests, ultrasounds, hospital fees, and other procedures will work their way into your mailbox at least once a month. Here's what you can expect to pay (before your insurance pays its part) for having your baby:

OB/GYN
Expect to pay $2,500 to $6,500 for general prenatal care and a problem-free, vaginal delivery. Add a few thousand more for C-section. Most doctors will meet with you to discuss their rates and the services they provide. For a list of important questions to ask, see pages 24–25. In addition, be sure to discuss which insurance plans, if any, they participate in (it might actually be easier to start with the doctors your insurance covers and choose from there). You should also ask whether they'll bill your insurance company directly or will want you to make a deposit (most will want to collect about 25 percent of the anticipated bill up front); whether you can make your payments in installments; and whether they expect their fee to be paid in full before the delivery.

MIDWIFE
The average cost of a delivery by a midwife is $2,000 to $4,000, but it can vary greatly depending on where you live and whether you expect her to be with you throughout labor or just the part that's right before the birth. If you're delivering at home, you'll also need to add the cost of the supplies the midwife thinks you'll need for the birth (sterile pads, bandages, and so on).

Lab and Other Expenses
♦ Blood: Over the course of the pregnancy, you can expect to be billed anywhere from $200 to $1,500 for various blood tests.
♦ Ultrasound: At least $250 each. In an ordinary pregnancy, you'll have between none and three.

Prenatal Testing
If you and/or your practitioner decide that you're a candidate for amniocentesis or any other prenatal diagnostic test, you can expect to pay $1,000 to $1,500. In most cases genetic counseling is required beforehand, and that costs an additional $400 to $600. If you're having any prenatal testing done just because you'd like to find out the sex of the baby or want reassurance of its well-being (and not because you're in a high-risk group), your insurance company may not pay for it. But if your partner is 35 or older, they probably will pay for testing.

At the Hospital

♦ If you're paying for it yourself, a problem-free vaginal delivery and a twenty-four-hour stay in a hospital will run anywhere from $4,500 to $9,000, depending on where you live. Add $5,000–$7,000 for Cesarean.

♦ If you're planning to spend the night in the hospital with your partner, add about $250 per day.

♦ Anesthesiologists usually charge from $1,000 to $1,500, depending on what they do and the time spent doing it.

♦ Although a lot of people worry about preterm delivery, there's also the issue of late delivery. If your baby decides to stay inside any more than seven to ten days past his due date, your partner may need to have labor induced. If that happens, add another $1,000–$3,000.

♦ If your partner does deliver early (by more than a couple of weeks) and your baby needs to spend time in intensive care, the bills—most of which you will hopefully never see—can go into the hundreds of thousands.

If Your Partner Needs a Cesarean Section

If your partner ends up having a C-section (which happens over 30 percent of the time—up from 21 percent in 1993), all bets are off. Even though it's routinely done, it's still considered major surgery, and is expensive. The operation, which your OB/GYN will perform, is not included in his or her flat fee, and you'll have to pay for at least two other doctors to assist, plus a nurse, who must be in attendance to care for the baby. In addition, a C-section entails a longer recovery period in the hospital—usually four to five days—as well as extra nursing care, pain medication, bandages, and other supplies. If the baby is in good health, you can probably take him home while your partner stays in the hospital, but chances are you'll want the baby to stay with your partner, especially if she is breastfeeding. The baby's additional time in the nursery costs more, too. In our case, by the time all the bills had been paid, we (actually, mostly our insurance company) had shelled out more than $15,000 for the birth of our first child. That alone was just about enough to make us decide on a home birth for the second one (although we ultimately opted against it).

An Important (and Possibly Profitable) Word of Advice

Make sure that you and your partner check your birth-related bills very carefully. Hospitals can make mistakes—in fact, a study by credit giant Equifax found that nine out of ten hospital bills contain errors, and they're rarely in your favor. After we'd recovered from the shock of the C-section bills (which started off at closer to $17,000), we asked a doctor friend to go over them with us. He found that we'd been charged for a variety of things that hadn't happened and overcharged for a lot of the things that had. For example, we'd been billed $25 for a tube of ointment that the hospital's own pharmacy was selling for $1.25. And for the second pregnancy, our nit-picking review of the bills cut about 20 percent off the total.

Look for double billings, services you never received (say, a private room when you were actually in a shared one, or brand-name drugs when you really got generics), and any kind of suspicious jargon. A wonderful exposé done by ABC News found that people had been billed hundreds of dollars for a "disposable mucus recovery system" (a 79-cent box of tissues) and "thermal therapy" (ice cubes in a bag). Also keep an eye out for procedures that never happened. I've heard stories about new parents being billed for their baby's circumcision. That would have been fine, except that they had a girl.

While some of these things may seem silly, they can really add up—especially if you're footing a big portion of the bill. In the Equifax study, the average error was over $1,300. And according to a joint study done by Harvard's Medical and Law Schools, "[n]early half of all Americans who file for bankruptcy do so because of medical expenses." About 10 percent of those are childbirth related.

Even if all the bills are being paid by your insurance, reviewing those bills can still be profitable. Although most insurance companies have their own internal auditors, all they'll be able to catch is charges that are above the "usual and customary" or procedures that simply aren't covered. They won't know about most of the things mentioned above and will be ecstatic if your review ends up saving them money. In fact, some insurers are so thrilled that they'll actually give you a percentage (sometimes as much as half) of the money they save. Naturally, though, you'll have to ask for your reward. So, read your policy carefully and, if you still have questions, talk to your agent or one of the company's underwriters.

And while you're reading your insurance policy, here are a few other things to look out for:

♦ **How long before the birth does the insurer need to be notified about the pregnancy and estimated due date?** Not complying with the carrier's instructions could mean a reduction in the amount they'll pay for pregnancy and birth-related expenses.

Your Rights to Free and Subsidized Medical Care

If worse comes to worst, hospital emergency rooms are required by federal law to give your partner an initial assessment—and any required emergency care—even if you can't afford to pay. But that's no substitute for the kind of ongoing prenatal care that will ensure a healthy pregnancy, healthy baby, and healthy mom.

So if you're uninsured or underinsured (and according to www.MaternityHealth.org, that's the case for two-thirds of pregnant women), or just need some help paying for that prenatal care your partner needs, your first step should be to find out what Medicaid benefits she's eligible for. (If you're in this category, don't feel bad. An average of about 40 percent of maternal hospitalizations related to childbirth are paid out by Medicaid.) Since benefits vary by state, you should also make contact with your state's health department as well. You'll be able to get most of your questions answered at the Medicaid Web site (www.medicare.gov/contacts/) or at www.MedicaidApplication.org.

♦ **When can the baby be added to the policy?** Until the baby is born, all pregnancy- and birth-related expenses will be charged to your partner.

After the birth, however, your partner and the new baby will be getting separate checks (all baby-related expenses, such as medication, pediatrician's exams, diapers, blankets, and various other hospital charges, will be charged to the baby). Some carriers require you to add the baby to your (or your partner's) policy as far in advance as thirty days before the birth; most give you until thirty days after. Again, failing to follow the insurer's instructions carefully could result in a reduction of coverage.

Low-Cost Alternatives

Obstetrical Clinics

If you live in a city where there is a large teaching hospital, your partner may be able to get prenatal care at its obstetrical clinic. If so, you'll spend a lot less than you would for a private physician. The one drawback is that your baby will probably be delivered by an inexperienced—yet closely supervised—doctor or a medical student. This isn't to say that you won't be getting top-quality care. Clinics are often equipped with state-of-the-art facilities, and the young professionals who staff them are being taught all the latest methods by some of the best teachers in the country.

Notes:

Salad Days

What's Going On with Your Partner

Physically
♦ Morning sickness (nausea, heartburn, vomiting)
♦ Food cravings or aversions
♦ Dizziness, irritability, headaches
♦ Fatigue
♦ Breast changes: tenderness, enlargement

Emotionally
♦ Thrilled, stunned, a little frightened, or even completely bummed out (not all pregnancies are planned) that she's pregnant. Sometimes all of these at the same time.
♦ A heightened feeling of closeness to you
♦ Apprehension about the nine months ahead
♦ Mood swings and sudden, unexplained crying

What's Going On with the Baby

It's going to be a busy first month. About two hours after you had sex, one very lucky sperm will have fertilized the egg, and, voila, you've got yourself a *zygote*. By the end of the day, the zygote will divide into two cells and is now, technically, an *embryo*. Your tiny bundle of cells will continue to divide, and four to seven days after conception it will implant itself comfortably into the wall of your partner's uterus, where it'll stay until birth. By the end of this month, your little embryo will be about one quarter inch long—10,000 times bigger than when it was just a zygote—and will have a heart (but no brain), and tiny arm and leg buds.

What's Going On with You

Thrills

I still have the white bathrobe I was wearing the morning my wife and I found out we were expecting for the first time. I remember standing nervously in the kitchen, the countertop cluttered with vials of colored powders and liquids, droppers, and the small container filled with my wife's "first morning urine." (Fortunately, do-it-yourself pregnancy detection kits are a lot less complicated

"Young kids today don't know how good they have it . . .
I remember the old days before home pregnancy tests."

today than they used to be, but I'm not sure they're anywhere near as much fun.) Feeling like a Nobel Prize–winning chemist on the edge of making a discovery that would alter the course of the entire world, I carefully dropped several drops of the urine into one of the vials of powder. I stirred the mixture with the specially provided swizzle stick, rinsed it, and slowly added the contents of the other vial.

In all honesty, the results we got twenty minutes later weren't a complete surprise. But that didn't make it any less thrilling. I'd always wanted to have children, and suddenly it seemed that all my dreams were finally going to come true. It was like hitting the million-dollar jackpot on the nickel slots.

Relief . . . and Pride
The pregnancy test's positive result filled me with an incredible feeling of relief. Secretly, I'd always been afraid that I was sterile and that I'd have to be

Fresh or Frozen
Whether your baby was conceived in a lab or a bed, your future child will develop in the same way. A few days after conception, the embryo— now about eight cells—may be implanted in your partner's uterus. Some clinics wait a few more days, until the embryo develops into a *blastocyst*. The reason is that in the wild, fertilization usually takes place in the fallopian tubes and the embryo travels for a few days until arriving in the uterus where it implants in the wall. Not all embryos, however, develop into blastocysts, so waiting until they do gives your fertility doc a better shot at implanting something that has a strong chance of survival.

Ideally, if you're doing IVF, the lab will fertilize a "fresh" egg— one that has just been retrieved from your partner (or a donor). Fresh embryos result in far more pregnancies and live births than frozen ones. However, fresh isn't always a possibility (the eggs may have been fertilized before you or your partner went through a medical procedure—like chemotherapy—that could potentially have damaged either her eggs or your sperm. Or the eggs may have been retrieved from a faraway donor). Interestingly, fresh may not always be better. In independent studies, researchers in Finland, the U.S., and Australia all found that while defrosted embryos result in fewer pregnancies, the babies that are produced that way are less likely to be born prematurely, be born underweight, or die soon after birth. No one has any idea why that is.

Morning Sickness

Somewhere between half and 90 percent of all pregnant women experience "morning sickness." Despite the catchy name, the nausea, heartburn, and vomiting can strike at any hour of the day. No one's quite sure what causes morning sickness. Some suggest that it's the pregnant woman's reaction to changing hormone levels, in particular *human chorionic gonadotropin* (HCG), which is produced by the placenta and is the same stuff that's picked up by home pregnancy kits. Others, such as researchers Margie Profet, Samuel Flaxman, and Paul Sherman, contend that morning sickness is the body's natural way of protecting the growing fetus from *teratogens* (toxins that cause birth defects) and *abortifacients* (toxins that induce miscarriage). Morning sickness seems to go hand in hand with food aversions, which a lot of pregnant women also have. The most common aversions are to meat, fish, poultry, and eggs—all foods that can spoil quickly and can carry disease.

Whatever the cause, for most women, morning sickness disappears after about the third month. Until then, here are a few things you can do to help your partner cope:

♦ Give her some good news. It turns out morning sickness may actually be a good thing. Women who have severe morning sickness are less likely to miscarry, deliver too early, or have very-low-birth-weight babies. Some research indicates that the more severe the symptoms, the higher the baby's IQ will be. Knowing this probably won't make your partner feel any better, but it might give her something to smile about as she's leaning over the toilet bowl.

♦ Help her maintain a high-protein, high-carbohydrate diet.

♦ Encourage her to drink a lot of fluids (although some women with morning sickness have trouble tolerating milk). You might also want to keep a large water bottle next to the bed. She should avoid caffeine,

satisfied with taking someone else's kids to the circus or the baseball game. I also felt a surge of pride. After all, I was a man, a fully functional man—all right, a stud, even. And by getting my wife pregnant, I'd somehow lived up to my highest potential.

If you're not the biological father of your child (your partner conceived using donor sperm), you probably won't have these feelings. But that in no which tends to be dehydrating, and she might want to start the day with a small amount of nonacidic juice, such as apple or grape, or flat soda; the sweet flavor will probably encourage her to drink a little more than she might otherwise.

♦ Be sensitive to the sights and smells that make her queasy—and keep them away from her. Fatty or spicy foods are frequent offenders.

♦ Encourage her to eat a lot of small meals throughout the day—every two or three hours, if possible—and to eat before she starts feeling nauseated. Basic, bland foods like rice and yogurt are particularly good because they're less likely to cause nausea than greasy foods.

♦ Go for a walk. Some women find that exercise reduces nausea.

♦ Make sure she takes her prenatal vitamins—with food—if her doctor says to do so. He may also suggest that she take some additional vitamin B and K. For some women, the prenatal vitamins may actually be making the morning sickness worse. OB Lissa Rankin often switches her patients to a chewable vitamin. If that doesn't work, she takes them off the vitamins altogether for a few months. "It's more important to stay hydrated and take in some nutrients than to take a vitamin," she says.

♦ Put some pretzels, crackers, or rice cakes by the bed—she'll need something to start and end the day with, and these are low in fat and calories and easy to digest.

♦ Explore alternative treatments. Wristbands that press on the inside of the wrist have reduced symptoms in some women, and so has eating or drinking ginger. In addition, some research indicates that sniffing peppermint oil and isopropyl alcohol (the stuff they rub on your arm before giving you a shot) can shorten the duration of symptoms. But be sure to check with her practitioner before sniffing or eating or pressing on anything.

♦ Be aware that she needs plenty of rest and encourage her to get it.

way means that you're any less manly—or that you're going to be any less of a dad—than the rest of us.

Many expectant ART dads feel a different kind of relief: all those months and years of infertility treatment—the emotional ups and downs, the optimism and disappointment—are now a thing of the past. Other dads take longer to get to this point, and some never completely shake the infertility mentality.

Irrational Fears

At some point after the initial excitement passes, a surprising number of men find themselves experiencing an irrational fear that the child their partner is carrying is not theirs. Psychologist Jerrold Lee Shapiro interviewed more than two hundred men whose partners were pregnant, and found that 60 percent "acknowledged fleeting thoughts, fantasies, or nagging doubts that they might not really be the biological father of the child." The majority of these men don't actually believe their partners are having affairs. Rather, Shapiro writes, these feelings are symptoms of a common type of insecurity: the fear many men have that they simply aren't capable of doing anything as incredible as creating life, and that someone more potent must have done the job. Most guys get over these feelings pretty quickly.

IVF dads, who actually *didn't* do the biological creating, have their own kind of irrational fears. A lot of guys worry that the sperm samples have been switched and that they'll end up with a child of a different race. Actually, the issue isn't so much race as physical similarity. Most IVF couples don't feel the need to make the circumstances of the pregnancy public. And, like any other dads, they hope their children will look like them—at least enough so that they won't have to deal with the inevitable "Gee, the baby doesn't look anything like you" comments. They may choose to tell the kids the true story of their birth later on. But that's a topic we'll tackle in the sequel to this book, *The New Father: A Dad's Guide to the First Year*.

Staying Involved

Exercise

If your partner was already working out regularly before the pregnancy, she probably won't need any extra encouragement to exercise. And if her doctor approves, she can continue her regular fitness routine, and do pretty much any kind of working out she wants to (see "Workout No-Nos" on page 42 for some exceptions). Be aware, though, that some health clubs—out of fear of getting sued—may ask a pregnant woman to provide a letter from her doctor. If your partner wasn't physically active before pregnancy, this isn't the time for her to take up rock climbing or start training to climb Mount Everest. That doesn't mean, however, that she should spend the entire pregnancy on the sofa. Getting exercise is critical. It will help improve her circulation and keep her energy level high.

Exercising during pregnancy may also help your partner keep her weight gain steady and reasonable, help her sleep better, improve her mood, and reduce some of the normal pregnancy-related discomforts. In addition, it will improve her strength and endurance, both of which will come in very handy during labor and delivery. Researchers James Clapp and Elizabeth Noble found that women who exercise during the pregnancy have shorter labors and give birth to healthier babies. Others have found that exercise may even lessen the chance that your partner will deliver prematurely or need a Cesarean section.

But because pregnancy can make even the buffest woman feel a little run down, she may not always feel like working out. One way to help motivate her to get the exercise she needs is to work out with her. (See below for a list of good activities you can do together.) The most important thing is to start easy and not push her if you see she's feeling tired or winded. If your budget doesn't permit joining a gym or health club, you can always buy pregnancy workout DVDs or even download pregnancy exercise apps to your phone.

Whatever you do, remember that you and your partner will get the greatest benefit and least chance of injury if you exercise regularly—thirty minutes on as many days as you can—rather than sporadically. Here are some great ways of exercising together:

♦ **Walking**—doesn't matter whether it's fast or slow, through your neighborhood, on a trail, or on a treadmill.

♦ **Running**—but do yourselves and your knees a favor: get good shoes and run on a soft surface.

♦ **Low-impact aerobics and low-impact exercise machines** such as stairsteppers, treadmills, and bicycles.

♦ **Swimming, water aerobics, or snorkeling.**

♦ **Cycling**—stationary or street is fine, but you should probably skip those bumpy dirt-bike rides.

♦ **Tennis or golf.**

♦ **Light weight-lifting.**

♦ **Yoga**—but avoid extreme stretches; this can cause damage to your partner's connective tissues, which are somewhat weakened during pregnancy.

Before starting any kind of workout program, discuss the details with your practitioner and get his or her approval. If you're doing anything that will work up a sweat, be sure to get enough fluids. Both of you should drink a glass or so an hour before starting and another four to eight ounces every fifteen to twenty minutes while you're working out.

Workout No-Nos

♦ **High-impact sports.** I've spoken with dozens of OB/GYNs over the years and have yet to find one who seriously believes that it's possible to induce a miscarriage by ordinary falling—especially in the first trimester. Severe, sudden impacts such as car crashes can sometimes cause a miscarriage, though. That said, it's a good idea to limit or avoid high contact sports, like boxing, hockey, and roller derby.

♦ **Any sport that might cause her to take a hard fall.** This includes horseback riding, in-line skating, ice skating, and, starting in about the seventh month, bicycling. For a non-pregnant person, taking a tumble doing one of these sports could be dangerous. For someone who's having balance issues, the risks are even greater.

♦ **Downhill skiing.** Unless you're an expert, don't, and even then take it easy. My wife skied when she was seven months pregnant but avoided the most challenging runs, where she'd have risked a serious fall. Unless your partner's doctor prohibits it, cross-country skiing should be fine.

♦ **Heavy lifting.** This can put unnecessary pressure on internal organs.

♦ **Overdoing it.** If she can't carry on a normal conversation while exercising, she's working too hard.

♦ **Overheating.** Your partner shouldn't overdress, and she should keep her workouts moderate. Remind her to take plenty of breaks and drink lots of water before, during, and after the workout.

♦ **Hot tubs/steam baths/saunas.** During the first six to eight weeks of the pregnancy, it's best to stay away from anything that could raise your partner's body temperature above 102°F (39°C). To cool itself, the body moves blood away from the internal organs—including the uterus and the fetus that's inhabiting it—and toward the skin. After eight weeks, she should be okay. But even then, if she does decide to slip into the hot tub, make sure she drinks plenty of water.

One final word of advice: *Do not panic* if your partner engaged in any of these activities before you found out she was pregnant. First of all, there's nothing you can do about it now, and torturing yourselves won't undo it. Second, the chances are slim that anything she did will have an impact on the baby in any significant way. Just be careful from here on out.

Nutrition

The principles of good nutrition haven't changed all that much since you learned about the food pyramid (or, if you remember them, the four basic food groups) in sixth grade. But now that your partner is pregnant, she'll need about 300 more calories a day than before. (Of course, if she was underweight before the pregnancy or is pregnant with multiples, she might need a little more than that. Defer to her doctor on this one.)

If she was overweight before getting pregnant, this is not the time to go on a diet. At the same time, the fact that she's "eating for two" is not a license to eat anything she wants. Her practitioner will undoubtedly suggest a diet for your partner to follow, but here are a few important nutritional basics to keep in mind:

PROTEIN

The average woman needs 45 grams of protein a day, but your pregnant partner should take in 70–80 grams per day. If she's pregnant with twins, however, she'll need to up her protein intake by another 20–25 grams a day, but not until she's in the fourth or fifth month. When the fetus is eight weeks old, it has about 125,000 brain-cell neurons. But then production goes into hyperdrive—one thousand new neurons every *second*—so by the end of the nineteenth week, there are more than twenty-five billion, the most your child will *ever* have.

Many nutritionists believe that a high-protein diet—especially during the first nineteen weeks of pregnancy—supports this surge in brain-cell growth in the baby. Fortunately, most women already eat plenty of protein, so you shouldn't have to pay too much attention. But if you feel you need to be involved, lean proteins are always the best bet. Low-fat milk is one of the easiest sources of protein: one glass has about 8 grams. (Drinking milk may have other benefits as well. Dr. Fariba Mirzaei of the Harvard School of Public Health found that daughters of mothers who drank four glasses of milk per day while pregnant, were 56 percent less likely to develop multiple sclerosis than daughters of women who drank less than three glass per month. If your partner can't drink milk, high doses of vitamin D produced similar results. But check with her practitioner before she takes any supplements.) Other good sources are skinless chicken, lean meats, low-fat cheese, tofu (soybean curd), peanut butter, and cooked fish (but be careful with fish; see "Nutritional and Chemical No-Nos" on pages 48–51). Eggs (cooked, not raw) are another excellent choice; hard-boiled, they travel well and make a handy between-meal snack.

IRON

If your partner doesn't get enough iron, she may become anemic and begin to feel exhausted. She should try to get three servings of iron-rich foods per day. Spinach, dried fruits, beef, fortified cereals, and legumes are all good sources, but since a lot of your partner's iron intake is being used to manufacture the fetus's blood, she may need still more than she can possibly get from food alone. If so, her doctor will prescribe some over-the-counter supplements, but probably not until sometime after the third month. (The doctor may also have her take prenatal vitamins, which contain some extra iron.) If possible, your partner should take the tablets with a glass of orange juice—it (along with other sources of vitamin C) will help her body absorb the iron. One warning: iron supplements frequently cause constipation.

CITRUS FRUIT (AND OTHER FOODS HIGH IN VITAMIN C)

Vitamin C is critical to the body's manufacture of collagen, the stuff that holds tissue together. It also helps ensure the baby's bone and tooth development. Your partner should have a total of at least seven servings a day of fruits and vegetables.

CALCIUM

Calcium is critical to the manufacture of the baby's bones. And since so much of your partner's calcium intake goes directly to the baby, she needs to make sure there's enough left over for herself—1,200 to 1,500 mg per day. If not, the growing fetus will leach it from your partner's bones, potentially increasing her risk of developing osteoporosis later in life. The best sources of calcium are milk and other dairy products. But if your partner is allergic to milk or is lactose intolerant (a condition that affects as many as fifty million Americans), many doctors will advise her to stay away from it—especially if she's planning to breastfeed (her milk allergy could be passed to the baby). Good alternate sources of calcium include pink salmon (canned, with soft bones, is okay), tofu, broccoli, calcium-fortified orange juice, eggs, oyster-shell calcium tablets, and TUMS 500s.

GREEN AND YELLOW VEGGIES

Besides helping form red blood cells, green and yellow vegetables (which, strangely enough, include cantaloupe and mango) are excellent sources of iron and vitamins A and B, which will help your partner's body absorb all that extra protein she'll be eating. Vitamin A may also help prevent bladder and kidney

Going Organic

Grocery store shelves are filled with organic everything. But how much of this craze is hype, just another excuse to mark things up even more? Well, there's no way to give you an exact statistic, but it just seems to make sense that we should try to minimize the amount of pesticides, hormones, antibiotics, and other nasty gunk that shows up in our food. The Environmental Working Group estimates that you can reduce your exposure by as much as 80 percent by avoiding the worst fresh fruits and veggies. They've got a complete list (foodnews.org/fullest.php) of the produce items that you and your partner should avoid, as well as the ones that pose little or no danger (meaning there's no sense paying extra for organic). I've included the ten worst and the ten best below. If you can't stay away from the bad ones, at least wash them very, very carefully.

NO NEED TO BUY ORGANIC	DEFINITELY BUY ORGANIC
Onion	Celery
Avocado	Peaches
Sweet Corn	Strawberries
Pineapple	Apples
Mangos	Blueberries
Sweet Peas	Nectarines
Asparagus	Bell Peppers
Kiwi	Spinach
Cabbage	Kale
Eggplant	Cherries

infections. In addition, these vegetables are an excellent source of folic acid, which can help reduce the incidence of brain and spinal cord defects, especially in the early months of the pregnancy. The prenatal vitamins your partner is probably taking will help augment the folic acid she's getting from her food. The darker the green, the better it is for your partner; she should try to have a serving or two per day. And hey, it wouldn't do you any harm to do the same.

GRAINS AND OTHER COMPLEX CARBOHYDRATES

Grains (including breads and cereals) are basically fuel for your partner's body, and she should have at least four servings a day. Since her body will

"Is it organic?"

burn the fuel first, if she doesn't get enough there may not be enough for the baby. Grains are generally low in calories and high in zinc, selenium, chromium, and magnesium—all essential nutrients. They're also high in fiber, which will help your partner combat the constipating effect of iron supplements. Good sources includes whole-grain breads (keep her away from white bread for a few months if you can), brown rice, fresh potatoes, peas, dried beans, and quinoa.

WATER

As if she doesn't have enough to do already, your partner should try to drink at least eight 8-ounce glasses of water (or unsweetened, non-caffeinated fluids) a day—more if she's doing a lot of exercise or if she's pregnant during the summer. This will help her to replace the water she loses when she perspires (which she'll do more during pregnancy) and to carry away waste products. Keep in mind that at any given moment, about half of the population is walking around somewhat dehydrated, which puts them at increased risk of developing all sorts of problems, including kidney stones and urinary tract cancers.

FATTY FOODS

Despite all the hype about low- or no-fat diets, the fact is that your partner, like everyone else in the world, needs to consume at least some fat. She'll probably be getting most of what she needs in the other things she's eating during the day. But no more than 30 percent of her total caloric intake should come from fat. A diet too rich in fatty foods isn't good for her or your growing baby-to-be. Monounsaturated fats (avocado, peanuts, olive oil, canola oil) are best, followed by polyunsaturated fats (margarine, mayonnaise, walnuts). The worst kind are saturated fats (bacon, lard, butter) and trans fats—basically anything that has the words "partially hydrogenated" or "hydrogenated" on the ingredients panel.

Nutritional and Chemical No-Nos

Here's the deal. Generally speaking, if your partner eats it, drinks it, breathes it, or smells it, so does your growing baby.

♦ **Cigarettes.** When a mother-to-be inhales cigarette smoke, her womb fills with carbon monoxide, nicotine, tar, and resins that inhibit oxygen and nutrient delivery to the baby. Maternal cigarette smoking increases the risk of low-birth-weight babies and miscarriage. There's also some evidence that paternal smoking (exposing your partner and your baby to secondhand smoke) is just as bad. If you think the baby is somehow protected from your smoke by being inside your partner, or if you think that smoking doesn't matter this early in the pregnancy, you're dangerously wrong. Bottom line: if you're a smoker, quit now. If she is, encourage her to quit and help her any way you can. Interestingly, a lot of men put off quitting—or asking their partners to quit—out of fear that withdrawal might lead to some marital tension. Bad choice. The potential danger to your baby far outweighs the danger to your relationship. Oh, and if you're thinking of eCigarettes (and why not? Everything else in our lives seems to have an "e" or an "i" in front of it), think again. Although they do cut down on secondhand smoke, most brands contain nicotine, which is dangerous and addictive to your partner and baby, and many contain diethylene glycol (a very toxic ingredient used in antifreeze) and nitrosamines (the same carcinogen found in real cigarettes).

Here's a great example of what happens when people get something only half right. Remember what I said about smoking causing low-birth-weight babies? Well, in Great Britain, smoking during pregnancy—especially among teen girls—is disturbingly common. These young girls somehow got the idea into their head that having a smaller baby would make labor and delivery less painful. What they didn't understand was that low birth weight is only the beginning. Smoking also increases the odds of miscarriage, birth defects, stillbirth, and premature birth. Babies born too soon have a higher risk of all sorts of problems later in life: respiratory illness, cerebral palsy, mental retardation, and heart problems, just to name a few. And they often go through nicotine withdrawal right after birth, just like crack babies. It also affects the mom, by increasing her risk of developing *placental previa* (where the placenta covers the opening to the uterus) and *placenta abruption* (where the placenta separates from the wall of the uterus before delivery), as well as of going into labor prematurely. Am I scaring you? I sure as hell hope so.

♦ **Alcohol.** Complete abstinence is the safest choice (although your partner's practitioner may sanction a glass of wine once in a while to induce relaxation). Regular, high-dose alcohol consumption can cause Fetal Alcohol Syndrome, a set of irreversible mental and physical impairments and abnormalities. Even moderate social drinking has been linked to low-birth-weight babies, learning impairments, and miscarriages in the early stages of pregnancy. "[I]f you have a glass of chardonnay here and there, you do so at your own risk," writes OB Lissa Rankin in her book, *What's Up Down There? Questions You'd Only Ask Your Gynecologist If She Was Your Best Friend.* "It's probably just fine to enjoy the occasional glass of wine. There's a big difference between being reckless (a definite no-no) and having one drink at dinner. But there's just no data to help us make safe recommendations." If you're worried about any drinking your partner may have done before you found out you were pregnant, talk to her practitioner about it.

♦ **Fasting.** Unless she has a doctor's approval, your partner should never, ever go twenty-four hours without eating. This is especially important in the first nineteen weeks of pregnancy, when the baby's brain is developing.

♦ **Over-the-counter or prescription drugs.** Your partner should talk with her doctor before taking any medication, including aspirin, ibuprofen, and cold medicines—especially anything that contains alcohol or codeine. Antidepressants in particular have come under a lot of scrutiny lately. Several recent studies have linked one class of antidepressants, SSRIs (which include Prozac, Zoloft, Celexa, and Paxil), with increased risk of several fetal abnormalities. Others haven't found any connection. Here's the tough part: researcher Tiffany Field found that untreated depression causes plenty of problems too. So if your partner has struggled with depression, talk with her doctor about whether the risks of taking antidepressants are outweighed by the risks of not taking them.

♦ **Caffeine.** Avoiding caffeine is especially important in the early months. Some studies have shown that pregnant women who drink more than 200–300 mg per day (that's two or three good-sized cups of coffee) have a greater risk of having a miscarriage, of delivering prematurely, or of having a low-birth-weight baby than women who can walk by a Starbucks and keep their wallet in their purse. Zero caffeine is the safest. But if she really needs it, cutting back to a cup a day should be fine. Check with her practitioner to get the final word.

♦ **Recreational drugs.** Abstain during pregnancy—unborn children can be born addicted.

♦ **Certain foods.** Raw meats and fish may contain *Toxoplasma gondii*, which can blind the fetus or damage its nervous system. Unpasteurized milk and soft cheeses such as Brie may contain *Listeria*, another dangerous bacterium. Raw eggs and chicken may contain salmonella. Practitioners do disagree, however, on the magnitude of the risk involved. My wife's first OB/GYN was Japanese and had absolutely no problem with her eating sushi. Some fish you do need to watch out for, though. The FDA recommends that pregnant women stay away from shark, swordfish, mackerel, and tilefish, all of which contain high levels of mercury. Limit albacore tuna to a serving or two per week. If she wants fish or seafood, salmon, pollack, and shrimp are low-mercury choices.

♦ **Cat feces.** Although cat feces don't have much to do with nutrition, they do contain high quantities of the same parasite found in some raw meats. So if you have a cat and you want to be chivalrous, take over the duty of cleaning the litter box for the duration of the pregnancy. Actually, litter boxes don't pose much of a problem for most women. She's got a much better chance of coming into contact with cat poop when she's outside, digging the garden (which, in many cats' view, is nothing more than a giant litter box anyway).

♦ **Insecticides, weed killers, and the like.** As long as you're taking over the gardening, put on your gloves and take a load of chemical fertilizer and pesticides to the nearest toxic waste disposal place (your regular trash company won't take it if they know it's there). Prolonged and repeated exposure to those toxic substances has been linked to birth defects. If you really need pesticides and fertilizers, now's the time to switch to organics. Also, keep your partner far away from other potential chemical contaminants, such as diazinon (a common cockroach killer), as well as no-pest strips, flea sprays and collars, and pesticide bombs. Two chemicals in particular—PCBS and DDE (an insecticide byproduct)—can have some very negative effects. Kids exposed to those chemicals in utero tend to be taller (about two inches) and weigh more (an average of eleven to fifteen pounds) as teens than kids who weren't exposed, and they often enter puberty too early.

♦ **Hair dyes.** Long-term use of hair dyes by adults has been linked to increased risk of several types of cancer. But could hair dye be absorbed through a pregnant woman's scalp, enter her bloodstream, and harm her unborn baby? The jury's out on that one. Some people say that hair dyes (and other chemical-intensive products) are fine during pregnancy. After all, your partner isn't planning to drink the stuff—she's putting it in her hair, right? Others, including Joanne Perron, a postdoctoral fellow at the University of California, San Francisco, don't agree. They point to research that indicates that using hair dye may affect a growing fetus on the cellular level and could increase a child's risk of developmental and reproductive disorders. May. Could. Big words. But why take the risk? The easiest solution is for your partner to avoid dyeing her hair while she's pregnant—at the very least, during the first three months, when the baby's organs and nervous system are forming. If you can't convince her that her hair looks wonderful just the way it is, have her take a look at the list of less-toxic alternatives at the Web site of the Environmental Working Group (www.ewg.org; search for "nontoxic hair dye").

You can get a comprehensive listing of domestic eco-hazards online from www.greenhome.com. Contact information is in the Resources section.

A WORD ABOUT A VEGETARIAN DIET

If your partner is a vegetarian, there's no reason why she and the baby can't get the nutrition they need—especially if she eats eggs and milk. But if she's a strict vegan, you should check with your doctor or a good nutritionist for special guidance.

A FINAL NOTE ON NUTRITION

Helping your partner eat right is one of the best things you can do to ensure that you'll have a healthy, happy baby (and a healthy, happy partner). But don't be too hard on her. Being pregnant is tough enough without having someone standing over her shoulder criticizing every choice she makes. While she'd undoubtedly be better off eating nothing but healthy foods all the time, an occasional order of fries or a candy bar isn't going to do any long-term damage. Finally, be supportive. This means that you should try to eat as healthily as she does. If you absolutely must have a banana split and you're not planning to share, do it on your own time (and don't brag about it).

"Why have you brought me here?"

A Special Note for Adoptive and ART Dads

If you're one of the many expectant adoptive parents who has met your future baby's birth mother, or you've hired a surrogate, do whatever you can to support her pregnancy without being annoying. Encourage her to exercise, stop smoking, eat right, take her prenatal vitamins, go to her regularly scheduled medical appointments, and so on.

The Hunger Campaign

One of the things I constantly underestimated while my wife was pregnant was how incredibly hungry she would get, and how quickly it would happen. Even though she might have had a snack before leaving the office, by the time she got home she'd be ravenous again.

If you've been doing most of the cooking at your house, things probably won't change much during the pregnancy. But if your partner has been making the meals, there are a few things you can do to simplify her life significantly:

♦ **Learn to cook simple, quick meals.** There are plenty of cookbooks specializing in meals that can be made in less than thirty minutes (two good ones are *The 15-Minute Vegetarian Gourmet* and *Desperation Dinners!*:

Home-Cooked Meals in 20 Minutes Flat). In addition, most major newspapers run columns featuring easy-to-cook meals using local and seasonal produce. You can also stock up on healthy microwavable dinners or order take-out meals, but that can get expensive pretty fast.

♦ **Do some meal planning.** This means you'll have to spend some time reading cookbooks, looking for things that sound good. As you're reading, be sure to write down the ingredients you'll need. Although meal planning doesn't sound all that difficult, it's time-consuming—especially when you add in the extra time you'll have to spend at the grocery store.

♦ **Do the shopping.** Even if your partner still plans the meals and makes out the shopping lists, your going to the store will spare her an hour or so a week of walking around on floors that are tough even on non-pregnant people's feet. In addition, many women who have severe morning sickness find that being in a grocery store, surrounded by so much food, is just too much to stomach. If your partner did the shopping before the pregnancy, ask her to make a *detailed* list of the items she usually bought.

♦ **Make her a nutritious breakfast shake.** Let her spend a few more precious minutes relaxing in bed in the morning (see below for a good recipe).

♦ **Keep some snacks in the glove compartment when you're out together.** Her energy can crash at any time, and a handful of nuts, some raisins, or a granola bar can really help.

Recipes

Power Shake
½ cup skim milk
1 banana
12 strawberries
juice of 2 oranges

Combine ingredients in a blender or food processor and serve over crushed ice or straight up chilled.

Basic Quick Snacks
♦ Peel and slice carrots and celery the night before for your partner to take to work for lunch.

Stocking Up

If you keep the following items on hand, you or your partner should be able to throw together a healthy meal or snack anytime.

- Unsweetened cereals
- Whole-wheat pasta
- Tomato or vegetable juice
- Whole-grain bread
- Skim milk
- Nonfat cottage cheese
- Low-fat, naturally sweetened yogurt
- Fresh eggs (and some hard-boiled ones too)
- Natural peanut butter
- Pure fruit jams
- Bottled water
- Crackers
- Fresh vegetables that can be eaten raw, including carrots, cucumbers, celery, and tomatoes
- Fresh fruit
- Frozen berries and grapes
- Raisins and other dried fruits
- Doughnuts (okay, not very often, but you've got to give yourselves a break once in a while)

- Boil eggs: put a few eggs in a pot with enough water to cover them, cover the pot, bring to a boil. As soon as the water boils, turn off the heat and let the eggs sit in the pot for 20 minutes. Then rinse with cold water and shell.
- Mix up some GORP (dried fruits, nuts, raisins, sunflower seeds).

Open-Face Mexican Omelet

3 eggs
1 teaspoon cilantro, finely chopped
1 small tomato, chopped
¼ cup green and/or red pepper, chopped
¼ cup red onion, diced
black pepper to taste

If eating the egg yolks aggravates your partner's morning sickness, use only the whites. Whisk eggs in a bowl or measuring cup and pour into a medium nonstick frying pan. Turn heat on low. As eggs begin to cook, add all other ingredients. Simmer until egg becomes firm, and slide omelet onto plate for serving.

Microwave Oatmeal

⅓ cup oats (you can use 1-minute, 5-minute, quick, or regular)
⅔ cup water
½ banana, sliced
dash cinnamon
⅛ teaspoon vanilla extract
milk
1 tablespoon wheat germ

Put the oats in a 1-quart microwave-safe bowl. Stir in the water, banana, cinnamon, and vanilla. Microwave on high for 2 to 3 minutes, or until the concoction starts steaming or bubbling. Take out and stir again. Add milk to taste. Sprinkle with wheat germ for extra vitamins and protein.

Chocolate Banana Pancakes

½ cup white flour
½ cup whole wheat flour
2 teaspoons baking powder
¼ teaspoon cinnamon
pinch salt
½ tablespoon white sugar
½ tablespoon brown sugar (if you're missing either kind of sugar, just use a
    whole tablespoon of the one you have)
1 egg
1 teaspoon vanilla extract (optional, but great)
1 tablespoon vegetable oil
a bit less than 1 cup milk
½ cup chocolate chips
1 tablespoon butter or margarine
3 bananas, sliced

Reading the Small Print

Getting healthy food isn't always as easy as it might seem, and even though labeling requirements are getting more stringent, most food manufacturers aren't about to do you any favors. So as you're pushing your cart around the grocery store, be sure to read the labels carefully. In particular, watch out for the following:

◆ **Ingredients.** The first ingredient on the list is always the one there's the most of—no matter what you're buying. So, if that healthy ingredient (oat bran!!!) splashed all over the front of the box turns out to be at the bottom of the ingredients list, try something else.

◆ **Sugar—and all the synonyms.** Watch out for fructose, corn syrup, corn sweeteners, sucrose, dextrose, and even honey. They're just fancy ways of saying "sugar."

◆ **Words like "drink," "flavored," or "cocktail."** Despite the healthy-looking label, most fruit "drinks" or fruit-"flavored" drinks contain less actual juice than you might guess—often as little as 10 percent, with the rest usually water and... wait for it... sugar.

◆ **Servings.** This is one of the most potentially deceptive areas in food labeling. In most cases, the number of calories, grams of fat and protein, and other nutritional information is given per serving. That's all very nice, except that manufacturers don't all use the same serving size. For example, I recently saw an eight-ounce package of fairly healthy frozen lasagna. The calories, protein, and fat all seemed okay—until I noticed that the serving size was actually only six ounces. This means that since one person would eat the entire eight ounces, there were really 33 percent more fat and calories than expected.

Mix the dry ingredients in a large bowl. Add the egg, vanilla, oil, and milk. Mix into a smooth batter. Add the chocolate chips and mix again. Melt the butter on a heated griddle. Pour the batter onto the griddle in large spoonfuls. Then quickly place several banana slices on each pancake. When the bubbles that form on the surface of the pancakes pop, flip them over. Cook until the second side is as brown as the first, and remove from griddle.

Any of the following salads can be served as a main course for lunch or as a side dish for dinner.

- **Percentage of calories from fat.** Most nutritionists agree that pregnant women should limit their percentage of calories from fat to about 30 percent. Manufacturers are now required by law to make this calculation for you, so pay careful attention to the "nutrition facts" you'll find on any packaged food.
- **A word about additives.** When it comes to ingredients, my rule of thumb has always been that if you can't pronounce it, don't eat it. In addition, even some easy-to-pronounce items don't belong in your partner's stomach. So while she's pregnant, keep her away from saccharine (a popular sweetener), nitrates and nitrites (preservatives commonly found in lunch meats and bacon), and monosodium glutamate (MSG, a flavor enhancer especially popular in Asian food and, for some odd reason, gefilte fish). All of these may have negative effects on your unborn child.
- **A word about fat substitutes.** Olean and olestra are both fat substitutes that supposedly taste just like butter but pass through the body indigested. This means that they won't enter your partner's bloodstream, so—theoretically, at least—they won't affect your baby in any way. But they might affect your partner. As they pass through her system, these products may actually deplete her body of some valuable vitamins—A, D, E, and K—and interfere with her ability to absorb other important nutrients. Since pregnancy is a time for an increasing nutritional intake, not for cutting back, your partner should probably eat as little of these fat substitutes as possible. In addition, olean and olestra have been shown to cause diarrhea and other stomach problems in some people, and your partner is already feeling nauseated enough as it is.

Tomato and Basil Salad

The combination of these two ingredients makes a refreshing salad. When available, use fresh basil and local tomatoes for the best flavor.

2 vine-ripened tomatoes
6 to 8 basil leaves
4 tablespoons balsamic vinegar
4 tablespoons extra virgin olive oil
freshly ground black pepper to taste

Slice tomatoes and arrange on serving plate. Shred basil leaves and sprinkle over tomatoes. Cover with the vinegar and oil. Add freshly ground pepper. Cover and refrigerate for at least 1 hour. Remove from refrigerator a half hour before serving.

Mixed Green Salad with Balsamic Vinaigrette

Combining different types of greens, such as Boston, red leaf, radicchio, arugula, and endive, makes a green salad more interesting. Raw cucumbers, snow peas, French beans, shredded carrots, and cooked beets also add to the flavor, color, and nutrition of a mixed salad. Stay away from croutons, which are high in calories and low in nutrition.

Thoroughly wash and dry greens, place each serving on a plate, and arrange whatever selection of vegetables you like on top. Just before serving, pour about three tablespoons of balsamic vinaigrette dressing (see recipe below) over each salad.

BALSAMIC VINAIGRETTE

2 cloves crushed garlic
⅔ cup balsamic vinegar
1 teaspoon Dijon mustard
½ teaspoon chopped parsley
½ teaspoon chopped chives
½ teaspoon chopped basil
⅓ cup oil
salt and pepper

Mix garlic, vinegar, mustard, and herbs together. Whisk oil into the vinegar mixture. Add salt and pepper to taste.

Cucumber Salad

2 large cucumbers, sliced
1 medium Bermuda onion, diced
1 cup cider vinegar
½ cup nonfat plain yogurt
1 teaspoon fresh dill, chopped

If the cucumbers are not waxy, leave the skin on. Slice the cucumbers thinly (a food processor does the job best). Combine the diced onion with the cucumber slices in a large bowl that can be refrigerated. Pour the vinegar and yogurt over the mixture, cover, and leave in the refrigerator overnight. Serve cold as a side dish, garnished with the dill.

Low-Calorie Pizza

Create your own combination of toppings, including artichokes, olives, and squash, and use an assortment of cheeses, such as blue, cheddar, Swiss, and even low-fat cottage cheese.

4 soft tortillas (found in grocery freezer)
2 fresh plum tomatoes, sliced
3 cloves garlic, minced or crushed
1 cup mushrooms, sliced and sautéed
1 medium onion, chopped and sautéed
6 teaspoons fresh herbs (oregano, thyme, and basil), minced (or 3 teaspoons dried)
½ cup shredded cheese or low-fat cottage cheese

Preheat oven to 350°F. Place tortillas on a lightly greased cookie sheet. Cover with tomatoes, garlic, mushrooms, onions, and herbs. Add cheese. Bake for 20 minutes or until tortilla is crisp. Serve hot.

Low-Calorie Cream of Zucchini Soup

This recipe can be varied by substituting carrots, potatoes, or celery for zucchini.

3 medium-size zucchini, seeded and cut into ¼-inch slices
1 medium white onion, diced
1 small chicken bouillon cube (optional; bouillon cubes usually contain MSG)
1 cup nonfat plain yogurt
1 tablespoon fresh dill
salt and pepper

Put zucchini, onion, and bouillon cube in a saucepan. Add just enough water to cover. Bring to a boil and cook until soft (about 10 minutes). Let cool. Transfer to a blender or food processor, add yogurt and dill, and blend until smooth. Add salt and pepper to taste.

Quick and Easy Vegetarian Spaghetti Sauce

2 large onions, chopped
4 tablespoons olive oil
½ pound mushrooms, thinly sliced
2 16-ounce jars meatless spaghetti sauce
2 14.5-ounce cans stewed tomatoes
1 4-ounce can tomato paste
1 pound tofu, diced into ½-inch cubes
1½ teaspoons dried basil
a generous pinch of cayenne pepper
1 bay leaf
salt and pepper to taste
1 teaspoon sugar
½ teaspoon garlic powder
1 tablespoon rice vinegar

In a saucepan, sauté onions in the olive oil over medium heat until they're translucent. Add mushrooms, and sauté for 5 more minutes (until the mushrooms begin to release their liquid). Add all the other ingredients and simmer for 40 minutes. If sauce won't be used immediately, let cool, pour into two serving containers, and store in freezer. Defrost as needed.

Spa Potato Chips

3 baking potatoes, peeled and thinly sliced
nonstick cooking spray
paprika to taste

Preheat oven to 350°F. Slice potatoes as thinly as possible (a food processor is best). Spray a cookie sheet with nonstick cooking spray. Spread out potatoes evenly in pan. Sprinkle with paprika and bake for about 15 minutes, or until crisp.

Spicy Peanut Butter Pasta

1 pound angel-hair pasta
1 tablespoon sesame oil
4 tablespoons peanut or safflower oil
6 cloves garlic, minced
1 generous pinch (⅛ teaspoon) red pepper flakes

10 scallions, thinly sliced
½ cup creamy peanut butter
6 tablespoons rice wine vinegar
6 tablespoons soy sauce
4 teaspoons white sugar
1 cucumber, peeled, seeded, and diced (optional)
cilantro to taste (optional)

Cook pasta according to directions on package. Drain and drizzle with the sesame oil. Set aside. Sauté garlic and pepper flakes in the peanut or safflower oil in a large frying pan. Add scallions. Turn heat to high and stir for one minute. Remove from heat. Add remaining ingredients and use a wire whisk to thoroughly mix into a thick sauce. Pour over pasta while sauce is still warm. Garnish with cucumber and/or cilantro, if desired.

Garlic Roasted Chicken

1 roasting chicken (3 to 4 pounds)
5 garlic cloves
1 carrot, sliced
2 celery stalks, sliced
4 small white onions
2 teaspoons olive oil
½ cup white wine (optional)
¼ cup water

Preheat oven to 450°F. Clean chicken and rinse thoroughly with water. Pat dry. Using fingers, make pockets under skin and stuff with garlic cloves. Place chicken in a deep baking dish. Stuff cavity of chicken with carrot and celery slices and onions. Drizzle olive oil on top of chicken. Pour wine and water over chicken. Bake chicken at 450°F for ten minutes to sear. Then reduce heat to 350°F and cook for 30 to 40 minutes, or until the juices run clear when the thigh is pierced with a fork.

Rack of Lamb

A festive, delicious dish that is easy to prepare.

¼ cup bread crumbs
3 cloves garlic, crushed

2 teaspoons parsley flakes
salt and pepper to taste
1 rack of lamb (ask the butcher to crack the rack, remove excess fat, and
    French-cut the ribs)
5 teaspoons Dijon mustard

Preheat oven to 450°F. In a small bowl, mix the bread crumbs, garlic, parsley, and salt and pepper. Place rack of lamb in a baking pan, meat side up. Spread mustard on top and bake for 10 minutes. Remove from oven. Using a fork, press the bread-crumb mixture into mustard, reduce heat to 350°F, and cook for about 20 more minutes, or until medium rare.

Fruit Salad with Creamy Yogurt Dressing

A refreshing, low-calorie dish for breakfast, lunch, or dessert. As a side dish or dessert, this recipe serves four. As a main course for lunch, it serves two.

1 green apple, cored and diced
1 banana, sliced
juice of 1 lime
1 small bunch of red or green seedless grapes
5 strawberries, halved
1 seedless navel orange (or other citrus fruit), sectioned
2 kiwis, peeled and sliced
1 cup low-fat vanilla yogurt (or nonfat plain yogurt)
1 teaspoon cinnamon
½ cup shredded coconut (optional)
4 to 8 fresh mint leaves (optional)

In a large mixing bowl combine banana and apple, pour lime juice over them, and mix. Add remaining fruit and mix again. In a separate bowl combine yogurt and cinnamon. Just before serving, mix the yogurt dressing and coconut into the fruit. If fresh mint is available, garnish each serving with one or two leaves.

The Doctor Will See You Now

What's Going On with Your Partner

Physically
♦ Continuing fatigue
♦ Continuing morning sickness
♦ Frequent urination
♦ Tingly fingers
♦ Breast tenderness and darkening nipples

Emotionally
♦ Continued elation and at the same time some ambivalence about being pregnant
♦ Inability to keep her mind on her work
♦ Fear you won't find her attractive anymore
♦ Continuing moodiness
♦ Fear of an early miscarriage, especially if you used ART

What's Going On with the Baby

During this month, the baby will officially change from an embryo to a fetus. By the end of the month, he or she (it's way too early to tell which by looking) will have stubby little arms (with wrists but no fingers yet), sealed-shut eyes on the side of the face, ears, and a tiny, beating heart (on the outside of the body). If you bumped into a six-foot-tall version of your baby in a dark alley, you'd run the other way.

What's Going On with You

The Struggle to Connect

Just about every study that's ever been done on the subject has shown that women generally "connect" with their pregnancies sooner than men do. Although they can't feel the baby kicking inside them yet, the physical changes they're experiencing make the pregnancy more "real" for them. For most men, however, pregnancy at two months is still a pretty abstract concept. For me—as excited as I was—the idea that we were really expecting was so hard to grasp that I actually forgot about it for several days at a time.

Excitement vs. Fear

But when I remembered we were about to become parents, I found myself in the midst of a real conflict—one that would plague me for months. On the one hand, I was still so elated that I could barely contain myself; I had visions of walking with my child on the beach, playing catch, reading, helping him or her with homework, and I wanted to stop strangers on the street and tell them I was going to be a father. On the other hand, I made a conscious effort to stifle my fantasies and excitement and to keep myself from getting attached to the idea. That way, if we had a miscarriage or something else went wrong, I wouldn't be devastated.

Dads who have been through a miscarriage on a previous pregnancy, or done several unsuccessful ART cycles, are especially susceptible to this kind of self-protective (and completely understandable) denial.

Increased or Decreased Sexual Desire

It was during the times when I let myself get excited about becoming a father that I noticed that my wife's and my sex life was changing. Perhaps it was because I was still reveling in the recent confirmation of my masculinity, or perhaps it was because I felt a newer, closer connection to my wife. It may even have been the sense of freedom resulting from not having to worry about birth control. Whatever the reason, sex in the early months of the pregnancy

Looking for Validation

If you're adopting, the time between your decision to adopt and the actual arrival of your child could be considered a "psychological pregnancy." Unlike a biological pregnancy, you won't, in most cases, know exactly how long it's going to take from beginning to end. But what's interesting is that most expectant adoptive parents go through an emotional progression similar to that of expectant biological parents, says adoption educator Carol Hallenbeck. The first step is what Hallenbeck calls "adoption validation," which basically means coming to terms with the idea that you're going to become a parent through adoption instead of through "normal" means.

If you and your partner have hired a surrogate, there's a good chance that you'll be going through a psychological pregnancy as well. Unlike an adoptive couple, you have a much better idea of when your baby will be born, but you may still go through what might be called "surrogacy validation."

This may seem straightforward, but it's usually not. For many parents, according to researcher Rachel Levy-Shiff, adoption (or surrogacy) is a second choice, a decision reached only after years of unsuccessfully trying to conceive on their own and after years of disappointments and intrusive, expensive medical procedures. Infertility can make you question your self-image, undermine your sense of masculinity (how can I be a man if I can't get my partner pregnant?), force you to confront your shattered dreams, and can take a terrible toll on your relationship. If you're having trouble accepting the fact that you won't be having biologically related children, I urge you to talk to some other people about what you're feeling. Your partner certainly has a right to know—and she might be feeling a lot of similar things. In addition, the adoption agency you're working with will probably have a list of support resources for adoptive fathers. Give them a try.

became wilder and more passionate than before. But not all men experience an increase in sexual desire during pregnancy. Some are turned off by their partner's changing figure; others are afraid of hurting the baby (a nearly impossible task at this stage of the game). Still others may feel that there's no sense in having sex now that they're pregnant.

Whatever your feelings—about sex or anything else for that matter—try to talk them over with your partner. Chances are she's experiencing—or soon will be—very similar feelings. One thing you may *not* want to discuss with your partner is your dreams. According to Berkeley, California (where else?) psychologist Alan Siegel, a lot of expectant dads experience an increase in dreams about having sex—with their partner, old girlfriends, and even prostitutes. For some guys, these dreams are an expression of their concern that the pregnancy will mess with their sex life. The brain is probably saying to itself, "Well, big guy, if you can't get any in the flesh, you can still have some pretty wild fantasies...." For other guys, sexual dreams are a way of reassuring themselves that fatherhood—and all those mushy, protective feelings that go with it—in no way detracts from their masculinity.

Staying Involved

Going to the OB/GYN Appointments

The general rule that women connect with the pregnancy sooner than men has an exception: men who get involved early on and stay involved until the end have been shown to be as connected with the baby as their partners. And a surefire way to get involved is to go to as many of your partner's OB/GYN appointments as possible.

Although I always love being told that I'm healthy as a horse, I've never really looked forward to going to the doctor. And going to someone else's doctor is even less attractive. But over the course of three pregnancies, I think I missed only two OB medical appointments. Admittedly, some of the time I was bored out of my mind, but overall it was a great opportunity to have my questions answered and to satisfy my curiosity about just what was going on inside my wife's womb.

There's no doubt that you can get at least some basic questions answered by reading a couple of the hundreds of pregnancy and childbirth books written for women. But there are a number of other, more important reasons to go to the appointments:

♦ You will become more of a participant in the pregnancy and less of a spectator. In other words, it will help make the pregnancy "yours."
♦ It will demystify the process and make it more tangible. Hearing the baby's heartbeat for the first time (in about the third month) and seeing his or her

tiny body squirm on an ultrasound screen (in about the fifth month) bring home the reality of the pregnancy in a way that words on a page just can't do.

♦ As the pregnancy progresses, your partner is going to be feeling more and more dependent on you, and she'll need more signs that you'll always be there for her. While going to her doctor appointments may not seem quite as romantic as a moonlit cruise or a dozen roses, being there is an ideal way to remind her that you love her and reassure her that she's not in this thing alone.

♦ The more you're around, the more seriously the doctor and his or her staff will take you and the more involved they'll let you be (see pages 86–88 for more on this).

If you're planning to go to your partner's checkups, you'd better get your calendar out. Here's what a typical schedule looks like:

MONTH	IF YOU'RE EXPECTING ONE BABY	IF YOU'RE EXPECTING MULTIPLES
1–5	Monthly	Monthly
6	Monthly	Every other week
7	Every other week	Every other week
8	Every other week	Weekly
9	Weekly	Weekly

Of course, taking time off from work for all these appointments may not be realistic. But before you write the whole thing off, check with the doctor—many offer early-morning or evening appointments.

Testing

Besides being a time of great emotional closeness between you and your partner, pregnancy is also a time for your partner to be poked and prodded. Most of the tests she'll have to take, such as the monthly urine tests for blood sugar and the quarterly blood tests for other problems, are purely routine. Others, though, are less routine and sometimes can be scary.

The scariest of all are the ones to detect birth defects. One of the things you can expect your partner's doctor to do is take a detailed medical history—from both of you. These medical histories will help the practitioner assess your risk of having a child with severe—or not so severe—problems (see pages 69–73 for more on this).

If you're in one of the high-risk categories, your doctor may suggest some additional prenatal testing. Keep in mind that, with the exception of ultrasound, blood, and urine tests, each of the other prenatal diagnostics involves some potential risks either to your partner or to the baby. Ask your doctor about them and make sure the benefits of taking the test outweigh the potential risks.

If you did ART and PGD (preimplantation genetic diagnosis, see pages 334–35), you and your partner may not have to be tested at all—the lab was able to test the embryo itself for any potential abnormalities. If any were found, that particular embryo wouldn't have been implanted. However, because there is a small risk of getting a false negative on the PGD, many fertility doctors will recommend additional testing once the pregnancy is underway.

ULTRASOUND (SONOGRAM)

This noninvasive test is painless to the mother, safe for the baby, and can be performed any time after the fifth week of pregnancy. By bouncing sound waves around the uterus and off the fetus, ultrasounds produce a picture of the baby and the placenta. To the untrained eye, standard, 2-D images look remarkably like Mr. Potato Head, without the glasses and mustache. 3-D ultrasounds are able to generate a more complete image of the fetus. And 4-D ultrasounds (sometimes called dynamic 3-D) can actually let you see your future baby in action, sucking his thumb, napping, swimming, and doing whatever else fetuses do to pass the time.

In the first trimester, your doctor will probably recommend an ultrasound only if there's something going on that's a little out of the ordinary. The most common reason is that the size of the uterus doesn't correspond to the age of the fetus when measured from your partner's last period. The doc may also order an ultrasound if your partner has experienced any bleeding, if there's any doubt as to the number of fetuses, or if he or she suspects an ectopic pregnancy (a pregnancy that takes place outside the uterus). At this stage, the ultrasound can confirm that there's a heartbeat, and can measure the baby (starting with the charmingly named Crown-Rump Length, which will give you a better due date estimate).

Second-trimester ultrasounds are usually the ones that low-risk couples see first. They're used to determine the sex of the baby (this one is optional), to get a more accurate estimate of the due date, or just because you're curious about what the baby looks like. If this is the first ultrasound, your practitioner will want to confirm the number of residents in the uterus, see how well they're moving around, and make sure all the body parts and organs are the right size and in the right place. The test may also be used to firm up the due date and to confirm anything that may have come up in other prenatal testing, including the Triple or Quad Screen, amniocentesis, and CVS (see page 72).

During the last part of the pregnancy—and especially if the baby is over-due—your partner's doctor may order additional ultrasounds to determine the baby's position, to make sure the placenta is still functioning, or to confirm that there's still enough amniotic fluid left to support the baby.

TRIPLE OR QUAD SCREENS

The Triple Screen measures three chemicals that may show up in your partner's blood: AFP (Alpha-Fetoprotein), HCG (human chorionic gonado-tropin), and estriol. The Quad includes one more substance, Inhibin A, to the screen, and there's actually a Penta, which adds yet another substance, ITA (Invasive Trophoblast Antigen). Together they're used to flag potential abdomi-nal wall abnormalities and a variety of neural-tube defects (defects relating to the brain or spinal column), the most common of which are spina bifida and anencephaly (a completely or partially missing brain). Whether you have the triple, the quad, or the penta (is this is sounding like Olympic gymnastics judging, or is it just me?) will depend on what your doctor orders. Theoreti-cally, the more things you test for, the lower the false-positive rate.

These simple blood tests are conducted when your partner is 15 to 18 weeks pregnant (some labs will do it as late as 20 weeks), and the results are usually available within a week, sometimes even the next day. It's important to under-stand that a "positive" result is not necessarily an indication of the presence of an abnormality, just that there *might* be a problem. Most turn out perfectly fine, but if your partner does get a positive result, she'll be asked to take addi-tional tests, such as an ultrasound and amniocentesis, which should clear up any doubts you have. Since these screens are really designed to let your part-ner know whether she needs additional testing, she may not want to bother if she's planning to have an amnio or an in-depth ultrasound test.

TESTS *YOU* MAY HAVE TO TAKE

No, you're not pregnant, but there are still a few times when you may need to give a little blood to make sure all is well with your baby. A variety of geneti-cally transmitted birth defects, for example, affect some ethnic groups more than others. So, based on your family histories, your partner's doctor may order one or both of you to get additional blood tests. OB Saul Weinreb told me that

Reasons Your Partner (or You) Might Consider Genetic Testing

♦ One of you has a family history of birth defects, or you know you're a carrier for a genetic disorder such as cystic fibrosis, muscular dystrophy, or hemophilia.
♦ One of you is a member of a high-risk ethnic group, such as African-Americans, Native Americans, Jews of Eastern European descent, Greeks, Italians, and others (see "Tests *You* May Have to Take" pages 69–71).
♦ Your partner is 35 or older.
♦ Your partner has had several miscarriages.
♦ Your partner had a positive Triple (or Quad or Penta) Screen (see page 69).
♦ One of you might be a carrier of specific genes that have been linked with birth defects.

Other Reasons for Prenatal Testing

Prenatal testing is also available to people who, while not considered at risk, have other reasons for wanting it done. Some of the most common reasons include:
♦ Peace of mind. Having an amniocentesis or a Chorionic Villi Sampling (CVS) test can remove most doubts about the chromosomal health of your child. For some people, this reassurance can make the pregnancy a much more enjoyable—and less stressful—experience. If the tests do reveal problems, you and your partner will have more time to prepare yourselves for the tough decisions ahead (for more on this, see pages 81–83).
♦ To find out the sex of the baby (or, in some cases, to determine who the biological father is).

"every person in the world is estimated to carry thousands of potentially harmful genetic mutations, which means that every couple has an approximately equal chance of having a baby with a random genetic disease they had no idea they carried." The good news is that science has been able to identify certain diseases that occur more commonly in certain ethnic groups. So rather than think of these groups as somehow genetically worse off than others, think of them as being lucky that there are tests for conditions that may affect them. New tests are being developed every day. Among the most commonly identifiable conditions are:

♦ Sickle-cell anemia. If you're African American or if your family came from the Caribbean, Italy, Sardinia, or India, you may want to be tested whether your practitioner suggests it or not. If your partner knows she's negative, though, ask the doctor whether you should bother.
♦ Tay-Sachs and Canavan Disease. If either you or your partner is of Ashkenazi (Eastern European) descent, get tested. Tay-Sachs is also found in some non-Jewish French Canadians. Interestingly, once your partner is pregnant, it is more accurate to test you for these conditions than to test her. If your results come back positive, she'll need to be tested, though.
♦ Cystic fibrosis. The American College of Obstetricians and Gynecologists now recommends that OBs offer cystic fibrosis testing routinely.
♦ Thalassemia. Affects mainly families of Asian, Southeast Asian, African, Middle Eastern, Greek, or Italian origins.

You may also have to be tested if your partner has a negative Rh (for rhesus, like the monkey) factor in her blood. If you're positive (and most of us are), your baby might be positive as well. If this is the case, your partner's immune system might think the Rh-positive baby is some kind of intruder and try to fight it. This can lead to fetal brain damage or even death. Fortunately, this problem is preventable: your partner will have to get some anti-Rh injections, starting around the 28th week of the pregnancy.

AMNIOCENTESIS
This extremely accurate test is usually performed at 15 to 18 weeks, and can identify nearly every possible chromosomal disorder, including Down syndrome. It can't, however, detect deformities such as cleft palate. If your baby is at risk of any other genetic conditions, your partner's doctor can order additional testing (but these tests are not done routinely). Amnio is also sometimes used in the third trimester of pregnancy to help doctors determine whether the fetus's lungs are mature enough to survive an emergency premature delivery, if they're worried about that. The test involves inserting a needle through the abdominal wall into the amniotic sac, where about an ounce of fluid is collected and analyzed. Results are usually available in one to three weeks. Unless your partner is considered at high risk (see page 70), or either of you needs to be reassured that your baby is healthy, there's no real reason to have

Location, Location, Location

If your partner is going to have an amnio or CVS and you have a choice as to where to get the test done, go with the lab (or clinic) that does the highest number of procedures. Researchers at Copenhagen University Hospital found that miscarriage rates at facilities that did fewer than 500 amnios over a ten-year period were twice as high as those that did 1,500 or more. And the miscarriage rates for CVS were much higher at facilities that did fewer than 1,500 procedures than those that did more than 1,500.

this test. The chances that a 25-year-old woman will give birth to a baby with a defect that an amnio can detect are about 1 in 500. The chances that the procedure will cause a miscarriage, however, are 1 in 200. For a woman over 35, though, amnio begins to make statistical sense: the chances she'll have a baby with chromosomal abnormalities are roughly 1 in 190 and rise steadily as she ages. At 40, they're about 1 in 65; at 45, 1 in 20.

CHORIONIC VILLI SAMPLING (CVS)

Generally this test is performed at 9 to 12 weeks to detect chromosomal abnormalities and genetically inherited diseases. The test can be done by inserting a needle through the abdominal wall or by threading a catheter through the vagina and cervix into the uterus. Either way, small pieces of the chorion—a membrane with genetic makeup identical to that of the fetus—are snipped off or suctioned into a syringe and analyzed. The risks are about the same as for amnio, and the two tests can identify pretty much the same potential abnormalities. The main advantage to CVS is that it can be done a lot earlier in the pregnancy, giving you and your partner more time to consider the alternatives. That's why the number of amnios is falling, while CVSs are rising.

PERCUTANEOUS UMBILICAL BLOOD SAMPLING (PUBS)

No, PUBS has nothing to do with bars, although you may need one after thinking about all this. The PUBS test is usually conducted at 17 to 36 weeks and is sometimes ordered to confirm possible genetic and blood disorders detected through amnio or CVS. The procedure is virtually the same as an amnio, except that the needle is inserted into a blood vessel in the umbilical cord; some practitioners believe this makes the test more accurate. Later in the pregnancy, PUBS may be used to determine whether the fetus has chicken pox, *Toxoplasma gondii* (see page 50), or other dangerous infections. Preliminary results are available within about three days. In addition to the risk of complications or miscarriage resulting from the procedure, PUBS may also slightly increase the likelihood of premature labor or clotting of the umbilical cord, and since it can't be performed any earlier than 17 weeks, it's not nearly as popular as amnio or CVS.

Dealing with the Unexpected

For me, pregnancy was like an emotional roller-coaster ride. One minute I'd find myself wildly excited and dreaming about the new baby, and the next I was filled with feelings of impending doom. I knew I wanted our babies, but I also knew that if I got too emotionally attached and anything unexpected happened—like an ectopic pregnancy, a miscarriage, or a birth defect—I'd be crushed. So, instead of allowing myself to enjoy the pregnancy fully, I ended up spending a lot of time torturing myself by reading and worrying about the bad things that could happen.

ECTOPIC PREGNANCY

About 1–2 percent of all embryos don't embed in the uterus but begin to grow outside the womb, usually in the fallopian tube, which is unable to expand sufficiently to accommodate the growing fetus. Undiagnosed, an ectopic pregnancy would eventually cause the fallopian tube to burst, resulting in severe bleeding. Fortunately, the vast majority of ectopic pregnancies are caught and removed by the eighth week of pregnancy—long before they become dangerous. Unfortunately, there is no way to transplant the embryo from the fallopian tube to the uterus, so there's no choice but to terminate the pregnancy. As quickly as technology is advancing, though, I'm sure transplantation will be possible in the not-too-distant future.

PREECLAMPSIA

This is one of the most common pregnancy complications—about 10 percent of pregnant women, most between eighteen and thirty, suffer from it, although the highest risk groups are very young teens and women in their 40s. Preeclampsia is sometimes referred to as toxemia or PIH—protein-induced hypertension—because one of the symptoms is high protein in the urine. Basically, it's an increase in the mother's blood pressure late in the pregnancy. This can deprive the fetus of blood and other nutrients and put the mother at risk of a stroke or seizure. Women who have a history of high blood pressure or blood vessel abnormalities are especially prone, as are daughters of women who had preeclampsia when they were pregnant. And Norwegian researchers Rolv Skjærven and Lars J. Vatten found that "men born after a preeclampsia-complicated pregnancy had a moderately increased risk of fathering a preeclamptic pregnancy." But most of the time it comes as an unpleasant surprise to everyone.

In its early stages there usually aren't any symptoms, but it can be detected by a routine blood pressure check. If the condition worsens, the woman may develop headaches, water retention, vomiting, pain in the abdomen, blurred vision, and seizures. Interestingly, researchers now suspect that preeclampsia is actually a disorder in which the mother's immune system rejects some of the father's genes that are in the fetus's cells. They suspect that women may be able to "immunize" themselves *before* getting pregnant if they build up a tolerance by exposing themselves to their partner's semen as often as possible. This explains why preeclampsia is far more common during first pregnancies, or at least the first pregnancy with a new partner. It also explains why fewer women over 30 develop this condition. (Still, it can happen to older moms or those who have multiple children.)

There's no guaranteed way to prevent preeclampsia, but there are a few things that could reduce the risk. Staying well hydrated, cutting back on salt, and getting enough exercise may help your partner keep her blood pressure under control. So can increasing her fiber intake. One study found that women who ate over 25 grams of fiber every day cut their risk by 50 percent. And in one of the greatest pieces of good news for pregnant women, Elizabeth Triche and her colleagues found that "women who had five or more servings of chocolate each week in their third trimester were 40 percent less likely to develop preeclampsia than those who ate chocolate less than once a week." Apparently, there's a chemical in chocolate, theombromine, that dilates blood vessels and reduces blood pressure. But do you really think your partner needs an excuse to eat more chocolate?

MISCARRIAGES

The sad fact—especially for pessimists like me—is that miscarriages happen fairly frequently. Some experts estimate that between a fifth and a third of all pregnancies ends in miscarriage (sometimes also called "spontaneous abortion"). In fact, almost every sexually active woman not on birth control will have one at some point in her life. (In most cases the miscarriage occurs before the woman ever knows she's pregnant—whatever there was of the tiny embryo is swept away with her regular menstrual flow.)

Before you start to panic, there are a few things to remember: first, over 90 percent of couples who experience a single miscarriage get pregnant and have a healthy baby later. Second, many people believe that miscarriages—most of which happen within the first three months of the pregnancy—are a kind of Darwinian natural selection. Some have even called them "a blessing in disguise." In the vast majority of cases, the embryo or fetus had some kind of catastrophic defect that would have made it incompatible with life. Still, if you and your partner have a miscarriage, you probably won't find any of this particularly reassuring. And it won't make it hurt any less.

Until very recently, miscarriage, like the pregnancy it ends, has been considered the exclusive emotional domain of women. Truth is, it isn't. While men don't have to endure the physical pain or discomfort of a miscarriage, their emotional pain can be just as severe as their partner's. They still have the same hopes and dreams about their unborn children, and they still feel a profound sense of grief when those hopes and dreams are dashed. And many men, just like their partners, feel tremendous guilt and inadequacy when a pregnancy ends prematurely.

Some good friends of mine, Philip and Elaine, had a miscarriage several years ago, after about twelve weeks of pregnancy. For both of them, the experience was devastating, and for months after the miscarriage they were besieged by sympathetic friends and relatives, many of whom had found out about the pregnancy only after it had so abruptly ended. They asked how Elaine was feeling, offered to visit her, expressed their sympathy, and often shared their own miscarriage stories. But no one—not even his wife—ever asked Philip what he was feeling, expressed any sympathy for what he was going through, or offered him a shoulder to cry on.

Psychologists and sociologists have conducted many studies on how people grieve at the loss of a fetus. But the vast majority of them have dealt only with women's reactions. The ones that have included fathers' feelings generally conclude that men and women grieve in different ways. Dr. Kristen Goldbach found that "women are more likely to express their grief openly, while men tend to be much less expressive, frequently coping with their grief in a more stoical manner." This doesn't mean that men don't express their grief at all, or that they feel any less grief than women. Instead, it simply highlights the fact that in our society men, like my friend Philip, have virtually no opportunity to express their feelings—at least not in the "traditional" way. Many

If You're Expecting Twins

If your partner was carrying twins (or more), miscarrying one "does not seem to have negative implications regarding the health or genetic integrity of the surviving fetus," say doctors Connie Agnew and Alan Klein. Miscarrying a twin may, however, put your partner at a slightly higher risk of going into preterm labor.

If your partner is carrying three or more fetuses, you may have to deal with the question of "selective reduction." Basically, the more fetuses in the uterus, the greater the risk of premature birth, low birth weight, and other potential health hazards. Simply—and gruesomely—put, all these risks can be reduced by reducing the number of fetuses. It's an agonizing decision that only you and your partner can make. Since 1980, the number of twin births has doubled, and the number of unplanned triplets, quads, and so on has more than quadrupled. Fortunately, as ART methods improve, that trend will start to decline, which means that fewer and fewer couples will be faced with this heart-rending decision.

men respond to their grief by doing everything they can to get life back to normal. That often means going back to work, and putting in extra-long hours. It's a way of getting away from the self-blame and feeling of helplessness at not knowing how to comfort their partner. It's a way of avoiding the barrage of baby images that was probably always there but now seems much more pervasive. It's a way of coping with their grief and, unfortunately, of ignoring it.

Trying Again

If you've suffered a miscarriage and have decided to try to get pregnant again, your goal is to prepare a healthy environment for the baby to swim around in, and to prevent birth defects or other complications.

One of the most crucial times of the pregnancy is between 17 and 56 days after conception. That's when the organs start developing. But because this stage happens so early on, it's entirely possible that your partner might not know she's pregnant. And by the time she finds out, she may have already done all sorts of things that could affect the baby—things she'll wish she hadn't done.

For that reason, it's important to prepare yourselves for the next pregnancy as far in advance as you can. Six to nine months would be great, but even a month or two can make a big difference.

Pregnancy after a Miscarriage

Getting pregnant after having lost a baby can bring up a jumble of feel-ings for both you and your partner. For example, you'll probably be feeling incredibly happy that you're expecting again. But you may also be worried that this pregnancy will end the same way the last one did. That could keep you from allowing yourself to become truly engaged in and enjoy the pregnancy—at least until after you're past the point when the miscarriage happened last time. If your partner is feeling this, she may deliberately keep herself from bonding with the baby, trying to save herself the grief if the worst happens again. If it's been a while since the miscarriage, you might be angry—in an abstract sort of way—that you're still expecting, when by all rights you should be holding a baby in your arms right now. But if your partner got pregnant right away, you might be feeling guilty at not having let an appropriate (whatever that means) amount of time pass.

Everyone deals with post-miscarriage pregnancy differently, but there are a few things that may make it a little easier:

♦ Try not to worry. It may have happened before, but chances are it won't happen again. Only one in about 200 women are what are called "recurrent miscarriers," meaning that they have had three miscarriages and have never delivered a child.

♦ Don't pay attention to other people's horror stories (you'd be amazed at how insensitive some people can be).

♦ Don't tell anyone about the pregnancy until you're absolutely ready to, and then tell only people you'd want to support you if something bad were to happen (see pages 95–98 for more on this).

♦ Get some more ultrasounds or listen to the heartbeat—this might help to reassure you that all is well.

♦ Get some support. If your partner can help you, great, but she may be preoccupied with her own thoughts. Otherwise, find someone else who's been there and tell him or her how you're feeling.

♦ Support your partner. Encourage her to talk about what she's feeling and don't make any judgments about what she says. And try to keep her calm. As the pregnancy progresses, for example, and she can feel the baby's movements, she may become fixated on counting them—worried that there are either too many or too few. Just so you know, anywhere from 50 to 1,000 a day is normal.

Preconception

The rest of this book is devoted to how to have a healthy, safe pregnancy and a healthy mom and baby. But right now, we're talking about steps you can take *before* your partner conceives again that can boost your chances of getting pregnant, make for a less-eventful pregnancy, and potentially help you reduce or avoid the expense and emotional ups and downs of fertility treatments.

You never know when your partner is going to burst out of the bathroom waving a little white stick and announce, "Honey, I'm pregnant!" So before the two of you hop in the sack, there are a few things that she should do, you should do, and the two of you should do together to get ready.

What She Should Do

♦ **Make an appointment with her health-care provider for a preconception physical.** The doctor will:

   ◊ Evaluate any and all medications your partner is taking to see whether they're safe during pregnancy.

   ◊ Probably prescribe prenatal vitamins and possibly folic acid supplements (folic acid lowers the risk of some birth defects of the brain and spinal cord).

   ◊ Address any medical conditions, such as diabetes, asthma, high blood pressure, depression, epilepsy, obesity, or any problems with previous pregnancies. All of these reduce her ability to get pregnant, and if she does conceive, can increase pregnancy complications and the risk of miscarriage, preterm delivery, and birth defects.

   ◊ Make sure her immunizations are up to date, in particular chicken pox (varicella), German measles (rubella), and hepatitis B.

   ◊ Screen her for sexually transmitted diseases.

   ◊ Discuss the birth control methods she's been using. If she's been on the pill, she may need to go through a couple of pill-free months before trying to conceive.

♦ **Get healthy.** According to the Centers for Disease Control (CDC), "11 percent of women smoke during pregnancy, and 10 percent consume alcohol. Of women who could get pregnant, 69 percent don't take folic acid supplements, 31 percent are obese, and about 3 percent take prescription or over-the-counter drugs that are known teratogens" (substances that can interfere with fetal development or cause birth defects). Getting healthy means:

◊ **Limit caffeine.** Some studies show that caffeine can decrease a woman's fertility and increase the risk of miscarriage or other problems. Other studies find no connection. Just to be safe, though, it's probably best if she cuts back to no more than one or two cups of coffee per day or switches to decaf.

◊ **Exercise.** It's much better for a pregnant woman to continue an exercise routine she already has in place than to start a new one. If your partner hasn't been working out regularly, add this to the list of things to talk about with her health-care provider.

◊ **Watch her weight.** If she's overweight (her doctor will tell her whether it's a problem or not), now's the time to start slimming down. She definitely doesn't want to be dieting during the pregnancy. According to the CDC, "reaching a healthy weight before pregnancy reduces the risks of neural tube defects, preterm delivery, diabetes, Cesarean section," and other conditions associated with obesity.

◊ **Pay attention to diet and nutrition.** What your partner eats immediately before conception and in the first days and weeks of the pregnancy can have a big impact on fetal development and the baby's long-term health. See the sections on pages 43–51 for details on her diet and nutritional needs.

◊ **Quit smoking and drinking.** Both decrease fertility and increase the chances of a premature or low-birth-weight birth, or pregnancy loss. In one study of 20- to 35-year-old Danish couples trying to conceive for the first time, women who had fewer than five drinks (a glass of wine or bottle of beer) per week were twice as likely to get pregnant as women who had more than five.

◊ **Stay out of hot tubs.** A recent study by health-care giant Kaiser Permanente found that women who used a hot tub after conception were twice as likely to miscarry as women who didn't. Other studies haven't found much of a connection, but Kaiser's lead researcher, De-Kun Li, recommends that "women in the early stages of pregnancy—and those who may have conceived but aren't sure—might want to play it safe for the first few months and avoid hot tubs" as a way of reducing "unnecessary risk of miscarriage."

What You Should Do

♦ **Talk to your doctor.** Give him your medical history and tell him about your plans to do the dad thing. You want to find out whether there are any issues that you need to address before you start planning those romantic, candlelit, birth-control-free evenings. One especially important topic you'll want to discuss is how to make sure your sperm is healthy. Here are some ways to do that:

◊ **Keep your balls cool.** Sperm is very sensitive to heat, which is why your testicles—where those little swimmers of yours live—hang outside your body, where it's cooler. Heating them up by a couple of degrees (say, by spending any more than five minutes in a hot tub or hot bath, sitting with your legs crossed for extended periods of time, or wearing tight underwear that keeps your testicles up against your body) could reduce sperm production or cause abnormalities. We all know that women have fertility cycles, but did you know that we do too? Turns out that sperm are on a 90-day cycle, meaning that whatever happens to them today won't show up for three months or so.

◊ **Call in the vice squad.** Smoking, using illegal drugs (or misusing legal ones), and drinking alcohol have all been linked to lowered fertility, miscarriage, and birth defects.

◊ **Watch the toxins.** Hazardous chemicals, pesticides, and even noxious fumes could damage sperm and, if you inadvertently bring them home (for example, on your clothes), they could hurt your partner too.

◊ **Lose some weight.** Dr. A. Ghiyath Shayeb, from the University of Aberdeen, Scotland, found that obese men produce lower volumes of seminal fluid (the liquid that carries the sperm) and have a higher proportion of abnormal sperm. "[M]en who are trying for a baby with their partners, should first try to achieve an ideal body weight," writes Shayeb.

◊ **Have a little more fun.** Traditional thinking has it that if you want to improve your chances of getting your partner pregnant, you should not ejaculate for at least a couple of days before trying. But Australian OB David Greening disagrees. Greening studied men with DNA-damaged sperm. After seven days of ejaculating daily (no, it didn't matter how), the percentage of damaged sperm dropped significantly. And motility— a measure of how straight and how quickly sperm swim toward those ever-elusive eggs—increased.

♦ **Hang out with some dads.** Talk to other guys about what it's like to be a dad, the challenges they've faced, and how they overcame them. Ask a ton of questions.

What Both of You Should Do

♦ **Make sure you've discussed any possible medical issues with a qualified health-care provider.** If you haven't already, you should discuss any and all pregnancy-related risk factors. These include:

◊ **Her age.** Getting pregnant at thirty-five or older increases the risk of certain genetic abnormalities, such as Down syndrome.

◊ **Your age.** (See pages 330–31 for more).

◊ **Family history.** Could either of you be a carrier of any genetic disorders, birth defects, or conditions such as cystic fibrosis or hemophilia?

◊ **Belonging to a high-risk ethnic group.** African Americans may want to be tested for sickle cell anemia. Individuals of African or Mediterranean descent may want to be tested for thalassemia; Jews of Ashkenazi (Eastern European) descent may want to be tested for Tay-Sachs and / or Canavan disease.

♦ **Take a quick look at your HR manual and investigate your family leave options.** We'll talk about this more on pages 149–59. But the more time you have to prepare yourself and your employer, the better.

♦ **Look at your finances.** How are you going to pay for all this? Do you have insurance? If so, check your deductibles and copays—and whether you have maternity coverage at all. If you or she just started a job, does the policy have a waiting period before benefits kick in? If you don't have insurance, what are your options? Could you qualify for Medicaid?

♦ **Sit down with your partner and have some serious discussions about your plans.** Hopefully she'll get pregnant at the perfect time. But if that doesn't happen, how do you feel about fertility treatments? Would you consider artificial insemination using your sperm? Would you consider using donor sperm? How about in vitro (test tube) fertilization? What about using donor eggs? And if you do use any kind of technology, are you prepared to parent twins or more? Don't try to resolve anything in a single conversation.

BIRTH DEFECTS

If one of the tests discussed earlier in this chapter indicates that your baby will be born deformed or with any kind of serious disorder, you and your partner have some serious discussions ahead of you. There are two basic options for dealing with birth defects in an unborn child: keep the baby or terminate the pregnancy. Fortunately, you and your partner won't have to make this decision on your own; every hospital that administers diagnostic tests has specially trained genetic counselors who will help you sort through the options.

There's no question that the availability of genetic testing has changed the landscape with regards to birth defects. Two recent studies analyzed birth data from a 15-20 year period. One found a slight increase in the number of Down syndrome births, the other a slight decrease. As we've discussed, more and more women are putting off childbirth. And since women over 35 are about five times more likely than those in their 20s to have a Down syndrome baby, researchers would have expected the number of births to double. The reason that didn't happen is pretty simple: with genetic testing able to identify Down syndrome babies very early in the pregnancy, many couples are choosing abortion. If you're considering terminating the pregnancy for genetic reasons, remember that communicating clearly and effectively with your partner is probably the most important thing you can do during this stressful time. The decision you make should not be taken lightly—it's a choice that will last a lifetime—and you and your partner must fully agree before proceeding with either option. But ultimately, your partner should make the final decision.

COPING WITH YOUR GRIEF

If you and your partner choose to terminate your pregnancy or reduce the number of fetuses, or if the pregnancy ends in miscarriage, the emotional toll can be devastating. That's why it's critical for the two of you to seek out the emotional support you are entitled to as soon as possible. While there's nothing that can be done to prepare for or prevent a miscarriage, telling your partner how you feel—either alone or with a member of the clergy, a therapist, or a close friend—is very important. And don't just sit back and wait for her to tell you what *she's* feeling. Take the initiative: be supportive and ask a lot of questions.

Avoid the temptation to try to "fix" things. You can't. And don't try to console your wife with statements like, "We can always have another one." Your intentions are good, but it won't go over well.

You and your partner do not have to handle your grief by yourselves: counseling and support are available to both women and men who have lost a fetus through miscarriage, genetic termination, or selective reduction. Going to a support group can be a particularly important experience for men—especially those who aren't getting the support they need from their friends and families. Many men who attend support groups report that until they joined the group, no one had ever asked how they felt about their loss. The group setting can also give men the chance to escape the loneliness and isolation and stop being strong for their partners for a few minutes and grieve for themselves. If you'd like to find a support group, your doctor or the genetic counselors can refer you to the closest one—or the one that might be most sympathetic to men's concerns.

Some men, however, are not at all interested in getting together with a large group of people who have little in common but tragedy. If you feel this way, be sure to explain your feelings tactfully to your partner—she may feel quite strongly that you should be there with her and might feel rejected if you aren't. If you ultimately decide not to join a support group, don't try to handle things alone; talk to your partner, your doctor, your cleric, or a sympathetic friend, or read—and maybe contribute to—some of the blogs that deal with grief from the dad's perspective. One good one is at fathersgrievinginfantloss.blogspot .com. Keeping your grief bottled up will only hinder the healing process.

Notes:

Spreading the Word

What's Going On with Your Partner

Physically
♦ Fatigue, morning sickness, breast tenderness, and other early pregnancy symptoms are beginning to disappear
♦ Continuing moodiness
♦ She doesn't look pregnant yet, but she's having trouble fitting into her clothes anyway

Emotionally
♦ Heightened sense of reality about the pregnancy from hearing the baby's heartbeat
♦ Continuing ambivalence about the pregnancy and wondering how she's ever going to get through the next six months
♦ Frustration and/or excitement over her thickening waistline
♦ Turning inward—beginning to focus on what's happening inside her
♦ Beginning to bond with the baby

What's Going On with the Baby

By now, the little fetus looks pretty much like a real person—except that he or she (even a really sharp ultrasound technician would be hard pressed to tell you which) is only about two or three inches long, weighs less than an ounce, has translucent skin and a gigantic head (although "gigantic" is a relative term—it's roughly the size of a grape now). All the internal organs are there. Teeth, fingernails, toenails, and hair are developing nicely, and the brain is not far behind. By the end of this month, the baby will be breathing amniotic fluid and will be able to curl its toes, turn its head, open and close its mouth, and even frown.

What's Going On with You

A Heightened Sense of Reality
During the third month, the pregnancy begins to feel a little more tangible. By far the biggest reality booster for me was hearing the baby's heartbeat, even though it didn't sound anything like a real heart at all (more like a fast hoosh-hoosh-hoosh). Somehow, having the doctor tell us that what we were hearing was really a heartbeat—and a healthy one at that—was mighty reassuring.

Ambivalence
Most expectant dads have moments—or weeks or months—when they're less than completely excited about the pregnancy. Some are petrified that something terrible will happen to their partner or the baby, or that they'll be stuck in traffic on the way to the hospital and they'll have to deliver the baby all by themselves on the side of the road. Some see the whole thing as an inconvenience, or a never-ending suck of time and money. Others don't like the idea that they might lose their sex life, their youth, their independence, their friends, their savings, and that coveted spot at the center of their part-ner's universe. A lot of times these feelings of ambivalence or lack of interest are followed by guilt—for not being more supportive, or not being a better spouse—or fear that these less-than-warm-and-fuzzy feelings are a surefire sign that you'll be a lousy dad. Give yourself a break, will you?

There are a number of factors that can increase or decrease these feelings of ambivalence:

♦ Is your partner the woman of your dreams, or were you pressured into your relationship? Similarly, is this the relationship of a lifetime, or do you have a feeling that it's not going to last?

♦ Are you totally ready to be a dad, or do you feel that you were pressured into the pregnancy? Have you accomplished everything you wanted to accomplish at this stage of your life, or are you sitting on a bunch of unfulfilled dreams?

♦ Are you financially ready (whatever that means to you) for fatherhood, or are you worried about money?

As you can probably guess, the more ambivalence you feel, the less you'll be involved during the rest of the pregnancy and after your baby is born.

Feeling Left Out

While becoming more aware of the reality of the pregnancy is certainly a good thing, it's not the only thing that you'll be feeling around this point. Toward the end of this first trimester, your partner will probably begin to spend a lot of time concentrating on what's happening inside her body, wondering whether she'll be a good enough mother, and establishing a bond with the baby. She may be worried about the baby's health or concerned that every little ache and pain she feels is a sign of some horrible disease. She's probably internalizing her feelings about all this and may become a little self-absorbed. And if she has a close relationship with her mother, the two of them may develop a deeper bond as your partner tries to find good role models.

Everything she's going through at this point is completely normal. The danger, however, is that while your partner is turning inward, spending more time with her girlfriends, or bonding with her own mother and the baby, you may end up feeling left out, rejected, or even pushed out of the way. This can be particularly painful. But no matter how much it hurts, you should resist the urge to "retaliate" by withdrawing from her. Be as comforting as you can be, and let her know—in a nonconfrontational way—how you're feeling (see the "Your Relationship" section, pages 98–103). Fortunately, this period of turning inward won't last forever.

Excluded—or Welcomed—by Your Partner's Practitioners

For some men—especially those who are feeling emotionally left out by their partners—the joy they experience at the increasing reality of the pregnancy can be outweighed by the bitterness they feel at the way they're treated by their partner's doctors. Pamela Jordan, a nurse and a pregnancy expert, found that most men feel that their presence at prenatal visits is perceived as "cute" or "novel." Many men complain that medical professionals have a tendency to behave as if they're mere onlookers or intruders, and consider their partners the only ones worth interacting with. If they were talked to at all during visits, it was only to discuss how to support their partners. The fact that an expectant dad might have very specific, unique, and important needs and concerns didn't seem to occur to anyone.

If you are interested in being involved and your partner's practitioner isn't as welcoming as you'd like, I can just about guarantee that your experience of the whole pregnancy will be tainted. Whether you realize it or not, you probably have some pretty clear ideas about how you'd like the pregnancy and birth to go. If you're reduced to the role of spectator, you're not going to get what you want, and you're going to feel stressed and resentful. And that's going to influence your level of involvement throughout the rest of the pregnancy, and will make it a lot harder to adjust to all the changes that new fatherhood will bring.

I don't mean to suggest that this kind of thing happens everywhere, or that the fault always lies entirely with the medical staff. A lot of guys feel a little squeamish around (or are just plain put off by) gynecological stuff, and they hide in the corner to avoid having to deal with it. And if your partner has a male OB, it can also be a little odd to be in the room while another guy has his hands in places you thought were off limits to everyone else. (Yes, pelvic exams are standard medical procedures, and if you go to enough appointments, you'll get used to them, but still....)

Fortunately, more and more medical professionals (but not nearly enough) are welcoming dads into the fold. In my case, over the course of three pregnancies, all of the OBs went out of their way to include me in the process. They made a special point of looking at me when talking about what was happening with my wife and the baby. They encouraged me to ask questions, and answered them thoroughly.

Part of the reason for this was that from the very beginning I made it clear that I *wanted* to be involved and I peppered them with questions, so it was pretty much impossible for them to ignore me. I suggest that you do the same, especially if you have even the slightest suspicion that your partner's practitioner is ignoring you or not taking you seriously.

Our first OB even invited me to take a look at my wife's cervix. I was a little put off by the idea, but getting to see the cervix—through which our baby would emerge just six months later—somehow made the pregnancy seem less

"Just as your wife suspected, Mr. Sanders. You have a very little boy growing inside you."

mysterious and made me feel much more a part of the whole thing. (At the same time, I've got to admit that the experience was a little odd.) If your OB doesn't offer you a look, ask for one—but expect some raised eyebrows. Be sure to ask your partner first, though. She might feel that it's more than a bit intrusive—especially since it's a part of her body that she may never see. Plus, she may simply not want anyone but her practitioner looking at her in such a clinical way. Can't blame her for that one.

Physical Symptoms: Couvade

Although most of what you'll be going through during your pregnancy will be psychological, don't be surprised if you start developing some physical symptoms as well. Various studies estimate that as many as 90 percent of American expectant fathers experience *couvade syndrome* (from the French word meaning "to hatch"), or "sympathetic pregnancy." Couvade symptoms are typically the same as those traditionally associated with pregnant women—weight gain, nausea, mood swings, food cravings—as well as some not necessarily associated with pregnant women: headaches, toothaches, itching, diarrhea, even cysts. Symptoms—if you're going to have them at all—usually appear in about the third month of pregnancy, decrease for a few months, then pick up again in the month or two before the baby is born. In almost every case, though, the symptoms "mysteriously" disappear at the birth. Considering that our society generally denies the importance (if not the very existence) of what expectant fathers go through during pregnancy, it's not surprising that some men "express" their concerns and feelings by developing physical symptoms. Among the most common reasons an expectant father might develop couvade symptoms are:

SYMPATHY OR FEELINGS OF GUILT FOR WHAT THE WOMAN IS GOING THROUGH

Men have traditionally been socialized to bite the bullet when it comes to pain and discomfort. And when our loved ones are suffering and we can't do anything to stop it, our natural (and slightly irrational) instinct is to try to take their pain away—to make it ours instead of theirs. This is especially true if we have even the slightest feeling—no matter how crazy—that we're responsible for the pain in the first place. If your partner has been suffering from morning sickness or has had any other pregnancy-related difficulties, you may feel that it's your fault. And if her symptoms have been particularly rough, she might even reinforce your subconscious guilt by reminding you that you're the one who "got her into all this" in the first place.

JEALOUSY

There's no question that your partner is going to be getting a lot more attention during the pregnancy than you are. And some men who develop couvade symptoms undoubtedly do so in a subconscious attempt to shift the focus of the pregnancy to themselves. It's as if they're saying, "Hey, she's not the only one around here who's tossing her cookies," or "Excuse me, but my pants aren't fitting so well anymore either." My father, who was pacing the waiting room while my mother was in labor with me, suddenly got a gushing nosebleed. Within seconds the delivery room was empty—except for my mother—as three nurses and two doctors raced out to take care of my poor, bleeding father. I'm sure he didn't do it on purpose, but for one brief moment during the delivery, Dad was the complete center of attention. The same, of course, holds true during the pregnancy. Similarly, physical symptoms could be a kind of public way of asserting paternity.

Although it's not exactly a couvade symptom, a lot of expectant dads take up hobbies or begin projects that allow them to create something, just like their partner.

YOUR HORMONES COULD BE RAGING

No, I haven't got that backward. While she's pregnant, several of your partner's hormone levels gradually rise. These include *prolactin*, which helps get her breasts ready to lactate (produce milk), and *cortisol*, which appears to be associated with parent-child bonding. It used to be that everyone thought these hormone changes were triggered by the developing fetus. But in several fascinating studies, researcher Anne Storey and her colleagues found something that may change a few minds. Storey took blood samples from expectant mothers and fathers at various points during the pregnancy and found that expectant dads' levels of cortisol and prolactin (which you wouldn't think guys would even have) paralleled their partners'. "The differences for mums were much more drastic, but the patterns were similar," said Dr. Storey, who's Canadian—hence the cute "mums."

Some guys seem to be more susceptible to this kind of thing than others. In talking with the men in her study, Storey found that those who had experienced tiredness, weight gain, changes in appetite, or any other physical couvade symptoms had higher-than-average levels of prolactin and lower-than-average levels of testosterone compared to expectant dads who didn't have these symptoms. Fortunately, this doesn't mean that you'll be developing breasts anytime soon. Like your partner's, your hormone levels will return to normal not long after your baby is born, and your manliness will remain intact.

These hormone changes could also contribute to an extremely common, nonphysical type of couvade symptom. Most expectant dads find themselves somewhat more interested in children than before the pregnancy. Is it simply curiosity, or is it the body's way of preparing the expectant dad for his changing responsibilities? Hard to say. But studies have shown that the stronger an expectant dad's couvade symptoms, the better he'll care for his newborn. Maybe there's something about sharing (sort of) the physical part of pregnancy that helps develop the dad-baby bond. If any of this is hitting home, though, you may want to think twice before you let your partner read this page—especially if you've been making fun of *her* out-of-control hormones. If none of this is hitting home, that's fine too. There are no rules about how you're supposed to be feeling.

GOOD OLD-FASHIONED STRESS

Researcher Robert Rodriguez cites evidence that men with unplanned pregnancies seem to have more symptoms than others, and that working-class men (who, presumably, are more likely to worry about money) have more frequent symptoms than middle-class dads.

YOU MAY BE SENDING MESSAGES TO YOUR PARTNER

Generally speaking, women are more vulnerable during pregnancy and parenthood than men; you can always take off, she can't. (At the risk of sounding politically incorrect, a number of researchers have speculated that this is precisely why women have traditionally looked for men who will be "good providers.") As a result, expectant mothers are often particularly concerned about whether their partners are going to be there for them and whether they're really committed to being fathers. On one level, you can reassure your partner by telling her you love her, by going to all the prenatal doctor appointments, and by educating yourself and staying as involved as you possibly can. But words aren't always enough.

Some evolutionary psychologists have speculated recently that on a far more subconscious level, expectant dads' physical couvade symptoms could be a chemically driven way of showing their partners just how committed they truly are. After all, you could be lying when you tell her you love her and that you're excited about being a dad. But it's a lot harder to fake a nosebleed or a backache or weight gain. In short, your physical symptoms may be nature's way of giving your partner a way to evaluate your true feelings about her and the baby, as well as your reliability as a partner and fellow parent.

A LITTLE HISTORY

Most researchers today agree that in Western societies, couvade symptoms appear unconsciously in those expectant fathers who experience them. But as far back as 60 B.C.E. (and continuing today in many non-Western societies), couvade has been used deliberately in rituals designed to keep fathers involved in the experience of pregnancy and childbirth. Not all of these rituals, however, have been particularly friendly to women. W. R. Dawson writes that in the first century C.E. mothers were routinely ignored during childbirth, while their husbands were waited on in bed. And more recently, in Spain and elsewhere, mothers frequently gave birth in the fields where they worked. They then returned home to care for the baby's father.

Couvade for Adoptive and ART Dads Too? Yep.

Given that couvade symptoms seem to be an expression of fathers' desires to get some confirmation of their special status in their children's lives, it shouldn't come as much of a surprise that adoptive fathers often experience them as well. In fact, according to adoption educator Patricia Irwin Johnson, "sympathetic symptoms of pregnancy" are fairly common. "One or both partners may experience repeated, and even predictably scheduled, episodes of nausea," says Johnson. "Food cravings and significant weight gain are not unusual. One or both may complain of sleep disturbances or emotional peaks and valleys."

Men who are becoming fathers thanks to IVF or some other ART procedure aren't immune to couvade symptoms either. In fact, some research suggests that fathers who have (or whose partner has) experienced infertility may actually be *more* susceptible than dads who conceived naturally. The same may also be true for expectant dads who were adopted as babies.

But in some other cultures, men tried to do the same thing they try to do today: take their partner's pain away by attracting it to themselves. In France and Germany, for example, pregnant women were given their husband's clothes during labor in the belief that doing so would transfer the wives' pains to their husbands. The eighteenth-century Scots believed that a nurse could use witchcraft to transfer the pain of childbirth from the wife to the husband.

Perhaps the most interesting aspect of ritual couvade is the importance attached to the supernatural bond between the father and the unborn child. Whatever the fathers did during the pregnancy was believed to have a direct impact on the unborn child. In Borneo expectant fathers ate nothing but rice and salt—a diet said to keep a new baby's stomach from swelling. In other countries a man who hammered a nail while his wife was pregnant was thought to be dooming her to a long, painful labor, and if he split wood, he would surely have a child with a cleft lip. Afraid of making his own child blind, an expectant father wouldn't eat meat from an animal that gives birth to blind young. He also avoided turtles—so that his child would not be born deaf, with deformed limbs (flippers), and anencephalic (with a cone-shaped head).

While it's pretty doubtful that couvade rituals actually reduced any woman's childbirth pains or prevented any deformities, they do illustrate an important point: men have been trying to get—and stay—involved in pregnancy and childbirth for thousands of years. As Bronislav Malinowski noted in his 1927 book, *Sex and Repression in Savage Society*:

> Even the apparently absurd idea of couvade presents to us a deep meaning and a necessary function. It is of high biological value for the human family to consist of both father and mother; if the traditional customs and rules are there to establish a social situation of close moral proximity between father and child, if all such customs aim at drawing a man's attention to his offspring, then the couvade which makes man simulate the birth-pangs and illness of maternity is of great value and provides the necessary stimulus and expression for paternal tendencies. The couvade and all the customs of its type serve to accentuate the principle of legitimacy, the child's need of a father.

Staying Involved

Spilling the Beans

Another thing (this month anyway) that will make the pregnancy seem more real is telling other people about it. By the end of the third month, I'd pretty well gotten over my fears of miscarriage or other pregnancy disasters, and we'd decided it was safe to spill the beans to our family and close friends. Somehow just saying the words "My wife's pregnant" (I switched to "We're expecting" a while later) helped me realize it was true.

The decision about when to let other people in on your pregnancy is a big one. Some people are superstitious and opt to put off making the announcement for as long as possible. Others rush to the phone or start e-mailing, texting, tweeting, and updating their Facebook pages before the urine is even dry on the pregnancy test stick. Even if you're in the first category, sooner or later you're going to have to start spreading the word—and the end of the third month is a pretty good time.

There are, of course, advantages and disadvantages to making either an early or a late announcement. For example, if you tell people early, you'll probably get a lot of support, reassurance, referrals, and hand-me-downs. But after a while you may start looking around for an Off switch. If you tell early and something does go wrong, that support will be there for you. On the other hand, retracting good news is not an easy thing to do.

ANNOUNCING YOU'RE PREGNANT

J GREER

If you decide to tell people later, you'll have complete control over the information flow. You'll keep from drowning in advice, but some of that advice might have been good. And if something were to go wrong, you wouldn't have to worry about retracting the good news, but you wouldn't have as much of a support network to lean on either.

Ultimately, whom you decide to tell, and in what order, is your own business. But here are a few ideas you might want to keep in mind.

FAMILY

Unless you have some compelling reason not to, you should probably tell your family first. Your close friends will forgive you if they hear about the pregnancy from your Aunt Ida; if it happens the other way around, Aunt Ida may take real offense. There are a few cases, however, when telling your family first might not be a great idea. One couple we know, Lawrence and Beth, kept their pregnancy a secret from their friends for five months—and from their family for longer—hoping that Lawrence's brother and sister-in-law, who had been trying to get pregnant for years, would succeed in the interim.

FRIENDS

If you do decide to tell your friends first, don't count on your secret staying a secret for very long—good news travels a lot faster than you might think. As in the case of relatives, be considerate of friends who have been trying but who haven't been as successful as you.

THE OFFICE

You'll probably want to tell your coworkers and your boss (if you have one) at about the same time as you tell your friends. But remember that society has some pretty rigid work/family rules for men, so be prepared for a less-than-enthusiastic response from some people (see the "Work and Family" section, pages 149–59, for a complete discussion). Whatever you do, though, don't wait until the last minute to tell the folks at work—especially if you're planning to take some time off or make any work schedule changes after the birth.

YOUR OTHER CHILDREN

If you have other children, give them plenty of time to adjust to the news. But don't tell them until after you want everyone else to know. Until they're over six, kids don't understand the concept of "keeping a secret." When she was four, one of our older daughter's big thrills in life was to gleefully whisper in people's ears things that were supposed to be secrets. In her mind, whispering something didn't actually count as saying it.

Make a special effort to include your other children as much as possible in the pregnancy experience. Our older daughter came with us to most of the doctor appointments and got to hold the Doppler (the thing you hear the fetus's heartbeat through) and help the doctor measure my wife's growing belly.

Finally, keep in mind that it's perfectly normal for expectant siblings to insist that they, too, are pregnant—just like Mommy. Insisting that they're not may make them feel excluded and resentful of the new baby. This is especially true for little boys.

A FEW SPECIAL CIRCUMSTANCES

If your partner had a miscarriage and you're expecting again, the rules (to the extent that there are any) for telling family and friends change somewhat. You might want to tell selected people immediately—you may be craving your family's or friends' support, or you may just need someone to be happy for you. Most people, though, want to put it off as long as possible (although in another month or so it'll be pretty obvious). Here are some common reasons why:

♦ You may be worried that there could be another miscarriage and don't want to put yourself through the pain of calling everyone to give them bad news. This is especially true if your partner has had more than one.

♦ If your partner got pregnant right after a miscarriage, you may worry that other people will think you're being disrespectful by not grieving longer.

♦ You may want to wait until you're over the hump—past the point when the miscarriage happened last time. If you have other kids who know about the previous miscarriage, it's a good idea to wait until the pregnancy is pretty far along. They may worry about your partner or the new baby, and they might even be afraid that something they did caused the first miscarriage. If you have even the slightest inkling that this is the case, spend some time gently explaining to your other children that they are not responsible at all, that sometimes things happen that we just can't explain.

Telling friends and family that you've decided to adopt, that you're doing ART, or that you're using a gestational carrier can also be surprisingly tricky. Some couples are perfectly fine with the idea. But for most, it's a lot more complicated. To start with, you or your partner might be ashamed at what you might consider the inadequacy of not being able to get pregnant naturally. And then there's the grief one or both of you may feel. Depending on which options you're considering, you may have to come to terms with the loss of your dreams of having a biologically related child and keeping your genetic line alive. Or the disappointment at being deprived of the opportunity to go through a pregnancy and birth.

Although you'd think that everyone would be overjoyed at your decision to adopt (or, if you're using donor sperm or eggs, to tell people about it), that's not always the case. Some people—especially relatives—might not be too happy that you're bringing an "outsider" into your family. You have every right to expect your family to respect your decision and treat you and your partner with respect. At the same time, as Patricia Irwin Johnson points out, your family has the right to expect certain things from you:

♦ **Information.** They can't be sensitive about something they don't understand. You might want to recommend some books on adoption, such as Patricia Irwin Johnson's *Launching a Baby's Adoption* or Sherrie Eldridge's *20 Things Adoptive Parents Need to Succeed* (see Bibliography).

- ◆ **Sensitivity.** You must acknowledge that your decision to adopt might cause some people some pain. Your parents, for example, might be disappointed that they're not going to become grandparents the "right" way or that a genetic family link has been broken. Like you, they may need some time to mourn the loss of their hopes and dreams.
- ◆ **Patience.** Even if they do have information and a good understanding of adoption, they're still lagging behind you and your partner in terms of knowledge. So give them some time to catch up and don't expect instant support and understanding. If someone makes a dumb or insensitive remark about adoption or donor sperm, or anything else, resist the urge to bite her head off. Instead, take her aside and point out the mistake as nicely as you can.

No matter how or when you do it, telling people you're expecting will open a floodgate of congratulations and advice; after a few weeks, you may wonder what anyone used to talk about at parties before. Just about everyone has something to say about what you should and shouldn't do now that you're expecting. You'll hear delightful stories, horror stories, and just plain boring stories about pregnancy and childbirth. You'll probably also have to endure endless "jokes" about your masculinity, speculation about who the "real" father is, and questions about what the mailman or the milkman looks like— mostly, unfortunately, from other men. With attitudes like these, is it any wonder that 60 percent of men have at least fleeting doubts as to the true paternity of their children?

Immediately after breaking the news to our friends and family, my wife and I began to feel some slight changes in our relationship with them. What had once been our private secret was now public knowledge, and just about everyone wanted to share it with us. People would drop in unannounced, usually bearing either gifts or advice—just to see how things were going—and the phone never stopped ringing.

After a few days, you and your partner may start to feel a little claustrophobic. If this happens, don't hesitate to establish some ground rules. For example, you might want to ask your friends and families to call before coming over, or you might set up—and let everyone know about—specific visiting hours. You should also prepare yourself for the possibility that you may feel a little left out. Most people are going to be asking how your partner is feeling, what she's going through, and so on. Few, if any, will ask you the same questions.

If you start feeling that you're being treated more like a spectator than a participant in the pregnancy, there are three basic solutions. First, you can

What If You're Not Married?

Even in the twenty-first century, when it's the norm for couples to live together before getting married, having a child out of wedlock still raises a lot of eyebrows in some circles. Your most liberal-minded friends and relatives might surprise you by suggesting that you "make an honest woman of her" before the baby comes. Try to keep your sense of humor about these things. You and your partner are grown-ups and capable of making the decisions you think best. And anyway, most unmarried parents-to-be find that their relatives' joy at the prospect of a new little niece, nephew, or grandchild frequently overshadows those same relatives' disappointment over your lack of a marriage certificate.

just ignore the whole thing—no one's deliberately trying to exclude you; it just doesn't occur to most people that pregnancy, at least at this stage, affects men all that much. Second, you can sulk. This (although sometimes satisfying) will probably not get you the kind of attention you're craving. Third, you can take a proactive role and volunteer information about how the pregnancy is affecting you. Tell people about how excited you are, how much weight you've put on, and how bad those stomachaches you've been having hurt. Confide your hopes and fears to your friends—especially those who already have kids and can offer advice. If you're lucky, they'll then start asking you for updates.

Your Relationship

WITH EACH OTHER

Pregnancy is not only a time of great joy and anticipation, it's also a time of great stress. And even though you and your partner are both pregnant at the same time, you're not experiencing the pregnancy in exactly the same way or at the same pace. This can lead to an increasing number of misunderstandings and conflicts.

As Jerrold Shapiro writes, when a couple becomes a family, "generally all the things that are good get better, and all the things that are bad get worse." As your pregnancy continues, then, it's critical to learn to talk—and listen— to each other, and to find ways to help each other through this marvelous, but emotionally bumpy, experience.

Trying to Keep the Secret

Despite your attempts to control the flow of information, if you're not careful about what you do, people—especially your close friends—are going to guess. If you're serious about not wanting anyone to know, here are a couple of things to keep in mind:

♦ Stay away from expressions like "in her condition" or "I think she really needs to rest." That's exactly how I inadvertently leaked the news to a friend who had asked how we liked working out on the Stairmaster machine at the gym.

♦ Be unobtrusive if you change your habits. If your partner used to drink or smoke before she got pregnant, you might want to think a little about how your friends and family will react to her new, vice-free lifestyle. When my wife was pregnant with our second daughter, we agreed to meet some good friends at a bar one Saturday night. No one really noticed that my wife was drinking mineral water instead of her usual beer. But when she ordered an ice-cold glass of milk, the jig was up.

As men, we've been conditioned to try to protect our partners from harm. And when our partners are pregnant, protecting them may include trying to minimize the levels of stress in their lives. One way we try to do this is by not talking about our own concerns. Somewhere along the line, we got this idea that being strong for our partner means not ever acknowledging how much the pregnancy—and the whole transition to fatherhood—is affecting us.

Researchers Carolyn and Philip Cowan found that this overprotective, macho attitude has some very negative side effects. First, because we never give ourselves the chance to talk about our fears and concerns, we never learn that what we're going through is normal and healthy. Second, our partners never get the chance to find out that we understand and share their feelings. As a result, instead of decreasing stress around the house, we end up increasing it—for her and for ourselves.

There's also some evidence that there are other benefits to talking about how you're feeling—and getting your partner's support for those feelings. Researcher Geraldine Deimer found that men who receive their partners' emotional support during pregnancy have better physical and emotional health and are better able to maintain good relationships with their spouses than men who don't get that kind of support.

*"You're entirely too touchy. My saving grace
is my ability to laugh at myself."*

DANGEROUS ASSUMPTIONS

When I was in the Marines, one of my drill instructor's favorite comments was: "Never assume anything. Assuming makes an ass out of u and me." The sergeant's spelling problems notwithstanding (he also thought habitual thieves were called hypochondriacs and Italians ate bisgetti), he was right about the dangers of making assumptions.

Here are a few important things you may have assumed were no problem, but could end up biting you in the butt. Not all these issues are important to everybody, but if you haven't discussed them already, do it now. A lot of couples avoid bringing up these issues because they're afraid it'll lead to a fight—and no one wants to upset a pregnant woman, right? Well, in my view it's better to talk about these things now, a little at a time, than to seethe about them for the next six months and then have some kind of explosion. Because these issues are so important, give yourself partial credit toward your fifteen-minutes-a-day homework assignment outlined in the sidebar.

♦ **Your involvement in the pregnancy.** Dr. Katharyn Antle May has found that there are three basic styles of father involvement during pregnancy. The *Observer Father* maintains a certain emotional distance and sees himself largely as a bystander; the *Expressive Father* is emotionally very involved and sees himself as a full partner; the *Instrumental Father* sees himself as the manager of the pregnancy and may feel a need to plan every medical

An Important Homework Assignment

In the first year after the birth of their baby, 90 percent of couples in researcher Jay Belsky's studies experienced a tremendous dropoff in the quality and quantity of their communication. Half the time it was permanent.

If you think about this, it makes perfectly good sense. Right now, besides being in a relationship together, you and your partner have your own individual lives, hobbies, friends, jobs, and interests. You're both growing and developing as people—as individuals and as a couple. And that's what has made you the loveable guy you are and the loveable woman she is. But once your baby shows up, you're going to be making an abrupt change to the all-baby-all-the-time channel, constantly thinking about, talking about, and doing things with your baby. All that personal growth stuff is going out the window, at least for a while.

The cure for this is to set aside fifteen minutes every day to talk about something, anything, other than the baby. I know this sounds awfully simple, but if you get into the habit now, while your life is still relatively calm, you'll be taking a huge step toward keeping your relationship fresh. It really does work, and making a commitment to doing it every day is absolutely critical. The more satisfied you feel in your relationship *before* you have children, according to researchers Chih-Yuan Lee and William Doherty, the more time you'll spend with your child during the first year of his or her life.

appointment, every meal, and every trip to the gym. Whatever your style is, make sure to talk it over with your partner. After all, she's pregnant, too.

♦ **Your involvement in family tasks.** How much child care are you planning to do when the baby comes? How much is your partner expecting you to do? How much are you expecting her to do? This is going to sound harsh, but the reality is that you'll be as involved with your children as your partner will let you be. If she wants you to take an active role in child care, chances are, you'll want the same thing. But if she wants to keep these activities to herself, you'll probably be less involved. In addition, the Cowans have found that men who take a more active role in running their households and rearing their children "tend to feel better about themselves and about their family relationships than men who are less involved in family work."

*"Me carrying the baby and you having the cravings
is not my idea of shared responsibility!"*

♦ **Religion.** Both you and your partner may never have given a thought to
the religious education—if any—you plan to give your child. If you have
thought about it, make sure you're both still thinking along the same lines. If
you haven't, this might be a good time to start.

♦ **Discipline styles.** How do you feel about spanking your children? Never?
Sometimes? How does she feel about it? How you were raised and whether
your parents spanked you will have a great deal to do with how you raise
your own children.

♦ **Sleeping arrangements.** It's never too early to give some thought to where
you want the baby to sleep: In your bed? In a bassinet next to you? In a separate room?

♦ **Work and child-care expectations.** Is your partner planning to take
some time off after the birth before going back to work? How long? Would
you like to be able to take some more time off? How long? What types of
child-care arrangements do you and she envision?

♦ **Finances.** Do you need two paychecks to pay the mortgage? If you can get
by on one, whose will it be?

And throughout the pregnancy, don't forget your feelings—good, bad, or
indifferent. Talk about your excitement about having a child, your dreams,

your plans for the future, your fears, worries, and ambivalence, and how satisfied you are with your level of involvement during the pregnancy. Don't forget to ask your partner what she's feeling about the same things. Have these discussions regularly—what the two of you are thinking and feeling in the third month may be completely different from what you'll be thinking and feeling in the fourth, sixth, or ninth months. As difficult as it may seem, learning to communicate with each other now will help you for years to come.

Getting Time Alone

There may be times when you find the pressures of the pregnancy so overwhelming that you need just to get away from it for a while. If so, take advantage of the fact that you don't have a baby inside you, and give yourself some time off. Go someplace quiet where you can collect your thoughts or do something that will give you a break from the endless conversations about pregnant women and babies. Before you go, though, be sure to let your partner know where you're headed. And whatever you do, don't rub it in: she'd probably give anything to be able to take a breather from the pregnancy—even for a couple of hours. Here are a few things you might want to do with your free time:

♦ Hang out with some childless friends.
♦ See a movie or a play.
♦ Start a journal about what you're feeling and thinking during the pregnancy.
♦ Read.
♦ Go to the batting cages and let off a little steam.
♦ Go for a long drive or for a walk on the beach or in the woods.
♦ Be a kid for a while and spend a couple of hours playing video games. If you haven't got a PlayStation, X-box, or Wii of your own, download a few from your favorite gaming site, grab some quarters, and head for the nearest arcade.
♦ Sleep (good luck with that).
♦ If you feel guilty that you're getting a break when your partner isn't, use the time to do something for the family, like updating your blog or building a Facebook fan page and posting all those cute ultrasound pictures.

Money, Money, Money

What's Going On with Your Partner

Physically

♦ Nipples darkening; freckles and moles might get darker and more obvious (a normal side effect from her increasing skin pigmentation)

♦ As her morning sickness begins to wane, she'll start to recover her appetite—for food and for sex

♦ Clumsy—dropping and spilling things

♦ She may be able to feel some slight movements (although she probably won't associate them with the baby unless she's already had a child)

♦ She may notice some strange changes in her vision; if she wears contacts they may be bothering her

♦ She may get gingivitis (swollen, bleeding gums)—60 to 75 percent of pregnant women do

♦ She may be starting to show. Most people won't be able to say for sure, but if she's a celebrity and ends up on the cover of *The National Enquirer*, there'll definitely be a big arrow pointing to her "bump"

Emotionally

♦ Great excitement when she sees the sonogram

♦ Worries about miscarriage are beginning to fade

♦ Concerned about what it really means to be a mother

- Continuing forgetfulness and mood swings
- Increasingly dependent on you—needs to know you'll be there for her, that you still love her
- She may get very depressed when her regular clothes stop fitting her and may become nearly obsessed with her appearance

What's Going On with the Baby

During this month, the baby will grow to about four or five inches long and tip the scales at about four ounces. His heart will finish developing and will start pounding away at 120 to 160 beats per minute—about twice as fast as yours—and his whole body is covered with smooth hair called *lanugo*. The fetus can—and often does—kick, swallow, and suck his thumb. He can also tell when your partner is eating sweet things or sour things and reacts accordingly (swallowing more for sweet, less for sour). He can also respond to light and dark—if you shine a strong light on your partner's abdomen, the baby will turn away.

What's Going On with You

Increasing Sense of the Pregnancy's Reality

By the time the fourth month rolls around, most men are still in what Katharyn May calls the "moratorium phase" of pregnancy—intellectually we know she's pregnant, but we still don't have any "real" confirmation. Oh, sure, there was the pregnancy test, the blood test, the doctor's pelvic exams, her swelling belly and breasts, the food cravings, and hearing the baby's heartbeat a month before. Even with all that, I had the lingering suspicion that the whole thing was an elaborate, *Mission: Impossible*–style fake. Or maybe she was making the whole thing up as an excuse to get out of doing the laundry. Hmmm.

But the day my wife and I went in for the ultrasound, everything began to change. Somehow, seeing the baby's tiny heart pumping and watching those bandy little arms and legs squirm convinced me that we might really be expecting after all.

If you're expecting twins (or more), you may want to pay extra attention to the ultrasound (and you may want to see if you can schedule a couple more over the next few months), because the way the fetuses behave in utero may give you some insight into what you can expect after they're born. Each twin has its own temperament from the very early stages of development, and each set of twins establishes a characteristic pattern of behavior, according to researcher Alessandra Piontelli. Both the temperament and the way the twins interact continue for at least the first year after birth. Even odder (assuming that's possible), one group of researchers found that with triplets, two of the fetuses may interact with each other while ignoring the third. After the birth, that dynamic continued for a year or so, with the third baby isolated by his siblings.

Of course, seeing the ultrasound is only one of a number of things you can do to make the pregnancy seem more real. That's a good thing, because the more real it is, the more significance it will have to you—and the more you'll get involved. And as we've discussed earlier, involvement now leads directly to involvement later, after the birth. So, besides the ultrasound, what are some other activities you can do now to up the reality factor? Researchers Jacinta Bronte-Tinkew and Allison Horowitz identified five:

♦ **Discussing the pregnancy with the mother.** Check (hopefully you've been doing that for a while now).
♦ **Listening to the baby's heartbeat.** Check.
♦ **Feeling the baby move.** Coming soon to a belly near you.
♦ **Attending a childbirth prep class.** Give it another couple of months.
♦ **Buying something for the child.** An ongoing effort.

To give you a hint as to where all this is leading, "Men who participated in more of these prenatal activities," write Bronte-Tinkew and Horowitz, "were more likely to exhibit positive engagement in cognitively stimulating activities (e.g., reading to the child), warmth (e.g., hugging the child), nurturing activities (e.g., soothing an upset child), physical care (e.g., changing diapers), and caregiving activities (e.g., bathing the child)."

Can We Really Afford This?

Besides being fun, seeing the ultrasound filled me with a wonderful sense of relief. After counting all the fingers and toes (not an easy task, considering how small they were and how fast they were moving), I felt I could finally stop worrying about whether our baby would be all right.

But my newfound sense of ease didn't last long. I suddenly became possessed by the idea that we couldn't possibly afford to have a baby—not an uncommon thought among expectant fathers. Not surprisingly, though, expectant fathers in their early and mid-twenties feel more financial pressures than

Commissioning Connection

For most pregnant women, it doesn't take much imagination for the pregnancy to feel real—all they have to do is pay attention to what's going on with their bodies. Expectant dads can connect by being around the pregnant woman, and doing all the things listed above. But what if you've outsourced the pregnancy and someone else is carrying your baby? Connecting with *that* pregnancy is going to be particularly hard.

British researchers Fiona MacCallum and Emma Lycett studied relationships between commissioning couples and surrogate mothers. They found that whether the surrogate mother is a friend, relative, or someone completely unknown to the commissioning couple, the three players have to establish some kind of bond (which some have referred to as a "forced friendship").

In MacCallum's and Lycett's study, 98 percent of commissioning mothers and 90 percent of fathers rated their relationship with the surrogate mother as "harmonious." Sure, there were a few issues here and there—some couples thought the surrogate was overexerting herself, others found the relationship a little chilly—but just about everyone was satisfied with how things went.

Seventy-nine percent of the commissioning mothers saw the surrogate mother at least once a month, often going to all the OB visits. Only 55 percent of the men did this, but in a lot of cases, the surrogate requested that the dad not be there. Eighty-one percent of the moms were there for the birth, but only 31 percent of the dads. Again, this was in large part at the request of the surrogate.

dads-to-be who are over 32. These "older" fathers tend to be more settled in their careers and make more money than the young bucks.

American society values men's financial contribution to their families much more than it does their emotional contribution. And expressing strong feelings, anxiety, or even fear is not what men are expected to do—especially when their wives are pregnant. So, as the pregnancy progresses, most expectant fathers fall back on the more traditionally masculine way of expressing their concern for the well-being of their wives and little fetuses: they worry about money.

Some men express their financial worries by becoming obsessed with their jobs, their salaries, the size of their homes, even the rise and fall of interest

J. OATOR

rates. Expectant fathers frequently work overtime or take on a second job; others may become tempted by lottery tickets or get-rich-quick schemes. Clearly, a new baby (and the associated decrease in household income while the mother is off work) can have a significant impact on the family's finances. But as real as they are, write Libby Lee and Arthur D. Colman (authors of *Pregnancy: The Psychological Experience*), men's financial worries "often get out of proportion to the actual needs of the family. They become the focus because they are something the man can be expected to handle. The activity may hide deeper worry about competence and security." In other words, calm down.

In some ways, work and fatherhood are inseparable. But very few people (except the dads themselves) see providing for the family as involvement. Shawn Christiansen and pioneering fatherhood researcher Rob Palkovitz have come up with four explanations for this selective blindness:

♦ **There's an assumption that men should provide.** Because we're *supposed* to do it, all the financial support dads make gets taken for granted.

♦ **Providing is invisible.** This is partly because work generally takes place away from the family. "When family members do not see fathers in the act of providing," write Christiansen and Palkovitz, "they may not be as acutely aware of the energy, sacrifice, and labor extended in order to provide."

♦ **There are some negative connotations associated with the traditional provider role.** The more time dads spend at work, the less time they can spend at home. So people often see them as uninvolved, or uncaring, or emotionally distant.

♦ **People don't think the right way about providing.** We have a tendency to set up a dynamic of work vs. family (see pages 149–59 for more on this), as though it's one or the other. But men see providing for their family as just one component of what it takes to be a good father.

Safety—Your Partner's and the Baby's

As if worrying about finances weren't enough, many expectant fathers find themselves preoccupied with the physical health and safety of the other members of their growing family (but not their own—studies have shown that men go to the doctor much less frequently than usual when their partners are pregnant). In some cases, men's health and safety concerns take on a rather bizarre twist. For example, psychiatrist Martin Greenberg found that "more than a few men purchase weapons during a pregnancy." Fortunately, most of them sell their weapons after the baby is born.

I had seen the ultrasound and knew that the baby was fine. And I'd already read that at this point in the pregnancy, there was very little chance of a miscarriage. But still, I worried. I quizzed my wife about how much protein she was eating; I reminded her to go to the gym for her workouts; I even worried about the position she slept in. All in all, I was a real pain. (I was right about the sleeping position stuff, though: sleeping on the back is a bad idea. The baby-filled uterus presses a major vein—the *inferior vena cava*—and could cause hemorrhoids or even cut off the flow of oxygen or blood to both your partner and the fetus. It's rare, and anyway, most women will feel uncomfortable enough that they'll move long before any damage is done. But if you're looking for something to worry about, you could do worse.)

A word of advice: If you're feeling overly concerned and protective of your partner and your baby, be gentle and try to relax a little. She's probably feeling some of the same things. Bull riding—even on a mechanical one—is definitely out. But your partner can use her computer as much as she wants without harming the baby (although all that typing might lead to carpal tunnel). Airport metal detectors are no problem during pregnancy, and neither are luggage scanners, unless your partner is intending to climb inside of one. The most important thing you can do is to encourage her to eat right, exercise, and drink plenty of water. Most of the rest will take care of itself. If you're still worried, discuss your concerns with her practitioner at your next appointment. But leave your gun at home.

Ways to Show Her You Care

Here are nearly a hundred ideas—in no special order—that will make you popular around the house (and make your wife the envy of all of her friends—pregnant and otherwise). If you come up with one that's not on this list, e-mail us. We'll add it into the next edition.

♦ Offer to give her back rubs and foot massages.

♦ Get her a gift certificate for a real, professional massage.

♦ Suggest activities that might be harder to do when the baby comes, like going to movies or concerts.

♦ Bring home roses for no reason at all.

♦ Write a bunch of little love notes and hide them in her purse so she can find them.

♦ Vacuum the house—even under the bed—without being asked.

♦ Give your wife lots of hugs; research shows that the more she is hugged, the more she'll hug the baby after he comes.

♦ Go to the store and buy her a package of the most girly, moisturizing bubble bath you can find.

♦ If you're traveling on business, arrange to have a friend take her to dinner.

♦ Kiss her. Hard, long. Then do it again.

♦ Read to the baby (see 133–38 for more on this).

♦ Offer to pick up a pizza on your way home from work—and surprise her with a pint of her favorite frozen yogurt, too. Two pints, if you're planning on having any.

♦ Buy her a maternity pillow.

♦ Offer to run errands (pick up cleaning, shop, go to the drugstore, and so forth). Better yet, do them before you get asked to.

♦ Treat her to a manicure or pedicure. Extra points for both. Even more extra points if you go along with her and get your nails done too.

♦ Dry her tears when she has an unexplained meltdown.

♦ Do the laundry before it piles up. Then fold it, and put it away.

♦ Tell her you think she's going to be a great mother.

♦ Frame your first ultrasound pic of the baby.

♦ If she arrives home after you, have a candlelight dinner on the table, complete with sparkling cider.

♦ Hold her hand while you're out walking.

♦ Listen attentively when she wants to tell you about what a miserable day she had—even if yours was worse.

- Hand over the TV remote and watch what she wants.
- Load and unload the dishwasher.
- Write her a love letter and send it to her in the mail.
- Plan a romantic, pre-delivery babymoon weekend (together, of course). This could be the last time for quite a while.
- Buy a toy or outfit for the baby, have it gift-wrapped, and let her unwrap it.
- Thank her for making you the happiest guy in the world.
- Leave some love notes around the house.
- Indulge her cravings.
- Buy her a pretty maternity dress. Don't even think about the words circus tent.
- Go on a long walk with her.
- Slow dance in your living room.
- Arrange for some of her girlfriends to pick her up and take her out for an evening (nonalcoholic, of course) on the town.
- Plan a baby-naming ceremony.
- Start putting together a list of all the local take-out restaurants.
- Learn baby CPR.
- Offer to give her a back rub—again.
- If you smoke, stop.
- Netflix a chick flick, make some popcorn, and curl up to watch it together. Force yourself.
- Tell her she's beautiful. Then tell her again a few hours later.
- Pay extra attention to making sure she has enough to eat—pack some snacks for her before the two of you go out for an evening or for a hike.
- Organize a surprise baby shower for her.
- Keep a list of your favorite names or buy her an interesting name book.
- Paint a picture for or write a letter to your unborn baby.
- Set up some interviews with potential child-care people.
- Buy her a Mother's Day or Valentine's Day gift—even if it's November.
- Go to her prenatal appointments.
- Keep a journal (either written or recorded) of what you're thinking and feeling during the pregnancy.
- Do something with her that she knows you absolutely hate to do.
- Schedule a tour of the hospital where your baby will be born.
- Sign the two of you up for a childbirth prep class.
- Help her address envelopes for the birth announcements.

- Put together an e-mail or phone tree so you can get the word out when the baby arrives.
- Learn to prepare a few easy recipes (see pages 53–62).
- Smile and nod agreeably when she says, "You have no idea what it's like to be pregnant." She's right, you know.
- If you already have children, take them to the park and let your partner have time alone to relax or run an errand she's been putting off.
- Surprise her with breakfast in bed on a lazy Sunday. Or, on a workday, get up five minutes earlier and surprise her with a power shake.
- Let her win your next argument. And the fifteen or twenty after that.
- Take the day off from work and hang around the house with her.
- Give other expectant mothers seats on trains and buses.
- Make a donation to a local children's hospital or school.
- Don't tell her she looks tired or needs a rest.
- Discuss your fears with your partner. Listen to hers, too, but don't make fun of them—no matter how insignificant they may seem to you.
- Tell her about some of the cool things you're reading about in this book. She really wants to know that you're interested in the pregnancy.
- Paint or wallpaper the baby's room.
- Chocolates and flowers. It's mathematically impossible to overdo either one. Jewelry, either.
- Listen to her complain but don't tell her she's complaining.
- Help put together the changing table and crib.

Staying Involved

Focus on Her

Although every pregnant woman will need and appreciate different things, there is a lot more common ground than you might imagine. Basically, she needs three things from you now—and for the rest of the pregnancy—more than ever before: expressions of affection, admiration, and support (both verbal and physical); sensitivity to her changing physical condition (hunger, fatigue, muscle pains, and so on); and expressions of affection and excitement about the baby and your impending parenthood. Your support is absolutely critical. According to psychologist Edward Hagen, all this actually has a concrete

- Install smoke detectors in your house.
- If she's had a child before, don't tell her that she looks bigger this time than she did last time, even if she does.
- Make a new will that includes your baby.
- Don't complain about any physical pain you're having while she's still pregnant.
- Join a health club together.
- Tell her she's sexy.
- Clean out closets to make room for baby things.
- Stay away from comments like, "Didn't you just eat/cry a few minutes ago?"
- Call her on the phone during the day—just to tell her you love her.
- Offer to carry her bags.
- Do not tell her how great you think Angelina Jolie looks after having so many children.
- Buy a few tapes of her favorite music to listen to in the labor room.
- Say "no" if she asks if she's acting crazy. Ditto if she asks whether whatever she's wearing makes her look fat.
- Don't ask what to make for dinner, just do it. Take a cooking class if you have to.
- As the pregnancy progresses, pick stuff up off the floor. It's going to get harder and harder for her to bend over.
- Do a little sexting.
- Buy her a pregnancy journal.

effect on your partner's emotional and physical health, as well as on the kind of mother she'll be after the baby comes.

Finances

PLANNING A COLLEGE FUND

It may seem hard to imagine now, but in eighteen years or so the baby you haven't even met yet may be graduating from high school and heading off to college. And so, at the risk of reinforcing the old stereotype that a father's role in his children's lives is primarily financial, it's time to talk about money. Over the past twenty years or so, college tuition and expenses, such as room and board, have gone up an average of 6–8 percent a year—that's a lot faster than inflation—and most experts believe that they'll continue to rise at close to the same rate for the foreseeable future. This means that by the time your child walks off the stage with his high school diploma, a bachelor's degree at a public college will probably cost around $100,000; for a private college, you could be looking at more than $360,000. No wonder a growing number of Americans are saying they think that a college education isn't worth the expense. Now hang on a second before you panic. Things aren't as bad as they might seem. Here are some important factors to consider:

♦ The numbers above are based on average sticker prices. There are plenty of lower-cost institutions where your child can get a marvelous education.

♦ Two-thirds of college students receive grants, which can cut tuition and fees by as much as 50 percent. (Of course, even at half off, those numbers are still pretty shocking.)

♦ You don't have to—and probably shouldn't—pay for your child's education in cash. You wouldn't buy a house for cash, right? So why would you pay cash for an education that costs about the same?

"I just found out what braces cost."

♦ A college education is a good investment. According to the College Board (www.collegboard.com), a college graduate with a bachelor's degree will earn about 60 percent more per year than a high school grad. People with master's degrees earn twice as much as high school graduates, and having a professional degree triples earnings. There are also some hidden economic benefits. For example, people with college degrees are much more likely than high school grads to work at jobs where they get employer-paid health insurance and access to retirement plans.

♦ There are quite a few nonmonetary benefits to going to college. When compared to high school grads, those with degrees are healthier (they exercise more, smoke less, and are less obese) and more active in their communities (doing volunteer work, voting, giving blood).

But let's focus on the money. Unless your child gets a full-ride scholarship or attends a military college, you're still going to have to figure out how to finance her education. As counterintuitive as it sounds, your first step is to start socking away as much money as you can into your own retirement accounts. So how does feathering your own retirement accounts instead of starting a college fund in your child's name help put her through college?

Here's how it works:

♦ Money you invest in your retirement accounts is often at least partially tax deductible and always grows tax-free until you start withdrawing it. It also reduces your AGI, which means less income for the financial aid departments to look at. In contrast, investments made in your child's name are after-tax dollars, and interest and dividends may be taxable as income or capital gains at your rate.

♦ The more assets your child has, the less eligible she'll be for financial aid. Schools will assume that 35 percent of your child's assets will be available for educational purposes but only 6 percent of yours. Money in your retirement accounts doesn't count at all.

♦ Plenty of financial-aid options are available: student loans (usually available at below-market rates), grants, fellowships, work-study programs, and so forth.

♦ You can borrow against the equity in your home or against the equity in your retirement accounts.

♦ If you'll be over 59½ by the time your child starts college, you'll be able to withdraw money from your IRA or other retirement account without incurring any penalties. If you're under 59½, you can make penalty-free withdrawals

Digging Out of the Hole

Before you even start worrying about how you're going to finance the future, it's critical that you spend some time making sure the present is taken care of. If you have huge debts, the place to start is by paying them off. Adopting a child or conceiving one artificially, for example, can cost a ton of money—$25,000 to $50,000 is not at all uncommon. If you borrowed against your retirement accounts, took out a second mortgage, or put it on your credit cards, start working on those before, or at least at the same time as, you start saving for your child's education. You have a responsibility to your child, yourself, and your family to stay in the best financial shape possible. But big debts—particularly on high-interest-rate credit cards—can undermine your whole family's long-term financial health.

If you need to, consult a professional who can help you put together a budget that includes servicing your debt and savings (see pages 120–21 for more on this). Get in the habit of putting something aside every month, even if it's just a few dollars. The best way to do this is through *dollar cost averaging*. This means that on a regular basis—weekly, monthly, quarterly—you contribute a fixed amount to the same mutual fund or other investment. When prices are up you're buying fewer shares; when prices are down, you're buying more.

The problem with this or any other regular savings plan is remembering to do it. If things get tight—as they have plenty of times at my house—the education checks can get "overlooked" or "rescheduled." Having it automatically taken out of your paycheck is a great—and somewhat less painful—way to go. If you can get control of your finances now, who knows: you might even be able to afford to have another kid.

for qualified educational purposes. Keep in mind that you may still need to pay taxes on any withdrawals.

The bottom line, as certified financial planner Jackie Weitzberg so elegantly puts it, is that "You can always finance college, but you can't finance your retirement."

Of course, this approach may not work for everyone. You may have already maxed out all your retirement options or you may be wealthy enough that there's not much chance that your child will qualify for financial aid. Or maybe you just want to put some money away for your child to use later. In these cases, there are still a number of options. We can't possibly cover them all here, but we've focused on a few of the most common ones. Before you make any big decisions, I urge you to talk over your choices with a financial planner and/or an accountant to make sure that the plan you're considering fits in with your overall financial objectives.

BONDS   Of all the U.S. savings bonds that are available, only two—Series EE and Series I—have features that make them attractive options for financing your child's education. If you buy them electronically (at www.treasurydirect .gov), you'll pay the face value ($50 for a $50 bond), and it will earn a fixed rate of interest for as long as you hold it. If you buy paper bonds, which you can do at almost any bank, you buy them at a discount ($25 for a $50 bond), and the bond will be worth its face value only when it matures.

If you use the bonds for qualified educational expenses, interest is completely tax-free. But there are restrictions on the time you can hold them without penalty (no less than five years, no more than thirty); who can purchase them ($5,000 per social security number per year); who can own them (to qualify for the tax-free status, the bond must be held by someone 24 or older who is *not* the child, including grandma and grandpa); and how much money your family earns (above a certain income, the tax-free benefit begins phasing out). Before you buy, check with your financial adviser and www.savingsbonds.gov.

PREPAID TUITION PLANS   Some states have plans that allow you to prepay all or part of your child's state college tuition costs. How much you pay depends on when you expect your child to start college and on current interest rates. Some private colleges offer similar programs.

These plans usually offer pretty good value for the money, especially if you're able to prepay the tuition at today's rates, which is about a third of what it'll be eighteen years from now. But in most cases you're limited to the state or college you selected. If your child ends up not going to school at all or decides to go somewhere else, you'll usually get back only the principal you put in, plus a paltry 1–2 percent.

If you want to just get the whole tuition issue out of your hair right now and not think about it again, these plans may be the way to go. If you're interested in this option but live in a state that doesn't offer it, you might want to consider the CollegeSure CD. These accounts are like regular CDs, except that the interest rate is tied to the average cost of higher education.

One "unit" (you can buy partial units too) is guaranteed to pay the average cost of a year at a private four-year college, including tuition, fees, room, and board. Since college costs are rising faster than inflation this could be a very good investment. CollegeSure CDs are offered only by the College Savings Bank (www.collegesavings.com).

COVERDELL EDUCATION SAVINGS ACCOUNTS (OR COVER-DELL ESAS) If you and your partner together make $200,000 a year or less, you can put away a maximum of $2,000 each year into an account for each of your children. Your contributions aren't deductible from your income like regular IRAs, but they grow tax-free. Distributions are tax-free too, as long as the money is used to pay for education, room, board, books, and related expenses. If you don't end up using the money at all, you can roll it over into a new account for another family member. Another interesting advantage to Coverdells is that you can use the money to pay for elementary and/or high school expenses if you need to. If you make more than $200,000, the amount you can contribute to your child's Coverdell goes down. However, someone else who meets the income threshold may be able to make the contribution in your child's name instead.

Watch out, though. If you're thinking you'll need financial aid, this account will be considered an asset and will reduce the amount of aid your child is eligible for (but since the asset is in your name, the impact will be smaller than if it were in the child's name, as it would be with a UTMA or UGMA, See below for more on this). More important, you cannot contribute to Coverdell ESA and a prepaid tuition or state-sponsored savings plan in the same year without incurring some major penalties. Given that those other plans have much higher contribution limits, you might be better off putting your money there instead of here.

Beware of Good-Hearted Relatives

Because the IRS rules for Coverdells, prepaid tuition programs, and life in general are often confusing and contradictory, there's way too much potential to get yourself into major tax trouble. So let your parents and any other potentially generous relatives and friends know that they should check with you *before* opening up any accounts in your child's name. And if you aren't absolutely sure what to do and how, have an accountant or financial planner take a look.

CUSTODIAL ACCOUNTS   There are two types of custodial accounts: UGMAs (Uniform Gift to Minors Act) and UTMAs (Uniform Transfer to Minors Act), which are basically the same thing. The big advantage of these accounts is that there are no lifetime contribution limits, although going over the IRS's annual gift tax limits could have tax consequences for the giver and the receiver. And like Coverdells, the money in UGMAs and UTMAs can be used for high school and even elementary school education expenses.

There are a few disadvantages to these accounts. First, unlike some of the other choices in this section, the gains are subject to federal taxes every year—at your rate—until the child turns 18 (or older, if he or she is a full-time student and a dependent). Second, whatever gets put in there becomes an irrevocable gift to the child—and can never be transferred to any other child or beneficiary. As the custodian, you can invest it any way you want, but you can't take it out unless it's to be spent on something that directly benefits the child, such as education or summer camps. Spending it on yourself could land you in court. Third, when the child reaches the "age of majority" (18, 21, or 25, depending on the plan), the money becomes his to spend any way he wants. You have absolutely no control anymore. And finally, because money in these accounts is considered the child's, it may reduce the amount of college financial aid you're eligible for later.

STATE-SPONSORED SAVINGS PLANS (BETTER KNOWN AS 529 PLANS)   For most people, setting up a 529 is going to be the best option. The rules for 529s (which are creatively named after an IRS regulation) vary from state to state, but they all have a lot in common.

As with Roth IRAs, you make contributions with after-tax dollars, but the earnings are completely federally tax-exempt. Depending on your state of residency, you may be able to contribute as much as $250,000 over the lifetime of the plan, including $50,000 in one chunk if you don't make any additional contributions for the next five years. (Both of these numbers change all the time, so for the most recent figures, check www.collegesavings .org.) In some states, your contributions may actually be deductible from your state tax.

These plans are especially attractive because, unlike Coverdells, there are no income restrictions. Plus, the money can be used for nearly any educational expenses (including tuition, books, room, and board) at any accredited, post–high school institution, anywhere in the country. This includes state and private colleges, community colleges, or even vocational schools. If your child

Getting Professional Advice

Over the course of the next twenty years or so, you're going to be spending a lot of your hard-earned money on health, life, and disability insurance; college investment plans; and retirement plans. The way you spend all that money will have a powerful—and long-lasting—effect on you and your family. So unless you're a financial planner, stock broker, or insurance agent yourself, you've got no business making major financial decisions without advice.

Finding someone to give you that advice isn't always easy. Your goal is to find someone whom you like and believe will have your best interests at heart. Here are a few things you can do to help weed out the losers:

♦ **Decide what you want your advisor to do.** Will you be expecting your financial planner to advise you on taxes, wills, and trusts in addition to investments? Do you want daily updates or is once a week or once a quarter good enough? Do you want your advisor to execute trades for you, or just tell you what to do and leave it to you to perform the transactions through a discount broker? The more the advisor does, the more you'll be paying.

♦ **Get references from friends, business associates, and other people whose opinions you trust.** Alternatively, you can find local planners through the Financial Planning Association (www.fpanet .org) or the National Association of Personal Financial Advisors, (www .napfa.org). Select at least three potential candidates and set up initial consultations (which shouldn't cost you anything). Then conduct tough interviews. Here's what you want to know:

   ◊ **Educational background.** Not to be snobby here, but the more formal the education—especially in financial management—the better. In addition to a bachelor's degree (at least), certified financial planners (CFPs) go through a rigorous training program, and the CFP certification can help you differentiate between someone who's really a planner and someone who just sells stocks and insurance.

   ◊ **Licenses.** Is he or she legally able to buy and sell financial products such as stocks, bonds, mutual funds, and insurance?

   ◊ **Level of experience.** Unless you've got money to burn, let your niece break in her MBA on someone else. Stick to experienced professionals with at least three years in the business.

◊ **Profile of the typical client.** You want a planner who has experience working with people whose income level and family situation are similar to yours.

◊ **Compensation.** Financial planners may get paid on commission, charge an hourly rate or a flat percentage of however much they're managing, receive fees from companies they recommend, or some combination of the above. None of these options is necessarily better than any other. The important thing is that you understand where the compensation is coming from, how much it's likely to be, and how it's calculated.

◊ **Get a sample financial plan.** You want to see what you're going to be getting for your money. Be careful, though: fancy graphics, incomprehensible boilerplate language, and expensive leather binders may be used to distract you from the report's lack of substance.

◊ **A self-assessment.** How well has the planner done for clients like you when the economy has been hot? How about when things aren't so hot? Most people will have returns of 2 percent one year, 14 another, and 0 yet another. Be very suspicious of anyone who promises a regular return (unless all your money is in a CD). Remember Bernie Madoff?

◊ **References.** How long have customers been with the planner? Are they happy? Better off? Any complaints or criticisms? Always check your prospective planner's credentials. For certified financial planners, you can do this at the Certified Financial Planner Board of Standards Web site (www.cfp.net/search). For brokers or brokerage companies, the Financial Industry Regulatory Authority (www.finra.org/brokercheck) will tell you about your candidate's education, licenses, and disciplinary history.

doesn't go to college, you can transfer the account to another member of your family—including yourself.

Unlike custodial accounts, the money is in your name even though your child is the beneficiary. This means that you can withdraw it (with a penalty, of course) if you really need to. And since the 529 account is really a parental asset, it will have a smaller impact on your child's ability to get financial aid than if it were in his name. One way to ensure that the 529s don't affect aid eligibility at all is to have a grandparent or other trusted relative open the account. Anyone can contribute to it, but because it's in someone else's name, it won't be counted as your asset.

In each state, 529 programs are managed by a different financial services organization—e.g., Fidelity, Schwab, or Vanguard—and you'll usually have a number of investment options, ranging from the very aggressive to the completely conservative. There's usually also an option for an age-adjusted plan. For example, a newborn's account might have 70 percent in a growth stock fund, 10 percent in an international stock fund, and 20 percent in bonds. By age 16, the mix will have gradually shifted to 15 percent in growth stocks, 5 percent in international, 45 percent in bonds, and 35 percent in money markets. Look into your state's plan first, because it may offer benefits to residents. But if you don't like it, you may be able to invest through another state. You can find out more about 529s from the College Savings Plan Network at www.collegesavings.org, or from www.savingforcollege.com.

INSURANCE

LIFE INSURANCE   While you might think that this is a little early to be worrying about life insurance, you couldn't be more wrong. Because you have a lot of life insurance options, and because each of them is right only in certain circumstances, we're not going to go into much detail here. Suffice it to say that you and your partner should get life insurance if you don't have any, or meet with your agent to discuss if and how your new baby will change your insurance needs. The point is that if, God forbid, either of you dies unexpectedly, the survivor shouldn't have to worry about having to get a better job just to keep up the mortgage or private-school tuition payments.

Because insurance agents are salespeople, you may want to have a more neutral party (your financial planner, for example) evaluate how much and what kind of insurance you need first. That way you can walk into your meeting with the insurance agent with both eyes open.

A FEW INSURANCE TIPS
There are two basic kinds of life insurance: *term* and *cash value*. Each is further divided into several subcategories.

TERM   Comes in a variety of flavors: *renewable* (if you keep your death benefit the same, the premiums will rise, but if you develop a health problem, you may get canceled altogether); *level* (you can lock in death benefit and premium levels, sometimes for as long as thirty years); and *decreasing* (death benefit decreases every year but the premium stays the same). Term policies are, as their name indicates, in effect only for the specified period of time. They're also pretty cheap, especially in the early years. If you're young and don't have a lot in the way of assets, level terms are a good way to take care of your family if something should happen to you. As you get older and hopefully richer, you may find that you need less insurance. Of course, you'll check with your financial advisor before making any big decisions, right?

CASH VALUE There are an increasing number of cash-value insurance products available, all of which essentially combine term insurance with some kind of investment. Part of your premium goes to buy term insurance; the rest goes into a fund. Depending on the plan, you'll have more or less control over how the fund is invested. Your investments accumulate tax-free; plus you can borrow against the fund—usually at pretty competitive rates—if you need to.

You can set your premium at virtually any level you want. But because the cost of the underlying term insurance is rising every year, you may reach a point when your payment isn't enough to cover the cost of the insurance. When that happens, the shortfall is taken out of your investment fund.

The big drawback with cash-value policies is that the commissions and fees kill you. Commissions—which are built into your costs—routinely run as much as 100 percent of the first year's premium. And management fees are often much higher than the industry average. Oh, and let's not forget about the early cancelation fees, which can take a serious bite out of your cash value if you turn in the policy less than ten years after getting it.

So which is better? At the risk of getting death threats from some insurance salespeople, it's a fairly simple choice: if you feel confident that you have the discipline to do it, get yourself a guaranteed-renewable, level-premium term policy and either invest your money on your own or get a financial planner to help you.

There is one exception to this rule: if you have an especially large estate (including real estate and retirement accounts), a cash-value policy is a good way to leave your heirs the wherewithal to pay off federal estate taxes. Unfortunately, it's hard to be more specific than "especially large" because Congress keeps changing the rules and the limits.

Whether you go with term or cash value, be sure to choose a carrier you can count on to be around when the time comes to pay up. The best way to do this is to go with a company that's rated AAA or better by Standard & Poor's or AM Best. You can get ratings directly from the companies, or find them online, for free, at www.insure.com. Just make sure you're looking at the most recent rating.

DISABILITY   As long as you've got insurance on your mind, you really should take a long, hard look at disability coverage. If your employer offers a long-term disability policy, sign up now. If not, explore the subject of getting one of your own through your broker. In many cases, a long-term disability could be more devastating to your family's finances than death.

LIFE INSURANCE FOR CHILDREN   This one is pretty simple. In most cases, taking out a life insurance policy on a child is a complete waste of money. The point of insurance is to provide for the survivors.

WHERE TO GET IT   If you work for a big company or belong to a union, you probably already have at least some life and/or disability insurance. And you may even be able to get additional coverage for great rates and without having to take a physical. You may also be able to get small policies for little or nothing if you're a member of certain organizations, open up a bank account at the right place, and so on. But before you come out of pocket for any "guaranteed issue" insurance (the kind you don't have to take a physical for), do a little shopping around. You're usually paying a premium for the guaranteed issue part, and you may be able to get the same amount of coverage for less.

No matter how much coverage you get this way, though, these policies should never be all you have. If you suddenly leave your job, close your checking account, or whatever, you could find yourself without any coverage.

If you have an insurance broker, start there. But don't be shy about shopping around. Costs for the same policy can vary by as much as 200 to 300 percent. Web sites such as esurance.com, accuquote.com, and quickquote.com can help you find the cheapest, best-rated policy.

And while you're considering how much coverage you need, be sure to look into Social Security. Most people completely overlook the survivor benefits they'd be entitled to if their spouse died. If you factor in Social Security—assuming it isn't bankrupt by the time you need it—you may actually need a lot less insurance than you think.

Oh, But Wait. We're Not Done Yet...

Since we're already talking about depressing things, there are a few other documents you really shouldn't be without.

WILLS   A will is a document that spells out how you'd like to divide your assets if you die. In most cases, it'll all go to your partner. Or, if she gets hit by the same bus, everything will go to your child(ren). You can also appoint a guardian to look after the children's interests. For many young families without a lot of assets, a simple will is good enough for a while. But get on this right now. Not having a will leaves way too much to chance. Each state has its own rules about who inherits what when someone dies intestate (without a will). In addition, a probate judge—who has no idea what your wishes may have been—may appoint yet another stranger to be your child's guardian and manage the inheritance. Wouldn't you feel a little better if *you* were making these decisions? Another thing to keep in mind about wills is that they're contestable, which means that it could be held up in court for years. And, naturally, a lot of the costs will come out of your assets.

TRUSTS   A trust is similar to a will, but it gives you more control over how your assets are used. You can, for example, set up a trust so that your child can have access to the money only after age 35, only if it's used for educational purposes, or only if she marries a left-handed calf roper. Another nice benefit to having a trust is that they're non-contestable, and as long as they're properly structured and funded, they'll stay out of probate.

HEALTH-CARE DIRECTIVE   You'll use this document to appoint someone to make health-care decisions for you if you're incapacitated.

DURABLE POWER OF ATTORNEY FOR FINANCES   This one appoints someone to make financial decisions if you're not able to.

I know this sounds like a lot of paperwork (which it is) and a lot of money (it doesn't have to be). The good news is that you may be able to create these documents yourself, guided by some of the excellent do-it-yourself resources like those published by Nolo Press (www.nolo.com). If you've got the money, it might be worth hiring a good attorney—one who specializes in wills and trusts—to take you through the process or do it for you. One of the most common mistakes do-it-yourselfers make is that they forget to fund the trust. Setting one up is great, but it won't do you much good if your accounts and home aren't in it.

Lastly, if you're in the military and are deploying, you'll need to complete these documents without fail, right away. Fortunately, you can get legal help for free on base.

The Lights Are On and Somebody Is Home

What's Going On with Your Partner

Physically

♦ May feel the baby's movements—and she knows what they are

♦ May have occasional, painless tightening of the uterus (called Braxton-Hicks contractions) or "false labor" (during real labor, the cervix begins to open; in false labor, it doesn't)

♦ Continuing darkening of nipples, appearance of dark line from belly button down the abdomen

♦ Breasts are getting larger and may "leak" a little when she's sexually excited—and even when she's not

♦ Navel changing from innie to outie

♦ Vision changing. She's retaining so much fluid these days that it's changing the shape of her eyeballs. Contacts may irritate or no longer fit.

♦ Hormones are causing all sorts of trouble: she's forgetful, her fingernails may be brittle, and her skin may be splotchy, but her hair probably never looked better (pregnant women tend to lose less hair than non-pregnant women)

Emotionally

- Very reassured by the baby's movements and less worried about miscarriage—although those worries may come rushing back if she stops feeling the baby move.
- Developing feeling of bonding with the baby and may spend a lot of time daydreaming about her
- Overwhelmed by the flood of advice coming in from all sides
- Sensitivity about her changing figure
- Increase in sexual desire
- Increasingly dependent on you
- Feelings of jealousy (after all, it was her private pregnancy until now)
- Enjoying some of the benefits of being pregnant—people giving up seats on public transportation, grocery clerks helping with her bags, and more

What's Going On with the Baby

The baby's eyelids are still sealed, but her eyebrows and lashes are fully grown in and you might be able to see some hair on her head. Her skin is losing its transparency, and she may get occasional bouts of hiccups. By the end of this month she'll be about nine inches long and weigh in at close to a pound. She kicks, punches, grabs at the umbilical cord, sucks her thumb, and has developed something of a regular sleep pattern—waking and dozing at set intervals (although she'll be sleeping 90–95 percent of the time). She'll spend a lot of her awake time doing somersaults. Best of all, she can now hear what's going on outside the womb.

What's Going On with You

"Oh My God, I'm Going to Be a Father"

I have to admit that even after seeing the baby on the sonogram, I still found it hard to believe I was really going to be a father (the technology to fake a sonogram must exist, right?). But when my wife grabbed my hand and placed it on her belly, and I felt that first gentle kick, I knew the whole thing was true. And as usual, after the initial excitement passed, I found something to worry about.

What's *Really* Going On in There?

No matter where you stand on the pro-life vs. pro-choice debate, there's absolutely no question that your fetus is a living being who, like the rest of us, reacts to her environment. Your baby will be born with a full set of senses: touch, hearing, sight, smell, and taste. But those senses don't just show up at birth, completely out of the blue. They begin to form very early on in the pregnancy, and the fetus starts trying to use them immediately. The more practice she gets, the more developed the sense will be at birth. (Senses that aren't used tend to atrophy. In animal experiments, for example, when fetal chicks are prevented from moving inside their egg, cartilage turns to bone). Let me introduce you to the cast of senses, in order of appearance.

♦ **Touch.** About two months into the pregnancy, your baby's skin—which is considered the body's largest organ—is fully formed. Sensitivity starts with the cheeks and lips, and just a few months ago, if they were touched, the baby would turn away. Starting right about now (five months), the baby will turn *toward* the touch (after birth, that's called the *rooting reflex,* and it's designed to help the baby find the breast. When touched on the mouth, the baby turns toward the stimulus—usually a nipple, but it works with a finger too—and starts making sucking movements). The palms of the hands, soles of the feet, and genitals are next, followed by the rest of the body. To help develop their sense of touch, fetuses spend a lot of time exploring themselves—grasping the umbilical cord, stroking the face, sucking on fingers, and kicking and banging against the walls of the uterus. If the baby has a womb-mate or two, the fetuses often explore each other, sometimes poking, other times holding hands.

♦ **Movement and balance.** If your partner is up and about, the fetus will spend a lot of her day gently sloshing around in the uterus. Interestingly, the amount of movement the fetus experiences during pregnancy makes a big difference after the birth. Italian researcher Carlo Bellieni recently did a study of the children of ballerinas who didn't stop dancing while they were pregnant. "They needed to be rocked to sleep more energetically than the others," he says. Another researcher, Janet DiPietro, found that fetuses that are very active in the womb are more irritable as babies.

♦ **Smell and taste** (some lump the two under the heading "chemosensation"). Your baby's mouth and tongue developed a few months ago. And at this stage, her taste buds are just about as sensitive as yours. For the past month or two, your baby has been gulping down impressive amounts of amniotic fluid, peeing it right back out, and drinking it up again (it's best to get that image out of your mind). The amniotic fluid that flows through your baby's mouth and nasal passages changes flavor constantly, depending on what your partner eats. (The connection between diet and amniotic fluid is pretty strong. In one study, Julie Mannella and her colleagues found that adults were able to smell garlic in amniotic fluid collected from women undergoing amniocentesis who had eaten garlic just forty-five minutes before the test.) But mixed in there among the curry and chili peppers and peanut butter sandwiches are some odor molecules that are distinctly Mom. And after birth, the baby's sense of smell helps her adjust to life outside the womb. Mom's nipples smell (to the baby) like amniotic fluid, and that scent helps attract the baby to the breast. Babies definitely prefer the smell of their own fluid to anyone else's (hey, who wouldn't?).

♦ **Hearing.** If your baby's ears are filled with amniotic fluid and any external sounds would have to pass through your partner's abdomen, how much could a baby hear in there anyway? Well, despite what you'd think, the uterus is a pretty noisy place—and has been since early in your partner's pregnancy.

Armed with ultrasound machines, researchers Peter Hepper and Sara Shahidullah found that fetuses first start reacting to outside sounds as early as fourteen weeks. Their hearing range is rather limited, though, with mid- and low-frequency sounds (like your voice) getting through better than high-frequency ones. By about thirty-five weeks, fetuses not only can hear both high and low frequencies, but can actually tell the difference between the two.

In one study, for example, an obstetrician inserted a microphone into a woman's uterus while she was in labor (after her water had broken), and recorded the external sounds that could be heard from the inside. He got clear recordings—not only of voices and the mother's internal body sounds but also of Beethoven's Ninth Symphony, which was being played in the delivery room.

Hearing noises is one thing, but are fetuses affected in any way by what they hear from within the womb? Absolutely. Nearly 100 years ago, a German pediatrician by the name of Albrecht Peiper observed that fetuses would kick when a car horn was blown. And if you ask your partner, she'll probably tell you that the baby moves around more when she's listening to music, and may kick sharply if a door slams nearby or a car backfires.

Several researchers have found that the fetus's heart rate changes in response to sounds. Rock music, for example, tends to produce an increase, while classical lowers it. And developmental psychologist William Fifer and his colleagues noticed that the fetus's heart rate increased when a stranger was speaking, but decreased when Mom was. His conclusion? "The fetus not only hears and recognizes the sound, but is calmed by it." Babies aren't just passive listeners, either: they're actually learning from what they hear. For more on this subject, see "Prenatal Communication," pages 133–38.

♦ **Sight.** Your baby's eyes will be fused shut for another month or two. Even after her eyes open, it'll still be pretty dark inside of Mom. (Reminds me of that great Groucho Marx line: "Outside of a dog, a book is man's best friend. Inside of a dog, it's too dark to read.") Nevertheless, she can do some visual processing. For example, if you were to shine a bright light on your partner's belly (which you shouldn't actually do), your baby's heart rate would accelerate and she would turn away from it. Because of the lack of practice, eyesight will be your baby's least-developed sense when she emerges from the womb. At first, things will be a little blurry, although she'll be able to see objects—or people—10 to 15 inches away fairly well. But in six to nine months, her eyesight will be pretty much up to snuff.

More Interested in Fatherhood

After that first kick, I suddenly became consumed with the idea that I just wasn't ready to be a father. I still wanted children—nothing had changed there—but I suddenly realized that in only four months I would face the biggest challenge of my life, and I didn't know a thing about what I was getting into. I felt as though I were about to attempt a triple backflip from a trapeze— without ever having had any lessons, and without a safety net.

I had already done a lot of reading, but I felt I still didn't know what fathers are really supposed to do. Doesn't it seem a little strange—scary, really—that you need a license to sell hot dogs on the street or to be a beautician, but there are absolutely no prerequisites for the far more important job of being a father?

Feeling the baby's first kicks may make you much more interested in reading about pregnancy, if you haven't been doing so already. You may also find yourself wanting to spend more time with friends or relatives who have small kids, or just watching how other men interact with their children. You'll probably notice that younger dads (those under about 24) spend a little less time with their kids—playing, teaching, reading—than older dads (those over 32). You may also start becoming aware of the negative, stereotyped images of fathers that are so common in the media. We'll talk a lot more about that in "Fathering Today," starting on page 314.

Turning Inward

You've had a lot to think about lately—your family's finances, your new role as a father, your partner's (and your baby's) safety. So don't be surprised if you find yourself preoccupied with your own thoughts—sometimes to the exclusion of just about everything else, even your partner.

Just as it was for her, this sort of "turning inward" is perfectly normal. The problem is that while you're focusing on everything that's going on inside your head, your partner (who has been pretty focused on *herself* until now) is now starting to focus on you too. She may be feeling insecure and may need to be reassured that you aren't going to leave her or be feeling emotionally needy and crave confirmation of your love for her. Notice her subtle (or not so subtle) hints and make sure she gets the attention she needs. If she doesn't, she may think you don't care. As Arthur and Libby Colman write, "A man who ignores his partner's anxieties may find they escalate rather than abate with a condescending 'Everything is going to be all right, dear."

At the same time, though, don't forget about your own needs. It can be extremely tempting to try to get away from the external pressures by distancing yourself from your partner (you can't, of course, get away from your internal pressures). If you can, tell her what's on your mind; it'll probably make you feel a lot better. (If you're having a tough time opening up, you might want to review the "Your Relationship" section on pages 98–103.) If she doesn't react well, reassure her that even though you might be a little preoccupied, you still love her and you'll still be there for her.

Slice of Pie, Dad?

One topic that you'll probably spend a lot of time thinking about is what, exactly, being a father means, and how important fatherhood is to your sense of who you are. I'm not a big fan of self-help exercises, but here's one that's actually extremely helpful.

First, take a minute to think of all the different roles you play and how they come together to form your identity. For example, you're a husband or spouse, friend, son, mentor, father-to-be, worker, coach, relative, athlete, and so on.

Next, take a sheet of blank paper and draw a large circle in the middle. Imagining that the circle (which researchers refer to as a pie) represents the whole you, slice it up into pieces that are proportional to the importance you place on each of your identities. There are no right or wrong ways to do this exercise, and every man's pie will be divided differently. What's especially interesting, though, is that the number and size of your slices will change over time. If you had done this exercise a year ago, you might not have had a "father" slice at all, or if you did, it would have been pretty small. But as the reality of fatherhood gradually sinks in, that slice will grow and grow. When that happens, other slices will have to get smaller—or disappear completely. At least for a while.

Once you've finished this pie, grab another sheet of paper, draw another circle, and divide it up according to the weight you place on each of the fatherhood roles you expect to play and the kind of dad you want to be. When Cherine Habib and Sandra Lancaster had a group of Australian expectant dads do this, they came up with seven possibilities.

I've added a few more to the mix: reliable presence, breadwinner, coach, co-parent, disciplinarian, mother's emotional supporter, mother's helper, playmate, primary caregiver, protector, provider, reluctant father, role model, teacher, and uncertain/confused father.

You're probably not going to use all of these attributes—and feel free to add any you think are missing. As with the first pie, don't get too used to the way your pie looks; the number and size of the slices will change with time.

Staying Involved

Prenatal Communication: Can You Hear Me Now?

As we've discussed elsewhere, good communication with your partner is critical throughout the pregnancy. But what about communicating with your unborn child? While the very idea may sound a little wacky, research has shown that months before they're born, fetuses are extremely responsive to what they're hearing from the outside. Not only that, they're actually *learning* from it.

In one study, Peter Hepper found that newborns whose mothers had watched a particular soap opera while they were pregnant stopped crying when they heard the show's theme song. Babies who hadn't been exposed to the show had no reaction when they heard the music.

And in one of my favorite studies of all time, researcher Anthony DeCasper asked sixteen women to make a tape of themselves reading a poem called "The King, the Mice, and the Cheese," and two different tapes of Dr. Seuss's *The Cat in the Hat*. Then, during the last six and a half weeks of their pregnancies, the women were instructed to choose only one of the tapes and play it three times a day for their unborn child. When the babies were just three days old, DeCasper offered them a choice between the tape they'd heard over and over and one of the other tapes. Since three-day-old babies aren't particularly good about speaking up, DeCasper used a "suck-o-meter" (a specially rigged pacifier that enabled the babies to determine which tape they'd get to hear merely by changing their sucking speed) to allow the children to express their preferences. Fifteen out of the sixteen babies chose the tape they'd heard while in the womb. If nothing else, this research ought to convince you that even before they're born, babies' lights are on and there's somebody home.

Even more amazing, fetuses can tell the difference between two languages and exhibit a strong preference for their native one. Newborns will stare longer at people who are speaking the same language that Mom spoke while she was pregnant. Similarly, French researcher Jacques Mehler and his colleagues had a completely bilingual woman record several phrases in French and Russian, then played them to a few dozen brand-new French babies. Using a device similar to DeCasper's suck-o-meter, the babies adjusted their sucking so they could hear the French instead of the Russian.

So why should you try to communicate with your growing fetus? First of all, because it's a lot of fun. In the evenings, I used to place my hands on my wife's belly and tell the current resident all about what I'd done during the day.

Sometimes I'd even do "counting" exercises: I'd poke once and say (loudly), "One." Most of the time, I'd get an immediate kick back. A few seconds later, I'd poke twice and say, "Two." Frequently, I'd get two kicks back. I've often wondered whether this little math game could be the reason my oldest got an A in AP calculus in high school.

The second reason to try some prenatal conversations is that they can help you establish a bond with your baby before the birth. It may even help make the pregnancy seem a little more "real." I have to admit that in the beginning, the idea of talking to a lump in my wife's belly seemed silly. But after a while I got used to it and began to feel a real closeness with the baby. Another father I spoke with felt that by communicating with his unborn daughter, he was able to establish a loving relationship with her while she was still inside. And when she was born, he described their first encounter as "like meeting someone face to face with whom you had only spoken on the telephone."

If you're in the military and you're going to miss large chunks of your wife's pregnancy, one of the best things you can do before you deploy is to record yourself reading a couple of nice, rhythmic stories or poems. Then ask your wife to play them for the baby every day—before and after the birth. If you're already gone and you have access to Skype or phone, you can do a live read— just ask your wife to put the headset or speaker close to her belly. I've heard from a number of deployed service members who have done this, and many of them have been amazed that the first time they spoke to their baby, he or she turned to face them, having clearly recognized their voice. You'll find dozens of other tips on how to stay involved from a distance in my book, *The Military Father: A Hands-on Guide for Deployed Dads.* Communicating with your unborn child will also help him or her start developing a bond with you. Many fathers are justifiably envious of the immediate bond newborn children have with their mothers. It seems, though, that this bond may have more to do with the mother's voice (which the baby has heard every day for nine months) than anything else.

In another of DeCasper's suck-o-meter studies, nine out of ten newborns selected a story recorded by their own mother over the same story recorded by another woman. And other research has shown that for their first few days newborns prefer their mother's voice to their father's; if she whispers in one ear and the father whispers in the other, the baby will most likely turn toward the mother.

But that's no reason to give up. When you speak to your baby before he's born, he "learns to recognize the tone, pitch, and speech patterns that are unique to you, and will instantly identify your voice after birth," says Dr. Sarah Brewer, author of *Superbabies*. This means that if you whisper in one of your baby's ears and some stranger whispers in the other, the baby, who "recognizes" you, will turn toward you 80 percent of the time.

Communication with the fetus isn't limited to words, of course. Boris Brott (yes, he's a relative, but I've never met him), a famous Canadian orchestra conductor, traces his interest in music to the womb:

As a young man, I was mystified by this ability I had to play certain pieces sight unseen. I'd be conducting a score for the first time and, suddenly, the cello line would jump out at me: I'd know the flow of the piece before I turned the page of the score. One day, I mentioned this to my mother, who is a professional cellist. I thought she'd be intrigued because it was always the cello line that was so distinct in my mind. She was; but when she heard what the pieces were, the mystery quickly solved itself. All the scores I knew sight unseen were ones she had played when she was pregnant with me.

In an effort to harness the power of prenatal communication, several physicians, obstetricians, and entrepreneurs have developed organized communication programs. Psychiatrist Thomas Verny claims that by singing and talking to the fetus, "parents create a positive intrauterine environment, reducing the level of anxiety-producing hormones that lead to frenetic activity and even ulcers in the unborn." And Dr. F. Rene Van de Carr maintains that his "Prenatal Classroom" provides systematic stimulation that may "actually help the growing fetus' brain become more efficient and increase learning capacity after birth."

Dr. Brewer goes even further. "Your baby's brain is literally shaped by the stimuli and nutrients received from his environment," she says. "By enriching his prenatal environment with additional stimuli, you can encourage the growth and development of his brain cells (neurons) so they develop more complex 'communication antennae' (dendron trees), more 'satellite dishes' (dendritic spines), and stronger synaptic connections." Translation: it may make your baby smarter.

Perhaps the most dramatic claims, though, are made by developmental psychologist Brent Logan, whose BabyPlus technology uses what he calls the "cardiac curriculum" to pump a set of increasingly complex heartbeat-like sounds into the mother's womb. Logan may really be on to something with the heartbeat thing. It's the one sound that fetuses hear even more than their

A Few Things to Remember about Prenatal Communication

♦ **Respect your partner.** You've got a right to speak with your child, but she's got a right to privacy. If she's not completely into the idea, you might want to tell her that Logan and others have found that women who are carrying prenatally stimulated babies seem to have shorter labors and a lower C-section rate. In addition, certain kinds of stimulation may reduce the risk of breech births (where the baby comes out feetfirst instead of headfirst). Because they like sounds so much, some fetuses will "chase" after music playing through headphones placed against the mother's abdomen. The theory is that if you move the headphones to the bottom of the abdomen during the last month or so of the pregnancy, a stubborn yet music-loving breech fetus could be convinced to shift its head downward, right where it's supposed to be.

♦ **Try to overcome the feeling that what you are doing is absolutely ridiculous.** The idea that communicating with unborn babies could actually benefit them has been around for more than a thousand years.

♦ **Don't whisper.** Speak to the fetus loudly enough so that a person standing across the room could hear you clearly.

♦ **Don't do it when you're feeling bored.** The fetus will pick up on your tone of voice.

♦ **Don't go overboard.** Fifteen to twenty minutes, twice a day at most. Fetuses need plenty of time to rest, even more than newborns or kittens.

♦ **Set up a routine.** Try to do it at the same time every day so that the baby will get used to the idea that something's going to happen. Pat

mother's voices. And after birth, many newborns are soothed by recordings of their mothers' heartbeat (recordings of other people's hearts don't work nearly as well). Interestingly, although scientists have documented this, ordinary people seem to have known it all along. About 80 percent of mothers—whether they're right- or left-handed—naturally hold babies on the left side, where the baby's head can be nearer the heart. Even artists—a far less stodgy group than researchers and scientists—have noticed the left-side bias: studies of classical your partner's belly before you start, to let the baby know you're out there. Use the baby's name (if you know it).

♦ **Mix it up.** Playing the same piece of music or reading the same poem or story every day is great, but be sure to keep the rest of the program different. When fetuses hear the same thing over and over they just block it out.

♦ **Have fun.** With names like Prenatal Classroom, Prenatal University, and Tummy Tutor, it sounds like trying to communicate with your baby is going to take a lot of serious study and several advanced degrees. But it doesn't have to be nearly that complicated. Try some games, like gently patting your partner's belly and announcing to the baby, "I'm patting you now." Or play DJ with your iPod Shuffle or your CD collection—give a gentle rub and say, "Get ready, baby, you're about to hear some jazz," or classical, hip-hop, salsa, country, rock, or whatever. It's a little much to expect your baby to remember a lot of individual artists, but hey, genres could work.

♦ **Don't get your expectations too high.** Most of the prenatal communication systems make claims that your baby will be taller, smarter, more beautiful, come out of the womb fully dressed and speaking three languages, or whatever. Not long ago, I got a call from a publicist who insisted that if a baby went through the entire curriculum described, the company would guarantee that the child's SAT scores would be 15 percent higher. Excuse me? Higher than what? The absurdity of the claim was completely lost on her. Seems to me that if you're expecting a superbaby and you get a healthy but perfectly average baby, you're going to feel disappointed. And I can't think of a worse way for a baby to start off her life outside the womb than by being a disappointment to Dad.

paintings and sculptures have shown that 80 percent of the people depicted carrying babies hold them on the left side. Those carrying inanimate objects, however, do so half the time on the right, half on the left.

Whether it's the heartbeats or something else, Logan says his "graduates" frequently learn to talk as early as five or six months and to read at eighteen months (most kids don't usually talk until they're at least a year old, or read until they're five or six).

Besides that, Logan, Brewer, and other researchers have found that prenatally enriched babies tend to:

♦ cry less at birth
♦ be more alert at birth
♦ form attachments to Mom and Dad more quickly
♦ have longer attention spans and better concentration
♦ hold their heads up unassisted sooner
♦ have remarkable (for babies, anyway) physical strength
♦ sleep better
♦ mature more quickly
♦ be less likely to develop dyslexia
♦ demonstrate advanced musical and creative talents
♦ have an IQ in the 125 to 150 range (average is 100)

To be fair, you should know that there are plenty of people who say that there is absolutely no benefit at all to any of this prenatal communication stuff. That said, if you're interested in finding out more, take a look at the Resources section.

Sex

Pregnancy can do funny things to your libido. Some expectant fathers are more interested in sex and more easily aroused than ever before. Others are repelled by the very idea. Whether you're feeling either of these ways or something in between, rest assured that it's completely normal.

In this section, we'll talk about the sexual issues that may come up in the first six months of your pregnancy. Late-pregnancy sexual issues are covered on pages 196–97.

WHY YOU AND/OR YOUR PARTNER MIGHT BE FEELING *INCREASED* SEXUAL DESIRE

♦ After about the third month, her nausea and fatigue are probably gone, making sex more appealing—for both of you.
♦ You may find her pregnant body (with its larger breasts and fuller curves) erotic. If so, you certainly aren't alone. This is so common that there's actually a word for it: *maieusiophilia*.
♦ Your partner may be proud of her more ample figure and may be feeling sexier.

♦ You may be turned on by the feeling of power and masculinity at having created life.

♦ Your partner may be turned on by the confirmation of her femininity and by the awe at what her body is doing. She may also be aroused by how much she's arousing you.

♦ Throughout pregnancy, you both may experience a newfound feeling of closeness that frequently manifests itself sexually.

♦ One or both of you may be having more erotic dreams.

♦ The increased vaginal lubrication and blood flow to her pelvic area may make your partner's orgasms more powerful and easier to reach. (If that were happening to you, you'd want to have sex more often too.) It may also stimulate her to masturbate more than usual, or if she didn't (or says she didn't) before, she might start.

♦ If you experienced a miscarriage in an earlier pregnancy, you may have been abstaining from sex for the first trimester. Now that it's safely behind you, all that pent-up desire may have gotten you both to the point where you're about ready to explode.

♦ She's pregnant with a boy. According to neuroscientist Lise Eliot, women carrying boys have higher levels of testosterone (which is linked with increased sex drive) in their blood than those carrying girls.

WHY YOU AND/OR YOUR PARTNER MIGHT BE FEELING
DECREASED SEXUAL DESIRE

♦ In the first trimester, your partner may be too nauseated or tired to be interested in sex. In the second trimester, she may feel too uncomfortable or too awkward to want to have sex (about 25 percent of pregnant women feel this way. But most say that the second trimester—months 4, 5, and 6—are the best time of the pregnancy, sexually speaking).

♦ She may think that you don't find her attractive and don't want to have sex with her.

♦ You may not, in fact, be attracted to a woman whose body has been transformed from fun to functional.

♦ You may think your partner isn't feeling attractive and wouldn't be interested in sex.

♦ You or your partner may be afraid that sex will hurt her—or the baby. In fact, there's nothing to be afraid of. The baby is safely cushioned by its amniotic-fluid-filled sac, and unless your partner has cramps or bleeds during sex or her doctor feels there are extenuating circumstances, sex during pregnancy is no more dangerous for your partner than at any other time. The two of you may find this information reassuring. If you do, great. If not, now may be the time to talk about it and try some different sexual positions (lying on your sides or with your partner on top, for example; or she lies close to the edge of the bed and you stand) and different ways of bringing each other to orgasm (oral sex, vibrators, and so on). Often simply making a few such changes can go a long way toward alleviating your fears.

♦ Although in most cases sex is required to become a parent, you and your partner may feel, as it gradually sinks in that you are about to become parents, that parents aren't supposed to be sexual. (Even though we are all living proof that our parents had sex at least once, it's somehow hard to imagine the two of them, in bed, naked . . .)

♦ You or your partner may feel that sex serves only one purpose: creating children. And once you've done that, there's no more need for sex—until you want more kids.

♦ She may actually find it painful.

WHAT THE EXPERTS SAY

As you can see, the range of feelings about sex is broad. But if you still aren't convinced that you're not the only one feeling the way you do, here are a few interesting things researchers have found out about expectant couples' sexuality during pregnancy:

♦ According to psychologists Wendy Miller and Steven Friedman, expectant fathers generally underestimate how attractive their partners feel, and expectant mothers consistently underestimate how attractive their partners find them. (The bottom line is that most men find their pregnant partners' bodies erotic, and most pregnant women feel quite attractive. But many men and women fail to convey these feelings to their partners.)

♦ According to the Cowans, expectant fathers have more psychological inhibitions about physical intimacy during pregnancy than their partners do.

♦ The old myth that pregnancy somehow desexualizes women is just that—a myth. In fact, Miller and Friedman found that there are no significant differences in the level of sexual desire or sexual satisfaction between expectant men and women.

When to Be Particularly Careful

If your partner is at risk for, or has a history of, premature labor, *placenta previa* (when the placenta covers the cervix), or an incompetent cervix (when the cervix is not strong enough to hold the fetus inside until truly ready to be born), talk to her doctor before you hop in the sack. Nipple stimulation and orgasm have a direct impact on the uterus and could possibly trigger some contractions. If your partner has any of these conditions or is at risk for going into labor early, use a condom when you have sex. No, it's not a birth control thing. Strange as it sounds, there's a slim chance that one of the hormones in semen (prostaglandin) may cause contractions.

WHEN YOU AND YOUR PARTNER ARE OUT OF SYNC

Of course, you and your partner may not always be on the same wavelength. She may feel like having sex just when you're feeling put off by her Rubenesque figure. Conversely, you may want to have sex at a time when she's simply not interested. Here are a few suggestions that might help:

♦ **Talk.** At these and so many other times during your pregnancy, communicating with your partner is essential. As Arthur and Libby Colman so wisely write, "Unless the couple can talk about their sex life, their entire relationship may suffer, and that in turn will compound their sexual problems."

♦ **Try some nonsexual affection,** such as snuggling, touching, or just hugging each other. And say up front that that is what you're interested in doing, because it isn't as easy as it sounds. Professors Cowan and Cowan have found that many couples need practice finding sensual ways to please each other short of intercourse. And both men and women hesitate to make affectionate overtures if they aren't sure they're ready to progress to intercourse and are worried they'll be misinterpreted.

♦ **Be nice to each other.** Being critical of her figure will make her feel self-conscious, less attractive, and less interested in sex. Instead, tell her how hot she looks, send her sext messages during the day, go back and do a few more things from the lists on pages 110–13—especially anything that has to do with cleaning, cooking, and other household tasks. They don't call it *chore-play* for nothing.

♦ **Try something completely off the wall.** Some fascinating new research has found that oral sex may actually make the pregnancy safer. Work with me here. Gustaaf Dekker, a professor at the University of Adelaide, did a study comparing forty-one women who had preeclampsia (a condition marked by dangerously high blood pressure) and forty-four who didn't. He found that 82 percent of the women without preeclampsia gave their partner regular blow jobs, but only about 40 percent of the women who had the condition did. According to Dekker, "the protective effect of oral sex was strongest if the woman actually swallowed the semen rather than coughing it onto the pillow." So now, when he's counseling couples who have had trouble in the past carrying a pregnancy to term, he tells them, "Semen exposure is good, and you could think of oral sex." Hey, I'm just saying: could be worth a shot. But don't hold your breath.

This doesn't have to be a one-way street, either. Susan White and Kenneth Keamy, 1982, found that women who have regular orgasms during pregnancy have a lower risk of premature delivery than women who don't. Results of this study further indicated that couples who talk—versus do not talk—about sex actually engage in sex more frequently. The study also hypothesized that couples who talk about sex during pregnancy experience more pleasure during sex. It was concluded that talking about sex does not have a direct effect on the pleasure an individual experiences during sex. Finally, as predicted, couples who experience more pleasure during sex throughout pregnancy report being more satisfied with their relationship.

Notes:

Work and Family

What's Going On with Your Partner

Physically

♦ Period of greatest weight gain begins

♦ Increased sweating

♦ Increased blood supply gives her that pregnant "glow"; it may also be giving her some sciatica, numbness and tingling in the hands, or even carpal tunnel syndrome as all the extra fluid compresses some of her nerves

♦ Swelling of the hands and feet

♦ Fatigue, dizziness, and a runny nose are not uncommon

♦ A constant, nagging backache—especially if she's carrying twins or more

♦ Some incredibly bizarre food cravings (see page 150 for more on this)

♦ She's getting a full-body aerobic workout. Her heart and lungs are working 50 percent harder than before she was pregnant. Not surprisingly, she's a little short of breath.

♦ A little bit of urine leakage when laughing, coughing, or sneezing

Emotionally

♦ Moodiness is decreasing

♦ Continued forgetfulness and even some short-term memory loss (see pages 150–51 for more on this)

♦ Feeling that the pregnancy will never end

♦ Increased bonding with the baby

♦ Still very dependent on you
♦ Wondering what kind of mom she'll be, and how the way she was mothered will affect her own parenting

What's Going On with the Baby

The baby looks pretty trim—he hasn't started putting on much fat yet—and is starting to get covered with vernix, a thick, waxy, protective coating. His eyes are starting to open, he coughs and hiccups, and if you were inside the uterus you could see his unique footprints and fingerprints. The movements of your now foot-long two-pounder are getting stronger—no more of those butterfly kicks—and he can hear, and respond to, sounds from the outside world. Baby girls develop eggs in their ovaries this month, and according to some researchers, this is when your baby's emotions begin to form. He learns about love through the comfort that your voice (and your partner's) gives him. And when your partner is feeling stressed or angry or sad, the baby gets a tiny jolt of the same hormones that are affecting Mom.

What's Going On with You

Reexamining Your Relationship with Your Father

As the reality of your prospective fatherhood unfolds, you'll probably find yourself contemplating how you'll juggle the various roles—parent, provider, husband, employee, friend—that will make up your paternal identity. As mentioned in earlier chapters, you may be spending more time reading about parenting and watching how your male friends, family members, or even strangers do it.

But eventually you'll realize that your own father—whether you know it or not—has already had a profound influence on the kind of father you'll be. And you may find yourself nearly overcome with forgotten images of childhood—especially ones involving your father. Just walking down the street, I'd suddenly remember the times we went camping or to the ballet, how he taught me to throw a baseball in the park, and the hot summer afternoon he, my sisters, and I stripped down to our underwear in the backyard and painted each other with watercolors. There's nothing like impending paternity to bring back all the memories and emotions of what it was like to be fathered as a child.

Not all childhood memories of fathers are positive. Some men's images of their fathers are dominated by fear, pain, loneliness, or longing. Either way, don't be surprised if you find yourself seriously reexamining your relationship with your dad. Was he the kind of man you want as your role model? Was he the perfect example of the kind of father you *don't* want to be? Or was he somewhere in between? Many men, particularly those who had rocky, or non-existent, relationships with their fathers find that the prospect of becoming a dad themselves enables them to let go of some of the anger they've felt for so long. Don't be surprised if you start having a lot of dreams about your father. Researcher Luis Zayas found that an expectant father's uncertainty about his identity as father, his actual role, and the changed relationship with his wife and family are "among the psychic threads of fatherhood" that are fundamentally related to the man's relationship with his own father and are frequently present in his dreams.

So, whether you're awake or asleep, as you're thinking about your dad, remember that what's really going on is that you're worried about what kind of a father you will be when your baby arrives.

There's no question that the way your dad parented you will influence the kind of father you become. But despite all those silly aphorisms like "The acorn never falls far from the tree," whether that influence is positive or negative is completely up to you.

According to researchers Kory Floyd and Mark Morman, father involvement is based on a combination of modeling and what they call "compensation effects." On the one hand, if you feel that your dad did a good job parenting you, you'll use him as a model for your relationship with your own kids. On the other hand, if you were dissatisfied with the fathering you received, or you feel that your relationship was unaffectionate or distant, you'll "feel compelled to remake the fathering experience into something more positive" for your own children.

What's especially interesting is that your dad's relationship with your mother (when you were a boy) may also influence your fathering behavior, but not in the way you might expect. According to researchers John Beaton, William Doherty, and Martha Rueter, you'll be more committed to being an involved father if your parents "disagreed about how you should be raised." Apparently, in disagreeing with your mother, your dad was demonstrating that he wanted to be involved on his own terms. And you'll want to do the same thing.

Bottom line: If you work at it, you can be the father you want to be, rather than the one you think fate might have planned for you to be.

A Sense of Mortality

I've always been more than just a little fascinated by death—I love the movie *Harold and Maude*, and I wanted to paint my room black and hang an "R.I.P." sign over my bed when I was a kid (my parents wouldn't let me). But it wasn't until my wife got pregnant for the first time that death became something more than a mere abstraction. Suddenly it occurred to me that my death could have a serious impact on other people.

This realization had some interesting and fairly immediate results. The first thing that happened was that I became a much better driver—or at least a safer one. Overnight, yellow lights changed their meaning from "floor it" to "proceed with caution." I began to leave for appointments a few minutes earlier so I wouldn't have to hurry, I wove in and out of traffic less, and I found myself not quite so annoyed with people who cut me off in traffic. But besides becoming a better driver, I began to look back with horror at some of the risky things—parachuting, scuba diving—I'd done before I'd gotten married, and I began to reconsider some of the things I'd tentatively planned for the near future—bungee jumping, hang gliding. After all, now there were people counting on me to stay alive.

My preoccupation with my own mortality had other interesting consequences as well. I found myself strangely drawn to my family's history; I wanted to learn more about our traditions, our family rituals, the wacky relatives no one ever talked about. I even put together a family tree and began bugging my relatives about their birth dates. I didn't realize it at the time, but it's quite common for expectant fathers to experience a heightened sense of attachment to their relatives—both immediate and distant—even if they weren't particularly close before.

This really isn't so unusual, especially when you consider that one of the main reasons we have kids in the first place is so that a little piece of us will live on long after we're gone. I guess the hope is that one day seventy-five years from now, when my great-grandson is expecting a child, he'll start to explore his roots and want to get to know more about me.

Feeling Trapped

As we've already discussed, you and your partner probably aren't feeling the same things at the same time. Earlier on in the pregnancy, your partner may have turned inward, preoccupied with how the pregnancy was affecting her.

You may have felt a little (or a lot) left out. By now, though, your partner may be "coming out"—concentrating less on herself and the baby, and more on you.

Meanwhile, you may have just begun the process of turning inward that we began discussing last month (page 131). You're going to be a father in less than four months, and you've got a lot of things to think about, many of which you need to work through on your own. The potential problem here is that just as you begin to focus on yourself, your partner is becoming increasingly dependent on you. She may be afraid that you don't love her anymore and that you're going to leave her. Or she may be worried—just as you are—about your physical safety. Although being doted upon is nice, it can sometimes get out of hand. And your partner's increased dependence on you may cause you to feel trapped. As Arthur and Libby Colman found, a pregnant woman's "sudden concern may make a man feel over-protected, as though his independence is being threatened." If you are feeling trapped, it's important to let your partner know in a gentle, nonconfrontational way. At the same time, encourage her to talk about what she's feeling and what she wants from you.

Staying Involved

Having Fun

Besides being a time of great change—physical as well as emotional—pregnancy can be a fun time, too. Here are a few ways to amuse yourselves:

♦ **Take lots of pictures.** I took regular shots of my wife—from the front and the side, with emphasis on the belly—holding a mug-shot-style card labeled "Pregnant Woman Number 1 (2, 3, and so on)." For another series of photos, she stood up while I lay on my back between her legs and took pictures of her soft underbelly. Most cameras have a date stamp. If yours doesn't, be sure to take note of the critical day the belly completely blocks your view of your partner's face. Take pictures at least once a month until the eighth month, then once a week after that.

♦ **Get some special clothes.** His-and-hers "Yes sir, that's my baby" T-shirts and "Father-to-bee" hats (featuring a picture of a bumblebee) are favorites in some circles.

♦ **Get some exercise—together.** Taking a water aerobics or swimming class together can be a lot of fun. You'll be amazed at how agile pregnant women can be when they're floating in water. Unless you're quite confident about your partner's sense of humor, it's best to stifle your comments about whales—beached or otherwise.

♦ **Start a clipping file or scrapbook for the baby.** Just before our older daughter was born, my wife started putting together a file with newspaper and magazine photos of the hot fashions of the day; lists of the top ten movies, books, and albums of the year; articles on then-pressing political and social issues; pictures of the house we lived in and the baby's room—before and after we fixed it up; and ads—showing the prices, of course—for a variety of items (houses for sale in our neighborhood, computers, food, movie and theater tickets, and so on).

♦ **Go shopping for baby announcements.** Or, you can design your own. See pages 175–76 for more details.

♦ **Make a plaster belly cast.** Believe it or not, this is my all-time favorite. It's a little complicated, but well worth the trouble. Long after the baby is born, you, your partner, and your friends will be absolutely amazed that your partner was ever that big (and the baby that small). If you're interested in trying it, check out www.bellymask.com, www.proudbody.com, or just Google "plaster belly cast." An important warning: Don't even *think* about making a cast of your partner's belly using any kind of plastic, rubber, or resin. No matter what anybody tells you, these products can be harmful to both your partner and the baby.

Work and Family

FAMILY LEAVE

Let's face it: while your partner is pregnant, it's going to be kind of tough for you to put in a lot of quality time with your unborn child—a little before work, a bit more after work, a few hours on weekends. But what about after the pregnancy? Is a few hours a day going to be enough time to spend with your child? If it were, you probably wouldn't be reading this book. Contrary to the common stereotypes, work-family balance is *not* just a women's issue. It's something that most working dads strive for too. But it's not easy. Eighty-seven percent of

A Few Positively Odd Things
Your Partner Might Be Experiencing

You've probably heard all about pregnant women's strange and oddly
timed food cravings—such as pickles and ice cream at two in the morning, or strawberries and garlic for breakfast. As repulsive as some of
them may be, cravings like these are completely normal. Some pregnant
women, though, crave laundry starch, wax, gravel, dirt, coffee grounds,
paint, ashes, clay, cigarette butts, and even the smell of gasoline. Needless to say, such cravings are anything but normal. They are part of a
fairly rare condition called *pica*, which generally affects only kids one to
six years old and pregnant women (yet another reason I'm glad I'm not a
woman). Women who grew up or live in the South or in rural communities seem to be at greater risk, as are women who suffered from pica as
children. Some people believe that these wacky cravings are the body's
way of satisfying its nutritional needs; there is, for example, plenty of
iron in clay. The problem is that there's also a lot of really dangerous
stuff in it.

Other experts discount the nutrition angle completely: if she's missing
some nutrients, she needs to eat better or take some vitamins. So if you
catch your partner licking ashtrays, or if she wakes you up in the middle
of the night asking for a handful of gravel or a candle to chew on, offer
her a healthy snack, get her to sleep, and call her doctor first thing in the
morning.

As if that wasn't weird enough . . . if your partner has been forgetful
lately, or seems to be losing a lot of things—including her memory—it

working fathers report at least some work-vs.-family conflict. And according to
the Families and Work Institute, dads in dual-income households report "significantly higher levels of interference between their jobs and family lives than
do women in the same situation."

Despite all this, today's dads really want to make some changes. Consider
the results of a few recent studies:

♦ Three out of four fathers consider family to be the most important aspect
of their lives. Seventy percent say that being a father makes them a better
employee, and about the same percentage rate having a flexible schedule
that would allow them to spend more time with their family as the most-
appealing workplace benefit (followed by telecommuting, on-site child care,

may be because her brain is shrinking. Yep. Anita Holdcroft, an English anesthesiologist, found that during pregnancy, women's brains actually get 3 to 5 percent smaller.

Now that you know this, it's probably best that you keep it to yourself. After all, there's really no nice way to tell someone that her brain is shrinking. You could mention it in the hope that your partner will forget it right away, but if she doesn't, you're in big trouble. And anyway, the shrinkage seems to be attributed to the brain cells being compressed— not to an actual loss of cells. And, oh yes, it generally clears up within a few months after the birth. (Several researchers have recently disputed the pregnancy brain-shrink theory—also called "mommy brain" or "mommy mush brain"—but most mothers will tell you that they've had issues with memory, concentration, and the ability to think straight.)

We've talked a lot about how just about everything your partner does affects your baby. But can the fetus affect the mother in return? This could very well be. Claire Vanston, a Canadian researcher, did a fascinating study on the brain function of women throughout pregnancy and beyond. She tested the women five times: during pregnancy at twelve weeks, twenty-four weeks, and thirty-seven weeks, then six weeks after the baby was born, and several months after that. She found that "women pregnant with sons consistently outperformed women pregnant with daughters" on several tests of working memory. And the boy/girl difference was there from the first test all the way through the last. As to why this happens, no one knows yet. But it's still pretty interesting, isn't it?

and paid paternity leave). In fact, when searching for a job, 82 percent of working dads view companies more positively if they offer a flextime benefit.

♦ Seventy-four percent of fathers would rather have a "daddy-track" job than a "fast-track" one. Just among men aged 21 to 39, seven in ten say they'd give up some pay to be able to spend more time with their families (men were actually more likely than women to give up pay), and 68 percent would consider being a stay-at-home parent if money were no object.

♦ More and more dads are reducing their workload, passing up promotions, or turning down assignments that require overnight travel so that they can spend more time with their children.

♦ Eighty percent of fathers want to take more of a role in parenting than their own fathers did and expect to make parenting a fifty-fifty proposition with their wives.

Sounds pretty good, doesn't it? Well, unfortunately, despite their good intentions, only about 10 percent of new dads take any more than two weeks off after the birth of their child. So what accounts for the contradiction between what men say and what they actually do? First of all, the vast majority of family-leave plans (including the Family and Medical Leave Act, which we'll talk about in a minute) are unpaid, which makes them unworkable for most families.

Over the past decade or so, there's been a definite increase in the number of companies that offer family-friendly benefits. But when it comes to *male* employees, the messages about whether it's okay to actually use those benefits are mixed at best. For example, about 13 percent of U.S. employers offer paid paternity leave. But even at those companies, only about half of eligible men take it. Why? People generally see taking maternity leave (beyond the disability component) as a normal thing for women to do; but taking paternity leave is seen in many circles as a sure sign that the man isn't serious about his career. It's no surprise then, that so many men have a deep-rooted conviction that getting on the "daddy track" will hurt their careers. Tom, an attorney friend of mine who elected not to take advantage of his firm's paid family-leave plan, told me: "I wanted to take the leave, but I knew I'd never make partner if I did. All the male associates knew it would be career suicide."

Unfortunately, Tom's fears are not entirely unfounded. Julie Holliday Wayne and Bryanne Cordeiro studied the ways people perceive family leave in the workplace and found that men who take leave to care for a newborn are rated much more negatively than their male counterparts who don't take leave. And, sadly, men are more judgmental of other men than women are. The result of all this? Sixty-five percent of fathers work more than forty hours per week (vs. 36 percent of working moms). Compared to mothers, fathers were only one-tenth as likely to have ever used parenting leave, one-sixth as likely to have ever used part-time work hours, and about half as likely to have ever used child-care referral services.

But dads are certainly not giving up. Even those who don't take paternity or family leave manage to take some time off from work in order to be with their newborns. They do it by cobbling together sick days, comp time, vacation days, and so on. On average, that adds up to a little over a week. What it comes

*"Adorable, Kravitz, but from now on
baby pictures will suffice."*

down to is what attorney Kari Palazzari calls the "daddy double-bind." Men are still expected to be the primary breadwinner, so "success" at work means spending less time at home. But today's dads are now expected to be actively involved in every part of their family life, and "success" at home requires spending less time at work. You can see that there's no way out.

The good news is that it looks as though some cracks are developing in what I like to call "the other glass ceiling"—the obstacles that make it hard for men to be with their children as much as they'd like.

A growing number of companies are discovering that not having father-friendly policies can be incredibly expensive, and that having them is just plain good for business. Let me give you a few examples, some of which were drawn from a wonderful report, "Defining Paternity Leave: Shifting Roles, New Responsibilities in the Family and the Workplace," produced by the Boston College Center for Work & Family.

♦ Businesses lose more than $150 billion a year due to absenteeism, employee turnover, health care, and workers' compensation benefits directly resulting from overworked, overstressed dads.

The Family and Medical Leave Act

The Family and Medical Leave Act (usually referred to as the Family Leave Act) is a relatively straightforward document, and I suggest you familiarize yourself with it before you start making too many plans. You can find thousands of references to it online, but for the latest, take a look at the Department of Labor's Web site, www.dol.gov/dol/topic/benefits-leave/fmla.htm.

Here's a quick summary of what it means for fathers:

♦ **Who can take the leave?** Any person who works for a public agency (federal, state, or local) or a private-sector company that employs fifty or more people. You must have been employed by that company for at least twelve months, and have worked at least 1,250 hours during that time. This covers about two-thirds of the total U.S. labor force. If you're in the military, the FMLA may apply to you as well. Check with your CO and keep in mind that the needs of the service may trump your eligibility.

♦ **How much leave can you take?** Eligible employees can take up to twelve workweeks of leave at any time during the twelve-month period that starts the day your child is born or adopted. If you and your wife are employed by the same company, though, you may get only twelve weeks total.

♦ **When do you have to take it?** You can start anytime, just as long as you finish within a year. Beyond that, whatever you can work out with your employer is fine. You can take twelve weeks in one chunk, work part-time for twenty-four weeks, take every Friday off for a year, or make some other arrangement.

♦ Inability to balance work, family, and community is linked to reduced work performance, higher employee turnover, poor morale, and increased work conflict.

♦ Absenteeism alone costs an average of nearly $800 per employee every year—$80,000 per year for a company with 100 employees.

♦ Employees who felt that their supervisors supported their personal and family needs were three and a half times more likely to report high levels of job satisfaction (70 percent vs. 19 percent), according to the Families and Work Institute.

♦ **Is it paid?** Employers are not required to pay you your salary while you're on leave. But suppose your employer pays for six weeks of family leave: you're still entitled to take another six without pay. And even if your employer doesn't have paid leave, they may require you to burn through your sick time, vacation, and comp days before you can start using the leave.

♦ **What about benefits?** Your employer must maintain your coverage under the company's health plan for the duration of your leave.

♦ **Is your job protected?** In most cases, yes. Your employer cannot fire or replace you while you're on leave unless he or she can prove that your being gone has caused "substantial and grievous economic injury to the operations of the employer."

♦ **Do you have to give notice?** According to the act, you're required to give your employer at least thirty days' notice before taking your family leave. But the more notice you give, the more time everyone will have to get used to the idea.

Individual states may offer family-leave benefits that are more liberal than those of the federal program. In some states, for example, companies that employ as few as twenty-five people are required to offer their employees family leave. And a small number of states are now offering family leave that's paid (although you probably won't get anywhere near your current salary). And remember: these benefits are completely separate from the (potentially more liberal) ones your company may offer. Be sure to check with your employer's Human Resources department.

♦ Companies that offer paid parental leave say that those policies "have strengthened their recruiting and retention initiatives."

♦ Employers with fair leave policies believe that these policies "have been key components to increasing company loyalty and employee goodwill."

♦ Marriott estimates that for every dollar it spends helping employees with work/life issues such as fatherhood, the company saves four dollars due to lower turnover and absenteeism. A number of other companies have reported a similar return on investment.

LONG-TERM WORK SCHEDULE CHANGES

So far we've talked about taking a few weeks off just after the birth of your child. But what about after that?

Not long after our first daughter was born, my wife left her big, downtown law firm and found a less stressful, three-day-a-week job closer to home. Almost everyone we knew applauded. But when I made the announcement that I, too, would be cutting back to three days a week, the reaction was quite a bit different. At work, I was hassled repeatedly by my boss and coworkers, and a lot of my friends and relatives began to whisper that if I didn't go back to work full-time, my career might never recover.

I'm not suggesting that everyone should cut back their work schedules to three days a week. Clearly, that just isn't practical for most people (although it sure would be nice if you could, wouldn't it?). Frankly, you may never be able to resolve your work/family conflicts completely. But if you want to spend more time with your children on an ongoing basis, the only way to make that happen is to make some changes in your work schedule. Fortunately, there are a few ways you can maximize your time with your family, minimize your stress, and avoid trashing your career.

Here are some rather painless flexible-scheduling options you might want to run by your employer:

♦ Work four ten-hour days instead of five eight-hour days.
♦ Work 5:00 A.M. to 1:00 P.M. (or some other schedule) instead of the usual 9:00 to 5:00.
♦ Consider a split shift; for example, work 8:00 A.M. to noon and 5:00 P.M. to 9:00 P.M.

WORKING LESS THAN FULL-TIME

If you can afford to, you might want to consider one of the following options:

♦ **Job sharing.** You and another person divide up the responsibilities of the job. You'd probably use the same office and desk. A typical job-share schedule might have you working two days one week and three days the next, while the person you're sharing with does the opposite. One warning: be very careful to negotiate a continuation of your health benefits. Many employers routinely drop them for less-than-full-time employees.

♦ **Switch to part-time.** This is pretty much the same as job sharing, except you probably won't have to share a desk with someone else. Although this can be a great option, there are a few potential problems. According to www.abetterbalance.org, part-time workers earn an average of 20 percent

Family Leave If You're an Employee

♦ **Take it.** Every man I interviewed who took paternity or family leave told me he'd do it again. One even told me he thought that men who didn't take family leave were "nuts."

♦ **Know your rights.** Find out whether you're eligible under the Family and Medical Leave Act (see page 154–55), your company's voluntary plan, or any other federal- or state-mandated program. There's often a disconnect between what you're legally entitled to and what your employer will let you know about, so ask around.

♦ **Start talking to your employer now.** If you're covered by a leave plan, start working out the details in a nonconfrontational way. If you're not covered by a leave plan, you may be able to arrange for some time off anyway.

♦ **Come up with a plan.** I have an MBA, and before I switched to writing full-time, I worked in business for many years. That's why, as big a pro-father/pro-family advocate as I am, I believe that when an employer hires you to do a job, they have every right to expect that job to get done—and it's up to you to figure out how that's going to happen while you're out on leave. Start by talking with your partner and figuring out an ideal-case scenario that works for both of you. Then come up with a plan and present it to your employer, along with a way to evaluate whether everyone's needs are being met. If everything seems to be on track after a couple of weeks, keep it going. If not, revise the plan and try again. Acknowledging your employer's needs will make it a lot easier for them to acknowledge and support yours.

♦ **Sell the benefits.** If you're having trouble convincing your employer, take a quick look back at pages 153–55. Employers need to know that dad-friendly benefits aren't just something that's nice to offer (although they certainly are that); they're good business.

less per hour than full-timers with the same level of education and experience. But that's not all. Most part-timers don't get health insurance, aren't covered by employer-sponsored pension plans (including 401(k)s), and usually aren't eligible for unemployment benefits.

♦ **Become a consultant to your current employer.** This can be a great way for you to get a lot of flexibility over your workday. There are also many tax advantages—particularly if you set up a home office. At the very least, you'll be able to deduct auto mileage and a percentage of your phone and utility bills. There are some disadvantages too. As a company employee, you split the roughly 15 percent of your check that goes to Social Security: you pay 7.5 percent, your employer pays 7.5 percent. But when you're self-employed, you pay both halves. In addition, if you become a consultant, you'll lose your company-paid benefit package (if you keep it, the IRS will consider you an employee and you'll lose all those other deductions). So be sure to set your daily or hourly rate high enough to recoup those extra payroll taxes, your insurance costs (health, life, disability), vacation and holiday pay, and anything else, including your employer's matching contribution to your 401(k).

WORKING AT HOME (TELECOMMUTING)

Years ago, when I was a commodities trader, I used to spend eight or nine hours a day on the phone haggling with people—most of whom I never met—about grain prices. My coworkers were similarly occupied, and my boss was two thousand miles away. Realistically, there was no reason I couldn't have been working at home. It was pretty much the same story when I started writing full-time. Most of the people I've worked with—often very closely—I've never met (or did so only years later).

Granted, commodities trading and freelance writing aren't typical jobs, but the fact is that many Americans do work that doesn't require their physical presence in any particular place at any particular time. If you're not a construction worker or a retail salesman, you might be a prime candidate for telecommuting.

Now before you start to panic, I'm not suggesting that you rent out your office to someone else—most telecommuters work only a day or two a week at home. The point is that by telecommuting you may be able to reduce the time you spend getting to work and spend it with your family instead. Remember, though, that telecommuting is not meant to be a substitute for child care; you're supposed to be working when you're at home.

Telecommuting is good for your employer too. As the cost of office space rises and the cost of telecommunications equipment falls, many companies are finding that they save money by having their employees work elsewhere at least part of the time. And to top it off, employees who telecommute are more productive and get more and faster promotions than their office-bound coworkers.

Chances are you won't be the first person to raise the issue of telecommuting to your employer. Over 17 million people telecommute at least one day per month, according to undress4success.com and World at Work (worldatwork .org). That's more than double what it was a decade ago. And nearly 40 percent of those who didn't telecommute regularly said they had job-related tasks that could be done from home. Thirty-five percent of those non-telecommuters said they'd be willing to take a slight pay cut in exchange for being allowed to telecommute two days per week.

Another major advantage to telecommuting is that you don't have to shave and you can work in your underwear. But as great as working from home (or the library or coffee shop) is, there are still a few disadvantages. Some of my friends began to think that since I was always at home, I wasn't really doing anything, and since I wasn't doing anything, I could run errands for them. If this happens to you, you're going to have to learn to say no. Working at home can also get a little lonely—you might miss hanging out around the water cooler and schmoozing with your buddies at work. And if you have a tendency to be obsessive about your work (as I do), you'll have to train yourself to take frequent breaks.

I can't tell you how many times I've realized—at ten at night—that I hadn't eaten all day and that the only time I had gone outside was to take the newspaper in from the porch.

A WORK-FAMILY SOLUTION YOU MIGHT NOT HAVE THOUGHT OF

On pages 298–304 we'll discuss a number of the child-care options you and your partner will have to sift through sometime soon. But what if you'd both really prefer to have your child raised in the arms of a loving parent? Most families that make the decision to have a parent stay home automatically assume that it has to be Mom. Sometimes, though, that just won't work. She might have a more stable career than you, she might make more money, or she might simply have no interest in staying home. Well, all is not lost. If you and your partner truly want to have your children raised by a parent, the solution may be only as far away as the nearest mirror: you.

Now before you throw this book down and run out of the room screaming, take a minute to consider the idea. It may not be as crazy as it sounds, particularly if there aren't any other interested family members nearby. Let's start with some of the benefits:

Creating a More Family-Friendly Workplace for Dads If You're an Employer (or Supervisor)

♦ **If you don't have father-friendly policies, get some.** See pages 153–55 for some of the benefits. If you need help putting a program together, e-mail me, armin@mrdad.com.

♦ **Spread the word.** At the very least, let all of your employees—especially the men—know that you support their desire to find a better balance between their work and family lives, and that family-friendly policies aren't just for women. Then put your money where your mouth is. If you have a chance, for example, take family leave yourself. The ultimate responsibility for helping men get more involved with their families rests at the top—with male managers. If you demonstrate that it's okay for men to put their families first, everyone else will see that it's acceptable and follow your lead.

♦ **Encourage other men to take leave (whether it's official or not).** Most of your male employees will be reluctant to approach you with their family-leave plan. If you know they're expecting, raise the issue with them first. Chances are, they'll be grateful. If you can afford to make the leave paid, so much the better.

♦ **Encourage flexible schedules.** This doesn't mean that your employees will work less, just that they'll have more control over when and

♦ You won't have to agonize over picking the right babysitter or nanny or day-care center.

♦ It could be cheaper. Full-time day care for an infant in major metro areas can exceed $15,000 per year. Add in the dry cleaning you won't need to do as often, the three-times-a-week take-out meals you won't be needing, car expenses, train tickets, bridge tolls, and so on, and staying home could end up being a wash.

♦ You'll have a wonderful opportunity to get to know and build a strong relationship with your child.

♦ You'll be giving your child what you think is the best possible upbringing.

♦ You'll be able to help give your partner some peace of mind, while advancing her career at the same time. According to a recent article in womensenews.org, "More than one-third of the women on *Fortune* magazine's list of the 50 most powerful women in business have a husband at home either full- or part-time."

where they do their jobs. You can do this by wiring your workplace so that more people can telecommute or work remotely. Research has shown that flexibility is the most important factor in a family-friendly workplace.

♦ **Educate your workers.** Have an occasional brown-bag lunch at which dads get together to discuss their work-family issues. You—and they—will probably be amazed that a lot of other people are facing the same issues.

♦ **Don't worry about the cost.** "The more support employees receive on the job—the more flexible their work arrangements and supportive their supervisors—the higher their productivity, the more willing they are to go the extra mile, and the more likely they are to stay with their current employers," according to a recent study by the Families and Work Institute.

♦ **Don't forget about employees who don't have kids.** It's easy to think of work-life balance as something that affects only parents. But single, childless, or older workers have plenty of personal and family issues to deal with. And supporting them with flexible schedules and everything else we've talked about in this section will pay off in many of the same ways, such as being able to attract more top-quality workers and increasing productivity, morale, and loyalty.

Still with us? Deciding to be a stay-at-home dad is a big decision, one that will affect everyone in your family. If you're even remotely considering it, start by asking yourself the following very important questions:

♦ **Can you afford it?** Although you'll undoubtedly save on some things by working at home, if you're really committed to the idea, there are all sorts of ways to cut your expenses. Here are just a few: buy food in bulk, eat out less often, raise your insurance deductibles, take stay-cations (vacations closer to home), make presents instead of buying them, get rid of the housekeeper, move to a smaller house or a place where the cost of living is lower.

♦ **Can you take the career hit?** This is a big one, since earning power and masculinity are inextricably linked in so many people's minds. (If I'm not making money, I'm not a good man/father, the thinking goes.) If you can get over this hurdle, you may still be able to keep a finger or a foot in the work world by teaching, consulting, writing, or starting a home-based business. But don't be hasty. If you decide to reenter the workforce later, you may find that the employment gap on your résumé could cause you some problems with potential employers, many of whom are going to be a lot less enlightened and a lot more closed-minded than you.

♦ **Can you handle the pressure?** Some people will come right out and tell you that you really should be out there bringing in some money. After all, that's what guys are supposed to do, right? But even if you don't hear the actual words, you may feel the need to demonstrate that you're still a man, that even though you've chosen *not* to earn money (or at least not as much as you did before), you *could* if you really wanted to. Although some of that pressure may be external, some of it may be internal. Traditional sex roles do a real number on us, don't they?

♦ **Do you have a job description?** What are your responsibilities? Will you be doing all the laundry, shopping, and cooking? Some of it?

♦ **Can you handle the workload?** Staying home with a child is a lot more work than you think. It can also be a little mind-numbing. (Having done the stay-at-home dad thing for many years, I say this from experience. Sometimes, no matter how much fun you've had with the kids, you'll crave some adult conversation at the end of the day.)

♦ **Are you selfless enough?** You're not going to get a lot of personal time, and you'll have to put your children's needs above yours. Always.

♦ **How do you deal with isolation?** Being a stay-at-home-dad can be a bit lonely. According to researcher Robert Frank, about two-thirds of stay-at-home dads feel isolated, compared to only about one-third of stay-at-home moms. There's also not a lot of social support for men who decide to stay home, and you won't see many other guys around who are doing it.

♦ **Is your skin thick enough?** Women—whether they're moms, nannies, babysitters—tend not to welcome men into their groups at parks or playgrounds or malls and the other places people take their kids during the day. You'll have to deal with peoples' stereotypes about dads (very few of which are positive). You'll have to get used to the funny looks and stupid comments you'll hear from people who see you with your kids in the middle of the day. ("Hey, are you babysitting today?" is one that always bugs me. "No, bozo, I'm not babysitting, I'm taking care of my children.") And you'll have to deal with people's criticisms and critiques of your parenting—the kinds of "advice" and comments no one would ever make to a woman.

♦ **How thick is your partner's skin?** When you're the primary parent, your child will run to you when he wants a hug or has a skinned knee. And if

Mom tries to provide that hug or apply a Band-Aid®, he may push her away. I've been on both sides of this, and I can tell you that it hurts. A lot.

♦ **Do you have a reentry plan?** It's a good idea to have a rough plan for how long your at-home stint will last, and what you'll do afterwards.

In reality, you won't be quite as alone in making this choice as it might seem. At least two million stay-at-home dads are doing it every day, and the number is rising all the time, according to Peter Baylies, founder of the At-Home Dad Network. You may have to do some digging, but there are also a lot of great resources out there. Peter's organization, www.athomedad.net, and www.slowlane.com are terrific places to start. For more, see the Resources section of this book.

Notes:

Entering the Home Stretch

What's Going On with Your Partner

Physically

♦ Increasing general physical discomfort (cramps, dizziness, abdominal achiness, heartburn, gas, constipation, and so forth)
♦ Itchy belly, puffy face
♦ Increasing clumsiness and decreasing stamina
♦ Her hip joints are expanding and she's having to learn to walk in a new, awkward way, which may explain why she's a little more susceptible to muscle pulls and general klutziness
♦ Some thick, white, vaginal discharge (it's called *leukorrhea*, and is completely normal)
♦ Increased Braxton-Hicks (false labor) contractions

Emotionally

♦ May be getting kind of used to the emotional ups and downs of pregnancy
♦ Decreased moodiness
♦ Forgetful
♦ Dreaming/fantasizing about the baby
♦ Concerned about work—not sure she'll have the energy to go back, and anxious about how to balance roles of mother, wife, employee . . .

♦ Feeling energized and eager to get things ready for the baby—or completely overwhelmed by everything there is left to do
♦ Fearful about the labor and delivery

What's Going On with the Baby

The baby's lungs are maturing, and if she were born today, she'd have an excellent chance of survival. She's getting a little cramped inside now—especially if she's got a womb-mate. Her eyes are fully open, and her irises react to light and dark. She can now move in rhythm to music played outside the womb. The fat she's putting on has made her skin a little less red and wrinkly, and she's bulked up to two or three pounds and measures thirteen to fifteen inches long. Her brain is developing incredibly quickly, but the surface of it is still fairly smooth and she's not really capable of much rational thought (given her living situation, that's probably a good thing).

What's Going On with You

Increasing Acceptance of the Pregnancy

As we've discussed earlier, for most expectant fathers the process of completely accepting the pregnancy is a long one—with the baby becoming progressively more real over the course of the nine months. "It's like getting the measles," said one man interviewed by researcher Katharyn May. "You get exposed, but it takes a while before you realize that you've got it." Another researcher, Pamela Jordan, found that despite seeing the fetus on a sonogram many men don't really experience their children as real until they meet them face-to-face.

Visualizing the Baby

The growing reality of the pregnancy is reflected in men's dreams as well. Researcher Luis Zayas has found that in expectant fathers' dreams in the early and middle stages of the pregnancy "the child is not represented as a person. Instead, symbols of the child are present." But as the pregnancy advances to the final stage, expectant fathers—consciously and unconsciously—produce clearer images of their children.

If you want to get a little bit of insight into one of the differences between mothers and fathers, ask your partner to describe herself with the baby. Chances are, she'll talk about a brand-new, fresh-from-the-oven baby. Now do the same thing yourself. More than 90 percent of the expectant fathers in my research (myself included) describe a scene where they're engaged with a three- to five-year-old child, holding hands, leaving footprints on the beach, playing catch, reading together, or doing something else interactive.

It's a fascinating difference, one that I think is the result of hardwiring. Women, perhaps because of the physical link between themselves and the fetus, have no problem seeing themselves as mothers. And mothers can simply *be*. But for us, fatherhood is about *doing*—teaching, mentoring, preparing our children to meet the world. If you're ever out at a park or some other place where new parents are hanging out, carrying their babies in front packs, you'll see a perfect example of this being-vs.-doing approach. Moms almost always carry their babies facing in. Dads almost always carry them facing out, as if to say, "Hey, baby, this is your world."

"I want kids. He wants children."

Speculating about Gender

In case you hadn't noticed, our society is fixated on gender. So it's not surprising that most parents (if they don't already know) eventually—or constantly—speculate about the sex of their unborn baby. Is your partner carrying the baby high? Wide? Low? Are the baby's kicks hard enough to move your hand, or are they more gentle? Is your partner's complexion clear, or does she have a little acne? Does she crave salty foods or sweets? Is the hair on her legs growing more quickly than usual? And are *you* putting on weight or staying steady? There are literally hundreds of absolutely, positively surefire ways of determining what flavor your baby will be. Each has a fifty-fifty chance of being right, and before your baby is born, you'll hear every one.

A lot of the speculating people do about their unborn children is based on common stereotypes and prejudices that almost all of us have about gender long before our kids are born. Take the baby's kicks, for example. Expectant mothers who know they're carrying a boy often describe the baby's movements as "vigorous," "earthquake-like," or even just "very strong." They describe girls' kicks as "very gentle," "not terribly active," or "lively but not excessively energetic." Truth is, says Carole Beal, author of *Boys and Girls: The Development of Gender Roles*, there aren't any differences between boys' and girls' fetal activity levels.

Preconceived notions (so to speak) such as these may also have an influence on expectant parents' preferences. "Parents usually say they don't care what gender their child is as long as it's healthy," says Beal. "But the truth is that couples have a definite preference for the sex of their child." That preference is usually for a boy, and it's expressed by both men and women. Generally speaking, dads prefer boys because they feel more comfortable with them or because they feel that a boy would carry on the family name. Mothers may prefer boys because they know—instinctively or otherwise—how much it means to their husbands.

Interestingly, more women than men call their unborn baby "it." However, both men and women prefer to call the baby by some kind of nickname. In my case, the nicknames I gave our in-utero daughters stuck with them long after they were born. I called our older "The Roo"—as in kanga—because she kicked so hard she could knock an open book off my wife's belly. The next one was "Pokey" because, unlike her sister, she preferred to jab and poke. And the youngest is "Lumpty," because her first ultrasound picture looked like Humpty Dumpty.

Some expectant fathers are actually afraid of getting a child of the "wrong" gender, feeling that if they do, they won't be able to have the parenting experience they'd imagined. For many men, their images of themselves as parents are closely linked to the gender of their children. As boys, most of us spent a great deal of our childhood doing things, such as running, jumping, wrestling, and playing football. So it's natural to imagine ourselves doing the same with our own children. Yet some men feel uncomfortable with the idea of wrestling with their daughters, believing that playing physically with girls would somehow be inappropriate. The truth of the matter is that not only is it safe and appropriate to play physically with girls, it's quite beneficial for them in some unexpected ways (see pages 311–13 for more on this).

Your preferences may have a major impact on a lot of other people. According to Beal, boys tend to bring fathers into the family more: fathers of newborn boys actually visit the nursery more often and stay there longer than fathers of girls. In addition, couples who have girls first often have more children, trying to have a boy. But those who have boys first often end up with smaller families. Some experts speculate that this is at least in part due to the perception that boys are more "difficult." And two researchers in Stockholm, Sweden, recently found that men are generally more satisfied with their role as fathers when their babies—boys or girls—are the gender they'd hoped for.

At the same time, there's evidence that children who did not turn out to be the gender their parents preferred have worse relationships with their parents in childhood than preferred-gender kids. That is especially true for kids whose parents had wanted a boy but got a girl. This bias for boys plays out in a number of interesting and surprising ways. For example, researchers Gordon Dahl and Enrico Moretti found that unmarried expectant couples are more likely to get married before the birth if they know they're having a boy than if it's a girl. Among married couples, divorce rates are lowest for those who have only boys, and highest for those who have only girls. Divorced women with all-girl offspring are less likely to remarry, and if they do, they're more likely to get divorced again. And in countries where polygamous marriages are relatively common, women who have given birth to girls are more likely to be in polygamous relationships than mothers of boys.

It's going to be tough, but if you find yourself preferring one gender over the other—particularly if you're hoping for a boy—try to stop. If you can't, do yourself and everyone else a favor and keep it to yourself. If your child turns out to be the "wrong" gender, chances are he or she will eventually find out about it (probably from an unthinking friend or relative whom you once told in complete confidence). Besides the problems I just raised in the previous paragraphs, the feeling of being inadequate, of "letting you down," and even of being secretly rejected or loved less, may haunt your child for many years, especially in adolescence, when self-confidence is often at a low.

Fear of Falling Apart During Her Labor

Men are supposed to be strong, right? Especially while their wives are pregnant. And any sign of weakness could be taken as an indication of, well, weakness. Perhaps it's those old societal pressures that make most men dread labor—not only because they aren't looking forward to seeing their partners in pain, but because they're afraid that they'll simply fall apart. And everybody knows that real men don't crack under pressure.

If you're worried about how you'll perform during your partner's labor, do yourself these favors:

♦ Read the "Classes" section on pages 176–89—especially the "What If You Feel Like You Don't Want to Be in the Delivery Room at All?" section at the end. The more you know about what to expect during the labor and delivery, the less likely you are to worry that you won't be able to handle things.

♦ Lighten up. It's perfectly natural to be afraid for your partner's and baby's life. Actually, it would be rather surprising if you weren't.

♦ Remember that it rarely happens. In Jerrold Shapiro's study of more than two hundred expectant fathers, none of them fell apart during their partner's labor.

♦ Keep talking to your partner and let her know how you feel. The more supported and understood you are, the less likely you'll be to feel the need to do everything absolutely perfectly.

♦ Focus on the team. Your partner wants you—more than anyone else—to be there with her, to help get her through her labor. Knowing that you're a critical part of the process may help you pull it all together.

♦ Talk to some other dads who've experienced it. Most fathers who have will say it was some combination of tiring, exhilarating, amazing, boring, scary, exciting, bloody, annoying, and just about any other positive or negative feeling you can come up with. And just about all of them will also tell you they wouldn't have missed it for the world.

Staying Involved

Choosing a Name

Naming a child may sound like an easy task, but it's harder than you think. And you'd better start thinking about it soon, because the second question you're going to hear after the baby comes (the first being "Boy or girl?") is "What's the baby's name?" Here are a few things you might want to keep in mind as you begin your search:

♦ Think about the future. That name that strikes you as unbearably cute right now might be unbearably ridiculous when your child gets nominated to the Supreme Court. Take the real-life case of the other Jackson 5: Appendicitis, Laryngitis, Meningitis, Peritonitis, and Tonsillitis. I'm sure those names seemed to their parents like a great idea at the time. As did Anne Aass, Jo King, Ray Gunn, Stan Still, Barb Dwyer, Paige Turner, Carrie Oakey, Ben Dover, and Justin Case—all of which are real names, found by researchers digging through birth certificates in the United States and Britain.

♦ Watch out for rhyming names (Jane Payne, Bill Hill).

♦ Watch out for initials. Before you make your final decision, think about what your baby's initials could spell—especially in the age of texting and tweeting. Terms like BFF, FBI, BLT, and SAT might or might not cause problems. But do you really want to saddle your child with HIV, STD, DNR (do not resuscitate), LOL (laugh out loud), TMI (too much information), or WTF (what the fu**). Think about it.

♦ Do you need—or want—to honor a relative?

♦ Do you want a name that indicates your ethnic or religious background?

♦ Do you want something unique yet manageable?

♦ Do you want something easy to spell and/or pronounce?

♦ How do you feel about the nicknames that go with it?

♦ How does it sound with the last name? How would the nicknames sound with the last name?

♦ No, you can't use numbers. (There was a real-life court case a while back about a guy in Minnesota who tried to change his name to a number. He lost.)

HOW TO PICK 'EM

Start by making a list of the ten boys' and ten girls' names you like best. Exchange lists with your partner and cross off all the ones on her list you couldn't possibly live with. She'll do the same to your list. If there are any left, you're in business. If not, keep repeating the process until you come up with names acceptable to you both. Some couples who cannot agree on two names decide instead to let one partner choose the name if it's a boy and the other choose the name if it's a girl (and let the loser choose the next child's name).

Not only is this little exercise fun, but it will also give you and your partner some interesting insights into each other's minds. My wife, for example, had never really taken my interest in mythology seriously until the names Odin (the chief god in Norse legends) and Loki (the Norse god of mischief and evil) showed up on my top-ten list. I don't know what I'm more grateful for, that both those choices were vetoed or that all three of our children are girls.

Another approach—albeit an odd one—to picking names is offered by Albert Mehrabian in his book *The Name Game* (Signet, 1992). Mehrabian surveyed two thousand people, asking them to judge several thousand first names and rate them according to success, morality, health, warmth, cheerfulness, masculinity/femininity. Not surprisingly, Mehrabian found that certain names evoke certain stereotypes. Bunny, for example, scored high on femininity, but low on morality and success. Ann and Holly were highly rated in all categories. For boys, Grover and Aldo were big losers in all categories, while Hans (go figure) was rated highly across the board.

That ought to give you plenty to start with. But if you still need a little help, there are literally hundreds of resources out there that can give you access to tens of thousands of names, their history, meanings, popularity, and more. A lot of Web sites have search engines designed to help you wade through the endless possibilities. The one at www.greatdad.com is one of my favorites. There's also a very comprehensive list of sites, covering ethnic, religious, odd, celebrity, and fad categories, and even how to do a legal name change—hey, it could come in handy—at www.hubpages.com/hub/Top-50-Most-Popular-Baby-Name-Websites.

What's in a Name? Waaaay More Than You Ever Thought

Some onomasticians (people who study names) claim that a child's name has a direct and profound effect on the kind of life, and success, he or she will have. Of course, there's a big difference between causation and correlation (meaning that just because two things seem related doesn't necessarily mean that one caused the other). Nevertheless, here are a few examples of some positively bizarre name-life connections.

♦ In one study, fifth- and sixth-grade teachers were asked to grade identical essays called "What I Did Last Sunday." The essays "written" by Michael and David were given one full grade higher than those "written" by Elmer and Hubert. Similarly, Karen and Lisa outperformed Bertha by one and a half grades.

♦ Nicholas Christenfeld and his colleagues identified a connection between life expectancy and people's three-letter initials. People with positive initials (like HUG, VIP, or WOW) live almost five years longer than those with negative initials (like BAD, ZIT, or RAT). Ernest Abel and Michael Kruger analyzed nearly 2,000 major league baseball players whose initials were acronyms or words, and who died before 1950. They found that players who had positive initials (like ACE and WIN lived *thirteen* years longer than players with negative or neutral ones (like BUM or SOB).

♦ Boys who have peculiar names (Armin, for instance) have a higher incidence of mental problems than boys with common ones, and than girls with peculiar ones. Leif Nelson and Joseph Simmons looked at ninety years' worth of pro baseball stats and found that players whose

FAMILY PRESSURES/TRADITIONAL CUSTOMS

In many cultures (or families), your choice of names may be severely limited by tradition:

♦ Among the Kikuyu people of Africa, the family's first son is named after the father's father; the second son, after the father's grandfather; the first daughter, after the father's mother; and so on.

♦ In Myanmar, each day of the week is assigned a different letter of the alphabet and children's names must begin with the letter of the day on which they were born.

names begin with K (scoring shorthand for "strikeout") actually do strike out more (in 18.8 percent of their plate appearances) than other players (17.2 percent of appearances).

♦ Students whose names begin with A or B have higher grade point averages than students whose names begin with C or D. Oh, and it goes further than that. According to Nelson and Simmons, students whose names begin with A or B and go on to law school are much more likely to get into top schools (as ranked by *U.S. News & World Report*) than those with C or D initials.

♦ In a study by British researcher Philip Erwin, photographs of women labeled with names that score high on attractiveness scales (such as Jennifer, Katie, Julia, and Christine) were rated as far more physically attractive than the identical photos labeled with "unattractive" names (like Ethel and Harriet).

♦ People generally like their names a lot. So much, in fact, that names can influence where your children live and what they do for a living. For example, Brett Pelham, Matthew Mirenberg, and their colleagues discovered a disproportionate number of Mildreds in Milwaukee, Jacks in Jacksonville, Philips in Philadelphia, and Virginias in Virginia Beach. There's a similar connection between name and career: a disproportionate number of dentists are named Denis or Denise, and a surprising number of geoscientists are named George. Just looking at hardware stores and roofing companies, hardware store owners were about 80 percent more likely to have names starting with H than R, and roofing companies were 70 percent more likely to be owned by people with first names starting with R than H.

♦ In Thailand, the parents may ask a nearby priest—or even a fortune-teller—to give their child just the right name.

♦ Jews of Eastern European extraction generally don't name babies after living people because of the traditional fear that the Angel of Death might take the baby instead of the older namesake. Jews of Spanish or Moroccan descent don't have the same worries.

♦ If there is someone on either side of a family who absolutely has to be honored with a name for the sake of family peace, you may be able to find a reasonable compromise. Harry Truman's parents, for example, gave him the

Baby Showers

Not too long ago, baby showers—like so many other baby-related activities—were considered "for women only." But today, if your partner's relatives or friends organize a shower for her, there's a good chance you'll be invited, too. (But don't hold your breath waiting for your friends or relatives to plan one especially for you.)

The vast majority of baby showers take place several weeks or months before the baby is born, and the idea behind them is obvious: give the new parents a selection of baby clothing, furniture, toys, and the latest gadgets so the soon-to-be newborn can come home to a well-stocked nursery. If your relatives and friends are so inclined, enjoy—a shower can be a wonderful way to share your excitement about the coming event with others. Just don't forget to keep track of who gave what—after the birth, when you get around to those thank-you notes, all those yellow sleepers and *Where the Wild Things Are* dolls can look disconcertingly similar.

I've always thought, though, that having a baby shower before you've got a real baby in hand is kind of creepy—too much like tempting fate. After all, what if, God forbid, something were to happen to the baby? A friend of mine, when his wife was seven months pregnant, put a new patio in his backyard and carved the name of his yet-to-be-born son (they'd done an amnio) in the wet concrete. I could hardly bring myself to go back there until after the baby was safely home. Anyway, if you join me in the anti-shower camp, you may find that some people will be offended by your not wanting one. In such cases, try to steer them toward a post-birth shower instead (call it a "Welcome Baby" or "Baby Birthday" party if you want to stay away from the word "shower"). Be firm. Stressing how much more fun it will be for the guests to get presents for a baby whose name and gender are known may also make the no-shower news easier to swallow.

middle initial S—no name, no period, just the initial—to satisfy both grandfathers (whose names were Solomon and Shippe).

THE LAST-NAME GAME

If you and your partner already have the same last name, you haven't got anything to worry about; if you don't, there could be a few complications. Perhaps

I spent too much time in Berkeley, but I've known people who have done at least one of the following when they had kids:

♦ Given the kids the man's last name (probably the most common)
♦ Given the kids the woman's last name (less common)
♦ Used the woman's last name as the child's first
♦ Given the kids a hyphenated last name (but when Mary Jane O'Flaherty-Ignetowski marries Roberto Goldberg-Yamahito, what will their children's last name be?)
♦ Made up a completely new last name
♦ Given the boys the man's last name, and the girls the woman's

Birth Announcements

WHEN TO ORDER

Since you don't know the exact weight, height, or (unless your partner has had an amnio) sex of the baby before he or she is born, there's not much sense in having birth announcements printed until then. But running around trying to decide on birth announcements is about the last thing you're going to want to experience when you're sleep-deprived out of your mind. So now's the perfect time to start shopping.

There are two basic types of birth announcements: hard copy and electronic.

The hard copy variety can be as low-tech as a preprinted card with blanks to fill in, which you can get at stationery or office supply stores. You can also go to an online store and use one of their standard designs or upload your own artwork. Select your design now, then log on and drop in the baby's vital statistics as soon as you know them. If you're going the hard copy route, try to get the envelopes now and address them—or at least print up some labels—while your lives are still relatively calm.

The electronic route will probably be a little less labor-intensive. All you need is your digital camera and Web access and you can tweet, IM, send e-vites, and update your Web site or Facebook page from almost anywhere.

WHAT TO INCLUDE

As medical science becomes more exact, birth announcements will probably contain your baby's IQ, SAT scores, future profession, spouse's name, and number of children. But for now, all you really need to include is the baby's name, date and time of birth, weight, length (since they can't stand up, babies don't usually have "height"), and the names of the parents.

WHOM TO SEND ANNOUNCEMENTS TO

Family and friends are the obvious recipients. When it comes to more casual acquaintances and business associates, however, take it easy. Many people will feel obligated to send a gift if they receive a birth announcement, so don't send one to anyone from whom you wouldn't feel comfortable getting a gift. Exceptions include people who request an announcement as a memento, employers or employees who have already given you and/or your partner a baby gift and/or shower, and people your parents and in-laws ask you to send announcements to.

Classes

Until the late 1960s, there really was no such thing as childbirth education. Basically, all you had to know to have a baby was where the hospital was located. And all that expectant parents did to prepare for the arrival of their baby was set up a nursery. Women checked into the hospital, labored alone in stark, sterile rooms, received general anesthesia, and woke up groggy and tender, not knowing the sex of the child they'd delivered, and sometimes even the number of children. Meanwhile, men were left to pace anxiously in hospital waiting rooms until a nurse came to give them the happy news. Fathers who tried to buck their non-role in the birth of their children were in for a real surprise.

In 1522, a German guy named Dr. Wertt (no one knows what kind of doctor he was) wanted to learn about childbirth and see midwives in action. So he dressed up as a woman and slipped in to watch a delivery. Unfortunately, someone saw through the disguise and raised quite a stink. Poor Wertt was burned to death. Seems a touch harsh, doesn't it?

More than 400 years later, not much had changed. Dr. Robert Bradley, who originated the Bradley method, cites the 1965 case of a man who was arrested and fined for having "gained unauthorized admission to a hospital's delivery room in an attempt to witness the birth of his second child." Hey, at least he wasn't burned at the stake.

In her book *The Experience of Childbirth*, Sheila Kitzinger, a pioneering birth educator, quotes from a publication put out by the British Medical Association in 1959: "The last requirement of all for a successful delivery at home is the husband—the poor father. If he is of the right mentality, and very few are, he may sustain his wife's morale during the first part of her labour. Otherwise, he is best employed making tea, keeping the kettles boiling, and answering the front doorbell."

"Coach"—Don't Use That Word

Almost all of the most common childbirth methods now refer to the man as the childbirth "coach"—a term that seems to have been coined by Dr. Robert Bradley, the founder of the Bradley method. Today most expectant fathers (at least those who take childbirth classes) and their partners view themselves in those terms, but I agree with Professor Katharyn May that there are some very compelling reasons to erase the word from your non-sports vocabulary.

♦ We all know what happens to coaches when things don't go according to plan...

♦ The coach concept focuses attention on your role during the brief period of labor and delivery, but minimizes how important you've been throughout the pregnancy and how important you'll be to your child after the birth.

♦ The coach concept reinforces the sexist stereotype that you're some kind of prop, rather than a unique individual who's in the process of sharing a challenging life experience with your partner. It also places way too much pressure on you by implying that you should be providing direction if things don't go quite the way they're supposed to during labor and birth. Does anyone seriously expect that, after maybe twenty hours of classes and absolutely no medical training, you're going to know how to handle a true emergency? So if anyone calls you "coach," tell them you're not—you're the child's father.

And in 1975, Evelyn and Bruce Fitzgerald, Debra and Michael Greener, and at least eight other couples who had gone through a Lamaze course were told by Porter Memorial Hospital in Indiana that hospital policy prohibited "the presence of any person or persons in the Delivery Rooms located in the Obstetrics Ward other than members of the Medical Staff and Nursing Staff." In other words, no dads allowed. The Fitzgeralds and the other couples sued, and asked the court to decide a fairly simple question: does a father have a constitutional right to be present—per the wishes of himself, the mother, or their physician—in the delivery room of a public hospital during the birth of a child? The answer was no.

Today, as I'm sure you're well aware, the situation is radically different. It's hard to find a man who didn't already, or isn't planning to, attend the birth of

I THOUGHT YOU SAID "LE MANS" CLASS.

his children (according to recent statistics, over 90 percent of fathers-to-be are present at the birth) and just about everyone involved in the process—from parents to doctors—has given the word *preparation* a whole new meaning. Mothers and fathers frequently attend prenatal OB/GYN visits together, and many embark on a reading program reminiscent of cramming for college exams. In addition, most expectant couples sign up for childbirth preparation classes.

When my wife got pregnant for the first time, one of the first things we did was read everything we could get our hands on. By the time the baby was born, we'd probably read enough magazine and newspaper articles, books, and pamphlets to qualify for a degree in prenatal education. But unlike my various "real" degrees, which were fairly useless once I got out into the real world, my education in childbirth and parenting served me quite well.

SELECTING A BIRTHING CLASS

When the first childbirth preparation classes appeared in the late 1960s, the emphasis was on how to have a "natural," unmedicated childbirth. Recently, however, the focus has changed somewhat. While natural childbirth is still the

Infant CPR

Another class you should try to fit in this month is baby CPR (if you wait until after the baby comes, you'll never get around to it). Hopefully, you'll never have to use the skills you'll learn, but learn them anyway— for your own peace of mind and for your baby's safety. You can find out where to sign up from your birth class instructor, your baby's pediatrician (if you've picked one already), the hospital you've chosen, or your local American Red Cross.

goal of most classes today, the overriding principle is that the more you learn about pregnancy and the birth process—from good nutrition and exercise to the types of pain medications most frequently given to laboring women—the less you have to fear and the more in control you'll feel.

Although a lot of people use the terms "Lamaze" and "childbirth preparation class" interchangeably, there are in fact quite a few very different childbirth methods. What distinguishes one from another is the approach each takes to dealing with pain. Here's a little information about the most common methods:

LAMAZE   In the early 1950s, French obstetrician Ferdinand Lamaze took a trip to the Soviet Union to check out the latest medical advances. He was especially interested in *psychoprophylaxis*, which the Russians were billing as a revolutionary way of relieving childbirth pain. Psychoprophylaxis was too big a mouthful, so people started calling it the Pavlov method, since it was based on Ivan Pavlov's (yes, the guy with the dogs) theory that learned reflexes can be overcome by repetition and training. In this case, the learned reflex is pain and the way to overcome it is by focusing on something else—the woman's own breathing. According to historian John Bell, instructors were supposed to "emphasize that Pavlovian science and a benevolent Soviet government had freed women from the curse of labor pain."

Unfortunately, benevolent or not, the Soviets weren't terribly popular in the Russo-phobic West in the 1950s. So the method was renamed Lamaze. Today, Lamaze doesn't focus solely on drug-free, painless labor and delivery. The object is to give expectant parents the knowledge they need to be able to make well-founded decisions. You can take classes privately or at just about any hospital. Oddly, though, the method's supporters have backed off the painless

What Childbirth Classes *Don't* Teach You

Most childbirth prep classes are taught in groups and give you an opportunity to ask questions about the pregnancy in a less-hurried environment than your practitioner's office. They also allow you to socialize a little with other expectant couples and compare notes. But there are a couple of things you probably won't learn there.

♦ Socialization isn't worth much for the father. In the first birthing class I took, the teacher lectured most of the time, and the socializing consisted of the women discussing how much weight they'd gained, how painful their backs were, the color and consistency of their vaginal discharges, and how many times a night they had to get up to pee. From my perspective, that was a complete waste of time. What *was* helpful for me was the educational part of the class itself. By the time we'd finished, I felt that whatever happened, whether we had an unmedicated birth or a medicated one, whether my wife had a C-section or an episiotomy (an incision to enlarge the vaginal opening), I'd at least have some idea what was happening and what to do.

♦ Hey, dude, it's not just about Mom. Over the years, I've interviewed many men whose experiences were very similar to mine. Generally speaking, they felt all but left out by the instructors, who were focusing almost exclusively on the mothers. Of course, that's important. But she's not the only one becoming a parent. As British researchers John Lee and Virginia Schmied put it, "Men are not present at the birth solely to support women—they are there in their own right, as father of the child." Sure, guys learn some important things, but with their concerns all but ignored, they usually walk out feeling more like mommy's little helper than dads.

part. According to an article on pregnancy-info.net, "Contrary to what many people may believe, Lamaze does not actually aim to make the labor process less painful: Lamaze classes help women understand the value of pain and learn how to respond to pain in ways that both facilitate labor and increase comfort." Hmmm.

BRADLEY   Like Lamaze, the Bradley method (founded by Dr. Robert Bradley) believes in educating and preparing the expectant parents for the labor and delivery experience. But instead of trying to distract the woman's

What's the solution? Set up a time to hang out with the other guys in the class. I've taught classes for expectant dads for years, and I can guarantee you that men simply will not talk about the issues they're really concerned about in front of women—especially a spouse. A two-hour get-together with a group of men who are going through the same thing will be far more meaningful than the rest of the coed class.

If you get any resistance on this from your partner, tell her what Australian researcher Andrea Robertson says: "It is unfair to expect men to provide practical help and emotional support if their own needs are not being met during what is an anxious time for both parents." And as John Lee and Virginia Schmied have found, when men have a chance to explore their feelings about pregnancy, childbirth, and parenting (which isn't going to happen in a regular class), they're "more involved with their spouse and participate more with housework after the baby is born."

Lastly, it's okay to question authority. No matter how much you've read or how thorough your class is, something you don't understand is bound to happen during the labor or delivery. When it does, don't become a wallflower and let the practitioners take control of the whole process (unless it's a true medical emergency). Your child—not the doctor's or the nurse's—is about to be born, and you have the right to get your questions answered. So ask someone to explain what's happening and what they're doing, every step of the way. If you miss something the first time, ask again. Keep in mind, though, that there's a difference between being assertive and being annoying or confrontational, so be nice.

attention from her pain, Bradley believes that she should just "go with it." If she feels like groaning, she's encouraged to groan; if she feels like screaming, she's encouraged to scream. The Bradley method also devotes a lot of attention to exercise and nutrition. Over 90 percent of Bradley graduates have "natural" births. Bradley was the original "husband-coached" childbirth method and does more to include the father than any of the other methods.

LEBOYER Hospital delivery rooms are usually bright, noisy places. Dr. Leboyer, a French obstetrician, contends that all the light and noise are

While You're Planning Ahead: Making an Impact

Unless you're a paramedic or an emergency room doctor, you probably don't have a lot of opportunities to save lives. But for a few minutes after your baby is born you'll have a chance to do just that. Best of all, you'll be able to do it with something you otherwise might have thrown out: your baby's umbilical cord.

The blood inside the umbilical cord is an incredibly rich source of *stem cells*, which can be used to treat dozens of conditions, including leukemia and some cancers. And as technology advances, researchers are looking at cord blood stem cells as a possible cure for everything from torn ligaments and diabetes to heart disease, Alzheimer's, and spinal cord injury.

So what can you do? Well, you have two basic choices: donate the cord blood so some other person can benefit, or store the cord blood for your own family's use. Let me give you some of the pros and cons of each of these options:

♦ **Public donation.** This is a free option. Assuming enough blood can be collected (usually three to five ounces), and the mother meets certain requirements (for example, she must be free of HIV, most cancers, diabetes, and a number of other conditions), your baby's cord blood will be analyzed and frozen for storage. It will then be listed in a national registry where surgeons from all over the world can search for matches for patients who need stem-cell transplants. Unfortunately, because of the high costs of collecting and storing cord blood, there are only about twenty facilities in the United States that can take donations. That may be changing, though, as Congress recently approved $20 million to establish a national cord blood banking system.

♦ **Private banking.** If you can afford it, private cord blood banking can be an excellent insurance policy—especially if you have a family his-

quite stressful and upsetting for a newborn. Leboyer babies are generally born in dimmed rooms, often with the mother fully or partially submerged in warm water.

DICK-READ Grantly Dick-Read, an English obstetrician who, like most of his colleagues in the early part of the twentieth century, used chloroform to ease his patients' labor pains, developed a theory that fear is the source of tory of leukemia or any of the other diseases that can be treated with cord blood, and/or your child belongs to an ethnic minority or is multi-racial. People of a mixed-race heritage historically have a much harder time finding bone marrow matches than Caucasians. Privately bank-ing your newborn's cord blood stem cells is the only way to provide a 100 percent guarantee that you will have access to stem cells that are a perfect match for future medical treatments. Initial costs typically range from about $600 to over $2,000. Annual storage fees are usually about $100.

The public-vs.-private decision is one that only you and your wife can make. Both methods are medically safe and painless for the mother and baby, because the cord blood is collected after the baby is born. If you're having trouble deciding, you might want to take a look at the Parents' Guide to Cord Blood Banks (www.parentsguidecordblood.com) for an unbiased review of the options.

If you're interested in donating your baby's cord blood, start by talking with your partner's OB now. Most public banks like to get the testing and screening processes started before the thirty-fourth week of pregnancy. You should also make contact with the National Marrow Donor Program (www.marrow.org), which maintains the largest listing of cord blood units in the world. They have a huge amount of excellent information about stem cells and cord blood donation on their Web site.

If you're interested in exploring private banking, start with your part-ner's OB. You should also start doing some research right now to find the best possible bank. Important factors to consider include the company's financial stability (less chance it will go out of business), its age, the number of samples it currently stores, and whether it provides a com-plete listing of fees.

pain during labor and delivery. Here's how it works: when someone's afraid, the "fight or flight" instinct kicks in, drains blood away from organs that don't need it—such as the face—and pumps it to the organs that need it most, such as the legs. (Hence the expression "white as a sheet.") Fear also diverts blood away from the uterus (if you have one), leaving it unable to function correctly, which results in pain. Get rid of the fear, then—by relaxation techniques, affir-mations, or even hypnosis—and the pain will follow. Dick-Read's theory—

which is still very much in vogue today—was so radical at the time that it got him bounced out of the British Medical Society.

MCMOYLER METHOD   Started by an experienced Labor and Delivery Nurse named Sarah McMoyler, this method is aimed at the needs of today's busy parents and picks up where the others leave off. McMoyler's main emphasis is on education: since labor and delivery are completely unpredictable, it's best to learn about everything and anything that could possibly happen on that big day. Students are encouraged to work *with* the medical team and trust them, instead of being suspicious. With McMoyler, there's no such thing as failure. Natural childbirth is the goal, but if things don't go according to plan (and they rarely ever do), there's no guilt and no regret. If you walk out of the hospital with a healthy baby and a healthy mom, you win.

Childbirth classes usually run five to nine weeks (although McMoyler classes are conducted over two half days or one very full one). Your practitioner is probably the best source of recommendations and information on where childbirth classes meet and how to sign up.

Whatever you do, take one as soon as you possibly can. The knowledge you'll get will help ease some of your anxieties for the rest of the pregnancy.

PREPARING YOUR OLDER KIDS

While millions of second- and third-time parents sign up every time for some kind of childbirth classes, very few of them ever consider that their older children might need some preparation as well. Here are a few things you can do to help get those big sisters- and brothers-to-be ready:

♦ **Sign them up for a class too.** A lot of hospitals offer classes for soon-to-be older siblings.

♦ **Try to have them spend some time with new babies.**

♦ **Give them some practice.** Use a life-size doll to show them how to hold an infant and support its head. Demonstrate the proper way to touch a baby and explain the need to be gentle, but do not poke, or prod, or hit the doll to illustrate behavior to avoid. You'll just be showing the big kid exactly how to do what she's not supposed to do.

♦ **Get them excited.** Show them pictures of new babies, have them make a drawing for the new baby, even let them pick out some furniture or clothes or the color of the new baby's room.

♦ **Prepare yourself for some disappointment.** Most brand-new older siblings are thrilled—for a while. When the novelty wears off, they're going to want to go back to being the center of the universe. See the "Helping Older Kids Adjust to Their New Sibling" section on pages 285–87 for tips on how to help the kids—and yourself—through this transition.

GETTING SOME EXTRA HELP

Reading this book will help you prepare yourself for the emotional and physical experiences you and your partner will be going through during pregnancy and birth. But while the two of you are actually in the midst of labor, you're both in a state of trauma. You're both under pressure, and you both need support—physical as well as psychological.

Your partner has you to help her through. And she has her practitioner and the rest of the medical team. But what about you?

Each time my wife was in labor, I tried to do everything they'd taught me in the classes we'd taken: I reassured her, held her, told her stories, massaged her back and legs, mopped her brow, encouraged her, "helped" her breathe, and fed her ice chips. It was absolutely exhausting and sometimes scary, and I sure could have used a break (and an occasional back rub), but there wasn't anyone around to do it.

Fortunately, however, there is a way to help ease the burden—both yours and your partner's—of the trauma of labor and delivery: get yourselves a doula.

WHAT IS A *DOULA?*

As we discussed on pages 27–28, a doula is someone who's supposed to be there throughout labor, to give your partner *and* you emotional and physical support.

According to Dr. Marshall Klaus, the doula concept is hardly a new one. For hundreds of years, pregnant women in more than 125 cultures have gone through labor with another woman at their side the whole time. This used to be the case here as well. But in the 1930s women began to have their children in hospitals instead of at home, and everyone but the laboring woman and her doctors was barred from the delivery room. In 1980 Dr. Klaus and his colleagues reintroduced the doula concept in the United States. and gave it its name.

I've got to confess that when I met with Dr. Klaus, my first reaction was: no way. I've got too much invested in this pregnancy, and nobody is going to come

Doulas—Some Basic Q's and A's, Dos and Don'ts

♦ **What do they charge?** Most doulas charge a flat fee. The national average is around $700, although the range can be anywhere from $300 to $1,500, depending on where you live. This usually includes one or two prenatal visits, labor and delivery—from whenever you first feel you need the doula until one to three hours after the birth—and a few postpartum visits to answer any questions you or your partner might have and to help your partner get started breastfeeding.

♦ **Will my insurance company pick up the tab?** There's no hard and fast rule about this. But more and more insurers are finding that paying for a doula can significantly reduce their other birth-related costs. You may also be able to pay your doula through your company's flexible spending program or a Health Savings Account. But check with your company's HR department or your insurer to confirm.

♦ **Where can I find one?** Ask your partner's practitioner to recommend a doula he or she has worked with. You can get referrals from Doulas of North America (www.dona.org) or Doula World (www.doulaworld.com).

♦ **Interview any prospective doula.** You want someone who shares your vision for how you'd like the birth to go. Flexibility is key. You don't want someone who's going to storm out of the room in a huff if your partner decides she wants an epidural.

♦ **Have her meet the rest of the team.** If the doula and your partner's OB or midwife don't already know each other, giving them a chance to meet before labor starts can go a long way toward avoiding problems later.

♦ **Confirm that she's on board for *you* too, and that she acknowledges you as your partner's primary support person.**

between me and my wife during this critical stage. But as I continued talking to Dr. Klaus and reading the research on doulas, I began to change my mind.

It turns out that the presence of a doula can have some rather dramatic effects, potentially shortening the length of a woman's labor and reducing the odds she'll need pain medication, forceps delivery, or a Cesarean section. Considering my wife's history of long, painful labor, I began to feel that having a doula around the next time might be the way to go.

But I still had questions: would a doula do anything for me? Wouldn't she just push me out of the way? Not according to Dr. Klaus. "We make the mistake of thinking that a father can take a birthing class and be prepared to be the main source of support and knowledge for the entire labor. That's just unreasonable. A doula can reach out to the man, decreasing his anxiety, giving him support and encouragement, and allowing him to interact with his partner in a more caring and nurturing fashion." In one interesting study a researcher compared couples who had a doula present with others who didn't. The study found that men in both groups spent about the same amount of time with their partners.

Back on pages 27–28, I talked about some of the problems associated with doulas. But there are plenty of people—including medical professionals—who swear by them. One of the main advantages is that your partner will have more consistent support. The doctors and nurses are usually juggling five or six patients at the same time, meaning that they won't be able to focus very much on your partner and you. Shift changes just make the care even more disjointed. So if you're feeling that you really want someone (besides you) to be there throughout the whole ordeal, a doula may be the way to go. (Keep in mind that doulas do not deliver babies—that's something your practitioner and the medical team will handle. When it comes time to push, it's nice if your partner can be guided through by a nurse who's had a chance to get to know her. That's harder to accomplish when a doula is present.)

WHAT IF YOU FEEL LIKE YOU DON'T WANT TO BE IN THE DELIVERY ROOM AT ALL?

Years ago, no one expected men to be involved in their partners' pregnancies or to be there for the births of their children. But today, men who aren't jumping up and down about the idea of being in the delivery room are generally considered insensitive Neanderthals. The problem with such a black-and-white approach is that, as Katharyn May says, "there's a fine line between finding options for father participation, and pressuring men to adopt levels of involvement which may be unwanted or inappropriate for them." The truth of the matter is that not all of us feel the same need to be involved, and the last place some men should be is in the delivery room. You may be squeamish during medical procedures, prone to fainting at the sight of blood or needles, or worried about losing control during labor. You may not want to see your partner in pain, or you may simply be feeling ambivalent about the pregnancy. You may be downright frightened by what you saw in some of the movies you viewed during your childbirth prep class. You may even be feeling resentful about the pressure other people are putting on you to get involved. It's important to remember that these feelings—as well as any other reasons you might have for just not wanting to be there—are not only completely normal, they're shared by more men than you might think.

If you're feeling less than overjoyed about being involved in the labor and delivery, don't beat yourself up too badly or allow yourself to feel like a failure. You're not. In fact, as many as half of all expectant fathers have at least some ambivalence about participating in the pregnancy and childbirth. Clearly, being forced into a role that isn't comfortable for you will do you and your partner more harm than good. But there are a few things you might want to try that could help you get over some of your concerns.

♦ **Talk to other fathers.** Other dads you know may have been through something similar and may have some suggestions. Even if they don't, it's often very reassuring to get some living proof that you're not alone.

♦ **Talk to your partner.** Let her know what you're feeling and why. At the same time, reassure her about your commitment to her and to the baby.

♦ **Understand what your partner is thinking.** Instead of being sympathetic, she may interpret your apprehensiveness as a sign that you don't care about her or the baby.

♦ **Do it for her.** No matter how well you explain it to your partner, your desire to miss the birth or to miss the classes is probably going to hurt her. If you can stomach it at all, at least try to take the class—it will help her feel more understood, and you might just learn what it is that's been bothering you.

♦ **Consider a doula.** See pages 185–87 for information about doulas.

♦ **Don't worry about how your child will turn out.** While there's plenty of evidence about the positive impact on children of early paternal bonding, your not being there for the actual birth—whether it's because you didn't want to or because you simply couldn't—will not cripple your children; you'll still be able to establish a strong relationship with them. Just make sure you're there right after the birth.

♦ **Don't give in to the pressure.** If, after everything is said and done, you still don't feel comfortable participating, don't. But be prepared: your family, friends, and medical practitioner will probably suggest that you just quit pouting and do what you're "supposed to." If you're among the 10 to 15 percent of adults who pass out at the sight of blood, or the 10 percent who have a phobia of needles, and that's why you'd rather not be in the delivery room, you might want to tell your critics about the tragic case of Steven Passalaqua. Passalaqua, whose wife was in labor, was asked by hospital staff "to hold and steady his wife" while an anesthesiologist "inserted an epidural needle into her back." Seeing the needle caused Steven to faint, and he hit his head on a piece of molding at the base of the wall. He died two days later. Of course, that's an extreme case, but it ought to get people off your back for a while.

A Note for Deployed Dads

What can I say? You want to be there, your wife wants you to be there, but Uncle Sam needs you somewhere else right now. Despite the distance, though, there are a number of things you can do to stay connected with your wife (and, later, your baby).

♦ **Make sure your wife knows every possible way to contact you, just in case she needs to reach you quickly.**

♦ **Talk to your CO about whether you can get a few days off.** As mentioned earlier, the military does offer some paternity leave, but exactly how much you'll be able to take is impossible to pin down. The good news is that it won't count against your regular thirty days' leave. The bad news is that it's trumped by the needs of the military, so there's no guarantee that you'll actually make it. However, just having made the effort shows your wife that you're committed to her and the baby and will boost your stock in her eyes.

♦ **Check into whether you can set up a real-time phone or video conference for the delivery.** It's not the same as being there, but in this case, close counts for a lot. If you have access to high-speed Internet and a webcam, get signed up with one of the many free, real-time video services, such as Skype (skype.com), Oovoo (oovoo.com), camfrog.com, Freedom Calls (freedomcalls.org), and Google chat (google.com/chat). I've heard wonderful stories from service members who took advantage of video conferencing to watch the birth of their baby, see the kids in their Halloween costumes, or even participate in parent-teacher conferences. You could, I suppose, use this technology to keep an eye on what the painter's doing during your remodeling project, too.

♦ **Read as much as you can about what's left of the pregnancy—how the baby is developing, and what your wife is going through.** When you get close to the due date, start in on a book that covers childbirth and infancy. Again, you want to understand as much as you can about what's happening with your wife and baby. And don't forget to think about yourself too. You may not be able to see or hold your baby, but fatherhood is changing you too, and it's nice to know how. The more up-to-date you are on where everyone is, the easier it will be for you to plug into the routines when you get home. This book and the sequel, *The New Father: A Dad's Guide to the First Year*, will walk you through everything you need to know.

♦ **Send presents, love notes, and jewelry.** Flowers may seem like a complete waste of money, but send some anyway.

♦ **If you haven't deployed yet, do as many of the following as you can before you go:**

   ◊ **Burn a CD or DVD of you reading some simple children's books.** Before the birth, ask your wife to play them near her belly. Once the baby is born, she can play that same CD/DVD; plus you can record new stories, songs, poems, or whatever, until you're able to take over the story-reading duties yourself. This will help the baby recognize you—well, your voice anyway—when you come home. If you need help getting any of this set up—or you didn't get a chance to do it before you shipped out—it's not too late. Check out United Through Reading (www.unitedthroughreading.org).

   ◊ **Ask your wife to put up lots of pictures of you and to talk to the baby about you.**

   ◊ **Don't take a shower just yet . . .** Right before you leave, wear a few shirts to bed and have your wife keep them around until after the birth. Young babies acquire a lot of information about their world through their sense of smell, and the hope is that if your baby is exposed to your smell, it'll be easier for him to bond with you when you get home. You also might want to check out a fun program called Blankets for Deployed Daddies (www.blanketsfordeployeddaddies.com). They send blankets to deployed dads who have newborns or very young children at home. You sleep with the blanket for a few nights, filling it with your scent. Then you send it home. Yes, I know this sounds weird, but your wife will probably sleep with that blanket too. While you're at it, send one home for the dog, too. Your cat couldn't care less.

   ◊ **Strike a pose.** Have your wife or someone else take pictures of you doing your favorite things, eating your favorite foods, hanging out with your favorite people, and so on. Print out the best shots, laminate them, and get them bound together. This will give your child a chance to get to know a little bit about you—and gnaw on you—while you're away.

♦ **Ask your wife to send things to keep you in the loop.** Before the birth, this could be an ultrasound picture or a recording of your baby's heartbeat. After the baby comes, photos, worn outfits, and a full-length cutout of the baby are nice. If someone filmed the birth, she may want to send that video along too. But think about whether you really want to see your wife in incredible pain that you can't do anything to stop.

♦ **Send more presents, flowers, and a gift certificate for a spa day.** Poetry, even bad poetry, is appreciated.

♦ **Ask a friend to take the childbirth class with your wife if she hasn't already lined someone else up.**

♦ **Ask friends to help.** And make sure they understand what you mean. Most people define help as holding the baby for a few minutes, cooing, then giving him back. Your definition of help should include laundry, shopping, meal preparation, or reroofing the garage.

Notes:

Making a List and Checking It Twice

What's Going On with Your Partner

Physically

- Even stronger fetal activity
- Heavier vaginal discharge
- General discomfort getting more severe
- Frequent urination
- Sleeplessness—can that really be a surprise?
- Increased fatigue
- Shortness of breath as the baby takes up more room and presses against her internal organs
- Water retention, and swelling of the hands, feet, and ankles
- More frequent Braxton-Hicks contractions

Emotionally

- Feeling special—people are giving her their seats on buses or in crowded rooms, store clerks go out of their way to help her
- Feeling a bond with others, like a member of a secret club (strangers keep coming up to tell her about their own pregnancy experiences or to touch her

belly); she might also be scared by all those horror stories or angry at the
unsolicited touches
♦ Feeling exceptionally attractive—or ugly
♦ Relieved that the baby would survive if born now
♦ Worried about whether the baby will be normal, what he'll look like, whether
she'll be able to cope with the responsibilities of motherhood, and whether
her body will ever get back to normal
♦ Afraid her water will break in public

What's Going On with the Baby

At this point, most babies will have assumed the head-down position that
they'll maintain for the rest of the pregnancy. He's getting big and fat: eighteen
inches long, five pounds (a little less if he's sharing his quarters with a sibling), and his body now looks a little more like it belongs with that huge—and
probably pretty hairy—head. With practically no room to maneuver around,
the baby's movements are becoming a little less frequent but often so powerful that you can often tell which part of his body is doing the poking. His
little heart is pumping something like 300 gallons of blood every day (yours
pumps around 2,000), and his sense of hearing is getting so good that he now
responds differently to your partner's and your voices. Chances of survival outside the womb are excellent.

What's Going On with You

Dealing with the Public Nature of Pregnancy

As intensely private as pregnancy is, it is also inescapably public. Your partner's growing belly can bring out the best—and the worst—in people. Perfect
strangers will open doors for her, offer to help her carry things, give up their
seats in crowded subway cars and buses. In some ways, people's interest in
pregnant women and in the process of creating life is heartwarming. But there
may come a point when this outpouring of interest in her status and concern
for her comfort begins to feel like an invasion of privacy.

People would often come up to my wife when she was standing in the check-
out line at the grocery store and start chatting. The "conversations" would usually begin fairly innocuously, with questions like, "So, when are you due?" or

pronouncements about the baby's gender. But after a while the horror stories would inevitably come out—tales of debilitating morning sickness, ten-month pregnancies, thirty-hour labors, emergency C-sections, anesthesia that didn't work, and on and on. And as if that weren't enough, people would, without even asking, start touching, rubbing, or patting her belly as if she were a Buddha statue or a magic lantern.

Perhaps the strangest thing about the public nature of pregnancy is that a surprising (to me, anyway) number of women seem to take it all in stride. I kept waiting for my wife to bite some belly-rubber's hand off, but she never did. Not everyone stays so calm, though. I've heard stories of women reacting to being groped by strangers by screaming, wearing "keep your paws off my belly" T-shirts, slapping their hand, telling them of a highly contagious disease that's transmitted by touch, or even reaching out and fondling their belly in return. Why anyone tolerates this is a mystery to me. Can you imagine how you'd react if someone did the same thing when your partner *wasn't* pregnant? Or if you decided to touch some woman's breasts because they looked so inviting?

For men, this touching business can bring out feelings of anger and protectiveness: "Nobody touches my woman!" If this happens to you, it's best to take your cues from your partner. If she doesn't mind, try to relax. But prepare yourself. You're going to have to deal with a very similar situation after she gives birth, when complete strangers come up and start fondling your baby—without even washing their hands.

Panic

Just about six weeks before our first daughter was born, I suddenly had a great epiphany: our childless days were about to be over. It wasn't that I was worried about becoming a father—I already felt confident and prepared for my new role: I'd read a lot of material about becoming a parent, my wife and I had been taking childbirth classes, and we'd thoroughly discussed our concerns and fears. What struck me was much more superficial: once the baby came, it would be a long time before we'd be able to go to movies, plays, or concerts (or just about anyplace where you might have to be quiet), or even stay out late with our friends.

As it turned out, my wife was feeling the same thing at about the same time, so during the last two months of the first pregnancy, we ate out more often, went to more movies, saw more plays, and spent more late evenings with friends than in the next three years combined. A lot of expectant dads who are worried about the impending loss of their social lives find themselves looking up and visiting old friends they haven't seen for years.

In addition to trying to pack a lot of fun activities into the final few months of the pregnancy, you might want to consider cramming in a few practical things as well: when you (or your partner) are cooking a meal, try to double or even triple the recipes and freeze what's left over in two-person servings. Believe me, during that first postpartum week, defrosting a container of frozen spaghetti sauce is a lot easier than making a new batch from scratch.

Nesting

After morning sickness and 2 A.M. cravings for pickles, perhaps the most famous stereotype about pregnancy is a woman's "nesting instinct." Most women, at some point in their pregnancies, become obsessed (often unconsciously) with preparing the house for the new arrival: closets and cupboards are cleaned, and furniture that hasn't been budged for years suddenly has to be swept under.

Although much has been made of the woman's instinct, a variety of studies have shown that almost all expectant fathers experience some sort of nesting instinct themselves. Besides worrying about finances, many men spend a lot of time assembling—or even building—cribs, changing tables, and other baby furniture; shopping for baby supplies; painting and preparing the baby's room; childproofing the whole house; rearranging furniture; and even trying to find a larger living space for their growing families. Other guys take care of all those things that have been on their to-do lists for months: cleaning the gutters, getting the car tuned up and its tires changed, installing fire and smoke alarms, finally learning to square dance. For some men, these activities are a way to keep busy and to avoid feeling left out. But for others, they represent something much more fundamental. As Pamela Jordan writes, "These nesting tasks may be the first opportunity the father has to do something for the baby rather than his pregnant mate."

Here's how blogger Adam Hansen (www.New-Dad-Blog.com) describes his brush with nesting madness. "I have become obsessed with cleaning and organizing. It's more than a conscious thought, 'Oh, the counter is dirty, I need to clean it.' It's a compulsion, which once fed, spreads. I will start cleaning the counter, only to notice the dishes need to be unloaded, then I see that under the sink is disorganized, then trash needs to be taken out, which takes me to sweeping the floor...and it's impossible to stop. I want to clean, disinfect and organize the world! If I let myself go wild I'd be at home all day with cleaning gloves on. None of this is helped by my wife's unique cleaning methods. She apparently subscribes to 'Shove it in a Drawer' cleaning magazine. So when I open our kitchen cabinet and I find recipes, batteries, head sets, iPods, stationery, plates...my nesting-infected brain almost short-circuits."

Sex—Again

While the second trimester is frequently a time of increased sexual desire and activity, during the third trimester your sex life is bound to suffer. The most common reasons for this are:

♦ A mutual fear of hurting the baby or your partner.
♦ Fear that your partner's orgasm might trigger premature labor.
♦ Your partner's physical discomfort.
♦ Your partner's changing body makes the "usual" sexual positions uncomfortable.
♦ Your sense of changing roles. Soon your partner will no longer simply be your partner; she's going to be a mother—someone just like your own mother. Remember that as she begins to see you as a father, she may have similar (often subconscious) thoughts.

Unless your partner's doctor has told you otherwise, sex still poses no physical risk to the baby or to your partner. As we discussed on pages 138–42, if you're both still interested in sex (and I've heard from a lot of dads whose sex drive actually increases toward the end of the pregnancy), now would be a good time to try out some new and different positions. Again, if you and your partner aren't in sync, sexually speaking, it's critical to talk things through.

Several researchers have noted that a small number of expectant fathers have affairs during the late stages of their partners' pregnancies. But these "late-pregnancy affairs" rarely happen for the reasons you might think. Jerrold Shapiro found that most men who have had a late-pregnancy extramarital affair share the following characteristics:

♦ They felt extremely attracted to their partners and were very interested in "affectionate sexual contact" with them.

♦ They felt particularly excluded from the pregnancy and birth process.

♦ The affair was with a close friend or relative of the woman. (This would indicate that the person with whom the man had the affair was also feeling excluded from the pregnant woman's life during the pregnancy.)

Expectant mothers also have affairs during their pregnancies. In fact, Shapiro suggests that women are just as likely to have affairs as men. Couples who suddenly find themselves with no sexual outlet—and are feeling misunderstood by their partners—may be tempted to satisfy their needs elsewhere.

Birth Plans

Just about every expectant couple—together or individually—has a vision of how they'd like their baby to come into the world. Sometimes these dreams come true, but babies aren't particularly good about going along with the program. And in most cases—especially with first pregnancies—what actually happens during labor and delivery won't look very much like what you hoped it would. Which is why the words "birth" and "plan" really don't belong in the same document, let alone the same sentence.

Nevertheless, a lot of childbirth instructors and other folks still recommend that expectant couples write up a comprehensive birth plan that outlines every aspect of labor and delivery, lays out their demands for the way they want things to go, and makes it very clear that the expectant parents—not the medical staff—will be making all the decisions.

While birth plans may sound logical, they almost always cause more trouble than they prevent. You and your partner may feel bound by whatever you've planned, and if something unexpected (or contrary to the plan) happens, you'll be confused and tense, you may squabble with the medical team or each other, and you'll almost surely look back on the birth with some feelings of regret.

From the medical team's perspective, getting handed a rule-filled, demand-filled document immediately makes the rather intimate relationship they're

going to have with you for the next few days adversarial rather than coopera-
tive. Not a good idea.

Babies, meanwhile, have their own ideas. The notion that an expectant couple might have some choice in the labor, delivery, and immediate
postpartum-period procedures is a fairly recent one. But it's important not to
get too attached to that sense of control.

Saul Weinreb, an OB and one of my medical advisors, puts it this way:
"If you are comfortable with your care providers, and you share all of your
thoughts and wishes and ideas about labor and what you expect, and you trust
that they will be open and discuss your options, risks, benefits, etc. before
they do any interventions, I have no idea why birth plans are necessary. If you
haven't done the above, then a birth plan won't save you, it will only create
tension. If you aren't comfortable with your providers, you haven't made a good
choice, and you'll have problems whether you have a birth plan or not. Bottom
line, they don't help anyone."

Some doctors and nurses I've spoken with half-jokingly say that the longer
and more complicated the plan, the greater the chance of a Cesarean—

after every possible intervention and drug has been used. And I mean *half*-jokingly.

Okay, so after all that, should you have a birth plan? Well, yes and no. Here's what I mean. Yes, you and your partner should absolutely go through the exercise of putting together a plan. Talk about your ideal scenario, your philosophy, and anything you can think of. Would you like to burn incense and have your baby ushered into the world by a troupe of Tibetan monks? Great. Have your partner give birth standing on one foot while riding horseback? Have the delivery filmed live for a new reality show? Have the entire medical team speak only Mandarin Chinese so that your baby will be able to begin life bilingual? Have the baby licked clean by your pet schnauzer rather than cleaned up by the nurses? Wonderful.

Then, once you've got it all worked out and the wording is just perfect, fold it up and put it in your pocket. And keep it there. Feel free to use it as a cheat sheet in case you forget something, but do *not* show it to anyone else. Ever.

The idea here is to get you and your partner to set some goals and think about what you want for the labor and delivery while you still have clear heads. Remember, though, that things rarely, if ever, go the way they're supposed to. So, be flexible. Here are some topics the two of you may want to discuss. If you have questions about any of them, be sure to bring them up with your partner's practitioner now. There may be certain policies that can't be breached.

- ♦ **Emergencies.** Do you want the doctors or midwives to handle things on their own or would you prefer to have them explain what's going on? If your partner is unconscious or unable to make a decision, should the practitioners get your permission before doing anything out of the ordinary?
- ♦ **Pain medication.** Do you want the hospital staff to offer it if they feel your partner could use some? Or do you want them to wait for her to ask for it?
- ♦ **Staying together.** Do you and your partner want to remain together for the entire labor and delivery?
- ♦ **Freedom of movement.** Will your partner be able to labor in the hallways (or in the shower), and in whatever position she'd like? There's no reason to spend the whole time in bed. In fact, walking around as much as possible yields better results.
- ♦ **Labor.** If labor slows down, does she want to be offered oxytocin or other drugs to speed it up?
- ♦ **Pictures and videos.** Do you want to take them? Do you want someone else to? Do you want to be able to take them even if there's a C-section?

Should Your Older Children Attend the Birth?

Having older children attend the birth of the new baby can be a tricky thing. In general, it's probably okay to have children present both during labor and immediately after the birth (although depending on hospital policy, that may not even be an option). But for a variety of reasons, children—especially those under five—probably shouldn't be there for the birth itself.

♦ They may be frightened that their mother is being hurt, and that all of the blood and moaning might mean she is dying. The last thing you want is for your scared preschooler to be running to mommy for comfort. She's going to have a few other things on her mind.
♦ Even well-prepared children can have unpredictable reactions, and you and your partner won't want to have to be distracted by anyone else's needs but hers, yours, and the new baby's.
♦ The older child might be jealous of all the attention paid to the new baby.
♦ Aside from the fear factor, kids under four aren't able to understand what's really going on, and they certainly won't appreciate the specialness of the occasion.

If you're still thinking about having an older sibling there for the birth of his or her new sibling, be sure to discuss the idea with your doctor

♦ **Fetal monitoring.** Does your partner want the baby's heart rate monitored by machines throughout her labor, or would she prefer that monitoring be done only when necessary?
♦ **Water breaking.** Your baby has been swimming around in a sac filled with amniotic fluid. Before the baby can be born, that sac has to rupture. Ideally, that will happen on its own and, depending on the position of the baby, the fluid will gush or dribble out. Sometimes, though, the rupture may need to be induced manually.
♦ **The birth.** Do you want the doctors to try forceps or suction to speed up the delivery, or do you want to hold out for a while longer? Do you want any other people (friends, relatives, midwife, other children) to attend the birth? Will a mirror be available (so your partner can get a better view of the delivery)?

first. Then, get yourselves some visual aids—books, movies, or pictures of births, for example—and plan on having some long discussions with the child. It's important that you keep in mind that watching mom give birth will not be like anything they've seen on one of those PBS specials or on Animal Planet. Birth scenes (human or animal, but especially human) are usually carefully edited to avoid showing private parts, blood, and extreme pain. Encourage the child to ask questions; answer them; tell him what's going to happen; talk about acceptable and unacceptable behavior; and plan on spending some private time with him— older children can get really jealous.

Also, make sure there's an adult around to help each child who will be at the birth. This person should be prepared to talk to the child about what's happening and to take the child out of the room if necessary. Your place—and your focus—is with your partner.

If you've got a "tween" or teen, your decision to have him or her in the delivery room will depend on a lot of factors.

♦ Maturity. Is the child able to handle seeing mom in pain? How do you think big bro or sis will respond if something completely unexpected happens and your partner needs an emergency procedure?

♦ Sex of the child. Your partner may not feel comfortable with a son being at the north end of the bed. For a girl, however, watching mom give birth could be the best birth control you'll ever come across.

♦ **Episiotomy.** If your partner's vagina won't stretch enough to allow the baby's head through, the doctor may suggest making a small cut in the perineum—the space between the vagina and the anus. Some doctors do episiotomies as a preventative measure; others don't do them unless absolutely necessary. Some people believe that a small but natural tear in the vagina is better than a surgical cut. Others say that the cut helps control the tearing. Either way, your partner should learn as much as she can about episiotomies and think about whether—barring emergencies, of course—she would want one, and if so, whether she would want it done with or without anesthesia.

♦ **Cesarean section.** In case of a C-section, can you stay with your partner, or will you have to be separated? Will you be separated only for the spinal or epidural anesthesia, or for the entire procedure? Where will you be allowed to stand?

- **The baby.** Who will cut the cord, and when? Do you want the hospital staff to take the baby away for cleaning and testing right after birth, or would you like him or her handed to you and/or your partner first?
- **After the birth.** Do you want the baby to breastfeed right away, or will you be bottle feeding? Do you want the baby with one of you all the time, or would you rather have him or her kept in the hospital's nursery? What about circumcision?
- **Going home.** Do you want to stay for as long as the hospital will let you, or do you want to go home as soon as possible?

I'm not saying that you should blindly follow every single thing a doctor, nurse, midwife, or hospital janitor tells you. Nurses love it if you tell them—in a nice way—about your ideal scenario. They love it when you ask questions—it shows you're interested and engaged and that you respect them. And they especially love it when you tell them that you're prepared to defer to their judgment in case of emergency. All you want is to be part of the process.

I know that despite everything I've said in the preceding paragraphs, some readers will want a written birth plan anyway. If you're in that category, that's okay, I'll get over it. But please keep the following guidelines in mind, some of which were suggested by birth instructor Kim Kaehler:

- In the first paragraph, indicate your flexibility should an emergency arise.
- Try not to make it sound like a legal document. That's a great way to make a doctor or other health-care provider very nervous and defensive. Your practitioner will not be comfortable if she feels her hands will be tied in the case of an emergency.
- Try to word your desires in a positive way. Avoid beginning every statement with "No" or "Do not."
- Refrain from including things in your plan that are not part of your birth site's normal procedures.
- Be sure to thank everyone for their respect and support.
- After you and your partner have hammered out a draft of your birth plan, show it to your doctor. Let him or her go over it and make suggestions.
- Remember that a birth plan is not a contract. It's a way for you to communicate your preferences to your partner's practitioners.

You can find dozens of sample birth plans on the Web, including some templates for which all you have to do is fill in the blanks. Just perform a search for "birth plan."

Making Final Plans

REGISTERING AT THE HOSPITAL

Despite what you've seen on TV and in the movies, getting to the hospital doesn't have to be a frantic exercise at breakneck speed. Fortunately for men (but not nearly as fortunately for our partners), the onset of labor and the delivery itself are usually hours (if not days) apart, so if you plan carefully, there should be plenty of time to get everything done. And once you've got your bags packed and ready to go (see pages 207–9 for details), the next most pressing concern is registering at the hospital.

Most hospitals will allow—or may even require—you to register up to sixty days before the anticipated birth of the child. This doesn't mean that you're making a reservation for a particular day. All it means is that when you do show up at the hospital, you won't have to waste time signing papers while your partner is screaming and having contractions. So as soon as you can, check with your hospital's or clinic's administrative offices and/or Web site to find out their policy. Doing so is particularly important because besides making you fill out 785 forms, the hospital will have to get a verification of coverage and eligibility from your insurance company. And that can take some time.

Finding a Pediatrician

I know, you don't actually have a baby yet, but you will soon, so you'd better start putting some real thought into picking a doctor for her. Most people take their kids to pediatricians, but plenty of family practitioners see babies too. During their first year, all three of my kids saw their pediatrician nine times—and they were all as healthy as horses. A typical first-year schedule includes visits a few days after you bring the baby home, two weeks after that, then once a month until six months, once in the ninth month, and again in the twelfth month. Clearly, since you're going to be spending a lot of time with your child's doctor, you should select someone you think you can get along with at least until your child turns sixteen or so. Given the state of health coverage in this country, your options may be limited. But if your plan gives you some flexibility, try to interview several prospective pediatricians. Here are some questions you should ask (you might want to write some of them down and bring them along to the interview):

♦ **Are you affiliated with the hospital where the baby will be born?** If not, that's probably a deal breaker.
♦ **Will you visit the baby at the hospital?**

♦ **What insurance do you take?** Another potential deal breaker.

♦ **What's your philosophy about vaccinations?** Although the vast majority of pediatricians advocate routine vaccination, there is a vocal minority
that doesn't. The debate is interesting but beyond the scope of this book.
It's similar, in a way, to debates about the death penalty, abortion, cloth vs.
disposable diapers, circumcision, and a few others. It's almost impossible for
anyone on either side to change anyone else's mind.

♦ **Where do you stand on breastfeeding?** Current thinking is that babies
should have nothing but breast milk for at least six months (longer is okay
too). You'd be hard pressed to find a pediatrician who won't support breastfeeding. But you also want someone who's flexible enough not to make your
partner feel bad if she can't breastfeed for some reason or decides not to.

♦ **How many waiting rooms do you have?** This may sound silly, but hospitals and medical offices are full of sick people—exactly the kind of people
you'll want to keep your baby away from. Ideally they should have a waiting room for sick kids and another one for kids who are there for well-child
visits.

♦ **Do the waiting room toys get cleaned often?** Another seemingly silly
question, but do you really trust all those sick kids to cover their mouth and
nose when they sneeze? And to keep their fingers out of their nose—and
their ears and their butts? And to wash their hands before they touch any of
the toys? Yeah, right.

♦ **How long are routine office visits?** For at least the first few visits you're
going to have a ton of questions. Some doctors, though—particularly those in
HMOs—often see six or more patients per hour, meaning that appointments
can be as short as ten minutes. Other doctors are more relaxed and can
spend twenty minutes or more with you and your baby.

♦ **How many doctors are in your practice?** You may think that male and
female doctors are the same, but your child may not agree. When she was
about two, my older daughter absolutely refused to see her regular (male)
pediatrician, and insisted on seeing a "girl doctor." Don't worry about
offending your pediatrician—about 75 percent of kids prefer to see a doctor
of their own gender.

♦ **What about emergencies?** Is there an on-call doc?

♦ **What about nighttime and weekend hours?** Does the practice have
an advice line, staffed by a nurse, who can talk you off the ledge when you
inevitably panic about something?

DAVE CARPENTER...

♦ **What about non-life-threatening emergencies?** Who's covering the phones and what happens if your child needs to be seen? During business hours, most practices will have a special line staffed by pediatric nurses who will be able to diagnose just about anything and who, if necessary, will make a same-day appointment.

GETTING TO THE HOSPITAL

Sooner or later—unless you're planning to have a home birth—you and your partner are going to have to get to the hospital. There are several ways of getting there, each with its own advantages and disadvantages:

♦ **Walking.** If you live close enough to the hospital, walking may be the best option. You won't have to worry about any of the disadvantages of driving yourself or getting a ride (see below). You will, however, have to deal with the possible embarrassment of having people stare at you as your partner leans up against the side of a building every three minutes and bellows. But your partner may actually like this option, since walking can help make the contractions of early labor easier to cope with.

If you're walking, be sure to bring enough cash to take a cab—just in case things don't go the way they should.

♦ **Driving yourself.** No matter how much you've prepared, when labor really starts, you're going to be a little nervous, and that could be a little dangerous when you're behind the wheel of a car. You could get lost, get caught speeding, or even cause an accident. Worst of all, while your eyes and mind are on the road, they can't be where they really ought to be—on your partner. And when you finally get to the hospital, you'll have to deal with parking—and later retrieving—the car.

If you're driving, make sure you have a full tank of gas and that you've got the hospital programmed into your GPS (along with several alternative routes). Don't worry: if you get there a little early, they probably won't throw you out. Also, check with the hospital parking lot (if they have one) to find out their rates and hours of operation. You may be able to park, get your partner settled into her room, and then run down and move the car.

♦ **Getting a ride—taxi, friend, or relative.** If you're in the backseat of someone else's car, you'll at least be able to tend to your partner. Problems might arise, however, if your partner goes into labor at 2 A.M. and your friends or in-laws take more than a minute or two to roll out of bed. In addition, since most people have never driven a pregnant woman to the hospital, they'll be at least as nervous (probably more) than you would have been. And watch out for potholes; my wife assures me they're hell for a laboring woman.

If you're taking a taxi, have the phone numbers of at least three companies that can get a cab to your door within minutes, at any hour of the day or night. Also, be sure to have enough money for the fare. If you're planning on having someone else do the driving, make sure you have a few backups.

WHAT IF YOU HAVE OTHER KIDS?

If you have other kids—especially young ones—getting to the hospital can be doubly stressful and requires extra planning.

Toward the end of my wife's second pregnancy, we decided that we'd take a cab to the hospital. We also decided that if she went into serious labor in the middle of the night, we'd signal our friends who had agreed to take care of our older daughter by calling them, letting the phone ring once, hanging up, calling again, and letting it ring three times.

So, at one in the morning, we made the phone calls, got into the cab, and arrived at our friends' house, where, holding thirty-five pounds of sleeping deadweight, I pounded on the door for five minutes before giving up (our friends had apparently slept through the secret signals). Fortunately, we'd made a backup plan, and when we got to the hospital, we called my parents and had them take their grandchild to their house.

AND FINALLY, SOME LAST-MINUTE DETAILS

♦ Keep your doctor's number by the phone.
♦ Keep your gas tank full. Have an extra set of keys stashed someplace, or cash for a cab ready.
♦ Make sure you've checked to see whether there are any road closures or construction projects along your route to the hospital.
♦ Get ready at work. Labor usually starts without warning and can last a long time—sometimes more than a day. Be sure you've delegated urgent matters to a coworker or supervisor, and that your time-off plans are in order. (See pages 149–63 for more on work/family concerns.)

Packing Your Bags

FOR HER

♦ A favorite picture and/or anything else she might need or want to help her through labor and the birth.
♦ A battery-operated CD or MP3 player and some favorite music to help you both relax during labor. I know this sounds so twentieth century, but some hospitals may not allow you to plug anything into their outlets.
♦ A bathrobe, a nightgown, or even one of your old T-shirts that she won't mind getting a little blood on. Or a lot.
♦ A large sports bottle (you know, the kind with the built-in straw) for sipping clear liquids.
♦ Warm socks and/or old slippers (again, ones she won't mind getting bloody).
♦ A change of clothes to go home in—not what she was wearing before she got pregnant. Sweats or maternity pants are particularly good.
♦ A nursing bra.
♦ Her toiletries bag. Don't forget things like mouthwash, toothbrush and toothpaste, glasses, contact lens paraphernalia, hairbrush or comb, and a hair ribbon or two.
♦ Leave the jewelry at home.

FOR YOU

♦ Comfortable clothes.

While You're Waiting

If your partner is at risk for giving birth prematurely, try to carve out a few minutes to do some research or make a few calls on the following topics. You're going to be plenty busy with other things, but the time you spend now will be well worth it.

◆ **Call Social Security and the Motor Vehicle Department.** Since premature babies sometimes need extra (and expensive) medical care, Social Security may help you out. You may also be able to get a temporary handicapped parking pass, which should cut down on the time you have to spend looking for parking. Phone numbers are in the Government Listings section of your local phone book or online.

◆ **Find a doctor who has a lot of experience with premature babies.** Check with the pediatrician you've already selected, your insurance carrier, or the hospital where the baby will be born.

◆ **Find out about infant massage.** Researcher Tiffany Field found that preemies who got three fifteen-minute periods of gentle massage a day grew 50 percent faster than preemies who didn't. Hospital stays for the massaged babies were also a week shorter (and a week cheaper).

◆ Some magazines or a collection of your partner's favorite short stories to read to her.

◆ A swimsuit (you might want to get into the shower with your partner, and the nursing staff might be surprised at the sight of a naked man).

◆ A camera, plenty of batteries, and memory cards or film.

◆ This book.

◆ A cooler filled with snacks. This is not for your partner. (She shouldn't be eating while she's in labor, but you'll need to keep your energy up.) You're not going to want to leave your partner, mid-contraction, to run down to the hospital cafeteria. If you have some extra room, bring along a small birthday cake and maybe even some champagne for afterward.

◆ Cash. For vending machines, parking meters, cab rides, and so on.

◆ Program your phone with the numbers of the people you'll want to tell the news to right away, or set up an e-mail list you can blast to.

◆ Chargers for your phone, PDA, MP3 player, and any other electronic gadgets you're planning to bring with you.

◆ Tennis balls for back rubs.

♦ A toothbrush, extra underwear, shaving kit, and the like. You'll probably end up staying at least one night.

FOR THE BABY

♦ An infant car seat (if you don't have one, the hospital won't let you leave). And make sure it's been properly installed.
♦ A little outfit to go home in—a sleeper or sleep sac is fine, just as long as it has legs so the car seat's harness can go between them. (It's a good idea to wash all new clothes before putting them on the baby.)
♦ Diapers.
♦ Several receiving blankets, weather-appropriate.

Preterm Labor/Premature Birth

In the vast majority of pregnancies, labor doesn't start until about the fortieth week. However, a small but significant number of babies (8 to 10 percent) are born prematurely—meaning sometime before the thirty-seventh week. More than half of twins and about 90 percent of triplets, however, are born prematurely. Interestingly, identical twin boys are more likely to be born prematurely than identical twin girls. This gender distinction doesn't seem to hold for fraternal twins.

The symptoms of premature labor are exactly the same as those of real labor (see pages 232–33 for more)—they just happen before they're supposed to. If your partner has any of the following symptoms, she may be considered at high risk for giving birth early.

♦ An "incompetent cervix"—meaning that the cervix is too weak and may open, allowing the baby to be born too soon. Diagnosed early enough, an incompetent cervix can be "corrected" (and premature births prevented) by sewing the opening of the cervix shut.
♦ "Placenta previa" (when the placenta is covering up the cervix) or "placental abruption" (when the placenta has prematurely separated from the wall of the uterus).
♦ Any kind of surgery during pregnancy.
♦ She's carrying twins (or more). See "When Premature Labor Really Isn't" on page 211.
♦ There's too much or too little amniotic fluid.
♦ She didn't eat well during the pregnancy or is (or has recently been) smoking, drinking, or using drugs.

♦ She's been spending a lot of time on her feet. Several recent studies have found that pregnant women who spend five hours or more standing or walking every day are as much as three times more likely to deliver prematurely than women who are on their feet less than two hours a day. So if your partner is a waitress or nurse or runway model, she might want to switch to a desk job until after the baby's born. Moderate, recreational physical activity, on the other hand, has been shown to protect against preterm birth.

♦ Exposure to Diethylstilbestrol (DES) while her mother was pregnant with her (many of the daughters of women who took DES to prevent miscarriage were born with abnormalities of the reproductive tract).

♦ She's had a previous premature labor.

♦ She's carrying an unusually small fetus.

The bad news about premature babies is that if they're born too soon they really aren't ripe yet. The fetus's lungs aren't fully developed until it's at least twenty-eight weeks old. Babies born before that time have a far higher risk of developing serious respiratory problems, including chronic lung disease, as well as neurological and cognitive problems. Babies born at twenty-eight to thirty-two weeks are far better off, but still at risk for vision and gastrointestinal difficulties.

Overall, premature and low-birth-weight babies are at risk for a number of short- and long-term problems. As infants, they may be less responsive to visual and auditory stimulation, and their reflexes aren't as sharp as normal-birth-weight babies. They may have trouble breathing, sucking, or swallowing, and are more likely to develop a chronic illness or to die of SIDS (Sudden Infant Death Syndrome). As they get older, they may have smaller vocabularies than other kids the same age, have shorter attention spans and lower self-esteem, and are more likely to fail in school or have to repeat a grade. As adolescents they often have more behavioral and psychological problems, and as adults they're more likely to suffer from depression.

Premature babies are also less likely to be breastfed. Breastfeeding boosts babies' immune system and protects them from developing ear infections, pneumonia, and stomach problems, and from becoming obese later in life. There's some evidence that breastfed babies have higher IQs and lower risk of developing leukemia or diabetes.

The good news is that medical technology has advanced so much in recent years that the chances of survival are excellent. Ninety percent of thirty-week babies do quite well. And by thirty-five weeks, it's up to 99 percent.

Obviously, it's to the fetus's benefit to spend as many days as possible right where it's supposed to be: in its mother's uterus. Therefore, if your partner shows signs of being in real labor (see pages 232–33), call your doctor immediately. Caught early, premature labor can sometimes be arrested (usually with the help of intravenous drugs), and the fetus will be able to stay where it belongs for a few more weeks.

After an arrested premature labor, your doctor will most likely order your partner to stay in bed for the rest of the pregnancy. She may even be put on a home fetal monitor to keep an eye on the baby. If this happens, be prepared to step in and take over all of the household responsibilities, as well as responsibility for other children if you have them. If you aren't in a position to do this, you may have to hire someone or ask friends or relatives to help out. Your involvement, though, is actually a lot more important than you might think. Researcher Michael Yogman tracked a group of preemies and found that at three years old, for example, the IQ scores of the kids with highly involved dads were six points higher than the ones with less involved dads.

When Premature Labor Really Isn't

If you're expecting twins (or more) and your partner goes into labor, chances are it's not premature at all. Although single babies spend an average of forty weeks under construction, most twins are born at about thirty-seven weeks. Triplets usually arrive at thirty-five weeks, and quads make their entrance a week earlier. Even if it turns out that you're going to be skipping the traditional ninth month, read the next chapter anyway— especially the "What's Going On with You" section—to make sure you aren't missing out on anything important.

The Nursery: Everything You Need and What It Costs

There are literally thousands of things you *could* buy for your newborn's nursery, but you'll max out all your credit cards, clean out your IRAs, and have to take a second mortgage on your house to get them all. Most are simply unnecessary. You could, for example, buy a special machine that warms up the wipes you use to clean your baby's bottom. But believe me, your baby's bottom will get just as clean with room-temperature wipes. Here are some of the items you'll truly need or at least have a pretty good chance of using. The prices listed are retail; you can probably save quite a bit by buying these things online, at garage sales, from friends, or at used-furniture stores.

Please remember that when acquiring *anything* for your baby, safety should be your primary concern. Before you spend a fortune on Queen Victoria's

Essentials to Have Waiting at Home

FOR THE BABY

Note: You'll have to increase the quantities somewhat if you have twins or more.

♦ Enough diapers to last for at least a week (you're not going to want to go shopping). Just so you know, your newborn will go through about a dozen every day. Do the math. If you're buying disposables, don't go out and buy a truckload of the infant size. Babies tend to bulk up pretty quickly, and you might be on to the next size before you use the smaller ones. If you know your baby will be big, you can skip the newborn size completely. If you're going with a cloth diaper service, a week's supply is typically 80 (for one baby).

♦ Baby soap and shampoo

♦ Thermometer. (You may want to invest in the electronic kind that takes the temperature via the ear almost instantly. Preventing your baby from squirming for three minutes while trying to keep a thermometer in her mouth or bottom is going to be an unpleasant experience for everyone concerned.)

♦ An ear bulb. (These are usually used for rinsing adults' ears, but for babies, they're used for suctioning mucus from their noses. Well, what do you expect? They can't do it themselves!)

♦ Nail scissors. (Essential: a baby's nails are like tiny razors and grow like Jack's beanstalk.)

♦ A first-aid kit. You can get one from the Red Cross for about $20. But just to be sure, ask your pediatrician what should be in it.

♦ A diaper bag. It used to be that most diaper bags looked like oversized purses. They were pink or flowery and no self-respecting man would be caught dead with one. Fortunately, there are quite a few more masculine options. Check out www.diaperdude.com and www.dadgear.com for some possibilities.

♦ Cotton swabs and alcohol for umbilical cord dressing

♦ Some formula, just in case. But keep in mind that some breastfeeding experts think this is a bad idea, because it might be too big a temptation to give up breastfeeding.

♦ Pacifiers

♦ Stroller

♦ Fitted crib sheets

♦ Bottles and a breast pump

- 5 or 6 onesies (those cute little one-piece suits)
- 5 or 6 pairs of booties (those stretchy socks)
- 3 or 4 undershirts
- 3 or 4 outfits with separate top and bottom (that way you can wash only the part that gets dirty). Try to get the kind that have snaps.
- 3 or 4 nightgowns or sleep sacs
- 1 or 2 coveralls with snaps
- 4 or 5 baby blankets
- 1 or 2 hooded bath towels
- 1 or 2 sun or snow hats
- 1 or 2 sweaters
- Snowsuit (as needed)
- 0 shoes (people who don't walk shouldn't wear shoes—it can hurt their feet)

A word of advice: your baby will poop or vomit on his clothes every single day. More than once. So skip the silk T-shirts and the lamb's wool sweaters and stick with good-quality *washable* materials. And, as with diapers, don't invest a huge amount on newborn-sized clothes. Your baby will be out of them in no time.

FOR YOUR PARTNER
- Nursing pads
- Maxi-pads (she may need these for weeks)
- Any medication or dressing materials needed in the event of a C-section or episiotomy
- Milk and vitamins, especially if she is nursing
- Flowers, and favorite chocolates or other foods she might have avoided during pregnancy
- A good book about your baby's first year of life. Modesty aside, my books *The New Father: A Dad's Guide to the First Year* and *Fathering Your Toddler: A Dad's Guide to the Second and Third Years* are the best resources out there for dads.
- A comfortable rocking chair or glider, for nursing
- A breastfeeding pillow
- For both of you, *Caring for Your Baby and Young Child, Birth to Age 5,* from the American Academy of Pediatrics

Green Babies

People generally select the products they buy based on price, quality, availability, and brand. In recent years, though, consumers are paying more attention to how products impact the environment, whether it's their home environment or the one we all live in. A recent national poll, conducted by The Shelton Group, found that 60 percent of American consumers say that, given the choice, they would rather buy environmentally friendly products—as long as they wouldn't be inconvenienced or uncomfortable. And 42 percent of adults aged eighteen to thirty-four actually tried a new product because they felt the product, its packaging, or the manufacturer benefited the environment. Overall, 36 percent of Americans say they "always" or "almost always" buy green products—that's up from 12 percent in 2007. So what does this have to do with you and your baby? Plenty.

You might be concerned that the paint you used in the nursery could emit toxic fumes. Or maybe you're worried about the bleaches in your laundry and you'd prefer that your baby wear nothing but organic fabrics. Or perhaps you're concerned about how disposable diapers are impacting the environment. Whatever your concern, there are environmentally friendly alternatives to just about any product you're currently using (although the most common reason given by those who don't buy green is that the products cost too much).

You can find some of these products at places like Walgreens, Sears, Whole Foods, Babies "Я" Us, and even Wal-Mart, or at your local natural grocer. But the widest selection and the most resources are going to be online, at places like Green Home (www.greenhome.com). See the Resources section for a lot more.

original bassinet or drag out the crib that you (or your parents or grandparents) slept in as a kid, consider this: your baby will do just about everything possible to jeopardize his or her own life (and scare the hell out of you), from sticking his head between the bars of the crib and throwing himself off tall changing tables to burying herself under a pile of blankets left in the corner.

So before you buy anything for your baby—whether it's new or used—make sure it complies with the most recent safety standards. Some of them are listed in the sections that follow. For additional guidance on the safest—

and best-quality—deals, consult the latest *Consumer Reports Guide to Baby Products,* in print or online at ConsumerReports.org, or Kids in Danger, www.kidsindanger.org.

The U.S. Consumer Product Safety Commission posts a list of product recalls on its Web site, www.cpsc.gov. And you can find out the latest standards and requirements for car seats and other travel-related equipment from the National Highway Traffic Safety Administration, at www.nhtsa.dot.gov.

BABY FURNISHINGS

CRIB: $150 to well over $2,000. There's nothing that says baby quite like a crib. And so it's no surprise that this is one of the first pieces of baby furniture an expectant couple thinks about. Some cribs are just cribs; others can be converted to a toddler bed or other furniture as your baby grows up. Here are some safety tips:

♦ No corner posts. Babies can accidentally strangle themselves if their clothes become caught on a post. New cribs are constructed without them, but if you have your heart set on using a vintage model, unscrew or saw off the posts.

♦ Slats or bars should be spaced no more than 2⅜ inches apart, and none should be broken or missing.

♦ Never place your crib near draperies, blinds, or anything else that has long, hanging or wall-mounted cords. Babies can tear these down or become entangled in them.

♦ Keep the crib away from radiators, heaters, and area rugs. The last thing you want to do while holding your baby is burn yourself or slip.

♦ Crib sides should slide up and down easily and lock solidly at the top. Any teething rails (the hard plastic caps over the top rails of the crib side) should be firmly attached. They're going to get chewed on a lot, and you don't want them to come off.

♦ Before you buy, check the CPSC Web site for recall info.

A SOFA FOR EVERY BUDGET!

$67.50 $859.35 $64,242,906.25

CRIB MATTRESS: $100 to $150. Couples are often surprised that mattresses are usually sold separately from the crib. The theory is that some babies prefer firm mattresses while others prefer softer ones. Since your baby is going to be spending around fifteen hours a day on that mattress for a while, don't skimp—there's no reason why the one you buy now shouldn't last you through several kids. Just make sure it comes with a moisture-proof protector. A few safety tips:

♦ The firmer the better. Studies have shown that there is an increased risk of SIDS (Sudden Infant Death Syndrome) if the mattress is too soft. For the same reason, never put pillows in the crib.

♦ The mattress must fit tightly into the crib (no more than one finger's width between the edge of the mattress and the side of the crib).

♦ You'll have a choice between innerspring and foam. Neither is necessarily better than the other. The main thing is to go for quality over price. There are a lot of cheapies out there that either won't last or are made using questionable materials.

♦ Consider flame-retardant coverings and organic or eco-friendly materials if those things are important to your family.

CRIB ACCESSORIES

♦ Sheets: $8 to $75. Get at least three of the fitted kind. They usually come in regular and organic.

♦ Bumper: $100 (optional). Even though they can't move very well, babies somehow manage to ram their heads against the sides of the crib—hard enough to leave an impression of the slats or bars on the top or back of their head. It supposedly reminds them of the feeling of having their heads smashed up against your partner's pubic bone for the last month or two of pregnancy. Traditional crib bumpers are about 8 inches high, 1 inch thick, and run inside the crib along all four sides. They attach firmly (usually by ties or Velcro) to the crib and protect your baby's head. There's a newer kind of bumper, too: a lightweight wedge that also runs along the inside of the crib but sits on top of the mattress.

♦ Dust ruffle: $10 to $75 (extremely optional).

♦ Mobile: $25 to $200 (optional). Some of the most beautiful (and most expensive) ones are made to be looked at from the side—where the person who bought it is standing. But remember whom the mobile is really for, and think about whether your baby is really going to be interested in looking at the bottom of a bunch of cars or the underside of a group of jungle animals. Babies seem to prefer high-contrast patterns as opposed to simply bright colors. You can get mobiles that simply hang, some that play incredibly annoying music when you wind them up, some that run on batteries, and others that ring bells or make other noises when the baby swats at them.

BASSINET (sometimes called **MOSES BASKET**): $80 to $150. For the first few months of your baby's life, you may want him or her to sleep in the bedroom with you. If nothing else, this arrangement will make breastfeeding a lot more convenient. Bassinets come in a variety of styles (wheels, no wheels, handles, no handles, rocking, non-rocking). But because they generally accommodate a baby for only three months or so, you'll be better off borrowing a safe one from someone and passing it on to the next new parents.

SIDECAR or **CO-SLEEPER**: $50 to $750. These are essentially three-sided cribs that attach to the side of your bed (most likely your partner's side). The idea is that breastfeeding may be easier with the baby close by.

CAR SEAT: $40 to $300. A car seat may be the most indispensable baby item. (Again, you won't be able to take your baby home from the hospital without one.) This is a critical purchase, so don't skimp. Stay away from hand-me-downs unless they're practically new and conform to the very latest standards. Some are designed to face backward, others only face front. Some convert from one to the other. You may want to consider getting two—a small one (perhaps with handles so you can carry the baby around with you) that can be used until the baby reaches twenty pounds, and a larger one for later. There are also some car seat/stroller combinations out there.

CHANGING TABLE: $70 to $500. Changing tables come in an unbelievable variety of sizes and configurations. Some have drawers so that they can be used as a dresser when your child no longer needs to be changed. The problem with drawers, however, is that you have to remember to take out what you need before you get started; when you're in the middle of changing the baby, the last thing you want to be doing is fumbling around blindly for a clean outfit. Be sure to get a foam pad for the top of the table and a couple of washable pad covers. You also should stock your changing table with a good supply of the following:
♦ Diapers
♦ Baby wipes

♦ Diaper rash ointment, such as A&D or Desitin
♦ Cotton swabs and water for cleaning the umbilical cord stump
♦ Baby shampoo and soap (a mild one like Neutrogena or Dove is best)

Note: Stay away from talc-based baby powders. They can cause breathing problems and lung damage if inhaled. Cornstarch-based powders seem to be okay, but there's no solid evidence that either one does anything to help with diaper rash. The most important things you can do are change diapers regularly and pat or air-dry your baby's bottom before closing the diaper.

PORTABLE PLAYPEN: $50 to $200. Perfect for children less than thirty-four inches tall and lighter than about thirty pounds. Not only does it fold up compactly enough to check as luggage when you're traveling, but it can also be used at home—to keep your baby from crawling under your feet while you're cooking, for example. Some of our friends' children essentially lived in their playpens for the first eighteen months of their lives.

STROLLER: $100 to $2,000. A good stroller can make life worth living, so don't waste your time or money on one that won't last. We took our older daughter and her stroller all over the world, and it was still in good enough condition three years later for her younger sister to use. Getting a quality stroller doesn't mean you have to buy the one with every available option. Stick to the basics, such as weight, ease of folding, brakes, and balance (you don't want the thing tipping over backward with your baby in it). Finally, make sure the handles are long enough for you to push the stroller when you're standing up straight. Most strollers are made to be used by women, which means that if you're over 5'6" or so, you'll have to stoop a little to push. You might not notice it at first, but after a while, your back may give you trouble. Some smarter manufacturers have adjustable handles.

City dwellers who do a lot of traveling on subways or buses will want a sturdy but collapsible stroller—preferably one that you can fold with one hand while holding the baby with the other. Otherwise, it's next to impossible to get onto public transportation (at least without annoying everyone behind you). The stroller/car seat combos are especially bulky and hard to fold.

There are dozens of stroller manufacturers, and they come in a nearly infinite range of designs and functions. Some are designed for running, others for twins; some look like Harley-Davidson motorcycles and convert to a child's bike after the stroller years are past. Some look generic, some have military

Watch Out for Triboluminescence

Never heard of it? Well maybe it's time you should. In 1999 English housewife Jill Furlough got a fright late one night when she saw green sparks shooting out of her sleeping eleven-month-old son's disposable diaper. She called the diaper manufacturers, who assured her that the sparks were the result of *triboluminescence*, a perfectly harmless buildup of energy probably caused by the friction of the baby's bottom rubbing against the inside of the diaper. It's actually exactly the same chemical reaction that produces the sparks you see when you bite down on a Wint-O-Green LifeSaver in a dark room. You can see the same thing if you strike two sugar cubes together as if striking a match, or you yank on a roll of tape. Unlike static electricity, triboluminescence doesn't generate any heat. The boy apparently slept through the entire episode, and there's no record of any injury to anyone. Just something to think about.

camouflage, and others seem to serve no purpose but to show off how much money you have (or used to have, before you mortgaged your house to buy the stroller).

BATHTUB: $20. A small plastic washbasin is best for newborns because a sink is too big and can be dangerous. When the baby outgrows the basin, you can soak his or her little formula-stained clothes in it.

MONITOR: $15 to $300. These handy devices let you listen to or watch your baby wherever you are. And I really do mean wherever. Some of the higher-end video monitors allow you to get real-time feeds on your computer, PDA, or other device (that's good if you have to go back to work but you don't want to miss a second of your baby's life). If you're just going for a plain vanilla audio monitor, try hardware or sporting goods stores where you can get walkie-talkies and room monitors for quite a bit less than a similar item at a traditional toy or baby-gear stores, where they call them "baby monitors."

BABY CARRIER: $20 to $200. Whether it's a sling, a frontpack, or a backpack, you'll want to get something that you can use to carry your baby around in. Make sure it's comfortable and, if you're planning to share it with your partner, adjustable.

DIAPERS: Who would have thought that diapers would become a political issue or that something so ordinary could make or break friendships? But they have.

Until just a few years ago, there were two camps: disposable and cloth. People who used disposables were evil, pumping millions of tons of human waste, plastic, and chemicals into the landfill, where they'd stay in their present form for thousands of years. (There also were some "biodegradable" diapers, which broke down after only five hundred years). People who used cloth diapers, in contrast, were the white knights, saving the earth for our children.

Unfortunately, things were a bit more complicated: although cloth diapers are all natural, the problem is that they're made of cotton, which is taxing on farmland. And in order to sterilize them properly, diaper services bleach them and wash them seven times (it's true) in near-boiling water, thereby consuming a tremendous amount of power, water, and chemical detergents. The clean diapers are then driven all over town in trucks that fill the air with toxic pollutants. Bottom line? There was no clear winner.

Today, the situation is even more confusing. The regular disposables are still out there, and still playing the role of bogeyman. But there are also a number of eco-friendly disposables that offer some or all of the following features: chlorine-free, latex-free, dye-free, fragrance-free, gel-free, made of corn-based materials, GMO (genetically modified organism)-free, hypoallergenic, organic, compostable, and flushable.

On the other side of the argument, we need to talk about "reusables" instead of cloth. My wife and I started out by using cloth diapers for our older daughter. But every time she filled one up, the diaper had a nasty tendency to siphon the contents away from my daughter and onto my pants—not pleasant—and that meant even more laundry! It's possible that this phenomenon was the fault of my poor diapering technique. But I was convinced that disposables, which have elastic around the leg openings, do a better job of keeping what belongs in a diaper actually in the diaper.

Today, that's all changed. Cloth diapers are no longer rectangular and held together with pins or elastic clips. Now they're hourglass-shaped and hidden behind stylish washable covers that Velcro on and stretch to fit your baby. (Properly installed, these diapers can be just as leak-free as disposables.) There are also hybrid diapers, which use a washable exterior but have disposable (and sometimes flushable) liners. Assuming an average of eight changes a day (the dozen per day that you'll be changing for the first month will be offset by slightly fewer changes as your child gets older), plan on going through around 3,000 before you light the candle on your baby's first birthday cake. Double that if you have twins. The choice is yours.

Don't even bother to base your decision on cost. For disposables, figure 25 cents each, or around $60 per month. But if you keep your eye out for coupons (most parenting magazines have a bunch of them in every issue), you can save a lot. In addition, places like Babies "Я" Us have generic or house brands that are a lot cheaper and usually just as good.

Kids who grow up with disposable diapers tend to become potty-trained later than those who use cloth, because the disposables do such a great job of sucking up moisture that babies have no real incentive to get out of them. If you want to see this in action, just visit someone you know who has a toddler. Chances are, he'll be running all over the house with his diaper hanging down to his knees because he's got a quart of urine in there, but he's comfortable as can be.

On the reusable side, a typical diaper service will cost you $12 to $15 a week, roughly the same as for disposables, although prices vary greatly around the country. This price will cover door-to-door delivery and pickup of about eighty diapers each week. If you go this route, you'll also need at least three or four diaper wraps, which cost about $10 each, to help hold the diaper in place and minimize leaks. You can, of course, cut your costs a bit by buying diapers (about $10 to $14 for a package of six). If you're doing your own laundry, you'll need about forty.

The other reusable options are a lot more expensive—more than double the cost. But if you can afford them and are committed to a more sustainable, eco-friendly future, they're the way to go. Even if you don't end up using cloth diapers for the baby, keep a dozen on hand anyway—they're great for drying baby bottoms on changing tables and for draping over your shoulder to protect your clothes when your baby spits up. Probably the best place to do all your comparison shopping is www.Diapers.com.

FORMULA: Prices vary. You can use powdered, full-strength liquid, or liquid concentrate. But when you start checking prices, your partner may decide to keep breastfeeding a while longer. When we weaned our daughters, we put them on the powdered formula—I made a pitcher of it every morning and kept it in the refrigerator.

"Dear, It's Time..."

What's Going On with Your Partner

Physically

♦ Some change in fetal activity—the baby is so cramped that instead of kicking and punching, all she can do is squirm

♦ Increased sleeplessness and fatigue

♦ A renewed sense of energy when the baby's head "drops" into the pelvis and takes some of the pressure off the stomach and lungs

♦ She may have stopped gaining weight (and may even lose a pound or two), but she's still just plain miserable, with increased cramping, constipation, backache, water retention, and swelling of the feet, ankles, and face

♦ If her belly button was an innie before, it may have become an outie (the change isn't permanent, though)

♦ Absolutely no interest in sex (although some women's interest actually increases)

Emotionally

♦ More dependent on you than ever—afraid you won't love her after the baby is born (after all, she's not the same woman you married)

♦ Impatient: tired of being tired, frustrated with being so big, and can't wait for pregnancy to be over—or she may not want it to end

♦ Short-tempered: tired of answering "So when's the baby coming?" questions—especially if she's overdue
♦ May be afraid she won't have enough love to go around—what with loving you and all
♦ Fear she won't be ready for labor when it comes
♦ Creating endless lists of things that absolutely, positively have to be done (in most cases by you) before the baby shows up
♦ Increasing preoccupation with the baby and, perhaps, a sudden and unexplained interest in Martha Stewart and interior decorating

What's Going On with the Baby

Over the course of this last month of pregnancy, your baby will be growing at a tremendous clip, putting on about a quarter to a half pound a week, although she'll stop growing a week or so before birth. Before she finally decides to leave the warm uterus, she'll weigh six to nine pounds (less if she's a twin or triplet) and be about twenty inches long—so big that there will be hardly any room for her to kick or prod your partner anymore. Her fingernails and toenails are frequently so long they have to be trimmed right after birth, and the lanugo and vernix that have been covering and protecting her little body are starting to slough off. And despite the widespread myth that babies are born blind, her sight is coming along just fine. During her last weeks in captivity, she'll practice her sucking, hand clenching, head turning, swallowing, blinking, and even breathing.

What's Going On with You

Confusion

Well, it's almost over. In just a few weeks, you're finally going to meet the child you've talked to and dreamed about, and whose college education you've planned. But be prepared: the last month of pregnancy is often the most confusing for expectant fathers. At times you may be almost overcome with excitement and anticipation. At other times you may be feeling so scared and trapped that you want to run away. In short, all the feelings—good and bad— that you've experienced over the last eight months are back. But now, because of the impending birth, they're more intense than before. Here are a few of the contradictory emotional states you may find yourself going through during the final stages of the pregnancy:

♦ On the one hand, you may be feeling confident about your readiness to be a father. On the other, you may be worried and unsure about whether you'll be able to handle your dual roles as husband and dad.

♦ You may really be looking forward to spending some time with your baby while your partner is recuperating. But you may be worried that you won't know how to do all the things that she usually does for the family. (If this last part is true, you'd better learn how to do the laundry and run the dishwasher in a hurry.)

♦ You're looking forward to being involved, but you feel sidelined by your partner and jealous of her connection with the baby.

♦ If you've taken on a second job or increased responsibilities at work, all you'll probably want to do at the end of the day is go home and relax. But with your partner less and less able to handle physical tasks, you may be greeted at the door with a list of chores that need to be done.

♦ You may want to take a good chunk of time off after the baby comes, but you're worried about how that will affect your career, or whether your joint checking account can take the hit.

♦ You and your partner may be feeling an exceptionally strong emotional bond with each other. At the same time, your sex life may have completely disappeared.

♦ You may be horny as hell, but you saw some pretty graphic childbirth videos in your prep class and can't get those images out of your mind.

♦ As your partner gets more and more uncomfortable, she may feel less and less like going out with friends, so the two of you may be spending a lot more time together. This may be the last chance you have to enjoy some quiet, private time before the baby comes. But it may also be an unwelcome opportunity to get on each other's nerves.

♦ You may find yourself spending a lot more time with friends and family members who have small children, or you may find yourself avoiding families with kids.

♦ You may be practically giddy at the idea of holding your child in your arms, but petrified that you'll drop him.

Increased Dependency on Your Partner

By this time your attention—and that of your friends and family—is focused squarely on your partner and the baby. Since you're the person she's closest to and sees most often, your partner is going to be increasingly dependent on you—not only to help her physically, but to get her through the last-month emotional ups and downs. At the same time, though, you are going to be increasingly dependent on her as you get onto the last-month roller coaster.

Your partner's increased dependency is considered a "normal" part of pregnancy. But thanks to the ridiculous, gender-specific way we socialize people in this country, men are supposed to be independent, strong, supportive, and impervious to emotional needs—especially while their partners are pregnant. So, just when you're feeling most vulnerable and least in control, your needs are swept under the rug. And what's worse, the one person you most depend on for sympathy and understanding may be too absorbed in what's going on with herself and the baby to do much for you.

This results in what Dr. Luis Zayas calls an "imbalance in interdependence," which leaves the father to satisfy his own emotional needs *and* those of his partner. In addition, in many cases this imbalance essentially becomes a kind of vicious circle that "accentuates the stress, intensifies feelings of separation, and heightens dependency needs." In other words, the less response you get to your dependency needs, the more dependent you feel.

Feeling Guilty

Especially in the last month or so of the pregnancy, many men begin to blame themselves for what they think they've been putting their partners through. Yes, you're the one who got her pregnant, and yes, she's uncomfortable as hell. But strange as it might seem to you, your partner does *not* blame you for what she's going through. She understands and accepts—as you should—that this was her idea, too, and that (at least short of surrogate motherhood or adoption) there's simply no way to have a baby without going through this. So quit torturing yourself—there are a lot more productive things you can be doing with your time during these last few weeks.

Staying Involved

Sensitivity

The bottom line is that during the last few weeks of her pregnancy, your partner is likely to be miserable and uncomfortable. Although there's not a whole lot you can do to ease her burden, here are a few suggestions that might make the final stretch a little more bearable—for both of you:

- **Quit answering the phone.** Change the outgoing message on your voice mail to something like: "Hi. No, we don't have a baby yet, and yes, Jane's fine. If you're calling about anything else, please leave a message and we'll call you back." That may sound a little snotty, but believe me, it's a lot less snotty than you would be if you were really answering the same questions twenty times a day.

- **Stay nearby whenever you can.** Come home a little earlier from work, give away those basketball tickets, and postpone that long business trip.

- **Stay in touch.** A couple of quick calls, texts, or e-mails to her every day can make her feel loved and important. They'll also reassure her that you are all right. And never, ever go anywhere without your phone. The one time you do, she'll call and immediately panic that you've either left her or were hit by a bus.

- **Stay as calm as you can.** She'll be nervous enough for both of you.

- **Be patient.** She may do some pretty bizarre things, and the best thing you can do is bear with her. If the house has already passed the white-glove test and the car has been waxed twice, and she wants it all done over again, do it—she needs the rest.

- **Review the breathing, relaxation, mirroring, and any other techniques you plan to use during labor.**

- **If she wants it, give her some time to herself.** And if she wants time with you, make sure you're there for her.

- **If she hasn't stopped working, encourage her to do so.** Especially if she doesn't like her job. In a recent study of women in southern California, researchers found that women who took leave in the last month of pregnancy (starting around three to four weeks before delivery) had a C-section rate that was four times lower than women who didn't take leave. And while she's on leave, encourage her to get plenty of sleep. Exhaustion during the final weeks of the pregnancy also increases the C-section rate.

If you're running out of ideas, reread the "Ways to Show Her You Care" section on pages 110–13 and try the ones you didn't get to then, or those that got you the most mileage the first time around.

What If She's Overdue?

There's nothing more frustrating than starting the tenth month of a nine-month pregnancy. You've already given up answering the phone, afraid it's another one of those "What are you doing at home? I was sure you'd be at the hospital by now" calls. And you're sick of ending every conversation at the office with, "Now if I'm not in tomorrow, don't forget to . . ." The empty bassinet looks forlorn, and you're just dying to meet the baby face to little wrinkled face.

In most cases, however, couples who think they're late really aren't. When doctors tell a pregnant woman her due date, they often neglect to add that it's only a ballpark figure based on an assumed twenty-eight-day menstrual cycle, and there's always a window of plus or minus two weeks. If your partner's cycle is long, short, or irregular, her "official" due date could be off by as much as three weeks. And even if her cycle is like clockwork, it's nearly impossible to tell exactly when you conceived. First-trimester ultrasounds, which almost all women have, are more accurate, coming within three to four days (in either direction) of the actual due date. Second-trimester ultrasounds are less accurate, with a margin of error of around a week either way. In the third trimester, ultrasounds can be even less accurate—as much as ten to twelve days off.

There are also a number of other factors that can influence due-date accuracy. African-American and Asian women, for example, tend to have shorter pregnancies (by three to five days) than Caucasian women. Younger women have shorter pregnancies than older ones, and first-time moms typically deliver as much as ten days after their due date.

The problem with this is that your partner may have been fixated on a specific due date, and when she goes past it, she's likely to be bitterly disappointed. While going past the due date by a week or so is usually not a problem, being truly overdue can have serious consequences:

♦ The baby can grow so large that he or she will have problems passing through the birth canal, thus increasing the chances of a difficult delivery or a C-section.
♦ After a certain point the placenta gets so old that it can no longer provide adequate nourishment for the baby. This can result in the baby's losing weight in the uterus, increasing the risk of fetal distress.
♦ There may no longer be enough amniotic fluid to support the baby.
♦ There may be inadequate room for the umbilical cord to perform properly.

If your doctor feels the baby is overdue, he or she will most likely prescribe some tests to make sure the baby is still okay. The most common are an ultrasound (to determine the level of amniotic fluid as well as to get a general idea of how the baby is doing) and a nonstress test, which monitors changes in the baby's heart rate and movement in reaction to certain stimuli.

If the baby "passes" these tests, the doctor will probably send you home, telling you to repeat the test in three to seven days if the baby hasn't come by then. Or, he or she may suggest that you schedule a date for labor to be induced.

If all of this starts getting you down, remember the words of obstetrician J. Milton Huston of New York Hospital: "In all of my years of practice, I've never seen a baby stay in there."

What If It's a Boy?

Sadly, most people don't think about—and, consequently, never discuss—circumcising their sons until the thing is staring them in the face, so to speak. So if you and your partner haven't made up your minds about circumcision yet, now's the time to do so. Of course, if you know you're having a girl or if you and your partner have already decided what you're going to do, feel free to skip this section. But if either of you is still undecided, the pros and cons of circumcision are summarized below. If you and your partner aren't on exactly the same page, be careful: in recent years the whole circumcision debate has become extremely political, and tempers run pretty hot on both sides.

WHY YOU MIGHT WANT TO CONSIDER CIRCUMCISION

♦ **Religious reasons.** Circumcision is a traditional, ritual practice for Jews and Muslims. A few years ago, the wife of a local rabbi went to court to get an injunction preventing her husband from circumcising their newborn son. Needless to say, their marriage didn't last much longer.

♦ **Health.** A number of studies have shown that circumcision reduces boys' (and, later, men's) chances of getting HIV and some other sexually transmitted diseases, developing urinary tract infections (UTI) or cancer of the penis, and may reduce his future partner's chance of developing cancer of the cervix. Uncircumcised boys are ten times more likely to develop a UTI than circumcised ones (1 in 100 vs. 1 in 1,000), but the risk was very small to begin with. In addition, circumcision completely prevents *phimosis*, a condition in which the foreskin can't be retracted. Phimosis, which affects about 1 to 2 percent of uncircumcised males, can also be cured later on by circumcision, a procedure that gets a lot more painful with age. Short of that, the foreskin may be able to be loosened by gentle stretching (do not do this without proper medical supervision) or by using a topical steroid cream prescribed by your pediatrician to soften it.

♦ **Hygiene.** A circumcised penis is a lot easier to clean—both for the parents and for the boy himself.

♦ **Conformity.** If you've been circumcised, your son will probably want to look like you. Worldwide, only about 20 percent of boys are circumcised. But in the United States, it's a lot more popular, and having it done will probably make him look more like the other boys in the locker room. Nationwide, about 55 percent of boys are circumcised, but depending on where you live, the rate may be higher (75 percent in the Midwest) or lower (31 percent in the West).

WHY YOU MIGHT WANT TO CONSIDER
NOT CIRCUMCISING YOUR SON

♦ **Pain.** No matter how you look at it, getting circumcised is painful. The circumcision cut will take about three days to heal fully. Until the late 1990s, most circumcisions were done without anesthetic. Today, most are done with either a numbing cream or an injection. OB/GYN Marjorie Greenfield cites research showing that babies who get some pre-circumcision anesthetic "cry less, have a more normal heart rate during the procedure, and are less irritable" than those who were medication-free. Younger doctors and those practicing in the western states are more likely to use pain blocks than older doctors or those anywhere else in the country. Whether the circumcision is done by the baby's doctor or the mother's depends on the doctor's medical training and where he or she is practicing.

♦ **Other risks.** Complications, while extremely rare, can occur. There is about a 1 in 500 chance of bleeding, penile injury, or local infection due to circumcision, but death is almost never a risk. In 1979, for example, there was only one circumcision-related death in the entire United States. A recent comprehensive study comparing the risks and benefits of circumcision found that the procedure prevents six urinary tract infections for every complication endured and that about two complications can be expected for every case of penile cancer prevented. "Circumcision remains a relatively safe procedure," write doctors Christakis, Harvey, Zerr, and their colleagues who conducted the study. "However, for some parents, the risks we report may outweigh the potential benefits."

♦ **Conformity.** As above, if you haven't been circumcised, your son will probably want to look like you.

♦ **Pleasure.** Some people believe that the foreskin is there for a purpose: to protect the tip of the penis, and that removing it can cause the penis to be less sensitive, which will reduce sexual pleasure later in life. A number of anti-circumcision groups claim that penile circumcision has the same impact on boys that "female circumcision" has on girls. There is absolutely no evidence that this is true. Female circumcision (more accurately called genital mutilation) is practiced in some parts of the world and involves completely or partially removing a girl's clitoris or sewing the labia minora together. The specific purpose is to reduce the girl's sexual pleasure or ability to have intercourse before marriage, which, supposedly, will make her less likely to stray later. There is simply no comparison between the two procedures, and frankly, I think it's offensive to mention them both in the same sentence.

Billions of circumcised men around the world have perfectly delightful sex lives, and doctors have found little, if any, conclusive proof that circumcision has any negative effects on boys' or men's sexual, psychological, or emotional health. In fact, in a recent article in the journal *Urology*, Turkish researcher Temucin Senkul and his colleagues tested this hypothesis by asking uncircumcised men who were about to be circumcised for religious reasons to rate their sexual satisfaction and function before the procedure and at least 12 weeks after. The only difference between the before and the after was that it took the circumcised men a little longer to ejaculate, something many men would consider to be a good thing rather than a bad one.

♦ **Is it necessary at all?** Some claim that many of the health risks thought to be reduced by circumcision may in fact be reduced simply by better hygiene—something that can be taught. The American Academy of Pediatrics and the American Urological Association have both taken a fairly noncommittal position, saying that although scientific evidence shows the potential medical benefits of circumcising newborn boys, the benefits aren't sufficient to recommend that all infant boys be circumcised. Bottom line? It's a personal decision that's totally up to you and your partner.

CARE OF THE CIRCUMCISED PENIS

Your son's penis will be red and sore for a few days after the circumcision. And until it's fully healed—which will take a week to ten days—you'll need to protect the newly exposed tip and keep it from sticking to the inside of his diaper. A few tiny spots of blood on his diapers for up to two days is perfectly normal, but call your doctor if there's more blood that that, if the redness gets worse after three or four days, or if your son hasn't urinated within six to eight hours after the circumcision. How you care for your son's penis will depend on which method was used to do the circumcision, so ask the person who did the circumcision before you do anything. The general rule is that you'll need to keep the penis dry and the tip lubricated with petroleum jelly and wrapped in gauze at every diaper change. If there's a plastic ring over the tip of the penis (it's called a Plastibell), just leave it alone and let it fall off by itself. Again, check with the person who did the procedure for specific care instructions.

CARE OF THE UNCIRCUMCISED PENIS

Even if you elect not to circumcise your son, you'll still have to spend some time taking care of his penis. Eighty-five percent of boys under six months have foreskins that don't retract (pull back to reveal the head of the penis), so don't try to force it. Fortunately, as boys get older, their foreskins retract on their own; by age one, 50 percent retract, and by age three, 80 to 90 percent do. The standard way to clean an uncircumcised penis is to retract the foreskin as far as it will comfortably go, and gently wash the head with mild soap and warm water. There is absolutely no need to use antiseptics, cotton swabs, or any other special cleaning measures.

Dealing with Contingencies

LABOR: REAL OR FALSE

By now, your partner has probably experienced plenty of Braxton-Hicks contractions ("false labor"), which have been warming up her uterus for the real thing. Sometimes, however, these practice contractions may be so strong that your partner may think that labor has begun. The bottom line is that when real labor starts, your partner will probably know it. (This may sound strange, especially if she is carrying her first child. Nevertheless, the majority of mothers I've spoken to have told me it's true.) But until then, you—and she—may not be sure whether the contractions and other things she's feeling are the real thing or not. So before you go rushing off to the hospital, take a few seconds to try to figure things out.

FALSE LABOR

♦ Contractions are not regular, or don't stay regular
♦ Contractions don't get stronger or more severe
♦ If your partner changes position (from sitting to walking, or from standing to lying down), the contractions usually stop altogether or change in frequency or intensity
♦ Generally, there is little or no vaginal discharge of any kind
♦ There may be additional pain in the abdomen

REAL LABOR

♦ Contractions are regular

♦ Contractions get stronger, longer, and closer together with time

♦ There may be some blood-tinged vaginal discharge

♦ Your partner's membranes may rupture (the famous "water" that "breaks" is really the amniotic fluid that the baby has been floating in throughout the pregnancy)

♦ There may be additional pain in the lower back

PLANES, TRAINS, AND AUTOMOBILES

It seems like half the births you see in the movies take place on the backseat of a speeding taxi, in a snowbound cave, in an airplane bathroom, or at the end of a bungee cord. While those sorts of images may sell movie tickets, the reality is that about 98 percent of babies are born in hospitals. (And most of the nonhospital births were *planned* that way.) Nevertheless, at some point, just about every pregnant couple—okay, it's really more of a guy thing—starts worrying about giving birth unexpectedly.

EMERGENCY BIRTHS

Emergency births fall into two general categories: either you have a lot of time before the actual birth (you're snowed in, trapped in your basement because of an earthquake, or shipwrecked, and you know you're not going to get to a hospital for a while), or you have little or no time before the birth (you're caught in traffic, you're parachuting to safety, or your partner's labor was extremely short). Either way, there's not a whole lot you can do to prepare.

Of course, your first step should be to call 911 (assuming that's even possible). If you have some time, try to make sure that your partner is in the most sheltered area of wherever you happen to be, and that she's comfortable, which, given her condition, is a relative term. If you have facilities available, get yourself some clean towels or sheets and boil a piece of string or a shoelace and a pair of scissors or a knife. Then, just sit tight and let nature take its course.

If you don't have time, try to stay cool. Handling a birth is not as difficult as you might think. Doctors who do it for a living, in fact, usually show up just a few minutes before the birth and are there primarily in case any complications arise. The truth is that most of the time babies pretty much deliver themselves when they're ready. The ones who seem to be in a hurry usually come out without any complications.

An Emergency Kit

It's extremely unlikely that your partner will give birth anywhere but in the hospital. However, if you want to make sure all the bases are covered, here's a list of supplies to keep at home, in the car, or anyplace else you and your partner are likely to be spending a lot of time during the last month or so of the pregnancy. Please keep in mind, though, that this list is for emergencies only. If you're planning a home birth, you'll need a lot more supplies.

◆ Chux pads (large, sterile pads) for absorbing blood, amniotic fluid, and so forth. They're available at medical supply stores. If you can't find any, newspapers are fine—don't worry, a little ink won't hurt anything.
◆ Non-latex gloves.
◆ A suction bulb, so you can Hoover out the baby's nose and mouth.
◆ A clamp for clamping off the umbilical cord. You can get these at any hospital supply store. If you can't find one, you can do the job with a clean string or shoelace.
◆ A plastic zipper bag to store the placenta.
◆ Clean scissors or knife for cutting the cord, if necessary (see page 235).
◆ Some towels to warm the baby and mother after the birth.

Whether you have time to prepare or not, once the baby starts to come, the procedure for performing a delivery is the same. And you'll know the process has started when:
◆ Your partner can't resist pushing.
◆ The baby's head—or any other body part—is visible.

For the rest of this chapter, we'll describe what you should do if there's no way to avoid delivering the baby yourself. The information isn't intended to replace the years of training your doctor or midwife has. So don't try this at home—unless you absolutely have to.

STEP ONE: PREPARATION.   Call for help if a phone is available. Try to keep your partner focused on the breathing and relaxation techniques. Put a pillow or some clothing under her buttocks in order to keep the baby's head and shoulders from hitting a hard surface.

STEP TWO: THE HEAD.   When the head begins to appear, don't pull on it. Instead, support it and let it come out by itself. If the umbilical cord is wrapped around the baby's neck, *slowly* and *gently* glide it over the head. Once the head is out, try to remove any mucus from the baby's nose and mouth (although the baby's passage through the birth canal is usually enough to do the trick).

STEP THREE: THE REST OF THE BODY.   Holding the baby's head, encourage your partner to push as the baby's shoulders appear. After the head has emerged, the rest of the baby's body should slide out pretty easily. Support the body as well as the head as it slides out. Despite what you may have seen or heard, you don't have to slap the baby's bottom to make him cry: he'll take care of that—and the associated breathing—all by himself. Of course, if he's blue or not breathing at all, you'll need to make use of those baby CPR skills you hopefully learned a month or two ago.

Place the baby on your partner's chest and encourage her to begin breastfeeding right away. (Breastfeeding makes the uterus contract, which helps expel the placenta and reduces the chances of excessive bleeding.) And don't worry—the umbilical cord is generally long enough to allow the baby to nurse while still attached. Dry the baby off immediately and cover mom and baby to keep them as warm as possible.

STEP FOUR: CUTTING THE CORD.   Using the clamp or the shoelace or piece of string you boiled a while ago, tie a tight knot around the cord three or four inches away from the baby. If you know you can get to a hospital within two hours, don't cut the cord yet. If you're not going to make it by then, tie a second tight knot in the cord about two inches farther away from the baby and cut the cord *between* the knots with your knife or scissors. Don't worry about the cord stump that's still attached to the baby: it will fall off by itself in a week or so.

STEP FIVE: THE PLACENTA.   Don't think your delivery job is over as soon as the baby's out. Anywhere from five minutes to half an hour after the baby is born the placenta will arrive. Do not pull on the cord to "help" things along; in most cases the placenta, which is surprisingly large and meaty (it kind of reminds me of a hefty chunk of liver), will slip out on its own with a soft "plop." When it does, wrap it up in something clean (or drop it into a plastic bag—but don't throw it away; your doctor will want to take a look at it as soon as possible).

Things to Remember During an Emergency Birth

♦ Call for help as soon as possible.

♦ Try to relax. Do everything carefully, thoughtfully, and slowly.

♦ Keep the area where the baby will be delivered as clean as possible.

♦ Baby CPR. If you haven't taken a baby CPR class already, you should really consider it—just in case.

After the placenta is out, gently massage your partner's lower abdomen every few minutes. This causes contractions, which limit blood loss and start the process of returning her uterus back to its original shape.

Notes:

Labor and Delivery

What's Going On with Your Partner

The entire labor process typically lasts twelve to twenty hours—toward the high end for first babies and the low end for subsequent ones—but there are no hard and fast rules. Labor is generally divided into three stages. The first stage consists of three phases.

STAGE 1

PHASE 1 (EARLY or LATENT LABOR) is the longest part of labor, lasting anywhere from a few hours to a few days (but the average is about eight hours). Fortunately, you'll be at home for most of it. At the beginning of this phase, your partner may not even be able to feel the contractions. Even if she can, she'll probably tell you that they're fairly manageable. Contractions will generally last thirty to sixty seconds and come as much as twenty minutes apart. Over the next few hours they'll gradually get longer (sixty to ninety seconds), stronger, and closer together (perhaps as little as five minutes apart).

Every woman will have a slightly different early labor experience. My wife, for example, had from six to twelve hours of fairly long, fairly regular (three to five minutes apart) contractions almost every day for a week before our second daughter was born. Your partner may have "bloody show" (a blood-tinged vaginal discharge), backaches, and diarrhea.

PHASE 2 (ACTIVE LABOR) is generally shorter—three to five hours—but far more intense than the first phase. It's likely to last as much as ten minutes longer if you're having a boy than if you're having a girl. If you aren't already there, it's time to head off to the hospital. In the early part of this phase, your partner will still be able to talk through the contractions. They'll keep getting closer together (two to three minutes apart), longer, and stronger. As this stage progresses she'll start feeling some real pain. The bloody show will increase and get redder, and your partner will become less and less chatty as she begins to focus on the contractions.

PHASE 3 (TRANSITION) usually lasts one or two hours. And once it starts, you can stop wondering why they call it "labor." Your partner's contractions may be almost relentless, lasting as long as ninety seconds. And with just two or three minutes from the beginning of one until the beginning of the next one, there's barely any time to recover in between. The pain is intense, and if your partner is going to ask for some drugs, this is probably when she'll do it. She's tired, sweating, her muscles may be so exhausted that they're trembling, and she may be vomiting.

STAGE 2 (PUSHING AND BIRTH)

This is by far the most intense part of the process—and fortunately for your partner, it lasts only about two hours ("only" being a term that's used by anyone who's not in labor. Your partner would probably prefer "for-friggin-ever"). Your partner's contractions are still long (more than sixty seconds) but are further apart. The difference is that during the contractions, she'll be overcome with a desire to push—similar to the feeling of having to make a bowel movement. She may feel some unpleasant pressure and stinging as the baby's head "crowns" (starts coming through the vagina), but this will be followed by a huge sense of relief when the baby finally pops out.

STAGE 3 (AFTER THE BIRTH)

Less than twenty minutes after the baby is born, the placenta will separate from the wall of the uterus. Your partner will continue to have contractions as her uterus tries to eject the placenta and stop the bleeding. See "The Placenta" on pages 249–51 for more.

What's Going On with You

Starting labor is no picnic, for her or for you. She, of course, is experiencing—or soon will be—a lot of physical pain. You, in the meantime, are very likely to feel a heavy dose of psychological pain.

I couldn't possibly count the number of times—only in my dreams, thankfully—I've heroically defended my home and family from armies of murderers and thieves. But even when I'm awake, I know I wouldn't hesitate before diving in front of a speeding car if it meant being able to save my wife or my children. And I know I would submit to the most painful ordeal to keep any one of them from suffering. This instinct perhaps explains the adrenaline rush you'll probably feel. A team of Scandinavian researchers took fathers' pulses during the birth of their children and found that they went from an average of 72 beats/minute to 115 beats/minute just before the birth. But helping your partner through labor is not the same as deciding to rescue a child from a burning building.

The most important thing to remember about this final stage of pregnancy is that the pain—yours and hers—is finite. After a while it ends, and you get to hold your new baby. Ironically, however, her pain will probably end sooner than yours. She'll be sore for a few weeks or so, but by the time the baby is six months old, your partner will hardly remember it. If women could remember the pain, I can't imagine that any of them would have more than one child. But for six months, a year, even two years after our first daughter was born, my wife's pain remained fresh in my mind. And when we began planning our second pregnancy, the thought of her having to go through even a remotely similar experience frightened me.

Staying Involved

Being There—Mentally and Physically

Despite your fears and worries, this is one time when your partner's needs—and they aren't all physical—come first. But before we get into how you can best help her through labor and delivery, it's important to get a firm idea of how to tell when she's actually gone into labor, and what stage she's in once she's there.

Checking Things Out When You're Checking In

Here's what Sarah McMoyler recommends to her students. "On the day you check into the hospital, take a few minutes to survey the room and the labor and delivery unit. You're going to be in that room for hours and hours, go ahead and open up the cabinets to see where they keep the washcloths, gowns, bath blankets, extra pillows. While you're at it, try to find out where the wheeled stool is (for you to sit on), the shower, the nurse call button, and the controls for the electronic bed. Most of the time the nurse will get these for you, but if she's also busy caring for other patients, understand that she may not be able to get them as quickly as you need them."

While you're getting the lay of the land, be sure to locate the ice chip maker, the snack bar, and the place where they keep those warmed-up blankets. And make a special point of introducing yourself to the nursing staff. Let them know about any special concerns your partner might have. Does she have any allergies? Did she have a bad pregnancy experience sometime in the past? Is she afraid of needles? And tell them about your goals—in particular, your desire to be as involved as possible—while also letting them know that you'd love their input and advice. This is a great time to ask questions. They really are on your side, and they know a ton about labor and delivery. The warmer your relationship with the medical team, the smoother the whole experience will go.

STAGE 1

PHASE 1 (EARLY OR LATENT LABOR)   Although the contractions are fairly mild at this point, you should do everything you can to make your partner as comfortable as possible (back rubs, massages, and so forth). Some women may tell you exactly what they want you to do; others may feel a little shy about making any demands. Either way, ask her regularly what you can do to help. And when she tells you, do it. If taking a walk makes her feel better, go with her. If doing headstands in the living room is what she wants to do (fairly unlikely at this point), go ahead and spot her. The easiest way to tell whether she's really in labor is to watch the contractions. If they're getting longer, stronger, and closer together, it's the real deal. If not, take it easy. You should be recording the contractions anyway, because when you call her practitioner to ask whether to come down to the hospital, he'll want to know what's been going on.

During early labor, it's okay for your partner to keep her strength up, so light eating—salads, soups, and so on—is fine. And drinking water during early labor is crucial. No matter what your partner does, *you* should eat and drink something. You need to keep your energy level up too, and you're not going to want to try to make a dash to the snack bar between contractions. Finally, try to get some rest. Don't be fooled by the adrenaline rush that will hit you when your partner finally goes into labor. You'll be so excited that you'll feel you can last forever. But you can't. She's got some hormones (and pain) to keep her going; you don't.

PHASE 2 (ACTIVE LABOR) One of the symptoms of second-phase labor is that your partner may seem to be losing interest in just about every-thing—including arguing with you about when to call the doctor. After my wife's contractions had been two to three minutes apart for a few hours, I was encouraging her to call. She refused. Many women, it seems, "just know" when it's time to go. So chances are, if she tells you "it's time," you should grab your car keys. That said, you're going to be in regular contact with your partner's practitioner, and if he or she thinks it's time to come in, that trumps your part-ner's desires to stay home.

One of the biggest hints as to whether your partner is in active labor is whether she can walk and talk through the contractions. If not, she most likely is. If you're still not sure whether the second phase has started, here's a pretty typical scenario that may help you decide:

YOU: Honey, these contractions have been going on like this for three hours. I think we should head off to the hospital.
HER: Okay.
YOU: Great. Let's get dressed, okay?
HER: I don't want to get dressed.
YOU: But you're only wearing a nightgown. How about at least putting on some shoes and socks?
HER: I don't want any shoes and socks.
YOU: But it's cold out there. How about a jacket?
HER: I don't want a jacket.

Get the point?

Another common symptom of second-phase labor is an uncharacteristic loss of modesty. Birth-class instructor Kim Kaehler says she can always tell

Helping Her Cope

Throughout labor and delivery, your focus should be on your partner. But because childbirth is such a female-intensive thing, a lot of guys don't really understand how important they are to the process. The reality is that you're absolutely indispensible. Yes, there are doctors and nurses and midwives running around all over the place, but your partner is really counting on you most of all to help get her through this. Your being there—and being actively involved—can make a big, big difference. Women whose partners are supportive during labor and delivery tend to have shorter labors and report experiencing less pain. They also have a more positive attitude toward motherhood.

Here are a number of ways you can help your partner cope throughout the labor and delivery. Some of these are drawn from *The Best Birth*, which I wrote with a wonderful childbirth educator named Sarah McMoyler (a bit more about Sarah's approach—called the McMoyler method—can be found on page 184).

♦ **Remind her to slow her breathing down.** Just taking in long, deep breaths—inhale for five seconds, exhale for five seconds—can be very calming.

♦ **Encourage her to moan during the contractions and rest in between.** Screaming isn't very effective in coping with pain, and neither is the patterned breathing taught in many childbirth prep systems. Instead, go for low, growly, guttural sounds—deep and loud—the kind of sounds you'd make if you tried to lift a car. This is no time to be dainty or to worry about what the people in the next room—or on the next floor—will think. They're probably making plenty of noises of their own.

♦ **Help her relax.** People coping with pain often clench their jaws,

what stage of labor a woman is in just by looking at the sheet on the bed (when the pregnant woman is in it). If she's in phase one, she'll be covered up to her neck; in phase two, the sheet is halfway down; by phase three (see below), the sheet's all the way off.

Once active labor has started, your partner shouldn't eat anything unless her doctor specifically says that it's okay (she probably won't be allowed to eat anything after getting admitted to the hospital). If she ends up needing make fists, tense their shoulders, or hold their breath. None of this helps. In fact, it does more harm than good.

♦ **Get in her face and be direct.** (This may seem a little aggressive, but it really does work.) In early labor, lock eyes with her and tell her what to do: unclench your jaw, un-fist your hands, drop your shoulders, breeeeeeathe.... As labor progresses, skip the words and just show her what you want her to do by letting your body melt, unclenching, and moaning. Doing this is especially important *between* contractions. Staying tense—or tensing up in anticipation of the next uterus-wrenching contraction—will make it harder for her to recover during those all-too-brief breaks.

♦ **Offer sips of water, ice chips, and cold compresses.**

♦ **Offer a massage.** Back, hands, feet, or whatever she'd like (if she wants anything at all). Sometimes, when massage is annoying, sustained counterpressure can be just the ticket. Ask her which helps more: high or low on the back, or closer to the tailbone.

♦ **Verbal anesthesia.** Tell her she's doing a great job—it means a lot more coming from you than from a nurse she doesn't know. Simple things like "Great job!" or "Stay with it" are remarkably effective.

♦ **Make sure she hits the bathroom at least once every hour.** If she's not peeing that often, she's not drinking enough.

♦ **Get her up and moving around.** Being upright, if at all possible, makes gravity kick in and help the baby descend. Walking around keeps her body in motion and maximizes the effect that *relaxin* (a hormone that does just that) can have on the pelvic joints. You may be able to do this during the contractions in early labor. But once she's deep into active labor, do it between contractions.

any medication or even a Cesarean, food in her stomach could complicate matters.

PHASE 3 (TRANSITION) Whenever laboring women are portrayed in TV shows, they almost always seem to be snapping at their husband or boyfriend, yelling things like "Don't touch me!" or "Leave me alone, you're the one who did this to me." I think I'd internalized those stereotypes, and by the time

The Three Stages of Labor and Delivery

STAGE	WHAT'S HAPPENING	WHAT SHE'S FEELING
Stage 1/ Phase 1 (early labor)	• Her cervix is effacing (thinning out) and dilating (opening up) to about 3 centimeters • Her water may break	• She may be excited but not totally sure that "this is really it" • She may be anxious, restless, and wondering whether she'll remember anything from the childbirth prep class you took • She may not feel like doing much of anything • She may have diarrhea
Stage 1/ Phase 2 (active labor)	• She's increasingly uncomfortable • Her cervix continues to efface and will dilate to 7 or 8 centimeters • Her water may break (if it hasn't already) or may have to be broken	• She's getting serious and impatient about the pain • She's beginning to concentrate fully on the contractions and on the labor of labor • Bye-bye, sense of humor
Stage 1/ Phase 3 (transition)	• Her cervix is now fully dilated (if *not*, the baby may have to to descend a bit before she'll be allowed to push) • She may feel the urge to push • She may be nauseated, and may cry—from pain, fear, or both	• She may be confused, frustrated, and scared • She may announce that she can't take it anymore and is going home
Stage 2 (pushing and birth)	• Increase in bloody discharge • The baby is moving through the birth canal • Doctor may have to do an episiotomy	• She's feeling confident that she can finish the job • She may have gotten her second wind • She may be very worried that she'll poop while she's pushing. And there's a good chance she's right.
Stage 3 (after the birth)	• The placenta is separating from the wall of the uterus • Episiotomy or tearing (if any) will be repaired	• RELIEF • Euphoria • Talkative • Strong, heroic • Hungry, thirsty • Empty (of the baby) • Desire to cuddle with her baby (and her partner)

- Reassure her
- Tell jokes, take a walk, go out for your last romantic pre-baby dinner, or rent a movie—anything to distract her
- Keep her hydrated—and make sure she hits the bathroom regularly
- Record the contractions—how long they last and how often they come
- If it's nighttime, encourage her to try to sleep; active labor will wake her up, but any rest she can get now will really pay off later on
- While she's napping, double check that your bags are packed, that you've got your phone, and that you've made arrangements for someone to feed the dog until you get home

- Call the doctor before you leave to make sure it's okay to head out to the hospital
- Don't bother with conversation. She's not going to be able to keep up her end. So keep communication short and to the point.
- Reassure and encourage her
- Help her take one contraction at a time
- Feed her ice chips
- Praise her for her progress
- Massage, massage, massage

- Do whatever she wants you to do
- Try to help her resist pushing until the doctor tells her she should
- Mop her brow with a wet cloth
- Feed her ice chips
- Massage her (if she wants it)

- Continue to reassure and comfort her
- Encourage her to push when she's supposed to and tell her how great she's doing
- Encourage her to watch the baby come out (if she wants to and if there's a mirror around)
- Let the professionals do their job

- Praise her
- Put the baby on her stomach
- Encourage her to relax
- Encourage her to start nursing the baby, if she feels ready
- Bond with her and the baby

we got to the hospital I was really afraid that my wife would behave the same way when she got to the transition stage, blame me for the pain, and push me away. Fortunately, it never happened. The closest we ever came was when my wife was in labor with our second daughter. The only place she could be comfortable was in the shower, and for a while I was in there with her, trying to talk her through the contractions as I massaged her aching back. Then she asked me to leave the bathroom for a while. Sure, that stung a minute—I felt I should be there with her—but it was clear that she had no intention of hurting me.

Unfortunately, not every laboring woman manages to be as graceful under pressure. If your partner happens to say something nasty to you or throws you unceremoniously out of the room for a while, you need to imagine that while she's in labor her mind is being taken over by an angry rush-hour mob, all trying to push and shove their way onto an overcrowded subway train. Quite often, the pain she's experiencing is so intense and overwhelming that the only way she can make it through the contractions is to concentrate completely on them. Something as simple and well-meaning as a word or a loving caress can be terribly distracting.

So what *can* you do? Whatever she wants. Fast. If she doesn't want you to touch her, don't insist. Offer to feed her some ice chips instead. If she wants you to get out of the room, go. But tell her that you'll be right outside in case she needs you. If the room is pitch black and she tells you it's too bright, agree with her and find something to turn off. If she wants to listen to the twenty-four-hour Elvis station, turn it on. But whatever you do, don't argue with her, don't try to reason with her, and above all, don't pout if she swears at you or calls you names. She really doesn't mean to, and the last thing she needs to deal with at this moment of crisis is your wounded pride.

STAGE 2: PUSHING

Up until the pushing stage, I thought I was completely prepared for dealing with my wife's labor and delivery. I was calm, and, despite my occasional feelings of inadequacy, I knew what to expect almost every step of the way. The hospital staff was supportive of my wanting to be with my wife through every contraction. But when the time came to start pushing, they changed. All of a sudden, they were in control. The doctor was called, extra nurses magically appeared, and the room began to fill up with equipment—a scale, a bassinet, a tray of sterilized medical instruments, a washbasin, diapers, towels. (We happened to be in a combination labor/birthing room; if, in the middle of pushing, you find yourself chasing after your wife, who's being rushed down the hall to a separate delivery room, don't be alarmed. It may feel like an emergency, but it probably isn't.)

The nurses told my wife what to do, how to do it, and when. All I could do was watch—and I must admit that at first I felt a little cheated. After all, *I* was the one who had been there right from the beginning. *My* baby was about to be born. But when the most important part finally arrived, it looked like I wasn't going to be anything more than a spectator. And unless you're a professional birthing coach or a trained labor and delivery nurse, chances are you're going to feel like a spectator, too.

As I watched the nurses do their stuff, I quickly realized that simply holding your partner's legs and saying, "Push, honey: that's great" isn't always enough. Recognizing a good, productive push, and, more important, being able to explain how to do one—"Raise your butt...lower your legs...keep your head back...curl up around your baby like a shrimp..."—are skills that come from years of experience.

But just because you *feel* like a spectator doesn't mean you actually have to be one. Your partner needs you to be there, to support her, to encourage her—not in another corner of the room or hiding behind a camera, but right there with her. If you back away at this critical time, she may feel abandoned—even though she's surrounded by professionals. So let the medical team take the lead, but hang in there and ask them how you can be involved (ideally this was a question you should have asked when you first got to the hospital. See "Checking Things Out When You're Checking In" on page 240 for more).

STAGE 2: BIRTH

Intellectually, I knew my wife was pregnant. I'd been to all the appointments and I'd heard the heartbeat, seen the ultrasound, and felt the baby kicking. Still, there was something intangible about the whole process. And it wasn't until our baby started "crowning" (peeking her hairy little head out of my wife's vagina) that all the pieces finally came together.

At just about the same moment, I also realized that there was one major advantage to my having been displaced during the pushing stage: I had both hands free to "catch" the baby as she came out—and believe me, holding my daughter's hot, slimy, bloody little body and placing her gently at my wife's breast was easily the highlight of the whole occasion.

If you think you might want to do this, make sure you've worked out the choreography with your doctor and the nurses before the baby starts crowning. (See "Birth Plans" on pages 197–202 for more information.)

Your partner, unfortunately, is in the worst possible position to see the baby being born. Most hospitals, however, have tried to remedy this situation by making mirrors available. Still, many women are concentrating so hard on the pushing that they may not be interested in looking in the mirror.

If you were expecting your newborn to look like the Gerber baby, you may be in for a bit of a shock. Babies are generally born covered with a whitish coating called vernix. They're sometimes blue and frequently covered with blood and mucus. Their eyes may be puffy, their genitals swollen, and their backs and shoulders may be covered with fine hair. In addition, the trip through the birth canal has probably left your baby with a cone-shaped head. All in all, it's the most beautiful sight in the world.

After the Birth

THE BABY

Your baby's first few minutes outside the womb are a time of intense physical and emotional release for you and your partner. At long last, you get to meet the unique little person you created together. Your partner may want to try nursing the baby (although most newborns aren't hungry for the first twelve hours or so), and you will probably want to stroke his or her brand-new skin and marvel at his or her tiny fingernails. But depending on the hospital, the conditions of the birth, and whether or not you've been perfectly clear about your desires, your baby's first few minutes could be spent being poked and prodded by doctors and nurses instead of being held and cuddled by you.

One minute after birth, your baby will be given an APGAR test to allow the medical staff a quick take on your baby's overall condition. Created in 1953 by Dr. Virginia Apgar, the test measures your baby's Appearance (skin color), Pulse, Grimace (reflexes), Activity, and Respiration. A nurse or midwife will score each category on a scale of 0 to 2. (A bluish or pale baby might get a 0 for color while a very pink one would get 2; a baby who's breathing irregularly or shallowly might get a 0 for respiration while one who's breathing well, or crying loudly, would get a 2.) Most babies score in the 7 to 9 range (just on principle, almost no one gets a 10—unless it's the child of someone the medical team knows). The test will be repeated at five minutes after birth.

Shortly after the birth, your baby will need to be weighed, measured, given an ID bracelet, bathed, diapered, footprinted, and wrapped in a blanket. Some hospitals also photograph each newborn. After that, most hospitals (frequently as required by law) apply silver nitrate drops or an antibiotic ointment to your

Seeing the Baby

Some hospitals have very rigid rules regarding parent/infant contact—feeding may be highly regulated and the hours you can visit your child may be limited. Others are more flexible. The hospitals where all three of my children were born no longer have a nursery (except for babies with serious health problems). Healthy babies are expected to stay in the mother's room for their entire hospital stay. There are even hospitals that permit the new father to spend the night with mom and baby. Check with the staff of your hospital to find out their policy.

baby's eyes as a protection against gonorrhea. Although these procedures should be done within one hour of birth, ask the staff if they can hold off for a few minutes while you and your partner get acquainted with your baby.

If, however, your baby was delivered by C-section, or if there were any other complications, the baby will be rushed off to have his or her little lungs suctioned before returning for the rest of the cleanup routine (see pages 263–65 for more on this).

THE PLACENTA

Before our first child was born it had simply never occurred to me (or to my wife, for that matter) that labor and delivery wouldn't end when the baby was born. While you and your partner are admiring your new family member, the placenta—which has been your baby's life support system for the past five months or so—still must be delivered. Your partner may continue to have mild contractions for anywhere from five minutes to about an hour until this happens. The strange thing about this stage of the delivery is that neither you nor your partner will probably even know it's happening—you'll be much too involved with your new baby.

Once the placenta is out, however, you need to decide what to do with it. In this country most people never even see it, and those who do just leave it at the hospital, where it will either be destroyed or, more likely, sold to a cosmetics company (there are actually a surprising number of placenta-based beauty products). But in many other cultures, the placenta is considered to have a permanent, almost magical bond with the child it nourished in the womb, and disposal is handled with a great deal more reverence. In fact, most cultures that have placenta rituals believe that if it is not properly buried, the child—or the parents, or even the entire village—will suffer some terrible consequences.

In rural Peru, for example, immediately after the birth of a child, the father is required to go to a far-off location and bury the placenta deep enough so that no animals or people will accidentally discover it. Otherwise, the placenta may become "jealous" of the attention paid to the baby and may take revenge by causing an epidemic.

In some South American Indian cultures, people believe that a child's life can be influenced by objects that are buried with its placenta. According to researcher J. R. Davidson, parents in the Qolla tribe "bury miniature implements copied after the ones used in adult life with the placenta, in the hopes of assuring that the infant will be a good worker. Boys' placentas are frequently buried with a shovel or a pick, and girls' are buried with a loom or a hoe." In the Philippines some mothers bury the placenta with books as a way of ensuring intelligence.

But placentas are not always buried. In ancient Egypt, pharaohs' placentas were wrapped in special containers to keep them from harm. And a wealthy Inca in Ecuador built a solid-gold statue of his mother—complete with his placenta in "her" womb.

Even today, the people of many cultures believe that placentas have special powers. A lot of women—including many in the United States—believe that *placentophagy* (ingesting cooked or dried placenta) can reduce or eliminate postpartum depression. In other parts of Peru placentas are burned, the ashes are mixed with water, and the mixture is then drunk by the babies as a remedy for a variety of childhood illnesses. Traditional Vietnamese medicine uses placentas to combat sterility and senility, and in India, touching a placenta is supposed to help a childless woman conceive a healthy baby of her own. In China, some believe that breastfeeding mothers can improve the quality of their milk by drinking a broth made of boiled placenta, or speed up labor by eating a piece of it dried.

This sort of placenta usage isn't limited to non-Western cultures. In medieval Europe, if a child was born with a caul (with the amniotic membranes over his head), the placenta would be saved, dried, and fed to the child on his tenth birthday. If it wasn't done, it was believed that the child might become a vampire after death.

Whatever you and your partner decide to do, it's probably best to keep it a secret—at least from the hospital staff. Some states try to regulate what you can do with a placenta and may even prohibit you from taking it home (although if you really want to, you can probably find a sympathetic nurse who will pack it up for you). We deliberately left our first daughter's placenta at the hospital. But we stored the second one's in our freezer for a year before burying it, along with the placentas of some of our friends' children, and planting an apple tree above them. Twelve years later, at her bat mitzvah, we ate some of the apples from that tree. And yes, they tasted perfectly fine.

Dealing with Contingencies

Unfortunately, not all labors and deliveries proceed exactly as planned. In fact, most don't. The American Association of Obstetricians and Gynecologists estimates that more than 30 percent of babies are born by Cesarean section. And well over half of mothers who deliver vaginally are medicated in some way. As with so many other aspects of your pregnancy experience, having good, clear information about what's really going on and what the options are during labor and delivery will help you make informed, intelligent decisions about how to handle the unexpected or the unplanned. The key to getting the information you need is to ask questions—and to keep on asking until you're completely satisfied. Find out about the risks, the benefits, and the effects on your partner, as well as on the baby. The only exception to this rule is when there's a clear medical emergency. In that case, save your questions for later.

Here are a few of the contingencies that can come up during the birth and how they might affect you, your partner, and the baby.

PAIN

If you've taken a traditional Lamaze or Bradley childbirth class or read many pregnancy books (and even if you haven't), you and your partner may be planning to have a "natural" (medication-free) childbirth. Unfortunately, natural childbirth often sounds better—and less painful—than it actually turns out to be. According to Marci Lobel, Ph.D., director of the Stony Brook Pregnancy Project at Stony Brook University, "Popular books written for pregnant women often understate the degree of pain experienced during birth, and may overstate the effectiveness of childbirth preparation in reducing pain." And think about all those childbirth images you've seen in movies and on TV. The pain looks unbearable, but it never lasts any more than a few minutes.

Because your partner is the one who is experiencing the physical pain, defer to her judgment when considering ways to manage it. This doesn't mean, however, that you don't have anything to say about the issue. As labor progresses, your partner will become less rational and less able to make big decisions. So

Whew! That's a Relief

There is, as Sarah McMoyler puts it, "a big difference between coping and suffering." Despite all the emphasis on natural (unmedicated) childbirth these days, more and more women seem to be opting for some kind of chemical pain relief during labor and childbirth. Actually, there's evidence that women have been searching for alternatives to natural birth ever since they were first introduced in the 1840s, says obstetric anesthesiologist Donald Caton, author of *What a Blessing She Had Chloroform: The Medical and Social Response to the Pain of Childbirth from 1800 to the Present.*

Women today have literally dozens of options that fall into to two basic categories: *regionals*, which reduce or eliminate pain only in certain parts of her body, and *systemics*, which will relax her whole body.

REGIONALS

These medications work only on specific regions of the body, hence the name. The most common of all regionals (and of all childbirth-related pain medication, for that matter) is the epidural, which is usually administered during active labor (the second phase of the first stage), when the pain is greatest. Your partner will have to lean over or curl up on her side while an anesthesiologist numbs her lower back; inserts a medication-carrying catheter into the "epidural space" that's just outside the spinal cord, between it and the membrane that surrounds it; and tapes it to her back.

Epidurals are widely considered the safest and most effective labor painkiller available. They kick in almost immediately and will block the pain of your partner's contractions while still leaving her awake and alert. Perhaps most important, they don't "cross the placenta" (affect the baby).

Until just a few years ago, epidurals carried the risk of decreasing maternal blood pressure or reducing the woman's ability to feel when to push (which could slow down the course of labor), as well as causing headaches and nausea. And a lot of people thought that epidurals increased the risk of a Cesarean or instrument birth. But as of recent years, anesthesiologists are better able to fine-tune the dose, all but eliminating these risks. A growing body of research shows that women who have epidurals aren't any more likely to have a C-section or instrument birth; better yet, epidurals may actually move labor along more quickly. By blocking the pain, the woman can get a well-deserved break (sometimes even a nap), so when it's time to push, she'll be refreshed and strong.

Another problem with epidurals used to be that, since they numb the lower body, women were confined to their beds for the duration. But a new "walking epidural" is being introduced that will offer the same pain relief and allow at least some mobility, so ask your partner's practitioner whether it's available at your hospital.

While you're asking about the latest innovations, find out whether PCEA (patient-controlled epidural anesthesia) is a possibility. The way it works is that the anesthesiologist gets the epidural up and running and then allows the patient to adjust the amount of medication she gets (within reason). As with any kind of patient-controlled medication, patients don't use nearly as much as a doctor would have given them. Seems that just knowing relief is a button-push away decreases the need.

Other less-common regional options include the pudendal block (an injection given into each side of the vagina that deadens the vaginal opening), the paracervical block (an injection into the area around the cervix that relieves pain from dilation and contractions), the spinal block (injections into the fluid around the spinal cord in the lower back—it's similar to an epidural but doesn't last as long and carries a slightly greater risk of complications).

SYSTEMICS

This type of whole-body pain relief includes sedatives, tranquilizers, and narcotics such as Demerol and fentanyl, which are usually given as injections or added to existing intravenous (IV) lines. It also includes general anesthesia, which knocks the recipient out completely and is rarely used, except when performing an emergency Cesarean.

Besides taking the edge off the contractions almost immediately, one of the major advantages to systemic medications is that your partner can use them from the very beginning of labor. They may relieve a lot of her anxiety and won't usually have much of an impact on her ability to push or sense her contractions.

On the downside, though, these medications affect your partner's entire body and can cause a wide variety of side effects, including drowsiness, dizziness, and nausea. In some ways, these drugs do less to remove the pain than to make your partner simply stop caring about it. Even worse, since they go right into your partner's bloodstream, they also "cross the placenta," meaning that at birth, the baby could be drowsy, unable to suck properly for a short while, or, in rare cases, unable to breathe without assistance. Fortunately, those symptoms go away pretty quickly on their own. There's also a drug, Narcan, that can reverse these side effects.

Interestingly, your partner's use—or nonuse—of pain medication may have an impact on you as well. For most expectant dads, anything that makes our partners more comfortable and hurt less is great. But besides that, medication can also reduce the stress and make the whole experience more pleasant for us. In a study of how a laboring woman's use of epidurals affects her partner, Italian researchers Giorgio Capogna and Michela Camorcia found that "fathers whose partners did not receive epidural analgesia felt their presence as troublesome and unnecessary." On the other hand, when the mom did have an epidural, fathers' feelings of helpfulness were tripled. They were also more involved during the labor and felt less anxiety and stress.

For other guys, though, reducing her pain may be a source of disappointment—in a twisted, yet understandable, sort of way. We're supposed to be there to help her through the pain, the thinking goes, but if she doesn't need us to do that, maybe she doesn't need us at all. In other words, reducing the pain may also reduce the father's sense of usefulness and importance. A word of advice: if your partner wants some pain medication, support her. There are plenty of other ways to be helpful.

it's up to you to be her advocate, to make sure she has the kind of birth she wants (or at least as close to it as you can get). That's why I strongly suggest that the two of you have some thorough discussions about her attitude toward medication *before* she goes into labor, so you know whether she'd want you to suggest it when you get concerned or wait until she requests it. You might also want to come up with a code word that means "I really want drugs NOW." Some women may scream for the doctor (or you) to "do something about the pain" but not really want drugs.

If you do end up having a discussion about medication sometime *during* labor, make sure you do it in the most supportive possible way. It's painful to have to watch the one you love suffer, but starting an argument when she's in the middle of a contraction isn't a smart idea (and you're not going to resolve anything anyway). Despite the fact that most women get some kind of chemical pain relief, many women feel that taking medication is a sign of weakness, or that they've failed—as women and as mothers. It's as if having an unmedicated childbirth is part of the transition to womanhood. In addition, some childbirth preparation methods view medication as the first step along a path that ultimately leads to Cesarean section. Neither of these scenarios is, by any stretch of the imagination, the rule. If you check into the hospital with a pregnant partner, and leave a few days later with a no-longer-pregnant partner and a healthy baby, you win. It shouldn't matter at all how it happened, as long as it was medically necessary (and it almost always is).

I'm not suggesting that your partner should use—or that she'll even need—pain medication. But whatever you do, knowing a little about your options is always a good idea (see "Whew! That's a Relief" on pages 252–54).

EXHAUSTION

Pain isn't the only reason your partner might need some chemical intervention. In some cases, labor is progressing so slowly (or has been stalled for so long) that your practitioner may become concerned that your partner will be too exhausted by the time she needs to push. This was exactly what happened during the birth of my middle daughter. After twenty hours of labor and only four centimeters of dilation, our doctor suggested pitocin (a drug that stimulates contractions) together with an epidural (see pages 252–53). This chemical cocktail removed the pain of labor while allowing my wife's cervix to dilate fully and quickly. I'm convinced that this approach actually prevented a C-section by allowing my wife a well-deserved breather before she started pushing.

INDUCED LABOR

Any time after forty weeks of pregnancy, your baby is officially fully baked. They don't always get this piece of news, though, and are sometimes reluctant to come out. There are all sorts of supposedly surefire ways to bring on labor, and you'll start hearing every one of them as soon as you mention that the baby is late: eat certain kinds of salad dressings or vinegars, eat spicy food, go on long walks, drink cod-liver oil, and more. There is actually some research suggesting that sex may help: nipple stimulation and your partner's orgasm may trigger some contractions, plus semen has prostaglandin in it, which is similar to the gel or pill that's used to induce labor. And, as Lissa Rankin puts it, "Messing around with the cervix can trigger contractions and get things started." But before you try any kind of home remedy, check with your practitioner to make sure it's safe.

If your partner's due date is long past, your practitioner may decide that things have gone on long enough (this will happen about two months after your partner reached the same conclusion), and he'll suggest jump-starting the labor with pitocin (a chemical version of oxytocin) or Cytotec (a type of prostaglandin). Some people claim that pitocin results in more painful labors and increases the Cesarean rate, but just as many disagree, saying that all pitocin does is produce normal labor.

Other Common Birth Contingencies

FORCEPS OR VACUUM

If your partner's cervix is completely dilated and she's been pushing for a while, but the baby refuses to budge, her practitioner may suggest using forceps—long tongs with scoops on the end (imagine salad tongs that are big enough to pick up a coconut)—to help things along. It used to be that the very word *forceps* struck fear into every expectant parent's heart. But today they're used only to gently grasp the baby's head to guide it through the birth canal. Some forceps deliveries will leave the baby with bruises in the temple or jawline area for a few days or a week. In very rare instances, permanent scarring or other damage can occur. In addition, your partner will need additional medication and may require a larger-than-normal episiotomy (see below).

In some cases, instead of forceps, doctors may be able to use a vacuum-type suction device that attaches to the top of the baby's head, to move the baby around in the same way.

The doctor may also suggest using forceps or vacuum if the baby is in distress and a vaginal birth needs to be sped up, or if your partner is too exhausted (or medicated) to push effectively. Keep in mind that most OB/GYNs are trained in either forceps or vacuum extraction, not both. Used appropriately, forceps and/or suction can sometimes prevent the need for a C-section.

EPISIOTOMY

An episiotomy involves making a small cut in the perineum (the area between the vagina and the anus) to enlarge the vaginal opening and allow for easier passage of the baby's head. Only a decade or so ago, the episiotomy rate for women delivering for the first time under an obstetrician's care was 70 to 90 percent. The thought was that a controlled cut would help women avoid bowel, urinary, and sexual problems after delivery. But recent research has shown that episiotomy may actually increase the risk of those problems. Today, the episiotomy rate is under 20 percent. Overall, about 70 percent of first-time moms will have a small, spontaneous tear. The phrase "spontaneous tear" sounds absolutely frightening to me, but it turns out that with an episiotomy, the flesh can tear even more. So as contradictory as it might seem, those tears are preferable (and less painful) than a routine episiotomy. But the procedure may be legitimately indicated if:

♦ The baby is extremely large, and squeezing through the vagina might harm the baby or your partner.
♦ Forceps are used.
♦ The baby is breech (see below).
♦ The practitioner can see that numerous tears are going to happen.

BREECH PRESENTATION

If a baby is breech it means that the head is up and the butt or feet are pointing down (only 3 to 4 percent of single babies are born this way, but about a third of all twins are). Actually, there are several different types of breech births: frank breech means that the baby's feet are straight up next to his head and the baby will come out butt first. Complete breech means that the butt is down and the baby is "sitting" cross-legged. Footling breech means that one or both feet are pointing down. There's little you can do to prevent your baby from getting into any position he or she wants to. But most doctors in the United States will not deliver breech babies vaginally. This means that if the baby can't be turned, usually through a nonsurgical process called "external version," it's going to be delivered by C-section.

ELECTRONIC FETAL MONITORING (EFM)

EFMs have been around since the early 1970s, and today, they're used in 85 percent of births. They come in two flavors: external and internal.

The external variety is a rather complicated machine—complete with graphs, digital outputs, and high-tech beeping—that gets strapped to your partner's abdomen. It's used to monitor your baby's heartbeat and your partner's contractions.

Fetal monitors are really pretty cool. Properly hooked up, they are so accurate that by watching the digital display, you'll be able to tell when your partner's contractions are starting—even before *she* feels them—and if she has an IUPC (intrauterine pressure catheter, which is a tube that lies next to the baby and measures contraction strength), you'll actually be able to tell how intense they'll be. In one fascinating study, researchers Kristi Williams and Debra Umberson found that most expectant fathers like fetal monitors—partly because by getting information we feel like we're really involved. "By observing and communicating the changing intensity of the contractions, these men believed that they were able to provide valuable information to their wives," they wrote. "This creates a role for husbands to play in labor and delivery that is, from their perspective, more important than merely providing support and encouragement."

Notice the use of the phrases "these men believed" and "from their perspective." Williams and Umberson also found that women often perceived the monitors as a nuisance and the information they provided not particularly helpful. After all, they're getting the same information anyway, but in a slightly different way: it hurts like hell. And the monitors don't always reflect reality. The contraction may look like it's over on the screen, but it can be far from over for her.

So be careful. These monitors may help you guide your partner through the contraction. But think long and hard before saying something like "Ready, honey? Here it comes—looks like a big one" (unfortunately, I know whereof I speak).

In many hospitals, laboring women are routinely hooked up to external fetal monitors as soon as they check in. The nurses will take readings for half an hour or so and, assuming all is well with Mom and baby, they'll take the monitor off and just hook it back up every hour during labor. If, however, she has an epidural or is on pitocin, she'll need continuous monitoring. Ditto when it comes time to push.

Internal fetal monitors come in two varieties: an electrode attached to the baby's scalp, and the IUPC mentioned above. If your practitioner feels that it's important to keep closer tabs on the baby's heart rate, your partner will get one or both of these internal monitors.

Unless there's some compelling reason why you need it (if there have been signs of fetal distress, for example), you and your partner will be a lot better off with as little monitoring as possible. Here's why:

♦ There's too much room for misinterpreting the results. One study had four doctors interpret fifty different tracings. The four concurred only 22 percent of the time. Worse yet, two months later, when the same docs were asked to evaluate the same tracings, they interpreted more than 20 percent of them differently.

♦ It can scare the hell out of you. When my wife was hooked up to a fetal monitor during her first labor, we were comforted by the sound of the baby's steady, 140-beats-per-minute heartbeat. But at one point the heart rate dropped to 120, then 100, then 80, then 60. Nothing was wrong—the doctor was just trying to change the baby's position—but hearing her little heart slow down that much nearly gave my wife and me heart attacks. If your partner's practitioner believes that monitoring is medically necessary, turn the volume down (better yet, all the way off).

♦ Fetal monitoring was originally implemented in the hope that it would prevent cerebral palsy. But despite the very best of intentions, it has led to an increase in C-sections and instrument deliveries. And, ironically, it didn't do anything for cerebral palsy either—the rate has stayed the same for the past fifty years. The moral of the story is that the doctor might see something happen to the baby on the monitor, get worried, and operate. In a lot of cases, what looks like fetal distress on the tracing (the printout generated by the monitor) ends up going away on its own.

Notes:

Cesarean Section

All things being equal, most parents would prefer to bring their babies into the world "normally." And most of the time that's what happens. But childbirth is one of those uncontrollable, unpredictable events, and things don't always go exactly the way they're supposed to. In the United States, in fact, more than 30 percent of all children born in hospitals are delivered by C-section.

What's Going On with Your Partner

Most childbirth preparation classes (see pages 176–84) put a great deal of emphasis on natural, unmedicated deliveries. As we discussed earlier, many women, therefore, feel a tremendous amount of pressure to deliver vaginally and may actually consider themselves "failures" if they don't—especially after they've invested many hours in a painful labor.

In addition, recovering from a Cesarean is much different from recovering from a vaginal birth (see pages 265–67 for more details). My wife (and I) spent three nights in the hospital after the C-section delivery of our first daughter. But after our second daughter was born (vaginally), we remained in the hospital for only five hours. (We rushed it a little; most people stay twenty-four to forty-eight hours after a vaginal birth, but my wife really wanted to leave.)

What's Going On with You

Your take on the C-section is undoubtedly going to be quite different from your partner's. Researcher Katharyn May found that only 8 percent of men whose partners delivered by C-section objected to the operation; 92 percent were "greatly relieved." Although I didn't participate in this study, it accurately reflects my own experience. It simply had never occurred to me that we might somehow have "failed." On the contrary, I remember feeling incredibly thankful that my wife's suffering would finally end. And seeing how quickly and painlessly the baby was delivered made me wonder why we hadn't done it sooner.

Despite the relief a father may feel on his partner's behalf, a C-section can be a trying experience for him. As a rule, he's separated from his wife while she is being prepped for surgery, and usually isn't given any information about what's happening. I remember being left in the hall outside the operating room, trying to keep an eye on my wife through a tiny window. Besides being terribly scared, I felt completely helpless—and useless—as the doctors, nurses, and assistants scurried around, blocking my view, getting dressed, washing, opening packages of scalpels, tubes, and who knows what else. Only one person—the pediatrician who ended up attending the delivery—took a minute to pat me on the shoulder and tell me that everything would be all right. I've never felt more grateful to another person in my life.

When I was finally permitted into the operating room, I was told—no discussion allowed—to sit by my wife's head. There was a curtain across her chest that prevented me from seeing what the surgeons were doing. I was ready to put some gloves on and help out with the operation, but whenever I stood up to get a better view, the anesthesiologist shoved me back down into my seat. I was too exhausted to argue, but a friend of mine whose partner had a C-section in the same hospital a few years later did argue and was able to go around to the "business end" of the operation.

(I've heard from several OBs that part of the reason they often try to keep dads up by the mom's head is that if there's ever a time when dads pass out, this is it. And the anesthesiologists simply don't want to have to deal with two patients at the same time. As OB Lissa Rankin puts it, "It's not personal. I'm happy to have dads at the business end, but they sometimes end up on the floor.")

Common Medical Reasons for a Cesarean Section

♦ **The mother's pelvis is too small to allow the baby's head to pass through the birth canal** (although there's no way to tell whether this is true until she tries to deliver vaginally).

♦ **Failure of the labor to progress.** Exhausted by an excessively long labor, the mother is unable to push the baby out, or the cervix stops opening after active labor has begun.

♦ **The baby is distressed in some way.** Her heartbeat has dropped too far, the heartbeat pattern is worrisome, or there are other problems.

♦ **You're about to have more than one baby.**

♦ **Your partner has a medical condition that puts her at risk,** including a heart condition, diabetes, high blood pressure, or an active case of genital herpes.

♦ **Placenta problems.** *Abrupto placenta* (separation of the placenta from the uterine wall before labor begins) causes bleeding and can threaten the lives of both mother and baby. *Placenta previa* (the placenta is fully or partially blocking the opening of the cervix) causes hemorrhaging and prevents the baby from leaving the uterus.

♦ **Position of the baby.** Under certain circumstances, if the baby is breech (coming out butt or feetfirst) or transverse (lying sideways instead of head down), a C-section is more likely.

♦ **Previous C-section birth(s).** Until the 1980s, the prevailing wisdom was, "once a C-section, always a C-section." Then, in response to an increasing C-section rate, many OB/GYNs proposed VBAC (vaginal birth after Cesarean) as a way of reducing that rate. The VBAC rate increased steadily until the '90s. But as more women opted for VBAC,

Staying Involved

My friend and I may be among the lucky ones; in some hospitals men aren't allowed into the operating room at all. Others permit them in only if they've taken a special C-section class (which most people wouldn't do unless they were planning for one). Hopefully, even before you check in, you and your partner will have already told your OB exactly what your preferences are should there be a C-section, and you'll be familiar with any relevant hospital policies. (See pages 24–25 for other things to discuss with your OB.)

the number of cases of uterine rupture increased (percentage-wise, the risk was still very low). Still, just to be safe, many OBs started recommending against VBAC, and the rate has dropped by almost 70 percent over just the past ten years. Some hospitals have banned them entirely. If your partner has had a C-section with a previous birth, ask her practitioner to explain the risks and benefits of VBAC and a scheduled, repeat C-section, and make the decision that's best for your growing family.

♦ **Your doctor thinks the baby is too big.** The American College of Obstetricians and Gynecologists defines "too big" as anything over 4,500 grams (about 9 pounds, 4 ounces). With babies this size there's an increased chance of *shoulder dystocia*—where the head delivers and then the shoulders get stuck. (This definition goes down to 4,000 grams/8½ pounds if mom is a diabetic.)

♦ **Your partner's age.** The older she is, the greater her chance of needing a C-section. Laurie Green, a San Francisco OB/GYN who delivered my youngest, puts it this way: "The uterus is a muscle, and like any other muscle, its strength decreases with age. A woman whose uterus struggles to force a baby out when she's 42, might very well have been able to deliver the same size baby with no problem when she was 22."

♦ **Suspected abnormality of the baby.** If the baby is expected to have a birth defect or other abnormality that might make vaginal delivery risky, the doctor might recommend a C-section, not just to minimize birth trauma but to make sure all the right specialists can be on hand to give your baby the best shot at thriving.

Don't forget that although a C-section is a fairly commonplace operation—American doctors do about 1.5 million every year—it's still major surgery. And after the operation, your partner will need some extra special care.

First of all, as strange as it may sound, after having a C-section your partner may feel terribly left out. She will probably have been fully awake during the operation and will be anxious to meet the new baby. But whereas after a vaginal birth the mother gets to see and touch the baby immediately, after a C-section the baby is usually quickly whisked away to have his or her lungs

Some of the Most Common Nonmedical Reasons for a Cesarean Section

As cynical as it sounds, sometimes C-sections aren't really necessary.

♦ **It's easier.** Some OBs consider C-sections safer than vaginal deliveries.

♦ **Demographics.** Although the national C-section rate is a bit over 30 percent, the actual number varies widely. In some states—Florida, New Jersey, Puerto Rico—the rate is over 35 percent; in others—New Mexico, Vermont, Alaska—it's under 25 percent. Married women and those with insurance are more likely to have a Cesarean than women without—34 percent vs. 25 percent. And women over 40 are about twice as likely as women under 25—50 percent vs. 25. High C-section rates aren't limited to the United States. In Thailand and Vietnam, for example, the rate is over 35 percent. In Paraguay and Ecuador, it's over 40; in China, it's close to 50; and in Brazil, where it's considered "low class" to give birth vaginally, it's 70 percent.

♦ **Your partner may just want one.** Picking the exact delivery date may enable a woman to have the baby at a time that's particularly convenient for her or her family. Then there's the "too posh to push" idea that's been driven by Hollywood. Quite a few celebrity moms have opted for a C-section because they're worried about the pain of a vaginal delivery, or the impact a natural birth could have on their

suctioned out. Sometimes the suctioning may happen even before the baby has been fully delivered. (Babies born vaginally have most of the amniotic fluid and other gunk in their lungs squeezed out on the way through the birth canal. But with C-section babies, it often has to be removed manually.)

You may get to make a "ceremonial" umbilical cord cut (the surgeons will have already cut the cord during the delivery). If the baby is being cared for right in the delivery room, make sure to tell your partner exactly what's happening—she'll want to know (although, depending on what the anesthesiologist used, she may be too drugged up to care very much). In some hospitals, C-section babies are removed from the delivery room immediately after the birth and taken straight to the nursery, where they're washed, examined, and put through basically the same procedures covered in the preceding chapter for vaginal birth babies. This whole process can take anywhere from a few minutes to a few hours.

sexual or urinary function. "Cesarean section prior to advanced labor is virtually 100 percent effective at eliminating these problems," writes OB and researcher Brent Bost. Dr. Bost has also found that "healthy women who undergo elective Cesarean section experience a relatively low rate of short-term complications. And long-term complications are rare." On the other hand, Sarah McMoyler says, "Consider the tradeoff: Several hours of pain—most of which can be eliminated with an epidural—vs. six weeks of not being able to go up and down the stairs, hold your baby without hurting, or drive." I guess if you have a chauffeur and servants that's not much of an issue.

♦ **Fear of lawsuits.** If something goes wrong with the birth—fetal or maternal distress, or even a birth defect that a lawyer might attribute to something that happened during delivery—the obstetrician is likely to be blamed for having let the labor go on too long. In some cases (but by no means all), OBs perform a C-section to minimize risk and speed things up.

♦ **Convenience.** Your partner may want a guarantee that a specific doctor will be available to do the delivery. You may plan a C-section to make sure you have child care lined up. Or your partner may have a personal or professional deadline she must meet. (In Lissa Rankin's case, she desperately wanted her father, who was dying of cancer, to meet his granddaughter.)

Although you might want to remain with your partner and comfort her immediately after the delivery, ask the doctor whether you can stay with your baby instead. It's bad enough for a newborn to be deprived of snuggling with one of his parents right away, but it would be worse if the baby couldn't be with either of you. Staying with our daughter also eased my paranoia that she might be switched in the nursery (a highly unlikely occurrence, given the rather elaborate security measures in place in most hospitals). But don't get too upset if the doctor says no—a lot of C-section babies are not medically stable at birth (not in danger, just requiring a little extra attention) and the medical staff won't want you hovering around, getting in the way.

Your Partner's Emotional Recovery

Having an unplanned C-section can trigger a whole host of conflicting emotions in your partner. She, like you, may feel greatly relieved that the pain

Facts to Remember about Recovery from a Cesarean Section

♦ Your partner's incision will be tender or downright painful for at least several days. Fortunately, she'll undoubtedly be receiving some intravenous (IV) pain medication.

♦ The nursing staff will visit quite frequently to make sure that your partner's uterus is getting firm and returning to its proper place, to see whether she's producing enough urine, and to check her bandages.

♦ Your partner will have an IV until her bowels start functioning again (usually within twenty-four hours after delivery). After the IV is removed, she'll start on a liquid diet, then add a few soft foods, and finally return to her normal diet (although some doctors will have their patients skip the liquid diet and go straight to real food—well, as real as hospital food can be).

♦ Your partner will need to get up and move around. Despite the fact that a C-section is major abdominal surgery, less than twenty-four hours after the delivery the nurses will probably encourage—and help—your partner to get out of bed and take a couple of rather painful-looking steps.

♦ The whole thing resembles a kindergarten art project. Besides stitches, your partner's incision may well be closed up with tape, glue, and/ or staples. Yes, staples. Until I heard the clink as the doctor dropped them into a jar, I'd just assumed that my wife had been sewn up. But staples may be on the way out. Pennsylvania OB/GYN Suzanne Basha recently found that women whose Cesarean incisions are closed with staples are four times more likely to have the wound reopen than those who had stitches.

is over and the baby is safe. At the same time, it's very natural for her to second-guess herself and the decisions she made, to start wondering whether there was anything she could have done to avoid the operation, or to believe she's failed because she didn't deliver vaginally. These feelings are especially common when the C-section was performed because labor "failed to progress" (meaning that the cervix wasn't dilating as quickly as the doctors may have thought it should, or stopped dilating altogether despite adequate contractions).

If you sense that your partner is experiencing any of these negative emotions, it's important for you to help her get past them. Some doctors believe that, left unchecked, these feelings can escalate and contribute to postpartum depression. She really needs to know that no one could have done more, or been stronger or braver than she was; that she didn't give in to the pain too soon; that she tried everything she could have to jump-start a stalled labor; that another few hours of labor wouldn't have done anyone any good; and that the decision she made (or at least agreed to) was the best one—both for the baby and for herself.

Some of these thoughts might seem obvious to you—so obvious that you might think they don't need to be said at all. But they do—especially by you. You were there with her, and you know better than anyone else exactly what she went through. So, being comforted and praised by you will mean a lot more to her than hearing the same words from a well-meaning relative, nurse, or even her own doctor. Having a baby isn't some kind of competition. As author Vicki Iovene writes, "It is not designed for your personal enjoyment and fulfillment. It is not an opportunity to demonstrate your abilities or fitness. It is designed to perpetuate the species and nothing more." Not the most romantic way of looking at having a baby, but quite accurate.

An Important Warning

Never, never, never suggest to your pregnant partner that she have a C-section—let your doctor make the first move. When my wife was pregnant with our second daughter, the pain she had been through during her first labor and delivery was still fresh in my mind. At one point I told her that I was really upset by the thought that she might have to endure another horrible labor, and I suggested that she consider a C-section.

I had no idea that someone could get so furious so quickly. Even though I had the very best intentions and was sincerely thinking only of her and how to minimize her pain, she thought I was being completely insensitive. Clearly, I had underestimated how incredibly important giving birth vaginally—especially after already having had one C-section—was to her.

Many of the men I've talked to have had similar thoughts about making the C-section suggestion to their partners. Most of them were wise enough not to act on their impulse. And hopefully, you won't either. Telling your partner how you're feeling and what you're going through is, in most cases, the right thing to do. But when it comes to C-sections, really and truly, it's an issue that's just too hot to handle.

One Final Thought

Whether C-section rates are too high or not is the subject of a lot of debate. But regardless of where you stand on the issue, Cesareans are here to stay. Noted OB/GYN and fertility specialist Elan Simckes believes that in a few hundred years, almost all babies will be born this way. Why? To start with, says Dr. Simckes, the human pelvis is shrinking over time. And thanks to a diet that consists more and more of sugar, carbs, and fat, babies are getting bigger. In 1965, the average baby born in the United States weighed about six and a half pounds. Today, it's almost eight pounds. Bigger baby + smaller pelvis = more Cesareans. It's inevitable.

Notes:

Gee Honey, Now What Do We Do?

What's Going On with Your Partner

Physically
- Vaginal discharge (called *lochia*) that will gradually change from bloody to pink to brown to yellow over the next six weeks or so
- Major discomfort if there is an episiotomy or C-section incision (the pain will disappear over the next six weeks)
- Constipation and hemorrhoids—hopefully not at the same time
- Breast discomfort starting about the third day after the birth (when her breasts become engorged with milk); if she's breastfeeding, her nipples may be sore for about two weeks
- Gradual weight loss
- Exhaustion—especially if her labor was long and difficult
- Continued contractions—especially while breastfeeding—but these will disappear over the next several days
- Hair loss (most women stop losing hair while they're pregnant, but when the pregnancy's over, so are all those great hair days)

Emotionally
- Relief that it's finally over
- Excitement, depression, or both (see pages 270–72)

- Worried about how she'll perform as a mother, and whether she'll be able to breastfeed (but over the next few weeks, her confidence will build and these worries should disappear)
- A deep need to get to know the baby
- Impatience at her lack of mobility
- An odd sense of grief or loss—at no longer being the center of attention, at the undeniable fact that, as everyone you've ever met has told you 18 million times, life will never be the same
- Decreased sex drive, assuming she had any left before the baby came anyway

Postpartum Blues and Depression

Anywhere from 50 to 80 percent of new mothers get what a lot of people call "baby blues"—periods of mild sadness, weepiness, mood swings, exhaustion or lack of energy, loss of appetite, difficulty concentrating or making decisions, irritability, or anxiety after the baby is born. (This shouldn't come as much of a surprise, when you think about the sleepless nights, lack of physical intimacy, worries about not being able to cope with her new responsibilities, and feelings of isolation that many new moms experience.) Many believe that the baby blues are caused by dramatic hormonal shifts in a new mother's body. Others say the cause is lack of sleep. Anthropologist Edward Hagen, however, believes that postpartum blues have little, if anything, to do with hormones. Instead, he says, it's connected to low levels of social support—especially from the father. And it could be the new mother's way of "negotiating" for more involvement.

Whatever the cause, the symptoms of baby blues won't really be severe enough to affect your partner's life too much. They typically start a day or two after the delivery, peak four or five days later, and in most cases, disappear on their own within a few weeks.

If you notice that your partner is experiencing any of these symptoms, be as supportive and involved as possible. Take on more of the child-care responsibilities, encourage her to rest if she can or to get out of the house for a while, do as much of the nighttime duty as you can without jeopardizing your career (that may mean doing a few nighttime feedings, which is great for daddy-baby bonding), and see to it that she's eating well. Again, most of this is completely normal and nothing to worry about. So be patient, and don't expect her to bounce back immediately. And don't demand that she "snap out of it."

For about 10 to 20 percent of new moms, postpartum blues can develop into postpartum depression, which is more serious. Symptoms include:

♦ Postpartum blues that don't go away after two weeks, or feelings of depression or anger that surface a month or two after the birth

♦ Feelings of sadness, doubt, guilt (that she's not loving every second of motherhood), helplessness, shame (if she didn't perform as she wanted to during the labor and delivery), or hopelessness that begin to disrupt your partner's normal functioning

♦ Inability to sleep when tired, or sleeping most of the time, even when the baby is awake

♦ Inability to take pleasure in activities she used to enjoy

♦ Marked changes in appetite

♦ Extreme concern and worry about—or lack of interest in—the baby and/or other members of the family

♦ Worries that she'll harm the baby or herself

Pay close attention to her behavior and her attitude. If you're really concerned—and since you know her better than anyone, you'll have a good sense of whether she's behaving abnormally or not—encourage your partner to talk with you about what she's feeling and to see her doctor or a therapist. If she doesn't want to go (and many women who have postpartum depression will deny that anything is wrong), take her yourself.

Sadly, a lot of moms who have postpartum depression don't get the assistance they need—they feel embarrassed to admit to anyone else what they're feeling. Untreated, these symptoms can last for years. In some cases antidepressants may be required.

You can play a major role in helping your wife get through her postpartum depression. Here are a few ways you can help:

♦ Remind her that the depression is not her fault, that you love her, that the baby loves her, that she's doing a great job, and that the two of you will get through this together.

♦ Also, do as much of the housework and child care as you can so she won't have to worry about not being able to get everything done herself.

♦ Encourage her to take breaks—regularly and frequently.

♦ Take over enough of the nighttime baby duties that your wife can get at least five hours of uninterrupted sleep.

♦ Get regular breaks to relieve your own stress. Yes, she's relying on you to help her, but if you're falling apart yourself, you can't be an effective caregiver.

A very, very important note. There's a good chance that you're going to be hearing stories about Andrea Yates, Deanna Laney, and other new mothers who killed their children. You'll also hear—usually from reporters or TV anchors who really should know better—that these women were suffering from postpartum depression. They absolutely were not. Women with postpartum depression do not harm their children. What Yates and the others had was *postpartum psychosis*—a condition that affects only one or two mothers in 1,000.

Symptoms usually start right after the birth and should be immediately recognizable by anyone. They include wild mood swings, hallucinations, being out of touch with reality, and making crazy or delirious statements. Postpartum psychosis is treatable—often with powerful antipsychotic drugs—but women who have it need help and they need it fast. Fortunately, despite the media hype, the majority of women with postpartum psychosis don't hurt their babies or anyone else.

What's Going On with the Baby

"Most people make babies out to be very complicated," says comedian Dave Barry. "But the truth is they have only three moods. Mood One: Just about to cry. Mood Two: Crying. Mood Three: Just finished crying. Your job, as a parent, is to keep the baby in Mood Three as much as possible." With just a few days of fatherhood under your belt, you may be inclined to go along with Barry's summary. But the truth is that babies' moods are a bit more subtle.

Babies actually have six clearly defined behavioral states that are apparent within just a few minutes after a baby is born. "By recognizing them and realizing when they occur and what the expected responses are in each," write Marshall and Phyllis Klaus, authors of *The Amazing Newborn*, "parents not only can get to know their infants but also can provide most sensitively for their needs."

In my first few weeks as a dad, I found that learning about these six states was a huge help in getting to know my daughter. Here's a summary of the six states, based on the Klauses' book.

Quiet Alert
Babies in the quiet alert state don't move very much—all their energy is focused on seeing and hearing. They can (and do) follow objects with their eyes and will even imitate your facial expressions.

Within the first hour of life, most infants have a period of quiet alertness that lasts an average of forty minutes. During his or her first week, the normal baby spends only about 10 percent of any twenty-four-hour period in this state. This is by far the coolest state, the time when your baby is most curious and is absorbing information about his or her new world. This is also the time when you and your baby will have your first few moments of connection, when you'll first become aware that there's a real person inside that tiny body.

Active Alert
In this state, the baby will make small sounds and move his or her arms, head, body, face, and eyes frequently and actively. The baby's movements usually come in short bursts—a few seconds of activity every minute or two. Some researchers say these movements are designed to give parents subtle clues about what the baby wants and needs. Others say these movements are simply interesting to watch, and therefore promote parent-infant interaction.

Crying
Crying is a perfectly natural—and for some, all-too-frequent—state (for more on this, see pages 304–8). The infant's eyes may be open or closed, the face red, and the arms and legs thrashing around.

Often, just picking up the baby and walking around with him or her will stop the crying. Interestingly, researchers used to think that babies were soothed because they liked being held upright. What really makes them stop crying, though, is actually the movement *toward* the upright position, or the repetitive rocking motion.

As unpleasant as it is sometimes, crying is not always a bad thing—it not only allows the baby to communicate but also provides valuable exercise. So if your efforts to calm him or her aren't immediately successful (and the baby isn't hungry or stewing in a dirty diaper), don't worry; chances are the tears will stop by themselves in a few minutes. See page 309 for more on how to handle crying.

Drowsiness
This is a transition state that occurs as the baby is waking up or falling asleep. He may move a little, but his eyes will often look dull or unfocused.

Leave the baby alone—let him drift off to sleep or move into one of the alert stages.

Quiet Sleep

The baby's face is peacefully relaxed and his eyelids remain closed and still. His body will hardly move at all, though his mouth may twitch, almost imperceptibly, from time to time.

Babies in the quiet sleep state tend to sleep very soundly—so soundly that the lack of movement and inaudible breathing will scare the hell out of you. If this happens, lean as close as you can and listen for the baby's breath. Otherwise, gently put a hand on his chest (you should always put your baby down to sleep on his back) and wait for it to rise and fall. Try to resist the urge to poke the baby to make sure she's still alive—most newborns spend up to 90 percent of their first few weeks sleeping.

Active Sleep

The baby's eyes are usually closed, but he may smile or frown, make sucking or chewing movements, and even whimper or twitch—just like you do in your active sleep state. And if you pay attention, you'll even see the eyes moving around under the eyelids.

Sixty percent of a baby's sleep time is spent in quiet sleep, 40 percent in active sleep, with the two states alternating back and forth. So, if your sleeping baby starts to stir, whimper, or seems to be waking up unhappy, wait a few seconds before you pick him up to feed, change, or soothe. Left alone, the baby may very well slip back into the quiet sleep state.

For thousands of years, most people believed that newborn infants were capable only of eating, sleeping, crying, and looking around. But if you pay attention, you'll see that your new baby has an incredible arsenal of talents.

Just a few hours out of the womb, your baby is already trying to communicate with you and everyone else around him. He can imitate your facial expressions, has some control over his body, can express preferences (most prefer patterned objects to plain objects and curved lines to straight ones), and has a remarkable memory. Marshall Klaus told me about a game he played with an eight-hour-old girl in which he asked one colleague (who was a stranger to the baby—who isn't at that age?) to hold her and slowly stick out her tongue. After a few seconds, the baby imitated the woman. Then Dr. Klaus took the baby and passed her around to twelve other doctors and nurses who were participating in the game, all of whom were told not to stick their tongues out. When the baby finally came back to the first doctor, she—without any prompting—immediately stuck out her tongue again. Even at just a few hours old, she had obviously remembered her "friend."

If you want your baby to respond to and play with you, the time to do it is during the active alert stage. (During the first few months infants are particularly responsive to high contrast, so black-and-white toys and patterns are often a big hit.) But be patient. Infants are incredibly bright little creatures, but they also have minds of their own. This means that despite your best efforts, your baby may not be interested in performing like a trained seal whenever you wish.

What's Going On with You

Unconditional Love

Sooner or later, almost every writer takes a crack at trying to describe love. And for the most part, they fall short. But there's a line in Maurice Sendak's classic children's book, *Where the Wild Things Are,* that captures the feeling of loving one's own child exactly: "Please don't go—we'll eat you up—we love you so." As crazy as it may sound, that's precisely what my love for my daughters feels like to me. Whether we're playing, reading a book, telling each other about our days, or I'm just gazing at their smooth, peaceful faces as they sleep, all of a sudden I'll be overcome with the desire to pick them up, mush them into tiny balls, and pop them in my mouth. If you don't already know what I mean, believe me, you will soon. Just you wait.

One of my biggest fears during my wife's second pregnancy was that I wouldn't be able to love our second child as much as the first—that there wouldn't be enough of the consuming, overpowering love I felt for our first daughter to share with the new baby. But I really had nothing to worry about. Three seconds after my second daughter was born, I already wanted to eat her up, too. Same with the third.

Feeling, Well, Paternal

Despite all the excitement, you may be filled with a sense of calm and peacefulness. You may feel less like going to work and more like hanging out with the new family. If so, you certainly aren't alone. Canadian researcher Anne Storey found that new fathers' testosterone levels often drop by as much as a third right after the birth of their children. Storey speculates that this kind of testosterone reduction would make a man feel more parental or more like "settling down."

Postpartum Depression for Dads? Yep.

According to Will Courtenay, a psychotherapist specializing in male postpartum depression, as many as one in four new dads experience the kinds of depression symptoms mentioned earlier in the days, weeks, and even months after the birth of a child. Unfortunately, men rarely discuss their feelings or ask for help, especially during a time when they're supposed to "be there" for the new mom. One big problem is that men and women express depression differently. Women tend to get tearful; men get angry or withdraw from their family and retreat to the office. Because depression—including the postpartum kind—is usually seen as affecting women more than men, many mental health professionals don't recognize the symptoms, or write them off as normal adjustment to the challenges of new parenthood.

The symptoms usually crop up a week or two after the birth and can include feelings of stress, irritability, or discouragement; aversion to hearing the baby cry; resentment of the baby and all the attention he gets; exhaustion; and disappointment with how you're doing as a new dad.

While no one knows exactly what causes postpartum depression, some groups of men are more susceptible than others. The clearest risk factors are a partner who is depressed herself or a personal history of depression. Other factors include financial problems, a poor relationship with your partner or parents, being unmarried, or a pregnancy that had been unplanned or unwanted. Postpartum depression doesn't discriminate based on socioeconomic level or ethnicity. It typically affects first-time parents, but can occur after subsequent births even if there were no symptoms after the first child.

If you suspect you may be experiencing postpartum depression, understand that it's not a sign of weakness. It doesn't make you a bad dad, or mean that you don't love your child. It's a recognized medical condition that affects hundreds of thousands of fathers, and you shouldn't have to suffer when treatment is available. If you aren't sure, Courtenay's Web site www.postpartummen.com offers an anonymous survey that can clarify the issues, and a listing of good resources for getting help. Whatever you do, don't sweep your feelings under the rug. Depression—regardless of what triggers it—is nothing to be ashamed of, and getting treatment is important. Don't let depression rob you of the joys a new baby brings, ruin your relationships, or destroy your family.

Awe at What the Female Body Can Do

Watching your partner go through labor is truly a humbling experience; chances are, your own physical courage, strength, and resolve have rarely been put to that kind of test. But there's nothing like seeing a baby come out of a vagina to convince you that women are *really* different from men.

I know that vaginal birth has been around for millions of years and that that's the way babies are supposed to be born. Yet in a strange way, there's something almost unnatural about the whole process—the baby seems so big and the exit so small (it kind of reminds me of the ship-in-a-bottle conundrum). Ironically, a C-section somehow seems more "normal" and humane: when the fetus is full-grown, cut an appropriately sized exit and let the baby out. Seems simple enough to me. You'd think that with all the technological advances we've made in other areas, we'd have invented a quicker, easier, less painful way to have children.

Jealousy

"The single emotion that can be the most destructive and disruptive to your experience of fatherhood is jealousy," writes Dr. Martin Greenberg in *The Birth of a Father*.

There's certainly plenty to be jealous about, but the real question is, Whom are you jealous of? Your partner for being able to breastfeed and for her close relationship with the baby, or the baby itself for taking up more than his or her fair share of your partner's attention, and for having full access to your partner's breasts while you aren't even supposed to touch them? The answer is, Both.

Now that the baby's born, communication with your partner is even more important than before. Jealousy's "potential for destruction," writes Greenberg, "lies not in having the feelings but in burying them." So if you're feeling jealous, tell her about it. But if you can't bring yourself to discuss your feelings on this issue with your partner, take them up with a male friend or relative. You'll be surprised at how common these feelings are.

Feeling Pushed Away or Left Out

Almost every new father in my research (and there have been more than 1,000) has talked about feeling pushed away or excluded from the new parenting experience. "The mother plays a critical role," writes Pamela Jordan. "She can bring her mate into the spotlight or keep him in the wings. The most promoting mothers . . . brought their mates into the experience by frequently and openly sharing their physical sensations and emotional responses. They actively encouraged their mates to share the experience of becoming and being a father."

While it's easy to give in to your feelings, throw up your hands, and leave the parenting to your partner, don't do it. Encourage her to talk about what she's feeling and thinking, and ask her specifically to involve you as much as possible.

A good way to cut down on your potential feelings of jealousy or of being pushed away is to start getting to know your baby right away—even before you leave the hospital. Change as many diapers as you can (if you've never changed one before, get one of the nurses to show you how), give the baby a sponge bath, or take him or her out for a walk while your partner rests.

Be prepared, though. When you get home, you may find yourself feeling pushed away by your baby. Here's a typical scene: You're home, having a perfectly delightful time with the baby, when she starts fussing and then crying. Hard. You try everything you can to resolve the issue, but after a few minutes it's clear that she's hungry and wants Mom. Now. So you turn her over to your partner and then spend the next twenty minutes feeling inadequate, useless, and completely superfluous.

Having been there many times, I guarantee that it's going to hurt. It's perfectly natural to want to distance yourself from anyone or anything that's causing you pain. But try not to take it personally. The baby isn't expressing a preference for your partner over you or saying that you're a lousy dad; it's just that Mom happens to be her favorite restaurant. So instead of withdrawing, try to focus on other ways to build your own, independent relationship with your child, one that's completely separate from your partner and is based on activities that don't involve feeding.

Amazement at How Being a Parent Changes Your Life

It's virtually impossible to try to explain the myriad ways becoming a parent will change your life. You already know you'll be responsible for the safety and well-being of a completely helpless person. You've heard that you'll lose a little sleep (all right, a lot) and even more privacy. And you've prepared yourself for not being able to read as many books or see as many movies as you did before. These are some of the big, obvious changes, but it's the tiny details that will make you realize just how different your new life is from your old one.

The best way I can describe it is this: sometimes one of my daughters would put food into her mouth, and after a few chews change her mind, take it out, and hand it to me. Most of the time I'd take the offering and pop it into my mouth without a second thought. You probably will too. Even more bizarre, since becoming a father, I have actually had serious discussions with my friends about the color and consistency of the contents of children's diapers. So will you.

Bonding with the Baby

No one knows exactly where or when it started, but one of the most wide-spread—and most enduring—myths about child rearing is that women are somehow more nurturing than men and are therefore better suited to parenting.

In one of the earliest studies of father-infant interaction, my colleague, pioneering researcher Ross Parke, made a discovery that might shock the traditionalists: fathers were just as caring about, interested in, and involved with their infants as the mothers were, and they held, touched, kissed, rocked, and cooed at their new babies with at least the same frequency as the mothers did. Several years later, Martin Greenberg coined a term, *engrossment*, to describe "a father's sense of absorption, preoccupation, and interest in his baby."

Parke and a number of other researchers have repeatedly confirmed these findings about father-infant interaction, and have concluded that what triggers engrossment in men is the same thing that prompts similar nurturing feelings in women: early infant contact. "In sum," writes Parke, "the amount of stimulatory and affectional behavior depends on the opportunity to hold the infant."

Not surprisingly, Parke and others have found that men who attended their baby's birth bonded slightly faster than those who didn't. But if you weren't able to be there for the birth, don't worry. "Early contact at birth is not a magic pill," writes Ellen Galinsky, author of The *Six Stages of Parenthood*. "It does not guarantee attachment. Neither does lack of contact prevent bonding."

But What If I Don't Fall in Love Right Away?

Although we've spent a lot of time talking about the joys of loving your child and how important it is to bond with the infant as soon as possible, a lot of new fathers (and mothers, for that matter) don't feel particularly close to the new baby immediately after the birth. Very few people will come right out and say, in public, that they feel nothing for their baby. It sounds kind of creepy, doesn't it? In fact, psychiatrists Kay Robson and Ramesh Kumar have found that 25 to 40 percent of mothers and fathers admit that their first response to their baby was "indifference." Putting things in slightly stronger terms, researcher Katharyn May says, "This bonding business is nonsense. We've sold parents a bill of goods. They believe that if they don't have skin-to-skin contact within the first fifteen minutes, they won't bond. Science just doesn't show that."

I have to admit that, in a way, this makes a lot more sense than the love-at-first-sight kind of bonding you hear so much about. After all, you don't even know this new little person. He or she may look a lot different than you expected. And if your partner's labor and delivery were long and arduous, you may unconsciously be blaming the baby for the difficulties or may simply be too exhausted to fully appreciate the new arrival. He seems to do nothing but cry, eat, and fill diapers. That's on a good day. And the kid never, ever laughs at your jokes. It's downright demoralizing.

Let me assure you that if you haven't whipped yourself up into a frenzy of love for your baby, there's absolutely nothing wrong with you. More important, there's no evidence whatsoever that your relationship with or feelings for your child will be any less loving than if you'd fallen head over heels in love in the first second. Just take your time, don't pressure yourself, and don't think for a second that you've failed as a father. Almost all new dads get that bonding feeling within two months.

There's a lot of evidence that parent-child bonding comes as a result of physical closeness. So if you'd like to speed up the process, try carrying the baby every chance you get, taking him with you whenever you can, and taking care of as many of his basic needs as possible.

The whole bonding thing is probably going to be a lot tougher if you've got twins (or more). Because they tend to be born somewhat more prematurely than single babies, multiples may have to stay in the hospital nursery for a few days or even weeks, which can limit the amount of time you can spend with them—separately or together. Things can get even more complicated if one of the babies comes home with you and the other(s) stay behind. You're going to feel torn between spending time with the baby in the hospital, the other baby, and your partner. Unfortunately, there's no magic formula for how much time each of them gets. Just do the best you can and spend a lot of time talking with your partner about how you're both feeling and what each of you needs.

Gee, This Isn't at All What I Expected...

Despite everything you've heard about how gorgeous babies are, you may have a slightly different opinion—at least for the first week or so after your baby is born. If your baby was born vaginally, the trip through the birth canal may have flattened his nose and made him look a little cone-headed. Calm

Adoptive and ART Dads Bond Too

Plenty of adoptive parents—particularly if they adopted because of infertility—feel a little insecure or inadequate. And a lot of ART families feel the same way. They often believe that the process of bonding and forming an attachment to the baby comes more naturally to birth or biological parents than to them. Fortunately, this isn't true.

Studies of adoptive and ART parents have shown that a majority feel some kind of love for their children right from the very first contact; it doesn't matter whether it's when they go to pick up the baby, when they first look at a picture that arrived months before, or right at the birth, if they're lucky enough to be there. At the same time, though, just like biological parents, a good percentage of adoptive parents or parents who are only partially biologically related to their child don't feel anything particularly parental when meeting their child for the first time.

If you're adopting a newborn, it's going to be a little easier to establish a bond. But a lot of adoptions aren't finalized until the babies are a few months older. Realistically, this makes the bonding process a bit tougher for all concerned, as babies and parents take a little time to get used to each other. It's by no means an impossible task. "Being a first-time parent, whether by birth or adoption, evokes a variety of feelings," writes Marshall Klaus. "And although many parents feel attached to their baby at first contact, many others find it takes a week or longer to feel the baby is theirs." If you aren't consumed with paternal feelings right away, the first thing to do is take a look at the "But What If I Don't Fall in Love Right Away?" section on pages 279–80.

In the long run, the news is good. According to researcher Susan Golombok and her colleagues, "fathers of assisted reproduction children were found to interact more with their children and to contribute more to parenting than fathers with naturally conceived children."

down. His nose will pop out and his head will get rounder over the next few months.

Do those green, tarlike bowel movements make you think there's something wrong with the baby's intestines? There isn't. Those first few loads are normal and will be replaced by a much more pleasant-looking concoction as your baby starts breastfeeding. Is the baby's skin splotchy—especially on the neck and

Welcome Home, GI Dad

Coming home to a baby who was born while you were deployed can be both exciting and terrifying. Of course, if this is your second or third or fourth child, you've already got a pretty good handle on what to expect and what you need to do. But if this is baby number one, you'll be stepping into a home that may look nothing like the one you left, and you may have no clue what to expect, what your wife will want from you, and how you'll react to the whole thing.

One of the first things you'll probably feel is a conflict between wanting to jump in immediately and take care of your wife, and wanting to run away as fast as you can. No question, it hasn't been easy for your wife to make it through the pregnancy and birth without you. But at least she had nine months to prepare. Your world is going to change in an instant. Military man one minute, daddy the next. Different uniforms, similar responsibilities.

Next, you'll start feeling guilty—in part for even thinking about running away, but mostly for not having been there for Mom and baby during the pregnancy and the birth. Get over it! The two of you knew that your being deployed was a distinct possibility, and there was absolutely nothing you could have done to change the situation. You may also feel some jealousy at the closeness of the connection between Mom and baby

the eyelids—and does she have strange-looking birth marks or tiny pimples? Relax. Just keep her clean—no scrubbing or zit popping—and she'll be fine. Does your infant seem a little cross-eyed? It's fine. As soon as his eye muscles get a bit more developed and coordinated, he'll be able to look you straight in the eye. Do his hairy back and shoulders have you worrying about what'll happen to him when the moon is full? Don't. That fuzz is called *lanugo* and it'll fall out pretty soon.

Staying Involved

The First Few Days

In the first few days you're going to have to learn to juggle a lot of roles. You're still a lover and friend to your partner, and, of course, you're a father. But for

(See page 277 for more on this). Try to let that one go, too. There's not much you can do about it, and you wouldn't want to even if you could. All you can do is jump in as soon as possible. Your wife will appreciate your being there to take on some of the parenting load. More important, you'll have a chance to start bonding with your baby.

But don't put a lot of pressure on yourself to start bonding right away, and don't worry about trying to make up for lost time—there's no such thing. Just do as much as you can: hug, bathe, change, feed, play, relax, play some more, read the Staying Involved section below, and just marvel at all the cool things babies can do. And remember, (a) it's never too late to start, (b) the sooner you get involved, the stronger your relationship with your child, and (c) you're going to make a ton of mistakes. That's another fun part of being a new daddy.

The first few weeks, however, are going to be a little less fun. Even if your partner showed the baby your picture every day and played the MP3s you made of yourself reading bedtime stories, it's going to take a while for your baby to get used to having you around. When you hold her, she may cry, fuss, pull away from you, or cling to your wife or another more familiar caregiver. And boy, is that going to hurt. You may be the toughest, most combat-hardened vet on earth, but that tiny infant of yours will be able to reduce you to Jell-O in seconds.

now, your most important role is that of support person to your partner. Besides her physical recovery (which we'll talk more about below), she's going to need time to get to know the baby and to learn (if she chooses to) how to breastfeed.

When our first daughter was born (by C-section), the three of us spent four days in the hospital (which meant three uncomfortable nights on a crooked, lumpy cot for me). But when our second daughter was born (vaginally), we all checked out less than twelve hours after the birth. In both cases, though, my first few days at home were mighty busy—cooking, shopping, doing laundry, fixing up the baby's room, getting the word out, screening phone calls and visitors, and making sure everyone got plenty of rest.

Coming Home . . . and Beyond

Within a few minutes after we'd brought our first daughter home from the hospital, my wife and I looked at each other and almost simultaneously asked,

"Well, now what are we supposed to do?" An important question, no doubt, and one that seems to come up time and time again.

A NOTE ON RECOVERY

As far as the baby is concerned, there's not much to do in the beginning besides feeding, changing, and admiring. But your partner is a different story. Despite everything you've heard about women giving birth in the fields and returning to work a few minutes later, that's not the way things usually happen. Having a baby is a major shock to a woman's system. And, contrary to popular belief, the recovery period after a vaginal birth is not necessarily any shorter than the recovery period after a C-section (although most women who have had both say that vaginal birth recovery is easier).

Whatever kind of delivery your partner has, she'll need some time—probably more than either of you think—to recover fully. According to a recent study, more than 40 percent of new mothers experience fatigue and breast soreness in the first month after giving birth. In addition, vaginal discomfort, hemorrhoids, poor appetite, constipation, increased perspiration, acne, hand numbness or tingling, dizziness, and hot flashes are common for a month after delivery. And between 10 and 40 percent of women feel pain during sexual intercourse, have respiratory infections, and lose hair for three to six months. Aren't you glad you can't have a baby?

Here are some things you can do to make the recovery process as easy as possible and to start parenting off on the right foot.

◆ Help your partner resist the urge to do too much too soon.

◆ Take over the household chores or ask someone else to help. And if the house is a mess, don't blame each other.

◆ Be flexible. Expecting to maintain your normal, pre-fatherhood schedule is unrealistic—especially for the first six weeks after the birth.

◆ Don't allow your relationship with your partner to be based solely on your child. If she's up to it, go on a date with your partner and leave the baby with a relative or friend.

◆ Be patient with yourself, your partner, and the baby. You're all new at this.

◆ Be sensitive to your partner's emotions. Recovery has an emotional component as well as a physical one.

◆ Make sure to get some time alone with the baby. You can do this while your partner is sleeping or while she's out for a walk.

◆ Control the visiting hours and the number of people who can come at any given time. Dealing with visitors takes a lot more energy than you might think. And being poked, prodded, and passed around won't make the baby very happy. Also, for the first month or so, ask anyone who wants to touch the baby to wash his or her hands first.

♦ Keep your sense of humor.

HELPING OLDER KIDS ADJUST TO THEIR NEW SIBLING

Handling your older children's reactions to their new baby brother or sister requires an extra touch of gentleness and sensitivity. Kids often start out wildly excited at their new status as big brother or big sister, but most will have some adjustment problems later on—as soon as they realize that the new kid is more than just a temporary visitor.

Some react with anger and jealousy. Who wouldn't? For the past few years he had you and Mom all to himself. Then, without even consulting him, you bring in someone who steals all your attention. Worse yet, the instant playmate he was hoping for turns out to be a blobby baby who does nothing but sleep, cry, eat, cry, poop, and cry. And to top it off, with everyone ooohing and aaahing over the new baby, your older child is feeling unwanted and unloved. As a result, new older siblings may shed a few tears themselves, have tantrums, and even try to hit the baby. They need to know immediately and in no uncertain terms that you understand how they feel and that it's okay to be mad and talk about how mad they are. It's even okay to draw hateful pictures or beat up a doll. But it's absolutely not okay to do anything to hurt the baby.

Others may react by regressing. My older daughter, for example, was completely potty trained before her sister was born, but began wetting her bed again a few weeks after we brought the baby home. Some kids suddenly start talking baby talk again, need more bedtime stories and cuddling, or make demands for attention that you may not be able to satisfy.

So what can you do to help your older child cope with those inevitable feelings of jealousy?

♦ If your older child comes to the hospital, keep the visit short. It won't take long for the initial excitement to wear off. And be sure to let him spend some time visiting with Mom too. He may have been worried about her, and seeing her in a hospital bed, possibly with IV tubes hanging out of her arms, can be a scary sight. Having a chance to hug her and be reassured that she's okay is important.

♦ Tell him—often—that you and Mom love him very much and that those feelings will never change. I remember having a similar conversation with my oldest when her younger sister was born. She was afraid that if I loved the

A Note on Dressing Children

Getting a baby dressed is not an easy task; their heads always seem
too big to go through the appropriate openings in their shirts, and their
hands regularly refuse to come out of the sleeves. There are a few things
you can do to make dressing a little easier:

♦ Reach through the sleeve and pull your baby's hands through—it's a
lot easier than trying to shove from the other side.

♦ Buy pants or overalls with legs that snap open. Some manufacturers
make baby clothes that are absolutely beautiful but impossible to put
on or take off. The snap-open legs also make diaper changing much
easier—you don't have to remove the whole outfit to access the diaper.
Clothing legs that don't snap all the way through the ankles are a big
pain—elasticized cuffs aren't so easy to maneuver when the kid is
squirming on the changing table!

Also, don't overdress your baby. For some strange reason, people tend
to bundle their children up in all sorts of blankets, sweaters, hats, and
gloves—even in the summer. But unless you're Eskimos, there's no reason to dress your children like one. A basic rule of thumb is to have the
baby wear the same kind of clothes you do, plus a hat. Layering clothing
is sometimes a good way to go—if the baby gets too hot, you can remove
a layer.

Finally, I mentioned this earlier, but it's worth repeating: If they can't
walk, they don't need shoes. It's not only a waste of money, but confining
a baby's feet in a hard pair of shoes all day long can actually damage the
bones.

baby I couldn't love her as much. I lit a candle and asked her to imagine that
the flame was my love for her. Then I took a second candle and lit it with the
flame from the first one. The second candle burned as brightly as the first,
which wasn't diminished in any way. It's the same with love.

♦ Keep a few small presents around in case your older child feels left out when
people bring gifts for the baby but not for him. It doesn't have to be a big
deal, just a little something to let him know he's special too. If you have an
album or a scrapbook of him as a baby, show him the photos and tell him
about the presents *he* received when he was born.

♦ Stress the perks of being a big kid. For example, the baby is too little to play with big-kid toys, or eat food that big kids do.

♦ Start fostering a relationship between your older child and the new baby by teaching big bro or sis to gently interact with the baby. Letting the older sibling help diaper, bathe, feed, and clothe the new baby is a great idea; it helps bring him into the process by making him feel that the baby is "his." But don't force the older child to get too involved. It can make him feel as though you want him around only to wait on the more important new baby, which can make him resent the little interloper even more.

♦ Model good behavior. Show your older kids the right ways to hold and behave with a new baby. Practicing with a doll is a great, risk-free way to get the hang of it—particularly the all-important head-supporting part. If you're bottle feeding, show the older kids the right way to hold a bottle and how to recognize when the baby's had enough. Never, ever leave the baby unattended with an older sibling (unless you've got a teenager—and if you do have a teen around, he or she will expect to get paid, so make sure you have plenty of cash on hand). Make sure the older child is always sitting down when holding the baby, and don't forget to praise loving, gentle behavior whenever you see it.

♦ Try to carve out some one-on-one time with your older child, doing all the activities you used to do before the baby's arrival—reading, going for walks, drawing, talking, seeing movies, or just hanging out. He may be an older sibling now, but he still needs your time, presence, and attention as much as ever. And make sure the big kid gets to spend some private time with Mom, too.

Immediate Concerns . . . with Long-term Impact

FEEDING THE BABY: BREAST VS. BOTTLE

When you were a baby, breastfeeding was probably out of style, and there's a pretty good chance that your mom's doctors gave her a wide variety of reasons not to breastfeed. But starting in the 1970s, breasts came back big time— so much so that it's pretty hard these days to find anyone who doesn't advocate breastfeeding. Even in the medical community, there's general agreement that breastfeeding is just about the best thing you can do for your child. The American Academy of Pediatrics recently recommended that new babies get nothing but breast milk for the first six months, and that breast milk should then be phased out and solid food in over the next six.

A Special Note on Breastfeeding

As natural as breastfeeding is, your partner and the baby may need any-where from a few days to a few weeks to get the hang of it. The baby may not immediately know how to latch on to the breast properly, and your partner—never having done this before—won't know exactly what to do either. This initial period, in which cracked and even bloody nipples are not uncommon, may be quite painful for your partner. And with the baby feeding six or seven times a day, it may take as long as two weeks for your partner's nipples to get sufficiently toughened up.

Surprisingly, she won't begin producing any real milk until two to five days after the baby is born. But there's no need to worry that the baby isn't getting enough food. Babies don't eat much in the first twenty-four to forty-eight hours, and the sucking they do is almost purely for prac-tice. Whatever nutritional needs your baby has will be fully satisfied by the tiny amounts of *colostrum* your partner produces. (Colostrum is a kind of pre-milk that helps the baby's immature digestive system get warmed up for the task of dealing with the real thing later.)

Overall, the first few weeks of breastfeeding can be very stressful for your partner. If this is the case, don't be tempted to suggest switching to bottles. Instead, be supportive, praise her for the great job she's doing, bring her something to eat or drink while she's feeding, and encourage her to keep trying. You also might want to ask your pediatrician for the name of a local lactation consultant (yes, there really is such a thing. Many hospitals have them on staff and they'll stop by your room to give your partner some coaching before you head back home). Your support is particularly important. Research shows that women whose husbands are supportive and encouraging breastfeed longer and are happier with the decision—an outcome that's good for everyone.

If you and your partner haven't already decided to breastfeed, here are the reasons why you should (besides the fact that you'll get a lot of nasty looks from people if you don't):

FOR THE BABY

♦ Breast milk provides exactly the right balance of nutrients needed by your newborn. In addition, breast milk contains several essential fatty acids that are not found in baby formula.

A Note on Juice

If you and your partner decide not to breastfeed, or your pediatrician suggests that you supplement breastfeeding with a bottle, don't fill it with juice. A recent study found that children who drink large quantities of fruit juice—especially apple juice—suffer from frequent diarrhea and other gastrointestinal problems, and in the worst cases, may fail to grow and develop normally. The problem is that babies love juice so much that, if you give them all they want, they'll fill up their tiny stomachs with it, leaving no room for the more nutritious foods they need. The American Dietetic Association recommends that parents refrain from giving their babies juice until they're at least six months old, and then limit it to four to six ounces of diluted juice (50 percent water) per day.

- Breast milk adapts, as if by magic, to your baby's changing nutritional needs. None of my children had a single sip of anything but breast milk for the first six or seven months of life, and they're all incredibly healthy kids.
- Breastfeeding greatly reduces the chance that your baby will develop food allergies. If your family (or your partner's) has a history of food allergies, you should withhold solid foods for at least six months.
- Breastfed babies are less likely to become obese as adults than formula-fed babies. This may be because with the breast, it's the baby—not the parent—who decides when to quit eating.
- Breastfed babies have a lower risk of developing asthma, stomach problems, diabetes, cavities, pneumonia, ear infections, childhood leukemia, and sudden infant death syndrome (SIDS).
- Breastfeeding is thought to transmit to the infant the mother's immunity to certain diseases. This is especially important for the first few months, until the baby's immune system matures.
- Breastfed babies may have higher IQs than their non-breastfed buddies.

FOR YOU AND YOUR PARTNER

- It's convenient—no preparation, no heating, no bottles or dishes to wash...
- It's free. Formula can cost a lot of money.
- It gives your partner a wonderful opportunity to bond with the baby. In addition, breastfeeding will help get your partner's uterus back into shape and may reduce her risk of ovarian and breast cancer, type 2 diabetes, and postpartum depression.

- In most cases there's always as much as you need, and never any waste.
- Your baby's diapers won't stink. It's true. Breastfed babies produce stool that—at least compared to "real food" stools—doesn't smell half bad.

Breastfeeding and Older Kids

Despite how wonderful breastfeeding is for the new baby, your older kids may see it as little more than an attempt to displace them from the center of the universe. And seeing Mom holding and cuddling and nursing often brings up all sorts of feelings—anger and jealousy being at the top of the list (see pages 285–88 for more on coping with this). Some new big brothers and sisters will want to be held the same way the baby is being held. Some will even want to nurse. If the older sibling is young enough, your partner may actually want to give in to the request. If so, it should be only on a very temporary basis. (Giving a teaspoonful or two of breast milk might be a better solution—most older kids won't like the watery consistency or the sweet taste.) Older children need to know that your partner's milk is for the baby and that big kids get to have—and do— lots of other things that newborns can't.

Hands-on Tips for Dads of Preemies

If your baby was born before about 35–36 weeks, he may have to spend some time in an incubator bulking up to at least four or five pounds before you can take him home.

One of the things you can do to make that happen a little sooner is to massage your baby. Tiffany Field, director of the Touch Research Institute at the University of Miami School of Medicine, found that preemies who had three fifteen-minute periods of gentle massage every day in addition to their normal treatment grew almost 50 percent more than those who didn't get the massage. Hospital stays were shortened by almost a week, and the bills were correspondingly lower as well. On their first birthdays, premature babies who'd been massaged were bigger and better developed than similarly premature kids who didn't get massaged. Pretty neat, eh?

Feeding Twins

Although there's no question that breastfeeding is best, nursing two infants at the same time often presents some real complications. First of all, for the first weeks or so each of them is going to want to eat every two or three hours. Sometimes they'll be hungry at the same time, sometimes not. Ideally, you'll be able to get them both on the same feeding schedule. That's not always easy, though, because typically one will want to eat more often than the other. If that's the case for you, a lot of nursing moms find it easier to start serving both babies whenever the hungrier one wants it. Either way, by the time the feedings are over and the diapers are changed it'll be just about time to start again, which will leave your partner feeling something like a 24-hour drive-through milk bar. In a valiant attempt to give themselves some downtime, a lot of new mothers of twins opt for a mix of breast- and bottle feeding. The bottles can be filled either with breast milk (which can be pumped out faster than a baby can suck it out) or formula. Either way, if you've got twins, you're really going to have to be a lot more involved in feeding them than you otherwise might have been.

SLEEPING ARRANGEMENTS

Your pediatrician will probably tell you that your baby should get used to sleeping by him- or herself as soon after birth as possible. The reasoning is that in American culture we emphasize early independence, so babies should adapt quickly to being away from their parents—especially if both parents work and the children are in day care.

But there is another school of thought that maintains that babies should sleep in the same bed as their parents (an idea shared by about 80 percent of the world's population). The rationale is that human evolution simply can't keep pace with the new demands our culture is placing on its children. "Proximity to parental sounds, smells, heat, and movement during the night is precisely what the human infant's immature system expects—and needs," says James McKenna, an anthropologist and sleep researcher.

So which approach is right? Well, given the wide divergence of expert opinions out there, it's a tough call—one you'll ultimately have to make on your own.

Here are a few of the most common questions you're likely to have if you haven't already decided where your child will be sleeping.

♦ **How will it affect the baby's independence?** There's absolutely no agreement on this. Richard Ferber, author of *Solve Your Child's Sleep Problems*, maintains that "sleeping alone is an important part of a child's learning to be able to separate from his parents without anxiety and to see himself as an independent individual." In contrast, Thomas F. Anders, M.D., a professor of psychiatry, contends that "every child is born with a strong need for lots of close physical contact with a caregiver, and children in whom this need isn't met early in their lives may end up trying to fill it as adults."

♦ **What about safety?** Most adults—even while asleep—have a highly developed sense of where they are. After all, when was the last time you fell out of bed? So the risk of accidentally suffocating your baby is pretty slim. Nevertheless, the Federal Consumer Product Safety Commission (CPSC) recommends that parents not sleep with babies under the age of two. The American Academy of Pediatrics agrees. This is based on an eight-year study that attributed the deaths of 515 children under two to sleeping in adult beds (121 of which were attributed to a parent, caregiver, or sibling rolling on top of or against the baby while sleeping). That's 64 a year. The CPSC also found that 50 babies die every year from being put into cribs that don't meet federal safety standards. There's no question that each of these deaths is a tragedy, and we should do everything we possibly can to minimize the risks. But with about four million babies born in the United States every year, the chances of anything happening are very, very small.

♦ **How will the baby sleep?** Despite what you might think, co-sleeping children tend to sleep more *lightly* than children who sleep alone (blankets rustling and parents turning over in bed wake them up). But light sleeping isn't necessarily a bad thing. In fact, there seems to be a correlation between lighter sleep and a lower incidence of SIDS (Sudden Infant Death Syndrome—see below for more).

Sharing a bed with your infant not only affects your child, but it can also have a serious impact on you. You'll lose a lot of sexual spontaneity (yes, eventually you will be having sex again), and maybe even more sleep. Even the soundest-sleeping kids generally wake up every three or four hours; 70 percent of them just look around for a few minutes and soothe themselves back to sleep. But if your baby is in the other 30 percent, he or she may wake up, see you, and want to play.

"Is There Anything We Can Do?"

One of the most common questions you'll hear from people is whether they can help out in any way. Some people are serious, others are just being polite—what they mean by "Can I help?" is, "Can I hold the baby for a little while, then give her back?" You can tell one group from the other by keeping a list of chores that need to be done and asking them to take their pick. Laundry, grocery shopping, rotate the tires, file your taxes, paint the living room, whatever.

When my two oldest were born, a group of our friends got together and, taking turns, brought us meals every day for more than a week. Not having to cook or shop gave us a lot more time to spend together and let us get some rest. And of course, when our friends had their children, we were there with our spinach lasagna and a bottle of wine.

When baby number three arrived, my wife's sister came out and stayed with us for a couple of weeks. At least I think she was there. I saw her only a few times. But before she left, she'd made us enough frozen meals to last several months.

A NOTE ON SIDS

Sudden Infant Death Syndrome, which affects otherwise healthy babies, is one of the scariest issues confronting new parents—and there's good reason: every year SIDS claims between 2,000 and 7,000 lives. It's the most common cause of death of children between one week and one year old, striking about one of every thousand babies. Despite all the millions of dollars spent on researching and fighting SIDS, no one's quite sure what, exactly, causes it. And there's no medical test to determine which babies are at the greatest risk. Here's what we do know:

♦ It's most likely to strike infants two to four months old.
♦ Ninety percent of deaths happen by six months.
♦ It's more likely to happen to boys than girls; to preemies, multiple birth babies, babies whose mothers are under eighteen, African American, or American Indian; and in families in which a parent or caretaker smokes.
♦ It's more common in cold weather, when respiratory infections and overheating are more prevalent.
♦ It is *not* caused by vaccinations.

If You Decide to Share Your Bed with Your Child

Do it because you and your partner *want* to, not because you feel you have to. You're not negligent or overindulgent parents for doing it, so don't be embarrassed by your choice. But please be *extremely* careful: no waterbeds or extremely soft mattresses; no gaps that the baby could slip into; your baby should be put down to sleep on his back; never leave the baby in the bed alone; no pillows, comforters, or anything else that could smother the baby; don't smoke; keep the bed far, far away from any window covering cords that could act as a noose; and for God's sake, keep the baby out of the bed if you've been drinking or taking medication— prescription or otherwise—that could make you less aware of your surroundings or less likely to wake up in case of emergency.

If Family Sleeping *Isn't* for You

Don't feel guilty. You're not a bad or selfish parent for not doing it. Teaching your children to be independent does not mean that you don't have a close bond with them. But don't feel like a failure if you allow an occasional exception, such as when a child is ill or has had a frightening experience.

Since two-thirds of SIDS babies don't fall into any of the highest risk categories, there are a few things you can do to minimize the risk:

♦ **Put your baby to sleep on his back.** Experts used to think that babies who slept on their backs would choke on their vomit if they spit up. Turns out that's not true—babies are smart enough to turn their heads. People also preferred to put their babies on their tummies as a way to avoid getting a bald or flat spot on the back of the head. Now we know that tummy sleeping may double or triple the risk. Since the Back to Sleep campaign began, SIDS deaths have dropped 43 percent. One thing, though: babies who sleep on their backs don't get to exercise their arms as much and take longer to learn to push themselves up and roll over. So make sure your baby spends plenty of his awake time on his belly working out that upper body.

♦ **Don't smoke, and don't let anyone who does near your baby.** While it's not possible to say that smoking directly increases SIDS risk, there does seem to be a connection.

♦ **Don't overdress the baby** (see page 286).

Do You Really Want Your Mother-in-law to Move in with You Right after the Birth?

Be careful about having people stay over to help with the newborn—especially parents (yours or hers). The new grandparents may have more traditional attitudes toward parenting and may not be supportive of your involvement with your child. They may also have very different ideas about how babies should be fed, dressed, carried, played with, and so on. If you do have someone stay with you to help out after the birth, make sure he or she understands that you and your wife are the parents and that what you say ultimately goes.

"Not so fast. I want to be called 'Nana.'"

- **Put the baby to sleep on a firm mattress:** no pillows, fluffy blankets, plush sofas, waterbeds, shag carpets, or beanbags. Crib mattresses should fit snugly into the crib so the baby can't slip in between it and the frame. And take out anything else, such as stuffed animals or extra blankets, that might accidentally cover the baby.
- **Breastfeed.** As with not smoking, while there's no definitive proof that breastfeeding actually reduces the risk, there seems to be a connection.
- **Give your baby a pacifier.** No one is sure why, but there's a lot of evidence that pacifiers reduce the risk. Wait until breastfeeding is well established before starting with the pacifier. And if it falls out of the baby's mouth, leave it alone—there's no need to try to jam it back in there.
- **Don't panic.** Although SIDS is a devastating, horrible experience for any parent, remember that 999 out of 1,000 babies don't die of it.

A Note on Middle-of-the-Night Wake-ups

If your baby wakes up in the middle of the night hungry, and your partner is breastfeeding, you might as well stay in bed and let your partner take care of things. I know that doesn't sound terribly gallant, but, really and truly, there's not much you can do to help. Here's what you do instead. Your partner takes the 1 A.M. and 3 A.M. feedings. While she's up, she pumps a few bottles of milk and puts them in the fridge. Meanwhile, you're hopefully getting four or five hours of relatively restful sleep. Then you take the 5 A.M. and 7 A.M. feedings, using the milk your partner pumped earlier. That'll give her a chance to get a few hours of uninterrupted sleep.

If, however, your baby is being bottle-fed (either with formula or expressed breast milk), you should do your fair share of the feedings. You might want to work out a system in which the one who does the 2 A.M. feeding gets to sleep in (or gets breakfast in bed, or whatever).

Sometimes, though, your baby might wake up at two or three in the morning for no other reason than to stay awake for a few hours and check things out. In this kind of situation, you and your partner can either split the child-entertainment duty or stay up together and see what's on late-night TV; if there were any sitcoms or detective shows you missed when you were growing up, you can probably catch the reruns at three in the morning. Thanks to my older daughter's middle-of-the-night awakenings, my wife and I once had the rare opportunity to see what may have been (hopefully) the only episode of *David Cassidy, Teen Detective*.

SEX AFTER THE BABY

Most doctors advise women to refrain from intercourse for at least six weeks after giving birth. But before you mark that date on your calendar, remember that the six-week rule is only a guideline. When you actually have sex again ultimately depends on the condition of your partner's vagina, and, more important, on how you're both feeling. In extremely rare cases, resuming your sex life too soon may actually be dangerous. A study published in the *Postgraduate Medical Journal* documents the cases of two new mothers who died of embolisms—air bubbles in the blood—after having sex.

It's not uncommon for couples to take quite a bit of time to fully reestablish their pre-pregnancy sex life. In one of the largest studies of post-baby sexuality, researcher Janet Hyde found that one month after giving birth, only

17 percent of new mothers had started having sex again. By the sixth month, 89 percent had. Many factors will influence when and how you and your partner decide to resume your sex life. Here are a few:

♦ When you had sex with your partner before, she was the woman you loved. Now, she's also a mother—a thought that reminds many men of their own mothers and can be a big turn-off. Several studies have shown that many women, too, have a tough time reconciling their roles as lover and mother, and may see themselves as un-sexual. According to Jerrold Shapiro, some men have "emotional difficulty being sexual with the part of their wives that produced their children." While I can't say that seeing my daughter coming out of my wife's vagina was particularly erotic, I always found the sight of her feeding our babies kind of arousing.

♦ In the first few weeks after the birth, your partner may focus more on the baby than on you.

♦ You may feel especially aroused at having concrete proof (the baby) of your virility.

Your partner's vagina may be much drier than before, making intercourse painful for her. This doesn't mean you don't turn her on; it's simply a common post-birth occurrence—particularly if she's breastfeeding. According to researcher Geraldine Barrett and her colleagues, in the first three months after the birth, 83 percent of new moms were reporting sexual problems, including vaginal dryness, pain during intercourse or orgasm, and loss of sexual desire. Some of these problems may be resolved by using a little K-Y jelly, Astroglide, or other similar lubricants. And be patient: almost all couples have resumed some kind of sex life by the baby's first birthday.

Unless your partner's practitioner encouraged you to have sex as a way of jump-starting labor, chances are, you were fairly abstinent during the last few weeks of the pregnancy and can hardly wait to get your sex life back on track. But you should expect the first few times you have sex after the baby is born to be a period of tentative rediscovery for both of you. Her body has changed, and she may respond differently than she used to. She may still be worried that having sex will hurt, and you may be afraid of the same thing. Go slowly, take your cues from her, and give yourselves plenty of time to get used to each other again. Here's a bit of good news: Australian researcher Judith Lumley found that while on average, couples had sex half as often as they did pre-baby, about 20 percent of new moms actually experienced *more* sexual pleasure "than they had ever experienced before pregnancy."

Questions to Ask Prospective Caregivers

♦ What previous child-care experience have you had (including caring for younger relatives)?

♦ What age children have you cared for?

♦ Tell us a little about your own childhood.

♦ What would you do if...? (Give several examples of things a child might do that would require different degrees of discipline, or things you might have done to discipline a child in the past.)

♦ When would you hit or spank a child? (If the answer is anything other than "never," find yourself another candidate.)

♦ How would you handle...(Name a couple of emergency situations, or ask for an example of a real emergency situation and how the candidate handled it.)

♦ Do you know baby CPR? (If not, you might want to consider paying for the caregiver to take a class.)

♦ What are your favorite things to do with kids?

♦ Do you have a driver's license?

♦ What days/hours are you available/not available? How flexible can you be if an emergency arises while we're at work?

♦ Are you a native speaker of any foreign language?

♦ Give an example of a conflict you had with a prior employer and how it was resolved.

CHILD CARE

With more and more women in the workforce, it's getting harder to find a traditional Dad-goes-to-work-while-Mom-stays-at-home kind of family anymore, and it's nearly impossible to find the Mom-goes-to-work-while-Dad-stays-at-home variety. And even if you or your partner wanted to be a full-time caregiver, you probably couldn't afford it anyway. (If you're considering staying at home, go back and take a look at pages 159–63.) So, sooner or later, most couples find themselves considering some form of child care. Here's a quick overview of your options. Each has its advantages and disadvantages, which are listed in the chart on pages 302–3.

IN-HOME CHILD CARE   Every time my wife and I tried to find in-home child care, it was a traumatic experience. But the first time was the hardest. Besides being afraid that the person we chose would turn out to be an axe

Other Important Topics to Cover

♦ Compensation and vacation. Check with other people who have care-givers for the going rate, but don't be surprised if it's way more than you were expecting. In some cities people are quitting perfectly good professional jobs to take child-care positions because they pay so much.

♦ Complete responsibilities of the job: feeding, bathing, diapering, changing clothes, reading to the baby, and so on, as well as what light housekeeping chores, if any, will be expected while the baby is sleeping.

♦ How much experience do you have caring for twins (if applicable)?

♦ English-language skills—particularly important in case of emergency (you want someone who can accurately describe to a doctor or 911 operator what's going on).

♦ Immigration/green card status.

You might want to draw up an informal contract, listing all of the care-giver's responsibilities—just so there won't be any misunderstandings.

murderer, we were worried that no one else could love our daughter as much or care for her as well as we did. While nothing can replace your love, there are many wonderful people out there who can give your baby the next best thing. You just need to know how to find them.

Start with friends and acquaintances who have kids, then check with local schools, churches, and synagogue groups. If you've already exhausted those resources, there are plenty of other Internet options. Start your search with local Web sites—you'll have a much better shot at finding someone who lives nearby, and it'll be a lot easier to check references.

Some of the best resources are Craigslist (www.craigslist.org), Great Au Pair (www.greataupair.com), and Nanny Locators (www.nannylocators.com). All three allow you to browse ads posted by people looking for employment. You can search by desired nationality, language spoken, and so on.

Check their rates, hours available, experience with children approximately your child's age, and other relevant items that are important to you. Respond to ads and exchange a few e-mails with the potential candidate, then do a phone interview. This will enable you to screen out the obviously unacceptable candidates: those who are only looking for a monthlong job, those who don't

Taxes and Child Care

♦ Be sure to get your caregiver or babysitter's social security number; you'll need it to take advantage of the tax deduction/credit for child-care expenses.

♦ If you pay a babysitter or other household worker over a certain amount a year, you are required to deduct social security taxes. The earning floor, the amount you need to deduct, and the IRS's regulations change every year, so check with an accountant to make sure you're completely up to date.

drive if you need a driver, and those who don't like kids but want the money. But go with your gut—if you have a good feeling about the candidate, ask her to come over for a face-to-face meeting with you, your partner, and the baby.

Make sure the baby and the prospective caregiver spend a few minutes together, and pay close attention to how they interact. My wife and I ruled out a couple of people right off the bat because they showed absolutely no interest in holding, cuddling, or playing with the baby. And we hired one woman largely because the moment she walked in the door she picked up our daughter and started playing with her.

One quick test you can give to any prospective caregiver is to ask her to change the baby's diaper. Does she sing or smile or try some other way to make the procedure interesting, or does she seem revolted by the whole thing? And does she wash her hands when she's done?

If you still like the potential sitter or nanny after the first meeting, ask for a list of references to call, and contact at least three. This is better done on the phone than online, since you'll be able to hear things in a person's voice that won't come across in an e-mail. Ask each one why the caregiver left, and what the best and worst things about him or her were. Also, make sure to ask the prospective caregiver the questions listed on page 298.

Even if the references sound great, do a thorough background check, including criminal and DMV records. Don't feel embarrassed about this— better safe than, well, you know. You can do a check through Great Au Pair or Background Check Gateway (www.backgroundcheckgateway.com), which offers do-it-yourself information and other options. Only you, as a parent, can decide when enough is enough.

What to Look For in Any Kind of Out-of-Home Day Care

♦ The level of training of the staff. Does the staff seem to like kids? And do the kids seem happy?

♦ Safety: windows, fences around yards, access to kitchen appliances and utensils (knives, ovens, stoves, household chemicals, and so forth).

♦ Overall cleanliness.

♦ Caregiver/child ratio. (In California, one licensed caregiver can take care of as many as four infants. I personally think that any more than two is too many.)

♦ Quality, condition, and number of toys. Is there enough variety to keep kids from getting bored? Are they cleaned regularly?

♦ Security: what precautions are taken to ensure that kids can be picked up only by the person you select? Do strangers have access to the center?

Before you make your final choice, be sure to take a tour. Spend half an hour or so—when all the kids are there—observing. Are the children happy? Are they doing the kinds of activities you expected?

Finally, in the weeks after you pick the perfect day-care center, make a few unannounced visits—just to see what goes on when there aren't any parents around.

When you've done all your due diligence and made your final choice, have the person start a few days before you return to work so you can all get to know each other (and so you can spy).

A NOTE ABOUT LIVE-IN CHILD CARE   If you're lucky enough to be able to afford it, you might consider hiring a live-in caregiver, such as a nanny or an au pair. While having a live-in caregiver may sound fun (and, let's be honest, the prospect of having around a cute twenty-year-old with an even cuter accent doesn't hurt), you're essentially adding a new member to the family. The process for selecting one is similar to that for finding a non-live-in caregiver, and you can use most of the questions listed on page 298 when conducting interviews. (If you're going the au pair route, though, you'll have to do it through one of only eight placement agencies that are approved by the

Various Types of Child Care

TYPE	+ Advantages
IN-HOME CARE	♦ Your child gets one-on-one care and enrichment, such as field trips to the zoo ♦ The environment is comfortable and familiar ♦ No commuting to drop off your baby—either the caregiver already lives in your home or she comes there every day ♦ Less exposure to germs ♦ The caregiver may do some light housekeeping, laundry, and make a few meals ♦ If you're really worried, you can install a "nanny-cam" to keep an eye on what's happening at home. But if you're that suspicious, you might have hired the wrong person
GROUP DAY-CARE CENTER	♦ The facility needs to be licensed, and will be inspected regularly ♦ The staff usually has to go through a thorough background check, and will almost always have had special training in child development, CPR, and more ♦ There's usually a structured curriculum, which includes a mix of learning activities to do besides playing (art, music, etc.) ♦ The facility will have a lot more toys than you do ♦ Your baby will have a chance to learn to socialize with other kids ♦ Your baby will get used to falling asleep in a noisy environment ♦ If one member of the staff is sick, you'll still have coverage ♦ Your baby may be able to stay at the same place through preschool ♦ It's usually a little cheaper than in-home care
FAMILY DAY CARE	♦ They may be licensed ♦ It's usually the cheapest option ♦ Your baby can socialize with other kids ♦ The environment is more like a home (because it actually is someone's home) and less like a commercial center ♦ The structure and rules are usually much more flexible ♦ The caregiver is almost always a parent, so you know that she'll understand what you're going through ♦ The groups are small enough that the caregiver can take everyone on field trips

GEE HONEY, NOW WHAT DO WE DO?

- Disadvantages

- This is the most expensive option (unless you're going with an au pair, but you'll have to provide room and board for her)
- There's no backup if the caregiver gets sick or is on vacation
- Background checks aren't required, unless you go through an agency
- There are no formal qualification requirements
- There's no formal curriculum, meaning that your child could end up parked in front of the TV
- You'll have to pay taxes and benefits, which means extra work for you (doing all the bookkeeping), or extra expense (hiring an accountant to do it for you)

- Your baby won't get nearly as much one-on-one time with a caregiver
- Your baby will be exposed to every germ known to man (although in the long run that may build a stronger immune system)
- The rules can be rather rigid, which may make it hard for the center to accommodate any special requests you might have
- The structure may also be rigid. For example, nap time will be at a specific time, but babies rarely nap at exactly the same time every day.
- There are often steep fees for showing up late
- You'll need to find backup coverage if your child is sick or the center is closed for a holiday and you still have to work
- Depending on staff turnover rate, there may not be much consistency

- The caregiver can quit without giving you any notice
- You'll need coverage if she gets sick or takes a vacation
- The child-to-staff ratios can be higher than in commercial centers—and may be a lot higher than you'd like
- Licensing requirements are less stringent than for commercial centers
- Some caregivers have degrees in early childhood education and have taken infant CPR. Others aren't much more than warm bodies.
- The caregiver's family pets may frighten your child or trigger an allergic reaction

United States Information Agency.) After you've made your choice, you might want to try out your new relationship on a non-live-in basis for a few weeks, just to make sure everything's going to work out to everyone's satisfaction. (You can't do this with an au pair, though; she'll need to stay with you.) You can find out more about au pair programs at www.exchanges.state .gov/jexchanges/programs/aupair.html.

OUT-OF-HOME CHILD CARE   Many people—even those who can afford in-home child care—would rather have their child cared for somewhere else. There are two basic out-of-home options: group day-care centers and family day care.

When considering out-of-home day care, keep in mind that there's no correlation between how much you pay and the quality of care. Some places charge a lot because they can. So there's no excuse for not thoroughly checking out all your alternatives.

You can find out about out-of-home child-care facilities from your friends or from ads in a local parenting newspaper. You might also want to check with Child Care Aware (www.childcareaware.org), a nationwide campaign created to help parents identify quality child care in their communities.

CRYING
Let's face it, babies cry; it's their job. The fact is that 80 to 90 percent of all babies have periods of crying that can last from twenty minutes to an hour every day. Still, there's nothing like holding an inconsolably crying child to make even the most seasoned parent feel inadequate.

I think fathers tend to feel this sense of inadequacy more acutely than mothers, perhaps because most men have been socialized to view themselves as less than fully equipped to care for children and therefore have less than complete confidence in their parenting abilities.

When (not if) your child starts to cry, resist the urge to hand him or her to your partner. She knows nothing more about crying babies than you do (or will soon enough). To start with, however, here are a few things you can do to reduce the amount of time your child will spend crying:

♦ **Respond immediately.** It is absolutely impossible to spoil an infant by picking her up when she's crying. At the very least you'll be teaching your baby that she's safe and that you're there for her. At the same time, when you pick her up and the crying stops, you'll get a jolt of much-needed self-confidence.

♦ **Take note of what your partner eats while breastfeeding.** After one horrible, agonizing evening of inexplicable crying from our usually happy baby and a frantic call to the doctor, we discovered that the broccoli my wife had eaten for dinner was the culprit.

♦ **Have your partner nurse more often.** The baby could be literally crying out for more intimacy. Besides that, smaller, more frequent meals may be easier on the baby's newly operating digestive system.

♦ **Watch out for bottles.** Formula, cow's milk, and soy milk are frequent causes of tear-inducing allergic reactions or stomach distress. Even if your baby is being breastfed, she could still be reacting to the milk in your partner's diet, so have her cut dairy out of her diet for a few days to see what happens.

♦ **Know your baby.** Within just a few days after birth, your baby will develop distinct cries: "I'm tired," "Feed me now," "Change my diaper," "I'm uncomfortable as can be," "I'm bored in this car seat," and "I'm crying because I'm mad and I'm not going to stop no matter what you do." Once you learn to recognize these cries, you'll be able to respond appropriately and keep your baby happy. It's also important to know your child's routine—

"I'm worried about him. He's not picking at his food."

Colic

Starting at about two weeks of age, some 20 percent of babies develop colic—crying spells that, unlike "ordinary" crying, can last for hours at a time, sometimes even all day or all night. The duration and intensity of crying spells peaks at around six weeks and usually disappears entirely within three months.

Since there's no real agreement on what causes colic or on what to do about it, your pediatrician probably won't be able to offer a quick cure. Some parents, however, have been able to relieve (partially or completely) their colicky infants with an over-the-counter gas remedy for adults. Talk to your doctor about whether he or she thinks taking this medication would benefit your child.

some babies like to thrash around and cry a little (or a lot) before going to sleep; others don't.

◆ **Carry your baby more.** Some studies show that the more babies are held (even when they're not crying), the less they cry.

◆ **Watch the calendar.** Your baby's cries will be pretty manageable for the first week or two. After that, she'll cry more and more, peaking at six to eight weeks before tapering back down to manageable again.

After you've tried soothing, feeding, changing the diaper, checking for loose diaper pins or uncomfortable clothing, and rocking, the baby may still continue to howl. Sometimes there's really nothing you can do about it (see the section on coping, pages 307–8), but sometimes all it takes is a new approach. Here are a few alternatives you might want to try:

◆ **Hold the baby differently.** Not all babies like to be held facing you; some want to face out so they can see the world. One of the most successful ways I've learned to soothe a crying baby—and I've tried this on many kids besides my own—is to use Dave's Magic Baby Hold. (Dave, the father of a close friend, supposedly used the Hold to calm his own three children.) Quite simply, have the baby "sit" in the palm of your hand—thumb in front, the other fingers on the baby's bottom. Then have the baby lie face down on the inside of your forearm, with his or her head resting in the crook of your elbow. Use your other hand to stroke or pat the baby's back.

+ **Distraction.** Offer a toy, a story, a massage, a song. If the baby is diverted by a story or song, you'd better be prepared to repeat it over and over and over...

+ **Give the baby something to suck on.** Just take a guess why they call them "pacifiers." If you don't approve of pacifiers, you can either help the baby suck on his or her own fingers, or loan out one of yours.

+ **Give the baby a bath.** Some babies find warm water soothing. Others freak out when they get wet. If you do decide to try bathing a crying infant, don't do it alone. Holding onto a calm soapy baby is no easy chore. But keeping a grip on a squirming, screaming, soapy baby takes a team of highly trained specialists.

+ **Invest in a frontpack.** A lot of crying babies just want to be held all the time, and no matter how strong you think you are, your arms—and back— won't last forever. You'll be able to use your frontpack for other purposes as well—both my daughters traveled hundreds of miles strapped to my chest, while I did my cross-country ski-machine workout. In addition, carrying the baby around in the pack might give you an inkling of what it was like for your partner to be pregnant.

+ **Take the baby for a walk or a drive.** A word of caution: this doesn't work for all babies. When she was an infant, my elder daughter would fall asleep in the stroller or the car in a heartbeat. But my younger daughter hated riding in the car, especially when she was tired, and cried even more when I put her in her car seat. If you don't feel like going out, try putting the baby on top of a running washing machine or dryer. There's also a special device called SleepTight (www.colic.com) that, when attached to the baby's crib, simulates the feel (and sounds) of a car going fifty-five miles an hour.

+ **Heat things up a little...or cool 'em down.** Some people believe that babies cry less when their feet are warm. So try putting an extra pair of socks on the baby. Do *not* hold the baby's feet over a fire or use some kind of electric heating device. Duh. On the other hand, some babies may cry if they're overheated, so you may want to experiment with taking off a layer.

COPING WITH CRYING

If you've tried everything you can think of to stop the baby from crying, but to no avail, here are some things that may help you cope:

+ **Tag-team crying duty.** There's no reason why both you and your partner have to suffer together through what Martin Greenberg calls "the tyranny of crying." Spelling each other in twenty-minute or half-hour shifts will do you both a world of good. Getting a little exercise during your "time off" will also calm your nerves before your next shift starts.

♦ **Get some help.** Dealing with a crying child for even a few minutes can provoke incredible rage and frustration. And if the screams go on for hours, it can become truly difficult to maintain your sanity, let alone control your temper. (To make things worse, the baby will pick up on your tension and anger and will be even harder to soothe than before.) If you find yourself concerned that you might lash out (other than verbally) at your child, call someone: your partner, pediatrician, parents, baby sitter, friends, neighbors, clergyperson, or even a parental stress hotline. If your baby is a real crier, keep these numbers handy.

♦ **Let the baby "cry it out."** Sort of. If the crying goes on for more than twenty minutes or so, try putting the baby down in the crib and letting him or her cry. If the screaming doesn't stop after ten or fifteen minutes, pick the baby up and try a different approach from the section above for another fifteen minutes or so. Repeat as necessary. Note: don't let your baby cry it out until you've tried everything else. Ordinarily, you should respond promptly and lovingly to your baby's cries. Several studies show that babies who are responded to this way learn that someone will be there to help them if they need it. This ultimately makes them cry less and helps them grow up more confidently.

♦ **Don't take it personally.** Your baby isn't deliberately trying to antagonize you—really. It's all too easy to let your frustration at this temporary situation permanently interfere with the way you treat your child.

PLAYING WITH YOUR BABY

Playing with your child is one of the most important things you can do with him or her. Kids learn just about everything they need to know from playing. And to top it off, it's fun for you too.

As a rule, men and women have different play styles: women tend to stress the social and emotional type of play, while men are much more physical and high-energy. "Father-child play may be a particularly important context," writes the dean of fatherhood research, Ross Parke, "because its range of excitement and arousal is higher than in the more modulated play of mothers and children." Neither kind of parent-child interaction is truly better than the other—each is different and indispensable, and there's no point in trying to compare or rate them.

Several researchers have done extensive studies on the impact of physical play on children and have come up with some interesting conclusions. Parke,

A Note on Crying in Public

Dealing with a crying child in public was particularly stressful for me. It wasn't that I didn't think I could handle things; rather, I was embarrassed by and afraid of how other people would react. Would they think I was hurting the baby? Would they call the police? If they did, how could I possibly prove that the baby was mine? Fortunately, no one ever called the police, but there was no shortage of comments, which ranged from the seemingly helpful ("Sounds like that baby is hungry") to the blatantly sexist and infuriating ("Better get that baby home to her mother").

Although my fears about my children crying in public may sound a little paranoid (okay, a lot), I know I'm not alone. Just about every father I've spoken to has had similar thoughts in similar situations. I have to admit, however, that most of the women I've mentioned this to (including my dear wife) think I'm completely nuts on this point.

for example, found that playful dads seem to have smarter kids than dads who don't play with their kids as much—they're better at math and score higher on intelligence tests. Physical play—particularly the dad kind—helps encourage kids' independence. Both boys and girls who are exposed to high levels of physical play are more popular among their peers and more assertive (in a good way) in their interactions later in life. They also do a better job of reading others' emotional cues and regulating their own emotions than kids who don't get as much chance to play.

In general, babies love physical play, and by the time they're just a few days old, they've already learned which of their parents will play with them which way—and they'll react accordingly. Here are some important things to keep in mind about playing:

♦ **Pay attention.** Even though your baby is nowhere near being able to catch a fly ball, sink a jumper, or even hold on to a rattle, you can still have fun together. Take all that wild arm and leg flailing. Surprisingly, it has a real purpose, as do many of the baby's other natural reflexes. The arm swinging, for example, may be a protective device designed to push dangerous things away. And you've probably noticed that your baby starts sucking the second anything—finger, nipple, thumb—gets in her mouth. This reflex helps ensure that they get nourishment in the days and weeks before they learn how to control their sucking muscles. We talk extensively about reflexes and how you can have fun with them in the sequel to this book, *The New Father: A Dad's Guide to the First Year.*

♦ **Use moderation.** It's perfectly fine to play with a baby as young as a few days old, but restrict each session to five minutes or so. Too much playing can make your child fussy or irritable.

♦ **Start simple.** Imitation games are a good beginning. Stick your tongue out or make an O with your mouth, hold it for a few seconds, and see if the baby will do the same. You'll have the best luck if you do this in the Quiet Alert phase (see pages 272–73).

♦ **Take your cues from the baby.** If you pay attention, your baby will give you some pretty strong hints about whether he's interested in playing or would rather not. If he tries to raise his head, turns to look at you, or his eyes and face look bright, this is a good time to interact together. If he cries, squirms a lot, looks away from you, seems bored, or his face and eyes look glazed over, stop what you're doing and take a break.

♦ **Put on some music.** Doesn't matter what kind, but try to expose the baby to a nice variety. Baby ears are pretty sensitive to noise, so keep the volume low, particularly if you have a preemie.

♦ **Schedule your fun.** The best time for physical play is when the baby is in the Active Alert state; reading and other calmer activities are best during Quiet Alert (see pages 272–73). Choose a time when your full attention can be devoted to the baby—no phone calls or other distractions. Finally, don't play too vigorously with the baby immediately after feeding. Believe me—I learned the hard way.

♦ **Get comfortable.** Find a place where you can get down to the baby's level—preferably on your back or stomach on the floor or bed.

♦ **Be patient.** As mentioned above, your baby is not a trained seal—don't expect too much too soon. And certainly don't expect him to perform on cue.

♦ **Be encouraging.** Use lots of facial and verbal encouragement—smiles, laughter. Although the baby can't understand the words, he or she definitely understands the feelings. Even at only a few days old, your baby will want to please you, and lots of encouragement will build his or her self-confidence.

♦ **Be gentle—especially with the baby's head.** Because babies' heads are relatively large (one-quarter of their body size at birth vs. one-seventh by the time they're adults) and their neck muscles aren't very well developed yet, their heads tend to be floppy for the first few months. Be sure to support the head—from behind—at all times, and avoid sudden or jerky motions.

A COUPLE OF WARNINGS

♦ *Never* shake your child. This can make their little brains rattle around inside their skulls, causing bruises or permanent injuries (commonly referred to as Shaken Baby Syndrome).

♦ Never throw the baby up in the air. Yes, your father may have done it to you, but he shouldn't have. It looks like fun but can be extremely dangerous and just isn't worth the risk.

THE DIFFERENCES BETWEEN BOYS AND GIRLS

Back in the 1970s and 1980s, all the politically correct people insisted that there were no real differences between boys and girls—except for the obvious anatomical ones, of course. Any behavioral differences were supposedly the result of socialization, and were imposed on children by their parents and their environment.

But in the past few years, researchers have started questioning this theory, and their answers are confirming what most parents have always known: boys and girls are just not the same. The differences between them go far beyond mere anatomy and may even be present in our children's brains before they're born. Here's what we know:

♦ Physically, boys are a little bigger than girls—about 10 percent heavier and longer at birth. Even after taking into account this size difference, first-time mothers spend almost a hundred minutes longer in labor with a son than a daughter. This often leads to increased birth trauma and drug taking, which, in turn, may be the reason why boys tend to be a little more irritable in their first weeks outside the womb, typically crying more and sleeping less than girls.

♦ After birth, boys squirm and wiggle around more than girls.

♦ Within hours of birth, girls are much more interested in people and faces, while boys seem just as happy looking at an object dangled in front of them, says Ann Moir, Ph.D., author of *Brain Sex*. At only four months, girls can tell the difference between photographs of people they know from those of strangers; boys can't.

♦ Boys tend to take in less sensory data than girls, according to gender roles researcher Carole Beal. They're generally less discriminating when it comes to food, and less sensitive to touch and pain. They also hear worse in one ear than the other, meaning they don't pick up background noises as well as girls can, which may explain why your parents always thought you were ignoring them when you were little. It may also account for why girls typically learn to speak before boys do, usually by a month or two.

Despite all this, the distinctions between boys and girls during the first eighteen months of life are so slight that when babies are dressed in nothing but diapers, most adults can't tell a boy from a girl. But that doesn't stop us from treating them quite differently.

In one of the first studies of its kind, two Cornell University researchers, John and Sandra Condry, showed two hundred adults a videotape of a nine-month-old baby playing with various toys. Half were told that they were watching a boy, the other half that they were watching a girl. Although everyone was actually viewing the same tape, the descriptions the two groups gave of the baby's behavior were incredibly different. The "boy" group overwhelmingly perceived the child's startled reaction to a jack-in-the-box as anger. The "girl" group saw the reaction as fear.

Parents not only perceive their boys and girls differently but often treat them differently as well (your reaction to an angry child would be much different than to a frightened one). Mothers, for example, respond more quickly to crying girls than to crying boys and breastfeed them longer, according to psychologist Michael Gurian. And when girls have a difficult disposition, mothers tend to increase their level of affection, holding and comforting the child. But when a boy is similarly fussy, they generally back off. (This kind of behavior can have some serious, long-term consequences. In one study, for example, researcher Laura Allen found that boys who received more cuddling had higher IQs than boys who received less.)

When playing with their children, dads tend to be more rough and tumble with boys, but treat their daughters gingerly. And when babies are just starting to take their first steps, both parents tend to let their sons fall repeatedly, but will step in and pick up their daughters even before they hit the ground.

The upside of this kind of thing is that it encourages boys to be independent, and teaches them to learn to solve their own problems without adult intervention. The downside, though, is that they often end up with less supervision and, as a result, are more likely to be injured than girls. In addition, "parents who step in to rescue their daughter before she is truly 'stuck,'" writes psychologist Katherine Karraker, "not only deprive her of a chance to overcome obstacles through her own efforts, but may also be sending the message that they have no faith in her ability to do so."

So what can you do to keep from falling into these traps? Start with this:

- **Don't let your own prejudices and preconceived notions get in the way.**
- **Make an effort.** If you have a son, there's no reason why you can't cuddle with him—it's a perfectly masculine thing to do. If you have a daughter, there's no reason why—a few months from now—you can't wrestle with her. She'll love it and so will you.
- **Give your child a broad range of things to play with.** Most girls end up playing with dolls, but some would be just as happy with a fire truck, if they only got the chance (although there's a better than average chance that she'll wrap it in a blanket and sing it a lullaby). And while most boys will end up biting their toast into the shape of a gun, some might have a lot of fun playing with a doll.

Notes:

Fathering
Today

For the first weeks and months after the birth of your child, you'll be spending a lot of your time in the role of support person for your partner. But after a while, you'll settle into a more "normal" life—one and/or both of you will go back to work, and you might feel like taking in a movie or visiting some friends. And gradually, you'll figure out exactly what it means to be a father and how involved you intend to be in your child's life. Do you want to be someone he runs to when hurt or sad? Will you know her shoe size or whether she likes pants that zip up or slip on? Will you schedule his medical appointments or playdates, or will you leave all that to your partner?

Whatever you decide, it won't take long before you come face-to-face with the fact that being a father in America—especially an involved one—isn't easy. The responsibilities of the job itself are difficult and at times frustrating, but the biggest obstacles you'll face—ones you've probably never even thought about before—are societal.

It's only within the past few decades that men and women have felt able to speak out against the traditional role fathers have played in the family. And it's only recently that society has finally recognized that the distant father is not the ideal father. But in the midst of this newfound freedom to lash out against yesterday's absent, neglectful fathers, today's fathers—that's you—are falling victim to old stereotypes.

P. Steiner
THE WASHINGTON TIMES

According to one stereotype, men haven't taken an active role in family life because they haven't wanted to. But is this true today? Hardly. More and more of us are figuring out that the traditional measures of success are not all they're cracked up to be, and we are committed to being a major presence in our children's lives, physically and emotionally. In study after study, the overwhelming majority of men aged twenty to forty-five say that having a work schedule that lets them spend more time with their family is more important than doing challenging work or even earning a high salary. And most of these men would gladly give up pay for more family time. The hitch is that society (and by this I mean all of us) not only won't support us but actively discourages us. Quite simply, Americans don't value fatherhood nearly as much as motherhood. (Even the words conjure up very different images: *motherhood* is equated with caring, nurturing, and love, while *fatherhood* doesn't seem to be much more than a biological relationship.) As a result, men are rarely accepted if they assume a different role than the one they are "supposed" to assume.

The emphasis on traditional roles starts early. Even before they can walk, children of both sexes are bombarded with the message that fathers are basically superfluous. Just think of the books your parents read to you, and that you'll probably read to your own children. Have you ever noticed that there aren't any fathers in *The Cat in the Hat*; *Babar*; *Where the Wild Things Are*; *Are You My Mother?*; *Goodnight Moon*; *The Runaway Bunny*; or *Peter Rabbit*?

The very first article I ever had published appeared in *Newsweek* and was called "Not All Men Are Sly Foxes." It was all about what I perceived to be the negative stereotyping of fathers in children's literature. I spent an entire day in the children's section of my local library talking to the librarians and reading children's books, and found that dads were almost completely absent. In the vast majority of children's books, a mom is the only parent, while the dad—if he appears at all—was much less loving and caring than Mom, coming home late after work and bouncing baby around for five minutes before putting her to bed. The library had (and still has) a special catalog of children's books with positive female characters—heroines *and* mothers. As the father of a daughter, I thought that was great. But as a father who was sharing the child-care responsibilities equally, I found it incredibly frustrating and annoying that they didn't have a catalog (or even many books) with positive *male* role models. Even my three-year-old wanted to know why there weren't more daddies in the books we read.

A book that was a favorite of all three of my kids is *Mother Goose and the Sly Fox*, "retold" by Chris Conover. It's the story of a single mother (Mother Goose) with seven tiny goslings who is pitted against (and naturally outwits) the Sly Fox. Fox, a neglectful, and presumably unemployed, single father, lives with his filthy, hungry pups in a grimy hovel littered with the bones of their previous meals. Mother Goose, a successful entrepreneur with a thriving lace business, still finds time to serve her goslings homemade soup in pretty porcelain cups. The story is funny and the illustrations marvelous, but the unwritten message is that women take better care of their kids than men, who have nothing else to do but hunt down and kill innocent, law-abiding geese.

You'll find the same negative portrayals of fathers in the majority of children's classics. Take *Babar*. Every once in a while someone will complain about the book's colonialist slant (you know, little jungle dweller finds happiness in the big city and brings civilization—and fine clothes—to his backward elephant village). But no one seems to find it strange that after his mother is killed by the evil hunter, Babar is an "orphan." Why can he find comfort only in the arms of another female? Why do Arthur and Celeste's mothers come alone to the city to fetch their children? Don't the fathers care? Do they even have fathers?

Unfortunately, in the more than fifteen years since "Not All Men Are Sly Foxes" came out, not much has changed. Sure, we now routinely refer to "firefighters" and "mail carriers" (instead of firemen and mailmen), and most new children's books make a conscious effort to take female characters out of the kitchen and the nursery and give them professional jobs and responsibilities. We've eliminated negative stereotypes (*Little Black Sambo*, for example, has all but disappeared from library and bookstore shelves), and there are dozens of books that feature positive portrayals of the disabled, minorities, and people from other religions and cultures. Only the portrayals of fathers have stayed the same.

What *has* changed is that I'm not the only one complaining about these negative stereotypes anymore. Researchers David A. Anderson and Mykol Hamilton did an exhaustive study of the portrayals of parents in two hundred children's books, and found pretty much what I had: fathers appeared in half as many scenes as mothers. When present, they were portrayed as "unaffectionate" and "indolent" and were "relatively less likely than mothers to touch, hug, kiss, make other contact with, talk to, or feed children." In fact, there wasn't a single action that fathers did more than mothers, and dads were *never* seen kissing or feeding a baby.

If books were the only place children got messages about the way the world is supposed to be, you might be able to edit out the negative messages. But sooner or later your kids are going to find themselves in front of some kind of screen. Did you know that the average six-month-old spends about an hour a day in front of a television? Within just a few years that'll be up to more than four hours a day! (That doesn't include time spent playing computer or console games or watching DVDs.) And much of that time they'll be bombarded by the same stereotypes: if dads are there at all, they're usually fairly useless. If only because of the sheer number of hours involved, these images have the potential to do a lot more damage than the ones they get from books.

In a recent study of sitcoms, the National Fatherhood Initiative found that fathers were eight times more likely than mothers to be portrayed negatively. In fact, if you just think of the most prominent television dads, you'll find what the NFI's study—and a lot of other research—has found: that most of them are outwitted or shown up by their wives, ridiculed by their children, and portrayed as complete incompetents in every way. Of course these dads love their kids, but good intentions aside, they can't handle even the simplest child-related tasks and need a Hazmat suit to change a diaper.

Portrayals of fathers (and men in general) in commercials may be even worse. In the thirty-second world of the commercial, family dads—if they're part of the family at all—are not only dumber than everyone else, they're also almost completely oblivious to the needs of their children. Mothers, it seems, are the only ones who care. Here are a few examples:

♦ Kix breakfast cereal is billed as being "Kid-tested, mother-approved."

♦ Flo-Nase would like us to believe that when Mom is sick, Dad won't be able to iron his own shirts without burning them.

♦ Robitussin cold medicines are "recommended by Dr. Mom," who sometimes has to drag herself out of her sickbed to keep an eye on her incompetent husband, who's burning dinner.

♦ A series of milk commercials (the ones featuring people with milk mustaches) is aimed at mothers. Vivian Godfrey, the CEO of MilkPEP (the group that produces those ads), says: "We are using the message of Building Strong Families to talk to mothers."

♦ Disney has pretty much the same attitude. In a *New York Times* article on advertising, Disney executive VP Tricia Wilber said, "What our clients are trying to achieve are two objectives: reaching children directly or reaching children and their moms."

♦ Hundreds of ads running during the 2010 Winter Olympics told us that Procter & Gamble is the "Proud Sponsor of Moms."

While it's possible to argue that mothers still do most of the shopping and feeding, the subtle yet critical message contained in these ads is that fathers are stupid and useless and simply don't care. Kids—and anyone else who's watching—get the clear message that dads don't feed their kids, don't clothe them, won't be there to take care of them when they're sick, and shouldn't be called in case of emergency. The "Proud Sponsor of Moms" one, though, is probably the worst. Nothing against mothers, but dads are usually the ones who encourage their kids to get involved in sports, who coach their teams, and who play catch, shoot hoops, or ski moguls with them. Ignoring their contribution is just plain insulting.

In fairness, I should point out that some advertisers are portraying dads in a nurturing, caring, non-moronic kind of way. Jif peanut butter, for example, sometimes replaces their decades-old tagline "Choosy moms choose Jif" with "Choosy moms and dads choose Jif." And there are others. But they're still very few and very far between.

Nevertheless, in a recent survey by the National Fatherhood Initiative, 65 percent of fathers said they feel that the media portrays fathers in a negative light. And in several other studies, 74 percent of men said that images of men in ads are "out of touch with reality," and 75 percent couldn't identify a single ad that's relevant to them. This doesn't say much for Madison Avenue. It seems that we've confused men's lack of training in child care with a lack of interest in or concern about their children. A lot of today's fathers who were raised in "traditional" families simply had no role models—no one to teach them the skills they lack today.

Perhaps the most active way we have of discouraging men's involvement with children is by continually portraying men as dangerous. In an article I wrote for the *New York Times Magazine*, I described an incident that took place a few years ago. I was pushing my older daughter on the swing at our favorite park when I heard a little girl start to scream. She was just a few feet away, teetering on the small platform at the top of a long, steep slide. As I watched, she lost her grip on the handrail and began to fall. Without thinking, I stepped over to the slide, caught the girl, and set her down on the sand. I knelt down and was about to ask her if she was all right, when a woman picked the girl up, gave me a withering look, and hustled the child away. "Didn't I tell you not to talk to strange men in the park?" the woman asked her daughter, glaring over her shoulder at me. "Did he hurt you?"

I remember standing there for a few seconds, stunned, as the woman bundled her child into the car and drove off. I wondered what she had been thinking. Hadn't she seen me playing with a happy girl who called me Daddy? As I looked around the park, I realized I was the only man there. And then it hit me: she hadn't seen *me* at all. Instead, she'd seen what years of media images had trained her to see: the stereotyped images of a man in the park, menacing and solitary.

In some twisted way, I can empathize. If I'd turned around and seen a strange man kneeling near my daughter, I might have jumped to the worst possible conclusions, too. And when my wife and I used to interview babysitters for our daughters, I was the one who had the most serious qualms about hiring a man for the job (but we did have some boys babysit anyway—and they got high marks from the kids).

Just like the woman in the park, my "understanding" of these fears is based less on the truth about how men actually behave with children than on how we've been trained to view men with children. I still remember the "safety movies" I saw in about the third or fourth grade—scary images of sinister, mustachioed men (and they were always men) lurking behind trees in the park or trying to entice us into their cars. I'm not saying that there aren't some sick men out there, men who do horrible things to children. Men are the perpetrators in most sexual abuse cases (which constitute 11 percent of all cases of abuse and neglect). Yet there are plenty of sick women out there too; women murder more children than men do and are the perpetrators in the majority of physical and psychological abuse cases.

None of this, of course, is meant to imply that men are just hapless victims, or that all the obstacles fathers face are someone else's fault. In fact, some of the most significant barriers have been erected by men themselves. In the workplace, for example, where men still occupy the majority of positions of power, men who try to take time off from work to be with their families— either as paternity leave or by reducing their work schedules—find that their employers abuse them, treat them like wimps, and question how serious they are about their jobs (see pages 152–53 for more on this).

Despite the many obstacles, some of us have risked our careers and jeopardized our finances to try to break through the "other glass ceiling" that keeps us at work and away from our families. But in many cases, when we finally get home, we run smack into another barrier—this one imposed by none other than our partners.

Here's an all-too-common scenario: When I was visiting some friends not long ago, their six-month-old son started fussing. Colin, who was holding the baby, began rocking him. Suddenly his wife, Marina, appeared and whisked the baby away. "Let me take him, honey," she said. "I think I know what he needs."

I've seen scenes of this kind played out many times before (and not only at Colin and Marina's house), but this time I began to wonder. Did Marina really know what the baby needed? And if so, did she know better than Colin did? According to a significant amount of research, the answers to my questions are "probably" and "no," respectively. In a variety of studies, researcher Ross Parke found that fathers—despite stereotypes to the contrary—are just as sensitive and responsive to their infants' needs as mothers. They know when something is wrong, and they take appropriate action. So why, then, had Colin—a man I knew wanted an active role in raising his children—simply handed his crying son over to his wife? When you factor out sheer laziness from the equation, the answer to that question is a little tougher. What it seems to boil down to is that most of us—men as well as women—simply assume that women know more about kids than men.

In some ways, that may be true. On average, women do spend more time taking care of children than men do (but over the past two decades, men's time with children has increased greatly, while women's has stayed steady), and their skills may be a little sharper than men's. But parenting skills are not innate—they are learned through experience and training. No first-time parents, mothers or fathers, know instinctively how to soothe a colicky baby or prevent diaper rash. In fact, when our older daughter was born, my wife was taught how to breastfeed by a male nurse.

Still, the stereotypes persist, and to a great extent women control the amount—and quality—of time men spend with their children. Although most mothers feel that fathers should play an important role in the kids' lives, research has shown that they want that role to be "not quite as important as Mom's." In fact, researchers in one nationwide study found that two out of three women seem threatened by equal participation and may themselves be "subtly putting a damper on men's involvement with their children because they are so possessive of their role as primary nurturer." Bottom line? As I've said before, like it or not, you'll be as involved with your children as your partner will let you be. The more encouraging and supportive she is, the more you'll do.

It may sound as though all these obstacles are almost too numerous to overcome. Well, there may be a lot of them, and they may be quite ingrained, but if you're willing to put in the time and effort, you'll be able to have—and maintain—an active, involved relationship with your children. Here are some things you can do:

♦ **Get off your butt.** If you don't start taking the initiative, you'll never be able to assume the child-rearing responsibilities you want—and that your kids deserve. So instead of letting your partner pluck a crying or smelly baby from your arms, try saying something like, "No, honey, I can handle this," or "That's okay; I really need the practice." There's nothing wrong with asking her for advice if you need it—you both have insights that the other could benefit from. But have her *tell* you instead of doing it for you.

♦ **Get some practice.** Don't assume that your partner magically knows more than you do. Whatever she knows about raising kids, she's learned by doing—just like anything else. And the way you're going to get better is by doing things, too. Research has shown, for example, that lack of opportunity may be one of the biggest obstacles to fathers' being more affectionate with their children. Once they get to hold them, fathers are at least as affectionate with their children—cooing at, looking at, holding, rocking, and soothing them—as their partners are. (So much for the stereotype about men being emotionally distant by nature.)

♦ **Don't devalue the things you like doing with the kids.** As discussed in the preceding chapter, men and women generally have different ways of interacting with their children; both are equally important to your child's development. So don't let anyone tell you that wrestling, playing "monster," or other "guy things" are somehow not as important as the "girl things" your partner may do (or want you to do).

♦ **Get involved in the day-to-day decisions that affect your kids' lives.** This means making a special effort to share with your partner such respon-

SON OF THE MORNING STAR

sibilities as meal planning, food and clothes shopping, cooking, taking the kiddies to the library or bookstore, getting to know their friends' parents, and planning playdates. Not doing these things can give the impression that you don't think they're important or that you're not interested in being an active parent. And by doing them, you make it more likely that your partner will feel comfortable and confident in sharing the nurturing role with you. But try to log some private, "quality" time with the kids, too. Sure, somebody has to schlep the kids all over town—to doctor appointments, ballet lessons, or soccer practice—but that shouldn't be the only contact you have with them.

♦ **Keep communicating.** If you don't like the status quo, let your partner know. But be gentle. If at first she seems reluctant to share the role of parent with you, don't take it too personally. Men aren't the only ones whom society has done a bad job of socializing. Many women have been raised to believe that if they aren't the primary caregivers (even if they work outside the home as well), they've somehow failed as mothers. A 2010 study done at the University of Texas at Austin found that the more involved dads are with their children, the lower the mother's self-esteem. "We believe that employed mothers suffer from self-competence losses when their husbands are involved and skillful because those mothers may consider that it is a failure to fulfill cultural expectations," said Takayuki Sasaki, the lead researcher. If your partner works outside the home, you might want to remind her of what Karen DeCrow, a former president of the National Organization for Women (NOW), once told me: "Until men are valued as parents, the burden of child-rearing will fall primarily to women and frustrate their efforts to gain equality in the workplace."

♦ **If you're in a position to do something for other men, do it.** All things being equal, try hiring a male babysitter once in a while. Or consider asking a male friend instead of the usual women friends to do some babysitting when you and your wife want a night out. If you need to ease yourself into it, try the responsible teenage son of some friends. Continuing not to trust men and boys will keep men and boys thinking of themselves as untrustworthy and will make it difficult for them to be comfortable enough in their role as parent to take on as much responsibility as they—and their partners—would like.

♦ **Get your partner to be your publicist.** Pamela Jordan writes that "men tend not to be perceived as parents in their own right by their mates, co-workers, friends or family. They are viewed as helpmates or breadwinners." The cure? "The mother can mitigate the exclusion of the father by others by including the father in the pregnancy and parenting experiences and actively demonstrating her recognition of him as a key player," Jordan says.

♦ **Get some support.** Even before your baby is born, you're likely to become aware of the vast number of support groups for new mothers. It won't take you long to realize, however, that there are few, if any, groups for new fathers. And if you find one, it will probably be geared toward men whose contact with their kids is limited to five minutes before bedtime.

Having read this book, you know that men have just as many pregnancy, birth, and parenting questions as their partners. So if you can't find a new fathers' support group in your own neighborhood, why not be a trailblazer and start one of your own?

Here are a few ways you might get going:

♦ Start meeting regularly with male friends who already have kids. Talk on the phone, go for walks with the kids, meet in a park for lunch.

♦ Encourage other expectant or new dads to join you, and ask them to contact their male friends who have or are about to have children.

♦ Put up signs in local children's clothing and/or toy stores.
♦ Check with your partner's doctor, your pediatrician, and your childbirth class instructor about helping you advertise your group.
♦ Contact the YMCA or some of the local family-planning agencies to see if they'll help with publicity.
♦ Check with the people who organize some of the new mothers' groups—maybe they'd be interested in a fathers' auxiliary.

Who knows—if you do a good enough job publicizing your new fathers' group, you might even be able to turn it into a real business. Don't laugh: plenty of people are making money on mothers' groups.

A Final Word

Throughout this book we've talked about the benefits—both to you and to your children—of your being an active, involved father, and about how fatherhood actually begins long before your first child is born. What we haven't touched on, though, is the positive effect your fatherhood role can have on your relationship with your partner.

Back in the Third Month chapter, I mentioned that in the first year after the birth of a baby, 90 percent of new parents suffer a major drop in the quantity and quality of their communication, and that half the time, it's permanent. One way to make sure you don't fall into the wrong half is for you, the dad, to get and stay involved, meaning that you're engaged with your children, you help maintain your household, and you and your partner are committed to raising your children together.

Sociologist Pepper Schwartz has found that couples who worked together to raise their children "seemed to create a more intimate and stable relationship. They did more together. They talked on the phone together much more and spent more child-related time together. Wives in the study said they believed that raising children together created a more intimate adult relationship." Parenting together can also help both of you cope if you happen to have a difficult child. "When couples with a supportive marital relationship have a difficult baby, they tend to rise to the challenge," says Ohio State University professor Sarah Schoppe-Sullivan.

Aside from all that, when you're actively involved, your partner will be less stressed, less depressed, and generally happier in her relationship with you.

Not surprisingly, a number of studies have shown that fathers who are actively involved with their children have a much lower divorce rate than those who aren't.

So it's in everyone's best interests for you to do everything you possibly can to jump in and get involved right now. And stay that way for the rest of your life. It's not easy, but the rewards—for you, your children, and your partner—are incalculable.

The Process Continues

We'll, we've reached the end of *The Expectant Father*. I hope you've enjoyed it as much as I've enjoyed bringing it to you. But don't think that just because you've got a baby now means you can stop learning. Not a chance. In fact, your journey is just beginning; being an involved father takes work, patience, and a lot of understanding. If you're interested in learning more—and I hope you are—I've written a number of other books to help you along the way. *The New Father: A Dad's Guide to the First Year* covers, as you might guess, your baby's first year. *Fathering Your Toddler* continues though your child's third birthday. *Fathering Your School-Age Child* picks up there and goes through age nine. All of these books continue and expand on the process we started here: getting to know yourself and what you're going through, how your child is developing, what's going on with your partner, and how to be the kind of father you want to be and your family needs you to be.

Now get out there and be a great dad!

Notes:

Appendix

Infertility: When Things Don't Go As Planned

A mong couples who consciously try to get pregnant (or who at least consciously stop trying *not* to get pregnant), about 25 percent conceive in the first month. Fifty to 60 percent get it done within six months, 60 to 75 percent within nine, and around 80 percent within a year. But that 80 percent number means very different things to different couples. According to researchers at Brigham and Women's Hospital, if you and your partner are in the 20–24 age group, your chances are 86 percent; if you're 25–29, it's 78 percent; 30–34, the odds are down to down to 63 percent; and if you're in the 35–39 group, it's only 52 percent. If you haven't conceived within a year (six months if your partner is thirty-five or older), you'll slip into the mysterious category called *infertility,* and you may need some outside intervention if you're going to have that baby you've been working so hard to get.

Despite what you may have heard, infertility is not just a female problem. Thirty-five to 40 percent of the time, the problem can be traced to the woman. The same goes for men. For 20 percent of couples, it's a mix of his and hers issues. Some of these reasons are listed in the chart on the next page. The rest of the time, there's simply no explanation.

Diagnosing a fertility problem can be a long and expensive process. Actually *treating* the problem will take even more time and money, which, most likely, won't be covered by your insurance. Technology is getting better all

Causes of Infertility

Because infertility is such a complex subject, there's no way I can do it justice here. Fortunately, the fertility doctor or clinic you work with will have tons of great resources for you, and they can explore every issue with you in great detail. What they probably won't have, though, is much information on how the ups and downs, ins and outs of infertility will affect you, your partner, and your relationship with each other. So after a brief look at what you might be in for, we'll talk about exactly that. Let's start with what might cause infertility.

YOURS

- Low sperm count or damaged/irregular sperm shape and movement. These can be caused by:
  - Smoking
  - Drugs
  - Alcohol
  - Environmental toxins such as fertilizers and hazardous materials
  - Medication
  - Medical conditions such as diabetes, prostate problems, sexually transmitted disease, genital infection, or trauma to the testicles
  - Radiation you may have received as part of chemotherapy
  - Tight underwear or keeping the testicles too warm
- Testosterone deficiency
- Having had mumps after puberty
- Having a mother who took DES, a medication designed to prevent miscarriage and other pregnancy complications. It was prescribed as recently as the 1970s.
- Undescended testicle
- Varicocele, which is the swelling of a vein in the scrotum that may keep the testicle from cooling off
- Age. See "That Clock You Hear Ticking May Not Be Hers" on pages 330–31.
- Stress

HERS

- Damaged or blocked fallopian tubes
- Ovulation problems
- Hormone imbalance
- Many of the same factors that could affect you:
  - Smoking
  - Drugs
  - Alcohol
  - Medication
  - Environmental toxins
  - STDs
  - Radiation
  - Poor diet
  - Being significantly over- or underweight
- Uterine problems, including endometriosis, cysts, fibroids, and scar tissue
- Having a mother who took DES during pregnancy
- Age
- Stress

That Clock You Hear Ticking May Not Be Hers

The average age of first-time mothers and fathers keeps rising. The birth rate for mothers over 35 today is over 40 percent higher than it was in 1970; for mothers over 40, it's nearly 50 percent higher. And although most people know about the difficulties that women over 35 have in getting pregnant, and the increased risk of miscarriage, preterm birth, and birth defects they face, we rarely hear anything about the effects of "older" fatherhood. In fact, having a child older in life is considered kind of cool and a confirmation of one's masculinity. (David Bowie, Mick Jagger, Jack Nicholson, David Letterman, and Eric Clapton all became dads in their fifties. Pablo Picasso, Van Morrison, Larry King, and Clint Eastwood were in their sixties. Charlie Chaplin became a dad at 73, Julio Iglesias Sr. was 89, and there are plenty more.) While there's no question that being an older dad can indeed be cool and masculinity-affirming, there are some risks that you should be aware of. Here's a quick overview.

♦ Researchers at Bristol University in the UK found that men's fertility begins to decrease starting at around age 24. The odds of conceiving within six months of trying go down 2 percent per year after that age.

♦ Sperm count decreases with age, and the little guys gradually lose their speed and accuracy, meaning fewer of them will make it all the way to the egg, and those that do will take a lot longer to get there.

♦ Sperm quality also decreases, meaning that the ones that reach the egg are less able to fertilize it. According to French researcher Stephanie Belloc, men over 35 are less likely to impregnate their partners; men over 40 are *significantly* less likely. And even if they do, the resulting pregnancies have a slightly increased risk of ending in miscarriage.

♦ A number of very rare health risks and genetic conditions are associated with older dads. For example, research shows that compared to men under 30, dads over 40 have a higher risk of fathering children with schizophrenia, dwarfism, heart defects, facial abnormalities,

the time; but while fertility treatments definitely improve the odds for many couples—sometimes to as high as 50 percent—there's no guarantee that it will actually have the desired effect. Ever.

The doctors will start the diagnostic process by taking, from both of you, a complete medical history designed to investigate the cause of the infertility.

autism, epilepsy, and some childhood cancers. Advanced paternal age may also be associated with children's lower IQ scores, increased risk of developing breast cancer, and shortened life span (for women born to dads 45 and over). But again, these conditions are rare. And the connection between a dad's age and elevated risks is small. Still, the American Society for Reproductive Medicine has set 40 as the upper limit for sperm donations, and many clinics have even lower limits. Just something to keep in mind.

♦ As your kids get older, you may not like it when people assume you're the grandfather instead of the dad.

♦ As you get older, it may be a bit harder for you to do some of the physical things young dads do, such as skateboarding, giving piggyback rides, and just crawling around on the floor.

On the other hand, being an older dad has its advantages. And in many people's eyes, those advantages far outweigh the disadvantages.

♦ Older dads are generally more financially secure, less worried about saving up for a down payment or making partner, and better able to provide for their families.

♦ Research indicates that older dads are more likely to share responsibility for taking care of their children and tend to be more actively involved with them.

♦ Older dads may also be warmer, more nurturing, and more focused on their children than younger dads.

♦ Older dads rate themselves as being more patient, more mature, and calmer than the young bucks.

♦ There is some indication that children with older dads do better in school. That's probably at least partly due to some of the factors above.

You'll both also have a physical exam. In yours the doctor will manhandle and squeeze your testicles. He may also order a semen analysis (see "Give Yourself a Hand" on page 333).

Here's the good news. Around 90 percent of couples seeking help with fertility get pregnant after relatively benign treatments, meaning lifestyle changes (diet, exercise, changing medication that may prevent fertility, timing of intercourse), drugs (to stimulate ovulation, increase sperm volume, or prevent miscarriage), artificial insemination (with either the male partner's sperm or a donor's), and minor surgery (to bypass obstructions, remove tumors and cysts, clear scar tissue, and correct other physical issues that are causing problems).

Only 3 to 5 percent of fertility patients need any of the high-tech options, such as IVF, egg donation, ICSI, PGD, and a few others (see pages 334–35 for these and other helpful terms). For those who don't conceive after all that, the remaining options are surrogacy or adoption.

Life on Planet Infertility

Ready for an understatement? Dealing with infertility—especially if you're among the minority that's undergoing expensive, time-consuming procedures—is not easy. To start with, there's the physical part: the semen samples, egg retrieval, blood tests, medication and hormone injections and the associated side effects, intrusive physical exams, and mad dashes to have sex at exactly the right time. All that, by itself, would be hard enough. But throw in the psychological toll of infertility, and you're in for a rough ride.

What's Going on with Your Partner

Most women in our society have grown up assuming that they will be mothers. So when that assumption—and the dreams that go with it—is shattered, it can bring up all sorts of feelings. Some experts believe that women take infertility harder than men. (In one study, half of women going through treatment said that being infertile was "the most upsetting event of their lives," compared to 15 percent of men.) Your partner has monthly reminders of her fertility, or lack thereof. And since she's the one who will carry the baby, society, family, friends, and maybe even her religion put more pressure on her to reproduce than on you. As she goes through the infertility process, she may experience some of the following:

♦ **Anxiety and depression.** A recent study cited in the *Harvard Mental Health Letter* found that "women with infertility felt as anxious or depressed as those diagnosed with cancer, hypertension, or recovering from a heart attack."
♦ **Grief and sorrow.** At the loss of her dreams.

Give Yourself a Hand

If you and your partner aren't able to conceive within a year, her OB may suggest fertility treatments. The first step—because it's the easiest—is to do a semen analysis. The lab will be looking for a number of things, including count (how much semen is produced and how many sperm per milliliter it contains), morphology (size, shape, and appearance of the individual sperm), and motility (how quickly and how straight the sperm swim).

There are a variety of ways to collect semen (either for analysis or artificial insemination), almost all of which involve masturbation. In many cases, the festivities will happen at your partner's OB's office. Chances are they have a room that's outfitted with at least a few raggedy porn magazines (though hopefully the pages won't be stuck together), where you'll be expected to masturbate into a clean collection cup. Your partner will not be invited to assist. And keep in mind that any feeble attempts at humor, such as asking the nurse whether she'd give you a hand, won't go over well. Especially if your partner finds out about it. If you need any other visual aids, you can download plenty of them onto your PDA or smartphone.

If you'd rather not produce your sample in the doctor's office, you may be able to do it at home, just as long as you can get the fresh sample there within an hour. The at-home approach gives you a few other options as well. You could do it yourself. Or your partner could help by bringing you to orgasm any way she wants and collecting the sample in the cup. Or you could have sex and collect the sample by withdrawing before climaxing or using a special condom that the doctor will give you.

+ **Shame and inadequacy.** At being unable to fulfill her biological role.
+ **Guilt.** Especially if the infertility is "her fault."
+ **Anger.** Especially if the infertility is "your fault."
+ **Protectiveness.** Again, if it's "your fault." She may want to keep you from feeling bad about yourself or your masculinity. Sometimes this plays out as wanting to have sex with you more often, as if to say that she still finds you sexually attractive—even if you have a low sperm count.
+ **Resentful.** Nearly a third of women going through infertility treatment don't feel that their partner shares "the same level of commitment and dedication to getting pregnant," according to a study conducted by Organon, a

A Few Helpful Terms

Baby-making, like any other science, has a vocabulary all its own. Here are a few of the most common terms you're likely to come across.

♦ **ART** (Artificial Reproductive Technology). Refers to any nonsexual method of producing a pregnancy. Includes IVF, donor eggs, donor sperm, PGD, and surrogates (see below for definitions).

♦ **AI** (Artificial Insemination—also referred to as **IUI**, for intrauterine insemination). The process of inserting sperm directly into a woman's uterus. This is the lowest-tech ART.

♦ **Donor eggs.** If your partner's eggs are not viable or healthy, or there's a significant risk of passing on a genetic disorder, doctors can use eggs harvested from another woman. Donor eggs will be combined with sperm—yours or a donor's—in IVF.

♦ **Donor sperm.** If your sperm is damaged or otherwise unhealthy, doctors can use sperm collected from someone other than you. This sperm will be combined with eggs—your partner's or a donor's—in IVF.

♦ **ICSI** (Intracytoplasmic Sperm Injection). Unlike regular IVF procedures, in which the lab puts the egg and millions of sperm together and gives them some privacy to do their thing, in this procedure, the doctor or embryologist injects a single sperm into the egg. This expensive procedure is sometimes used if AI has failed and the man's sperm count and motility are extremely low. The sperm can be collected the usual way (via masturbation) or through one of two amazing processes, called Testicular Sperm Extraction (TESE) and microsurgical epididymal sperm aspiration (MESA), both of which remove sperm directly from the testicle. With IVF, there's a 75 percent chance of the egg being fertilized. With ICSI, fertilization is guaranteed.

♦ **IVF** (In Vitro Fertilization, meaning "fertilization in glass"). This involves collecting a woman's eggs and a man's sperm and mixing them in a dish or tube. A few days after conception, anywhere from two

manufacturer of fertility products. In the same study, 40 percent of women said that someone other than their partner was "their greatest source of support," and 26 percent felt their partner "could have been more supportive."

♦ **A lack of intimacy.** As one fertility doc told me, couples undergoing fertility treatment can either have sex or make love. Not both. Having sex on a schedule can become a real chore and will suck all the romance out of it.

to five healthy-looking (under a microscope) embryos will be implanted in the woman's uterus.

♦ **Ovulation.** The release of the egg from the ovary, which typically happens twelve to fourteen days before a woman's period starts. The egg moves down the fallopian tubes to the uterus, where it hopes to be fertilized by sperm.

♦ **PGD** (Preimplantation Genetic Diagnosis). The main reason why many embryos don't result in a pregnancy is that they have some kind of chromosomal abnormality. The PGD process allows doctors to genetically analyze each embryo to determine whether it's normal or not (they can actually screen for about 400 diseases or abnormalities). Since only the healthiest embryos are implanted, they're more likely to result in a viable pregnancy, and the rates of miscarriage or birth defects are significantly lowered.

♦ **Semen.** The whitish, sticky fluid that carries the sperm (see below). Semen protects the sperm and helps them swim toward the egg.

♦ **Sperm.** The cells containing the man's DNA that do the actual impregnating of the egg. Sperm are tiny—there are as many as 300 million in a single drop of semen—and look like tadpoles, with a big head and a long tail. Average sperm count is around fifty million per milliliter, which is down from about one hundred million just fifty years ago.

♦ **Surrogate.** Essentially a womb for rent. If a woman is unable to carry a pregnancy to term, it's possible to "commission" another woman who can. In some cases, the surrogate mother and the commissioning father may be the genetic parents of the child. In others, the surrogate mother may not be genetically related at all, and is simply carrying the biological product of the commissioning couple. And given where IVF technology is today, it's even possible that the surrogate mother, the genetic mother, and the commissioning mother are all different. Pretty crazy.

What's Going on with You

In my view, one of the reasons that the study above found that more women than men rate infertility as the most upsetting event in their lives is that people take men's silence and withdrawal as an indication that they aren't suffering. Nothing could be further from the truth. Here's what you may be feeling:

- **Discomfort and embarrassment.** Those physical exams can be really unpleasant.
- **Inadequacy.** We try to convince ourselves that size doesn't matter, but most guys want to know how they stack up to others. Hearing that the average sperm count is 50 million per milliliter but that yours is only 10 million, or that there's some other reason you can't impregnate your partner, can come as a real blow to your masculinity.
- **Anger.** At yourself, if the infertility is on your end. At your partner, if it's on hers.
- **Lack of control.** We're supposed to be the provider/protectors, the guys with all the answers. But on Planet Infertility, there's little or nothing that we can do to change things.
- **Grief and depression.** If you lost a baby to miscarriage, you have something a bit more tangible to grieve about. But even if you didn't get that far, you can still mourn the loss of potential, of the future, of being able to pass on the family name and genes, of being able to be a dad.
- **Loneliness.** A lot of guys in infertile couples have no one to talk to—or at least they think they don't. You don't want to talk to your partner because you know you're supposed to be strong for her, you want to protect her, and you don't want her to have to take care of your needs in addition to her own. And it's hard to imagine talking about something as sensitive and personal as infertility over a beer with the guys.
- **Withdrawal.** Because infertility can make you question your self-image and your masculinity, a lot of guys pull away from their partner and begin spending more time at work or hanging out with their friends—places where they feel more in control and can get some praise for doing a good job.
- **Guilt.** At not being able to fulfill your partner's desires to be a mom.
- **Fear.** The intensity of your partner's reactions to the situation may expose a side of her that you never knew existed. You may wonder whether she loves you anymore or whether your relationship will survive all of this.
- **Frustration.** The things you used to do to comfort your partner may not work anymore.
- **Protectiveness.** You'll be amazed at the level of insensitivity that people— most of whom probably mean well—will display. You'll get all sorts of suggestions on how to get pregnant, hear horror stories about fertility treatments, and suffer through tons of anecdotes about people who got pregnant within fifteen seconds of trying. You'll do everything you can to protect your partner from hearing these things, but some of it's bound to get through.

♦ **Oversexed.** At one point in your life, the idea of having sex every day may have seemed like a dream. But when you're dealing with infertility, the sex can very quickly move from hot and steamy to routine and boring. And there's no one to talk to about this. Who's going to believe a guy who complains about having sex too often?

Coping with Infertility

Infertility can take a real toll on your relationship with your partner. But being aware of the potential pitfalls, and having some strategies in place to deal with rough spots, will make the whole process more tolerable.

♦ **Stick together.** The two of you may be experiencing different things at different times, but you're in this together. Be patient with each other and support each other every way you can. This may include coming up with some snappy responses to the inevitable questions from family and friends about when you're going to have children. And in fact, besides your relationship with your partner, infertility can affect your relationships with other family and friends. Understanding this—and recognizing that each of you is the other's closest ally—is critical.

♦ **No second-guessing or self-blame.** It's very easy to slip into "shoulda, woulda, coulda" mode. Okay, maybe you shouldn't have waited so long to begin trying to start a family. Maybe you shouldn't have had an abortion years ago. Maybe you should have lost weight or quit smoking a long time ago, or whatever. But there's nothing you can do about any of that now, and beating yourself up about it—or letting your partner beat herself up about it—is a complete waste of time and energy.

♦ **Learn.** Ask your doctors every question you can think of, and read everything you can get your hands on. But be careful to consider the source. Because infertility brings out the desperation in many couples, you'll find no shortage of "guaranteed" schemes that will separate you from your money, get you all optimistic, and then leave you worse off than before when they don't work.

♦ **Get ready for the ups and downs.** It's natural to get excited right before any procedure, and just as natural to feel devastated if it's unsuccessful. Typically, the more expensive and complex the procedure, the more stress couples experience.

♦ **Have a little fun.** Set aside some time to see a movie, have dinner together, hit the gym. Take advantage of the downtime between treatments to have wild, passionate sex in the backseat of your car. Don't let your entire lives revolve around treatments. You've got to give yourself some breaks from the routine.

♦ **Set some limits.** Is there a maximum amount of time you're willing to devote to trying to have a baby? A maximum budget?

♦ **Listen, talk, then listen some more.** Ask your partner what she needs from you. Tell her what you need from her. Be prepared to just listen. Although it might work in other situations, trying to solve her problems now may do more harm than good.

♦ **Stay away from places where there are going to be lots of people with children.** Of course, that's not always going to be possible, but don't be shy about turning down invitations (or backing out of obligations) if you think it would be better for your mental health.

♦ **Keep your mouth shut.** Whether you choose to tell people about your infertility is your choice. Some couples want to keep it to themselves, others feel better talking about it. But one thing is certain: there is absolutely no upside to telling anyone whose "fault" it is.

♦ **Get some support.** People who have never had to deal with infertility have no idea how devastating it is. Consider joining a support group so you can connect with others in your situation. If you don't want to do it in person, take a look at some of the options in the Resources section starting on page 355.

Bibliography

Books

Agnew, Connie L., Alan Klein, and Jill Ganon. *Twins: Pregnancy, Birth, and the First Year of Life*. New York: HarperPerennial, 1997.

American College of Obstetricians and Gynecologists. *The ACOG Guide to Planning for Pregnancy, Birth, and Beyond*. Washington, D.C.: ACOG, 1990.

Bainbridge, Jason. "Blaming Daddy: The Portrayal of the Evil Father in Popular Culture." In *Against Doing Nothing: Evil and its Manifestations*, edited by Shilinka Smith and Shona Hill. Oxford, UK: Inter-Disciplinary Press, 2010.

Beal, Carole. *Boys and Girls: The Development of Gender Roles*. New York: McGraw-Hill, 1994.

Bradley, Robert A. *Husband Coached Childbirth*. New York: Harper and Row, 1974.

Bryan, E. M. "Prenatal and Perinatal Influences on Twin Children: Implications for Behavioral Studies." In *Twins as a Tool of Behavioral Genetics*, edited by T. J. Bouchard Jr., and P. Propping. New York: John Wiley and Sons, 1993.

Camman, William. *Easy Labor: Every Woman's Guide to Choosing Less Pain and More Joy During Childbirth*. New York: Ballantine, 2006.

Cath, H. C., A. Gurwitt, and L. Gunsberg, eds. *Fathers and Their Families*. Hilldale, N.J.: Analytic Press, 1989.

Caton, Donald. *What a Blessing She Had Chloroform: The Medical and Social Response to the Pain of Childbirth from 1800 to the Present*. New Haven, Conn.: Yale University Press, 1999.

Churchwell, Gordon. *Expecting: One Man's Uncensored Memoir of Pregnancy.* New York: HarperCollins, 2000.

Colman, L. L., and A. D. Colman. *Pregnancy: The Psychological Experience.* New York: Noonday Press, 1991.

Cowan, C. P., and P. A. Cowan. *When Partners Become Parents.* New York: Basic Books, 1992.

Duff, Margaret. *A Study of Labor.* PhD dissertation, University of Technology, Sydney, Australia, 2005.

Eliot, Lise. *Pink Brain, Blue Brain: How Small Differences Grow into Troublesome Gaps—And What We Can Do About It.* Cambridge, Mass.: Houghton Mifflin, 2009.

Greenberg, Martin. *The Birth of a Father.* New York: Avon, 1986.

Hahn, Sinhue, and Laird G. Jackson, eds. *Prenatal Diagnosis.* New York: Humana Press, 2008.

Johnson, Patricia Irwin. *Launching a Baby's Adoption: Practical Strategies for Parents and Professionals.* Indianapolis: Perspectives Press, 1997.

Jordan, Pamela. "The Mother's Role in Promoting Fatherhood." In *Becoming a Father: Contemporary Social Developmental and Clinical Perspectives,* edited by Jerrold Lee Shapiro, Michael J. Diamond, and Martin Greenberg, 61–71. New York: Springer, 1995.

Keough, Carol. *New Baby Book.* Des Moines: Better Homes and Gardens, 1998.

Kitzinger, Sheila. *The Experience of Childbirth.* Harmondsworth, UK: Penguin, 1987.

Klaus, M., and P. Klaus. *The Amazing Newborn.* Rev. ed. Reading, Mass.: Addison-Wesley, 1999.

Klaus, M., J. Kennel, and P. Klaus. *Mothering the Mother.* Reading, Mass.: Addison-Wesley, 1993.

Kutner, Lawrence. *Pregnancy and Your Baby's First Year.* New York: William Morrow, 1993.

Lamb, Michael, ed. *The Role of the Father in Child Development.* New York: John Wiley and Sons, 1981.

Levene, Malcolm I., and Frank A. Chervenak. *Fetal and Neonatal Neurology and Neurosurgery,* 4th ed. Amsterdam: Churchill Livingstone, 2009.

Logan, Brent. *Learning Before Birth: Every Child Deserves Giftedness.* Bloomington, Ind.: AuthorHouse Publishing, 2003.

Luke, Barbara, and Tamara Eberlein. *When You're Expecting Twins, Triplets, or Quads, 3rd Edition: Proven Guidelines for a Healthy Multiple Pregnancy.* New York: HarperCollins, 2010.

Michaels, Paula. *Childbirth Pain Relief and the Soviet Origins of the Lamaze Method.* The National Council for Eurasian and East European Research, Seattle, Wash.: 2007.

Minnick, M. A., K. J. Delp, and M. C. Ciotti. *A Time to Decide, a Time to Heal.* Mullett Lake, Mich.: Pineapple Press, 1990.

Parke, Ross, and Armin Brott. *Throwaway Dads: The Myths and Barriers that Keep Men from Being the Fathers They Want to Be.* Cambridge, Mass.: Houghton Mifflin, 1999.

Pederson, A., and P. O'Mara, eds. *Being a Father.* Santa Fe: John Muir, 1990.

Profet, Margie. "Pregnancy Sickness as Adaptation: A Deterrent to Maternal Ingestion of Teratogens," In *The Adapted Mind,* edited by Jerome Barkow, Leda Cosmides, and J. Tooby, 327–65. New York: Oxford University Press, 1992.

Pruett, Kyle, and Marsha Kline Pruett. *Partnership Parenting: How Men and Women Parent Differently—Why It Helps Your Kids and Can Strengthen Your Marriage.* Philadelphia, Pa.: DaCapo Lifelong, 2009.

Rankin, Lissa. *What's Up Down There?: Questions You'd Only Ask Your Gynecologist If She Was Your Best Friend.* New York: St. Martin's Griffith, 2010.

Rodriguez, Robert. *An Anxious Time for Men: Pregnancy: A Research Study That Measured Anxiety, Stress, Marital Satisfaction, and Depression in First Time Expectant Fathers.* Ohio: Greenborough Publishing, 2003.

Roehrich, Susan K. *Men's Perspectives on a Spouse's or Partner's Postpartum Depression.* Unpublished PhD dissertation, Virginia Polytechnic Institute and State University, 2007.

Shapiro, Jerrold L. *The Measure of a Man.* New York: Delacorte, 1992.

———. *When Men Are Pregnant.* New York: Delta, 1993.

Siegel, Alan. *Dream Wisdom: Uncovering Life's Answers In Your Dreams.* Berkeley, Calif.: Celestial Arts, 2003.

Smith, Shilinka, and Shona Hill, eds. *Against Doing Nothing: Evil and its Manifestations.* Oxford, UK: Inter-Disciplinary Press, 2010.

Tassone, Shawn, and Landherr, Kathryn. *Hands off My Belly!: The Pregnant Woman's Survival Guide to Myths, Mothers, and Moods.* Amherst, N.Y.: Prometheus Books, 2009.

Thevenin, Tine. *The Family Bed.* New York: Avery, 1987.

Van de Carr, F. R., and M. Lehrer. *While You Are Expecting.* Atlanta: Humanics Learning, 1997.

Vanston, Claire M. *Maternal Cognitive Function in Pregnancy and Its Associa-tion with Gestation, Endoctine Factors, and Fetal Sex: A Longitudinal Study of Women from Early Pregnancy to the Postpartum Period*. Dissertation from Simon Fraser University, Summer 2005.

Verny, T., and J. Kelly. *The Secret Life of the Unborn Child*. New York: Delta, 1991.

Verny, T., and P. Weintraub. *Nurturing the Unborn Child*. New York: Dela-corte Press, 1991.

Journal Articles

Abel, Ernest L., and M. L. Kruger. "Symbolic Significance Of Initials on Longevity." *Perceptual and Motor Skills* 104 (2007): 179–82.

Alicesteen, R., and Y. Yum. "The Effect of Sex and Sex Talk During Pregnancy on Relationship Satisfaction." Paper presented at the annual meeting of the International Communication Association, Sheraton New York, New York City. Retrieved from www.allacademic.com/ meta/p12762_index.html.

Allen, V. M, R. D. Wilson, and A. Cheung. "Pregnancy Outcomes after Assisted Reproductive Technology." *Journal of Obstetrics and Gynaecology Canada* 28(3) (March 2006): 220–50.

American Academy of Pediatrics. Task Force on Circumcision. "Circumcision Policy Statement" (Reaffirmed). *Pediatrics* 116 (2005): 796.

Arabin, B., J. von Eyck, J. Wisser, H. Versmold, and H. K. Weitzel. "Fetales Verhalten bei Mehrlingsgravitat: methodische, klinische und Wissen-schaftliche Aspekte" (Fetal Behavior in Multiple Pregnancy: Methodologic, Clinical and Scientific Aspects). *Geburtshilfe und Frauenheilkunde* 51 (1991): 869–75.

Arguello, Ximena, et al. "Fetal Reaction to the World." Unpublished manuscript, Lincoln International Academy, November 23, 2009. Accessed 2/22/10 from www.liasociology101.com/Fetal%20 Reaction%20to%20Environment.pdf.

Badenhorst, W., S. Riches, P. Turton, and P. Hughes. "The Psychological Effects of Stillbirth and Neonatal Death on Fathers: Systematic Review." *Journal of Psychosomatic Obstetrics and Gynaecology* 27, no. 4 (2006): 245–56.

Barrett, Geraldine, et al. "Women's Sexual Health After Childbirth." *BJOG: An International Journal of Obstetrics & Gynaecology* 107, no. 2 (2005): 186–95.

Barrett, Geraldine, Elizabeth Pendry, Janet Peacock, Christina Victor, Ranee Thakar, and Isaac Manyonda. "Women's Sexuality after Childbirth: A Pilot Study." *Archives of Sexual Behavior* 28 (April 1999): 179–91.

Bartels R. "Experience of Childbirth from the Father's Perspective." *British Journal of Midwifery* 7, no. 4 (1999): 681–83.

Batman, P. A., J. Thomlinson, V. C. Moore, and R. Sykes. "Death Due to Air Embolism During Sexual Intercourse in the Puerperium." *Postgraduate Medical Journal* 74 (October 1998): 612–13.

Beaton, John M., William J. Doherty, and Martha A. Rueter. "Family of Origin Processes and Attitudes of Expectant Fathers." *Fathering* 1, no. 2 (June 2003): 149–68.

Becker, Gay, Anneliese Butler, and Robert D. Nachtigall. "Resemblance Talk: A challenge for parents whose children were conceived with donor gametes in the US." *Social Science & Medicine* 61 (2005): 1300–1309.

Bell, John D. "Giving Birth to the New Soviet Man: Politics and Obstetrics in the USSR." *Slavic Review* 40, no. 1 (Spring 1981): 1–16.

Bellver, Jose, et al. "Influence of Paternal Age on Assisted Reproduction Outcome." *Reproductive BioMedicine Online* 17, no. 5 (November 2008): 595–604.

Bergstrom, M., H. Kieler, and U. Waldenstrom. "Effects of Natural Childbirth Preparation Versus Standard Antenatal Education on Epidural Rates, Experience of Childbirth and Parental Stress in Mothers and Fathers: A Randomised Controlled Multicentre Trial." *BJOG* 116 (2009): 1167.

Breggin, Peter R., and Ginger Breggin. "Exposure to SSRI Antidepressants in Utero Causes Birth Defects, Neonatal Withdrawal Symptoms, and Brain Damage." *Ethical Human Psychology and Psychiatry* 10, no. 1 (2008): 203–7.

Borrelli, Francesca, et al. "Effectiveness and Safety of Ginger in the Treatment of Pregnancy-Induced Nausea and Vomiting." *Obstetrics & Gynecology* 105, no. 4 (April 2005): 849–56.

Boyce, P., J. Condon, J. Barton, and C. Corkindale. "First-Time Fathers' Study: Psychological Distress in Expectant Fathers During Pregnancy." *Australian and New Zealand Journal of Psychiatry* 41, no. 9 (September 2007): 718–25.

Brodzinsky, David, and Laureen Huffman. "Transition to Adoptive Parent-hood." *Marriage and Family Review* 6 (1988): 267–86.

Bronte-Tinkew, Jacinta, et al. "Resident Fathers' Pregnancy Intentions, Prenatal Behaviors, and Links to Involvement with Infants." *Journal of Marriage and Family* 69, no. 4 (2007): 977–90.

Bronte-Tinkew, J., K. Moore, G. Matthews, and J. Carrano. "Symptoms of Major Depression in a Sample of Fathers of Infants." *Journal of Family Issues* 28, no. 1 (2007): 61–99.

Broude, Gwen J. "Rethinking the Couvade: Cross-Cultural Evidence." *American Anthropologist* 90 (1988): 903–11.

Burns, L. H. "Psychiatric Aspects of Infertility and Infertility Treatments." *Psychiatric Clinics of North America* 30, no. 4 (December 2007): 689–716.

Callister, Lynn Clark. "Perinatal Loss: A Family Perspective." *Journal of Perinatal and Neonatal Nursing* 20, no. 3 (July/September 2006): 227–34.

Cannon, M. "Contrasting Effects of Maternal and Paternal Age on Offspring Intelligence: The clock ticks for men too." *Plos Medicine* 6, no. 3 (2009): 2.

Capogna, Girogio, Michela Camorcia, and S. Stirparo. "Expectant Fathers' Experience During Labor With or Without Epidural Analgesia." *International Journal of Obstetric Anesthesia* 16, no. 2 (April 2007): 110–15.

Carin, A., et al. "Correlation Between Oral Sex and a Low Incidence of Preeclampsia: A Role for Soluble HLA in Seminal Fluid?" *Journal of Reproductive Immunology* 46, no. 2 (2000): 155–66.

Chang, Grace, Tay McNamara, E. John Orav, and Louise Wilkins-Haug. "Identifying Risk Drinking in Expectant Fathers." *BIRTH* 33, no. 2 (June 2006): 110–16.

Christenfeld, N., D. Phillips, and L. Glynn. "What's in a Name: Mortality and the Power of Symbols." *Journal of Psychosomatic Research* 47 (1999): 241–54.

Christiansen, S., and R. Palkovitz. "Why the Good Provider Role Still Matters: Providing as a Form of Paternal Involvement." *Journal of Family Issues* 22 (2001): 84–106.

Condon, J. T., P. Boyce, and C. J. Corkindale. "The First-Time Fathers Study: A Prospective Study of the Mental Health and Wellbeing of Men During the Transition to Parenthood." *Australian and New Zealand Journal of Psychiatry* 38, nos. 1 and 2 (2004): 56–64.

Condon, John T., Carolyn Jennifer Corkindale, and Phillip Boyce. "Assessment of Postnatal Paternal–Infant Attachment: Development of a Questionnaire Instrument." *Journal of Reproductive and Infant Psychology* 26, no. 3 (August 2008): 195–210.

Cummings, David. "The Effects of Miscarriage on a Man." *Emotional First Aid* 1, no. 4 (1984): 47–50.

Dahl, Gordon B., and Enrico Moretti. "The Demand for Sons: Evidence from Divorce, Fertility, and Shotgun Marriage." NBER Working Paper no. 10281, National Bureau of Economic Research, Cambridge, MA (2004).

Davidson, J. R. "The Shadow of Life: Psychosocial Explanations for Placenta Rituals." *Culture, Medicine and Psychiatry* 9 (1985): 75–92.

Deave, T., and D. Johnson. "The Transition to Parenthood: What Does it Mean for Fathers?" *Journal of Advanced Nursing* 63, no. 6 (2008): 626–33.

Dekker, Gustaaf, et al. "Immune Maladaptation in the Etiology of Preeclampsia: A Review of Corroborative Epidemiologic Studies." *Obstetrical & Gynecological Survey* 53, no. 6 (June 1998): 377–82.

De La Rochebrochard, Elise, Ken Mcelreavey, and Patrick Thonneau. "Paternal Age over 40 Years: The Amber Light in the Reproductive Life of Men?" *Journal of Andrology* 24, no. 4 (July/August 2003): 459–65.

DeMott, S., and K. Lynch. "Defining Paternity Leave: Shifting Roles, New Responsibilities in the Family and the Workplace." Kaiser Family Foundation and the Boston College Center for Work & Family, Executive Briefing Series, Menlo Park, CA (2004).

Devlin, Kate. "Morning sickness 'increases the chance that child will have high IQ.'" Telegraph.co.uk. www.telegraph.co.uk/health/healthnews/5286670/Morning-sickness-increases-the-chance-that-child-will-have-high-IQ.html. Published May 6, 2009.

Diemer, Geraldine A. "Expectant Fathers: Influence of Perinatal Education on Stress, Coping, and Spousal Relations." *Research in Nursing and Health* 20 (1997): 281–93.

Doucet, Andrea. "Dad and Baby in the First Year: Gendered Responsibilities and Embodiment." *The Annals of the American Academy of Political and Social Science* 624, no. 1 (2009): 78–98.

Draper, J. "Men's Passage to Fatherhood: An Analysis of the Contemporary Relevance of Transition Theory." *Nursing Inquiry* 10 (2003): 66–78.

Dyck, Vera, and Kerry Daly. "Rising to the Challenge: Fathers' Role in the Negotiation of Couple Time." *Leisure Studies* 25, no. 2 (April 2006): 201–17.

Elliott, Stuart. "Campaigns for Challenging Times Put Children and Mothers First." *New York Times*, March 16, 2009, Business section.

Engeland, Anders, et al. "Prescription Drug Use Among Fathers and Mothers Before and During Pregnancy: A Population-based Cohort Study of 106 000 Pregnancies in Norway." *British Journal of Clinical Pharmacology* 65, no. 5 (2004–2006): 653–60.

Eriksson, Carola, Pär Salander, and Katarina Hamberg. "Men's Experiences of Intense Fear Related to Childbirth Investigated in a Swedish Qualitative Study." *Journal of Men's Health* 4, no. 4 (December 2007): 409–18.

Erwin, P. "First Names and Perceptions of Physical Attractiveness." *The Journal of Psychology* 127 (1993): 625–31.

Fagan, J., and R. Palkovitz. "Unmarried, Nonresident Fathers' Involvement with Their Infants: A Risk and Resilience Perspective." *Journal of Family Psychology* 21 (2007): 479–89.

Fagerskiold, Astrid. "A Change in Life as Experienced by First-Time Fathers." *Scandinavian Journal of Caring Sciences* 22 (2008): 64–71.

Field, Tiffany, et al. "Pregnancy Anxiety and Comorbid Depression and Anger Effects on the Fetus and Neonate." *Depression and Anxiety* 17 (2003): 140–51.

Field, T., et al. "Prenatal Depression Effects on the Fetus and the Newborn." *Infant Behavior and Development* 27 (2004): 216–29.

Field, T., et al. "Prenatal Paternal Depression." *Infant Behavior and Development* 29 (2006): 579–83.

Field, T., M. Hernandez-Reif, and M. Diego. "Newborns of Depressed Mothers Who Received Moderate Versus Light Pressure Massage During Pregnancy." *Infant Behavior and Development* 29 (2006): 54–58.

Finnbogadottir, H., E. Svalenius, and E. Persson. "Expectant First-Time Fathers' Experiences of Pregnancy." *Midwifery* 19, no. 2 (2003): 96–105.

Flaxman, S. M., and P. W. Sherman. "Morning Sickness: A Mechanism For Protecting Mother and Embryo." *Quarterly Review of Biology* 75 (2000): 113.

Fletcher, R., S. Silberberg, and D. Galloway. "New Fathers' Postbirth Views of Antenatal Classes: Satisfaction, Benefits, and Knowledge of Family Services." *Journal of Perinatal Education* 13, no. 3 (Summer 2004):18–26.

Fox, Douglas. "Gentle Persuasion." Accessed 2/23/10 from www.fortunecity.com/emachines/e11/86/c-men.html.

Friedewald, Mark, Richard Fletcher, and Hedy Fairbairn. "All-Male Discussion Forums for Expectant Fathers: Evaluation of a Model." *Journal of Perinatal Education* 14, no. 2 (Spring 2005): 8–18.

Ginath, Y. "Psychoses in Males in Relation to Their Wives' Pregnancy and Childbirth." *Israel Annals of Psychiatry and Related Disciplines* 12, no. 3 (September 1974): 227–37.

Gipson, Jessica D., Michael A. Koenig, and Michelle J. Hindin. "The Effects of Unintended Pregnancy on Infant, Child, and Parental Health: A Review of the Literature." *Studies in Family Planning* 39, no. 1 (2008): 18–38.

Glazebrook, Cristine, Sara Cox, Margaret Oates, and George Ndukwe. "Psychological Adjustment During Pregnancy and the Postpartum Period in Single and Multiple In Vitro Fertilization Births: A Review and Preliminary Findings from an Ongoing Study." *Reproductive Technologies* 10, no. 2 (2000): 112–19.

Goetzl, L. M. "Clinical Management Guidelines for Obstetrician-Gynecologists Number 36, July 2002. Obstetric analgesial and anesthesia." *Obstetrics & Gynecology* 100, no. 1 (July 2002): 177–91.

Goldbach, R. C., et al. "The Effects of Gestational Age and Gender on Grief after Pregnancy Loss." *American Journal of Orthopsychiatry* 61 (July 1991): 461–67.

Golombok, Susan, et al. "Children: The European Study of Assisted Reproduction Families: Family Functioning and Child Development." *Human Reproduction* 11, no. 10 (1996): 2324–31.

Goodman, J. H. "Becoming an Involved Father Of An Infant." *Journal of Obstetric, Gynecologic, and Neonatal Nursing* 34 (2005): 190–200.

Goodwin, T. M. "Hyperemesis Gravidarum." *Obstetrics & Gynecology Clinics of North America* 35 (2008): 401.

Green, R. F., et al. "Association of Paternal Age and Risk for Major Congenital Anomalies from the National Birth Defects Prevention Study." *Annals of Epidemiology* 20, no. 3 (March 2010): 241–49.

Gruenert, S., and R. Galligan. "The Difference Dads Make: Young Adult Men's Experiences of Their Fathers." *E-Journal of Applied Psychology* 3, no. 1 (2007): 3–15.

Habib, Cherine, and Sandra Lancaster. "The Transition to Fatherhood: Identity and Bonding in Early Pregnancy." *Fathering* 4, no. 3 (2006): 235–53.

Hagen, Edward. "Functions of Postpartum Depression." *Evolution and Human Behavior* 20 (September 1999): 325–59.

Hammarberg, K., J. R. W. Fisher, and K. H. Wynter. "Psychological and Social Aspects of Pregnancy, Childbirth, and Early Parenting after Assisted Conception: A Systematic Review." *Human Reproduction Update* 14, no. 5 (2008): 395–414.

Hanson, Suzanne, Lauren P. Hunter, et al. "Paternal Fears of Childbirth: A Literature Review." *Journal of Perinatal Education* 18, no. 4 (2009): 12–20(9).

Hay, D. A., et al. "What Information Should the Multiple-Birth Family Receive before, during and after the birth?" *Acta Geneticae Medicae et Gemellologiae: Twin Research* 39 (1990): 259–69.

Hay, D., and P. O'Brien. "Early Influences on the School Social Adjustments of Twins." *Acta Geneticae Medicae et Gemellologiae: Twin Research* 36 (1987): 239–48.

Helmstedt, Anna, et al. "Personality Factors and Emotional Responses to Pregnancy Among IVF Couples in Early Pregnancy: A Comparative Study." *Acta Obstetricia et Gynecologica Scandinavica* 82 (2003): 152–16.

Henley, K., and K. Pasley. "Conditions Affecting the Association Between Father Identity and Father Involvement." *Fathering* 3, no. 1 (2005): 59–80.

Hepper, Peter G. "Fetal 'Soap' Addiction." *Lancet* 11 (June 1988): 1347–48.

Hepper, P. G., and Sara Shahidullah. "Development of Fetal Hearing." *Archives of Disease in Childhood* 71 (September 1994): F81–87.

Hjelmstedt, Anna. "Psychological Functioning and Predictors of Father-Infant Relationship in IVF Fathers and Controls." *Scandinavian Journal of Caring Sciences* 22 (2008): 72–78.

Holditch-Davis, Diane, et al. "Beyond Couvade: Pregnancy Symptoms in Couples with a History of Infertility." *Health Care for Women International* 15, no. 6 (1994): 537–48.

Hossain, Z., T. Field, J. Gonzalez, et al. "Infants of Depressed Mothers Interact Better with Their Nondepressed Fathers." *Infant Mental Health Journal* 15 (1994): 348–57.

Howell-White, Sandra. "Choosing a Birth Attendant: The Influence of a Woman's Childbirth Definitions." *Social Science and Medicine* 45 (1997): 925–36.

Humphrey, M., and R. Kirkwood. "Marital Relationships Among Adopters." *Adoption and Fostering* 6 (1982): 44–48.

Jordan, Pamela. "Enhancing Understanding of the Transition to Fatherhood." *International Journal of Childbirth Education* 22, no. 2 (June 2007): 4–6.

———. "Laboring for Relevance: Expectant and New Fatherhood." *Nursing Research* 39 (January–February 1990): 11–16.

Kao, Bi-Chin, Meei-Ling Gau, et al. "A Comparative Study of Expectant Parents' Childbirth Expectations." *Journal of Nursing Research* 12, no. 3 (2004): 191–202

Kimbro, Rachel Tolbert. "Together Forever? Romantic Relationship Characteristics and Prenatal Health Behaviors." *Journal of Marriage and Family* 70 (August 2008): 745–57.

Knoester, C., and D. Eggebeen. "The Effects of the Transition to Parenthood and Subsequent Children on Men's Well-Being and Social Participation." *Journal of Family Issues* 27, no. 11 (2006): 1532–60.

Kurki, T., L. Toivonen, and O. Ylikorkala. "Father's Heartbeat Responds to the Birth of His Child." *Acta Obstetricia et Gynecologica Scandinavica* 74 (February 1995): 127–28.

Lee, Chih-yuan, and William Doherty. "Marital Satisfaction and Father Involvement During the Transition to Parenthood." *Fathering* 5, no. 2 (Spring 2007): 75–96.

Leighton, B. L., and S. H. Halpern. "The Effects of Epidural Analgesia on Labor, Maternal and Neonatal Outcomes: A Systematic Review." *American Journal of Obstetrics and Gynecology* 186, no. 5, part 2 (2002): S69–S77.

Levy-Schiff, Rachel, Ora Bar, and Dov Har-Even. "Psychological Adjustment of Adoptive Parents-to-Be." *American Journal of Orthopsychiatry* 60 (April 1990): 258–67.

Li, De-Kun, Teresa Janevic, Roxana Odouli, and Liyan Liu. "Hot Tub Use During Pregnancy and the Risk of Miscarriage." *American Journal of Epidemiology* 158, no. 10 (2003): 931–37.

Luke, B., N. Mamelle, L. Keith, et al. "The Association Between Occupational Factors and Preterm Birth: A United States Nurses' Study." Research Committee of the Association of Women's Health, Obstetric, and Neonatal Nurses. *American Journal of Obstetrics and Gynecology* 173 (September 1995): 849–62.

Lumley, Judith. "Sexual Feelings in Pregnancy and after Childbirth." *Australian and New Zealand Journal of Obstetrics and Gynaecology* 18, no. 2 (June 1978): 114–17. Published online: June 28, 2008.

Lund, Najaaraq, Lars H. Pedersen, and Tine Brink Henriksen. "Selective Serotonin Reuptake Inhibitor Exposure In Utero and Pregnancy Outcomes." *Archives of Pediatric and Adolescent Medicine* 163, no. 10 (2009): 949–54.

MacCallum, Fiona, Emma Lycett, Clare Murray, Vasanti Jadva, and Susan Golombok. "Surrogacy: The Experience of Commissioning Couples." *Human Reproduction* 18, no. 6 (2003): 1334–42.

Martin, Laurie T., Michelle J. McNamara, et al. "The Effects of Father Involvement During Pregnancy on Receipt of Prenatal Care and Maternal Smoking." *Maternal and Child Health Journal* 11 (2007): 595–602.

Matthews, Fiona, Paul Johnson, and Andrew Neil. "You Are What Your Mother Eats: Evidence for Maternal Preconception Diet Influencing Foetal Sex in Humans." *Proceedings of the Royal Society B* 275, no. 1643 (July 2008): 1661–68.

May, K. A. "Active Involvement of Expectant Fathers in Pregnancy: Some

Further Considerations." *Journal of Obstetric, Gynecologic, & Neonatal Nursing* 7, no. 2 (1978): 7–12. Published online: July 28, 2006.

———. "Factors Contributing to First-Time Fathers' Readiness for Fatherhood: An Exploratory Study." *Family Relations* 31 (July 1982): 352–61.

———. "First-Time Fathers' Responses to Unanticipated Caesarean Birth: An Exploratory Study." Unpublished report to U.C.S.F., 1982.

———. "Three Phases of Father Involvement in Pregnancy." *Nursing Research* 31 (November–December 1982): 337–42.

———. "A Typology of Detachment/Involvement Styles Adopted During Pregnancy by First-Time Expectant Fathers." *Western Journal of Nursing Research* 2, no. 2 (1980): 445–61.

May, Katharyn Antle, and Deanna Tomlinson Sollid. "Unanticipated Cesarean Birth from the Father's Perspective." *Birth* 11, no. 2 (1984): 87–95.

McIntyre, Matthew H., and Carolyn Pope Edwards. "The Early Development of Gender Differences." *Annual Review of Anthropology* 38 (October 2009): 83–97.

McVeigh, C., W. John, and C. Cameron. "Fathers' Functional Status Six Weeks Following the Birth of a Baby: A Queensland Study." *Australian Midwifery* 18, no. 1 (2005): 25–28.

Mennella, Julie, A. Johnson, and G. K. Beauchamp. "Garlic Ingestion by Pregnant Women Alters the Odor of Amniotic Fluid." *Chemical Senses* 20, no. 2 (1995): 207–9.

Mercer, R. T., K. Hackley, and A. Bostrom. "Relationship of the Birth Experience to Later Mothering Behaviors." *Journal of Nurse Midwifery* 30 (1984): 204–11.

Miller, W. E., and S. Friedman. "Male and Female Sexuality During Pregnancy: Behavior and Attitudes." *Journal of Psychology and Human Sexuality* 1, no. 2 (1988): 17–37.

Moses, S., R. C. Bailey, and A. R. Ronald. "Male Circumcision: Assessment of Health Benefits and Risks." *Sexually Transmitted Infections* 74 (October 1998): 368–73.

Mozurkewich, E. L., B. Luke, M. Avni, and F. M. Wolf. "Working Conditions and Adverse Pregnancy Outcome: A Meta-Analysis." *Obstetrics and Gynecology* 95 (April 2000): 623–35.

Nelson, Leif D., and Joseph P. Simmons. "Moniker Maladies: When Names Sabotage Success." *Psychological Science–Cambridge* 18, no. 12 (2007): 1106–12.

Olsen, Sjurdur F., et al. "Milk Consumption During Pregnancy Is Associated with Increased Infant Size at Birth: Prospective Cohort Study." *American Journal of Clinical Nutrition* 86 (2007): 1104–10.

Omranifard, Victoria, and Ghorbanali Asadollahi. "Association Between Paternal Age at Birth Time and the Risk of Offspring Developing Schizophrenia." *American Journal of Applied Sciences* 6, no. 1 (2009): 179–81.

Palazzari, Kari. "The Daddy Double-Bind: How the Family and Medical Leave Act Perpetuates Sex Inequality Across All Class Levels." *Columbia Journal of Gender and Law* 16, no. 2 (June 2007): 429–70.

Palkovitz, Rob, and Glen Palm. "Transitions Within Fathering." *Fathering* 7, no. 1 (Winter 2009): 3–22.

Pauleta, J. R., N. M. Pereira, and L. M. Graça. "Sexuality During Pregnancy." *Journal of Sexual Medicine* 7 (2010): 136–42.

Pelham, Brett W., Matthew C. Mirenberg, and John T. Jones. "Why Susie Sells Seashells by the Seashore: Implicit Egotism and Major Life Decisions." *Journal of Personality and Social Psychology* 82, no. 4 (2002): 469–87.

Pinzur, Laura, and Gary Smith. "First Names and Longevity." *Perceptual and Motor Skills* 108, no. 1 (2009): 149–16.

Piontelli, Alessandra. " A Study on Twins before and after Birth." *International Review of Psycho-Analysis* 16, no. 4 (1989): 413–26.

Premberg, A., and I. Lundgren. "Fathers' Experiences of Childbirth Education." *Journal of Perinatal Education* 15, no. 2 (2006): 21–28.

Quinn, Suzanne M. "The Depictions of Fathers and Children in Best-Selling Picture Books in the United States: A Hybrid Semiotic Analysis." *Fathering* 7, no. 2 (Spring 2009): 140–58.

Ramchandani, P., et al. "Paternal Depression in the Postnatal Period and Child Development: A Prospective Population Study." *The Lancet* 365 (June 25, 2005): 2201–05.

Righetti, P. L., M. Dell'Avanzo, M. Grigio, and U. Nicolini. "Maternal/Paternal Antenatal Attachment and Fourth-Dimensional Ultrasound Technique: A Preliminary Report." *British Journal of Psychology* 96 (2005): 129–37.

Roscoe, Joseph A., and Sara E. Matteson. "Acupressure and Acustimulation Bands for Control of Nausea: A Brief Review." *American Journal of Obstetrics and Gynecology* 186, no. 5, part 2, supplement (May 2002): S244–S247.

Schneer, Joy A., and Frieda Reitman, "The Impact of Gender as Managerial Careers Unfold." *Journal of Vocational Behavior* 47 (December 1995): 290–315.

————. "The Interrupted Managerial Career Path: A Longitudinal Study of MBAs." *Journal of Vocational Behavior* 51 (December 1997): 411–34.

Schoen, E. J., M. Oehrli et al. "The Highly Protective Effect of Newborn Circumcision Against Invasive Penile Cancer." *Pediatrics* 105 (March 2000): E36.

Sedgmen, B., et al. "The Impact of Two-Dimensional Versus Three-Dimensional Ultrasound Exposure on Maternal-Fetal Attachment and Maternal Health Behavior in Pregnancy." *Ultrasound, Obstetrics and Gynecology* 27 (2006): 245–51.

Seimyr, L., M. Edhborg, W. Lundh, and B. Sjögren. "In the Shadow of Maternal Depressed Mood: Experiences of Parenthood During the First Year after Childbirth." *Perinatal Maternal Depression and Parenthood* 25, no. 1 (March 2004): 23–34.

Shahidullah, Sara, and Peter G. Hepper. "Frequency Discrimination by the Fetus." *Early Human Development* 36 (January 1994): 13–26.

Shayeb, A. Ghiyath. "Male Obesity and Reproductive Potential." *The British Journal of Diabetes & Vascular Disease* 9, no. 1 (2009): 7–12.

Sheldon, Sally. "Reproductive Technologies and the Legal Determination of Fatherhood." *Feminist Legal Studies* 13 (2005): 349–62.

Simkin, P. "Just Another Day in a Woman's Life? Women's Long-Term Perceptions of Their First Birth Experience. Part I." *Birth* 18, no. 4 (1991): 203–10.

————. "Just Another Day In A Woman's Life? Part II: Nature and Consistency of Women's Long-Term Memories of Their First Birth Experiences." *Birth* 19, no. 2 (1992): 64–81.

Skjærven, Rolv, et al. "Recurrence of Pre-Eclampsia Across Generations: Exploring Fetal and Maternal Genetic Components in a Population Based Cohort." *British Medical Journal* 331, no. 7521 (Oct. 15, 2005): 877.

Skotko, Brian G. "With New Prenatal Testing, Will Babies with Down Syndrome Slowly Disappear?" *Archives of Disease in Childhood* 94, no. 11 (November 2009): 823–26.

Sonne, J. C. "The Varying Behaviors of Fathers in the Prenatal Experience of the Unborn: Protecting, Loving, and 'Welcoming with Arms Wide Open,' vs. Ignoring, Unloving, Competitive, Abusive, Abortion-Minded or Aborting." *The International Journal of Prenatal and Perinatal Psychology and Medicine* 14, nos. 1 and 2 (2002): 33–52.

Stainton, M. C. "The Fetus: A Growing Member of the Family." *Family Relations* 34 (July 1985): 321–26.

Storey, Anne E., Carolyn J. Walsh, Roma L. Quinton, and Katherine E. Wynne-Edwards. "Hormonal Correlates of Paternal Responsiveness in New and Expectant Fathers." *Evolution and Human Behavior* 21 (March 2000): 79–95.

Tang, C. H., M. P. Wu, J. T. Liu et al. "Delayed Parenthood and the Risk of Cesarean Delivery: Is Paternal Age an Independent Risk Factor?" *Birth* 33, no 1. (2006): 18–26.

Teichman, Y., and Y. Lahav. "Expectant Fathers: Emotional Reactions, Physical Symptoms and Coping Styles." *British Journal of Medical Psychology* 60 (1987): 225–32.

"Telework Trendlines 2009." A Survey Brief by WorldatWork. Data collected by The Dieringer Research Group, Inc., February 2009.

Temucin, Senkul, C. Iseri, B. Sen et al. "Circumcision in Adults: Effect on Sexual Function." *Urology* 63, no. 1 (2004): 155–58.

Thorn, Petra. "Understanding Infertility: Psychological and Social Considerations from a Counselling Perspective." *International Journal of Fertility and Sterility* 3, no. 2 (August–September 2009): 48–51.

Triche, Elizabeth W., et al. "Chocolate Consumption in Pregnancy and Reduced Likelihood of Preeclampsia." *Epidemiology* 19, no. 3 (May 2008): 459–64.

Trogstad, Lill, Per Magnus, Rolv Skjærven, and Camilla Stoltenberg. "Previous Abortions and Risk of Pre-Eclampsia." *International Journal of Epidemiology* 37, no. 6 (2008): 333–40.

Vahratian, A., J. Hasling Zhang et al. "The Effect of Early Epidural Versus Early Intravenous Analgesia Use on Labor Progression: A Natural Experiment." *American Journal of Obstetrics and Gynecology* 191 (2004): 259–65.

van den Akker, Olga, and Maggie Redshaw. "Beliefs and Attitudes During Pregnancy and Postnatally." *Journal of Reproductive and Infant Psychology* 26, no. 3 (August 2008): 155–56.

Vanston, Claire M., and Neil V. Watson. "Selective and Persistent Effect of Foetal Sex on Cognition in Pregnant Women." *Cognitive Neuroscience and Neuropsychology* 16, no. 7 (2005): 779–82. NeuroReport: May 12, 2005.

Vilska, S., et al. "Mental Health of Mothers and Fathers of Twins Conceived Via Assisted Reproduction Treatment: A 1-Year Prospective Study." *Human Reproduction* 24, no. 2 (2009): 367–77.

Wakefield, Melanie, Yolande Reid, Lyn Roberts, Robyn Mullins, and Pamela Gillies. "Smoking and Smoking Cessation Among Men Whose Partners Are

Pregnant: A Qualitative Study." *Social Science & Medicine* 47 (September 1998): 657–64.

Waller, Maureen, and Marianne P. Bitler. "The Link Between Couples' Pregnancy Intentions and Behavior: Does It Matter Who Is Asked?" *Perspectives on Sexual and Reproductive Health* 40, no. 4 (December 2008): 194–201.

Wayne, Julie Holliday, and Bryanne L. Cordeiro. "Who Is a Good Organizational Citizen? Social Perception of Male and Female Employees Who Use Family Leave." *Sex Roles* 49, nos. 5 and 6 (September 2003): 233–46.

Williams, E., and N. Radin. "Effect of Father Participation in Child Rearing: Twenty-Year Follow-up." *American Journal of Orthopsychiatry* 69 (1999): 328–36.

Williams, Kristi, and Debra Umberson. "Medical Technology and Childbirth: Experiences of Expectant Mothers and Fathers." *Sex Roles* 41, nos. 3 and 4 (1999): 147–67.

Wolfberg, Adam J., et al. "Dads as Breastfeeding Advocates: Results from a Randomized Controlled Trial of Educational Intervention." *American Journal of Obstetrics and Gynecology* 191, no. 3 (2004): 708–12.

Wong, Cynthia, Barbara Scavone et al. "The Risk of Cesarean Delivery with Neuraxial Analgesia Given Early Versus Late in Labor." *New England Journal of Medicine* 352 (2005): 655–65.

Woodward, Joan. "The Bereaved Twin." *Acta Geneticae Medicae et Gemellologiae: Twin Research* 37, no. 2 (1988): 173–80.

Yogman, Michael W., D. Kindlon, and F. Earls, "Father Involvement and Cognitive Behavioral Outcomes of Preterm Infants." *Journal of the American Academy of Child and Adolescent Psychiatry* 34 (1995): 58–66.

Zayas, L. H. "Psychodynamic and Developmental Aspects of Expectant and New Fatherhood: Clinical Derivatives from the Literature." *Clinical Social Work Journal* 15 (Spring 1987): 8–21.

———. "Thematic Features in the Manifest Dreams of Expectant Fathers." *Clinical Social Work Journal* 16 (Fall 1988): 283–95.

Zennaro, A., C. Mazzecchi, and M. Pinto. "Parental Styles in Prospective Fathers: A Research Carried Out Using a Semi-Structured Interview During Pregnancy." *Infant Mental Health Journal* 25 (2004): 149–62.

Zuk, M(arlene). "The Case of the Female Orgasm (review)." *Perspectives in Biology and Medicine* 49, no. 2 (Spring 2006): 294–98.

Resources

To paraphrase Dorothy in *The Wizard of Oz*: My! Resources for expectant and new dads come and go so quickly here. And because they do, this is by no means a comprehensive list. But I'd really like to create one—and you can help. If you know of a resource that can really benefit dads and their families, let us know. We'll be putting the constantly evolving list up on our Web site, www.resourcesfordads.com.

Adoption

National Adoption Center offers a comprehensive list of questions to ask adoption agencies, advice on tax and legal matters, and links to other organizations.
www.adopt.org

Adopting.org provides information, resources, and support for adoptive families.
www.adopting.org

Adoptive Families is an award-winning online magazine—a great source of info before, during, and after adoption.
www.adoptivefamilies.com

Blogs

Alltop Dads is the most comprehensive listing of dad blogs available.
www.dads.alltop.com

DadBlogs features tons of blogs by, for, and about dads.
www.dad-blogs.com

DadThing has a nice listing of dad blogs.
www.dadthing.com/2007/11/13/51-dad-blogs

Childbirth, Assistance

American College of Nurse-Midwives accredits midwife education programs, establishes standards, and provides information and referrals to midwives in your area.
www.midwife.org

ACOG (American College of Obstetricians and Gynecologists)
www.acog.com

Doulas of North America provides resources and referrals to doulas near you.
www.dona.org

International Childbirth Education Association is a professional organization that supports educators and other health-care providers.
www.icea.org

American Association of Child-bearing Centers provides information about birthing centers and resources for finding one near you.
www.birthcenters.org

Child Care and Day Care
Au Pair Search
www.aupairsearch.com

Child Care Aware is a nationwide campaign to help parents identify quality child care in their communities. Great source of local referrals.
www.childcareaware.org

International Nanny Association is a nonprofit association for nannies and those who educate, place, employ, and support professional in-home child-care providers. Provides links to placement agencies, and so forth.
www.nanny.org

National Association of Child Care Resource & Referral Agencies will put you in touch with the local child-care resource and referral agency that serves your area.
www.naccrra.org

National Resource Center for Health and Safety in Child Care and Early Education promotes health and safety in out-of-home child-care settings throughout the nation.
www.nrckids.org

Death and Grief
American (SIDS) Institute
www.sids.org

M.I.S.S. Foundation is a volunteer-based organization committed to providing crisis support and long-term aid to families after the death of a child from any cause. This page is specifically for dads.
www.missfoundation.org/family/dads/index.html

Fathers and Fatherhood, Advice and Skills
About.com offers extensive information on all sorts of father- and fathering-related issues.
www.fatherhood.about.com/parenting/fatherhood

DadLabs features very entertaining—yet practical—advice and insights.
www.dadlabs.com

FathersOnline.com is a site where real dads can gather on the Internet to ask questions and give advice to others. You can find—or be—a mentor.
www.fathersonline.com

GreatDad.com is a wonderful collection of articles and information on just about any dad-related topic you can think of. GreatDad also has a terrific pregnancy newsletter just for guys.
www.greatdad.com

MrDad.com is my Web site. You can get information there about pretty much every aspect of pregnancy, childbirth, and fatherhood; find out more about my other fatherhood books; and send me questions and comments.
www.MrDad.com
www.MrDad.com/radio: For "Positive Parenting," my syndicated radio show (also available as a podcast)
www.MrDad.com/ask: For "Ask Mr. Dad," my nationally syndicated newspaper column (also available as a blog)
Facebook: www.facebook.com/mrdad
Twitter: @mrdad

Fathers and Fatherhood, General
Men's Health Network is a comprehensive resource on fatherhood and other issues affecting men.
www.menshealthnetwork.org

National Center for Fathering offers plenty of advice on strengthening families by inspiring and equipping men to be better fathers.
www.fathers.com

National Fatherhood Initiative provides information on the importance of involved, committed, and responsible fathers and how they can improve the well-being of their children.
www.fatherhood.org

Fathers, Stay-at-Home
About.com's at-home-dad page has a lot of excellent, basic info.
www.fatherhood.about.com/od/stayat homedads/Stay_Home_Dads.htm

AtHomeDad.com provides online resources and support for stay-at-home and primary caregiver dads and their families.
www.athomedad.com

AtHomeDad.org is a resource and community for stay-at-home dads, fathers who are the primary caregiver in their families, and other involved dads: www.athomedad.org

Rebeldad.com
www.rebeldad.com

Fertility and Infertility
www.fertilityauthority.com is a web portal that provides tools and information to help you make the best, most efficient decisions about your fertility.

Fertility and Obstetrics (a.k.a. the unofficial medical advisory board)

Whitney Pollock, D.O. manages the Gynecology Center, Pottsville, PA.
www.drwhitneypollock.com
570-628-9448

Lissa Rankin, M.D. is the author of *What's Up Down There? Questions You'd Only Ask Your Gynecologist If She Was Your Best Friend* (St. Martin's Press). She also runs the Owning Pink Center, an integrative medicine center for vital wellness in Mill Valley, CA.
www.owningpink.com
www.lissarankin.com

David Elan Simckes, M.D. is a fertility specialist and OB/GYN. He practices at Fertility Partnership in St. Peters, MO.
www.FertilityPartnership.com

Saul Stromer, M.D. is a New York City–based board-certified OB/GYN at Lenox Hill Hospital and a sex therapist.
saulstromer@yahoo.com
212-717-7000

Susan Warhus, M.D. is a board-certified OB/GYN physician and author of several pregnancy and childbirth books. She currently serves on the Childbirth Graphics Advisory Board.
www.childbirthgraphics.com

Saul Weinreb, M.D. is an OB/GYN who practices at White Square Obstetrics and Gynecology in Baltimore, Maryland. He is also Director of Minimally Invasive Gynecologic Surgical Training at Franklin Square Hospital. Check out his Web site:
www.askmyobgyn.com

Carrie Wieneke, M.D. practices and teaches at the University of Kansas,
913-588-2532

Finances (College Savings, Financial Planning, Insurance, and so on)

American Council of Life Insurers provides basic information on the spectrum of life insurance products and operates the National Insurance Consumer Helpline, which can give you referrals to local agents.
www.acli.com

College Savings Plans Network offers great info on all of the state-sponsored college savings plans and referrals to the one in your state.
www.collegesavings.org

Financial Planning Association provides information on financial planning and referrals to certified financial planners in your area.
www.fpanet.org

Financial Planners (a.k.a. the unofficial finance advisory board)

Joe Pitzl, CFP
Mindful Asset Planning
800-525-5301
www.mindfulplanning.com

Jackie Weitzberg, CFP
Guide My Finances
800-423-4891
www.GuideMyFinances.com

Green Parenting

EcoMom Alliance is a global network of mothers working together to create an environmentally, socially, and economically sustainable future.
www.ecomomalliance.ning.com

Environmental Working Group's mission is to use the power of public information to protect public health and the environment.
www.ewg.org

GreenHome explains everything you need to create a healthy, nontoxic home environment.
www.greenhome.com

The Green Parent is a kid-friendly guide to earth-friendly living.
www.thegreenparent.com/category/green-home

Healthy Child Healthy World's mission is to create a movement that inspires parents to protect young children from harmful chemicals.
www.healthychild.org

Seventh Generation manufactures a variety of eco-friendly products. Their pregnancy and parenting section has a lot of good information.
www.seventhgeneration.com/learn/topic/pregnancy-and-parenting

Health and Safety

Danny Foundation educates the public about crib dangers and advises eliminating the millions of unsafe cribs currently in use or in storage.
www.dannyfoundation.org

Kids in Danger is a nonprofit dedicated to protecting children by improving children's public safety.
www.kidsindanger.org

National Highway Traffic Safety Administration offers the latest info on car and car-seat safety. Includes a shopping guide for car seats, recall information, and safety literature.
www.nhtsa.gov

National Safety Council provides facts, information, and resources on environmental issues and accident prevention.
www.nsc.org

U.S. Consumer Product Safety Commission provides comprehensive safety checklists, notices of recalls, and other important safety info.
www.cpsc.gov

Parenting, Children with Disabilities
Parents Helping Parents
www.php.com

The Fathers' Network supports fathers and families raising children with special health-care needs and developmental disabilities.
www.fathersnetwork.org

The National Dissemination Center for Children with Disabilities is a referral center that provides information on disabilities and disability-related issues for families, educators, and other professionals.
www.nichcy.org

Preemies
PreemieParenting.com aims to offer hope, inspiration, support, and resources to parents of premature infants.
www.preemieparenting.com

Prematurity.org's goal is to support preemie parents by providing information on prematurity and preemie care.
www.prematurity.org

Emory Perinatal Center is a great source of info on developmental milestones, medical concerns, and other issues.
www.emoryhealthcare.org/gyn/maternal-fetal.html

Preemie Store offers anything you could possibly need to buy for your preemie.
www.preemie.com

Pregnancy and Parenting, General
There are a number of excellent Internet sites offering comprehensive pregnancy, childbirth, and parenting information, advice, resources, and products. Most have community sections where you can post questions and get advice from other parents. Most also have special sections for dads (although they usually aren't as good as the Web sites listed above). Among the best are:

Babycenter.com
www.babycenter.com

iVillage
www.ivillage.com

Parents.com
www.parents.com

Pregnancy.org
www.pregnancy.org

PregnancyToday
www.pregnancytoday.com

SheKnows.com
www.sheknows.com

100 Top Parenting Sites maintains a constantly shifting list of, you guessed it, the top 100 parenting sites on the Internet.
www.100topparentingsites.com

Twins (and more)

About.com: Twins and Multiples has an excellent selection of information on all things multiple.
www.multiples.about.com/cs/dadsof-multiples

MOST (Mothers of SuperTwins) provides information, resources, empathy, and support to families with triplets and more.
www.mostonline.org

The National Organization of Mothers of Twins Clubs, Inc. (NOMOTC) promotes the special aspects of multiple-birth children.
www.nomotc.org

The Triplet Connection
www.tripletconnection.org

Work and Family

Families and Work Institute provides information on the changing nature of work and family life.
www.familiesandwork.org

Fathers at Work is my site, started to help companies create father-friendly workplaces.
www.fathersatwork.com

Sloan Work and Family Research Network at Boston College is one of the premier sources of information on work and family. Their new page, "Fathers, Caregiving and Work," is a wonderful resource on every possible issue facing working dads.
www.wfnetwork.bc.edu/topic
.php?id=46

Index

cribs and accessories, 215–17, 292, 295
crowning, 238, 247
crying, 272, 273, 278, 304–8; in boys vs. girls, 312; colic and, 306, 321; coping with, 307–8; in public, 309; reducing time spent, 304–7
custodial accounts, 119
cystic fibrosis, 70, 71

D

"daddy track" jobs, 151, 152
day care, 301, 302–3, 304
debts, 116
delivery, 238, 246–48; birth plans and, 197–201; breech presentation in, 22, 136, 257, 262; "catching" baby in, 247; cost of, 29; emergency, 233–36; episiotomy in, 201, 256, 257, 269; exercise during pregnancy and, 41; father not wanting to be at, 187–89; first few minutes after, 202, 248–49, 263–64; instrument (forceps or vacuum), 200, 252–53, 256, 257, 259; moment of birth in, 247–48; older children at, 200–201; pain of, 22–23; of placenta, 235–36, 238, 249; in planes, trains, and automobiles, 233; premature (*see* preterm labor/premature delivery); pushing in, 238, 246–47, 252, 253, 255, 256, 262; stages of, 238, 244–45. *See also* Cesarean sections; labor
dependence, of partners on one another, 67, 105, 127, 144, 148, 222, 225
depression, 49, 276; infertility diagnosis and, 322, 336. *See also* postpartum blues and depression
DES (diethylstilbestrol), 210, 329
diabetes, 22, 79, 182, 210, 262, 263, 289
diapers, 212, 213, 214, 218, 219, 390; changing, 278, 300; cloth vs. disposable, 220–21
Dick-Read method, 182–84
disability insurance, 124, 158
discipline styles, 102
divorce, 168–69, 326

dollar cost averaging, 116
doulas, 27–28, 185–87
Down syndrome, 71, 81, 82
dreams, 66, 165
dressing babies, 286
driving to hospital, 206, 207
drowsiness, of baby, 273
drugs, recreational, 50, 209, 329
due date, determining, 68, 69, 228
durable power of attorney for finances, 125

E

ear bulbs, 212
ectopic pregnancy, 68, 73
EFM (electronic fetal monitoring), 200, 257–59
eggs, donor, 37, 81, 96, 332, 334
ejaculation, 80, 231
embryos, 35–36, 63; fresh vs. frozen, in IVF, 37; PGD and, 335. *See also* fetuses
emergencies, 199, 202; pediatric care and, 204–5; rights to free and subsidized medical care and, 33
emergency births, 233–36
emergency kits, 234
emergency rooms, 33
engrossment, 279
environmental concerns, 214
epidurals, 23, 252–53, 254, 255
episiotomy, 201, 256, 257, 269
estate planning, 125
ethnicity, 170, 183; birth defects and, 69–71, 81
excitement, feelings of, 64
exercise, 40–42, 79; to do together, 41, 149; workout no-nos and, 42
exhaustion, in labor, 255, 256, 262
expectant fathers: birth plans and, 197–201; confusion experienced by, 223–25; connecting to pregnancy, 64, 66, 77, 107; couvade symptoms in, 88–93; dependent on partner, 225; dreams of, 66, 165; excitement vs. fear in, 64; experiences of, 36–40, 64–66, 73, 85–93, 105–9, 127–32, 144–48, 165–70, 193–97, 223–26, 239; feeling left out, 86; feeling

About the Authors

A nationally recognized parenting expert, **Armin A. Brott** is also the author of *The New Father: A Dad's Guide to the First Year*, *Fathering Your Toddler: A Dad's Guide to the Second and Third Years*, *Fathering Your School-Age Child: A Dad's Guide to the Wonder Years 3 to 9*, *The Single Father: A Dad's Guide to Parenting without a Partner*, and *Father for Life: A Journey of Joy, Challenge, and Change*. He has written on parenting and fatherhood for the *New York Times Magazine*, the *Washington Post*, *Newsweek*, and dozens of other periodicals. He also writes a nationally syndicated column, "Ask Mr. Dad," and hosts "Positive Parenting," a weekly talk show. Armin lives with his family in Oakland, California. To learn more, please visit his Web site, www.mrdad.com.

Jennifer Ash is the author of *Tropical Style: Private Palm Beach*. She also writes regularly for *Veranda* magazine and *Town & Country* magazine. Her articles have appeared in numerous publications, including the *Washington Post* and the *Palm Beach Daily News*. She and her husband, Dr. A. Joseph Rudick, live in New York City with their two children, Clarke and Amelia.

Cartoon Credits